Teach Yourself VISUALLY™ Dreamweaver® 3

From

maranGraphics™

&

IDG Books Worldwide, Inc.
An International Data Group Company
Foster City, CA • Indianapolis • Chicago • New York

Teach Yourself VISUALLY™ Dreamweaver® 3

Published by
IDG Books Worldwide, Inc.
An International Data Group Company
919 E. Hillsdale Blvd., Suite 400
Foster City, CA 94404
www.idgbooks.com (IDG Books Worldwide Web Site)

Original Text and Original Illustrations Copyright © 2000 IDG Books Worldwide, Inc.
Design and certain of the illustrations Copyright © 1992-2000 maranGraphics, Inc.
5755 Coopers Avenue
Mississauga, Ontario, Canada
L4Z 1R9

All rights reserved. No part of this book, including interior design, cover design, and icons, may be reproduced or transmitted in any form, by any means (electronic, photocopying, recording, or otherwise) without prior written permission of the publisher.

Library of Congress Control Number: 00-107553

ISBN: 0-7645-3470-X

Printed in the United States of America
10 9 8 7 6 5 4 3 2 1

1K/QV/QZ/QQ/IN

Distributed in the United States by IDG Books Worldwide, Inc.

Distributed by CDG Books Canada Inc. for Canada; by Transworld Publishers Limited in the United Kingdom; by IDG Norge Books for Norway; by IDG Sweden Books for Sweden; by IDG Books Australia Publishing Corporation Pty. Ltd. for Australia and New Zealand; by TransQuest Publishers Pte Ltd. for Singapore, Malaysia, Thailand, Indonesia, and Hong Kong; by Gotop Information Inc. for Taiwan; by ICG Muse, Inc. for Japan; by Intersoft for South Africa; by Eyrolles for France; by International Thomson Publishing for Germany, Austria and Switzerland; by Distribuidora Cuspide for Argentina; by LR International for Brazil; by Galileo Libros for Chile; by Ediciones ZETA S.C.R. Ltda. for Peru; by WS Computer Publishing Corporation, Inc., for the Philippines; by Contemporanea de Ediciones for Venezuela; by Express Computer Distributors for the Caribbean and West Indies; by Micronesia Media Distributor, Inc. for Micronesia; by Chips Computadoras S.A. de C.V. for Mexico; by Editorial Norma de Panama S.A. for Panama; by American Bookshops for Finland.

For corporate orders, please call maranGraphics at 800-469-6616.

For general information on IDG Books Worldwide's books in the U.S., please call our Consumer Customer Service department at 800-762-2974. For reseller information, including discounts and premium sales, please call our Reseller Customer Service department at 800-434-3422.

For information on where to purchase IDG Books Worldwide's books outside the U.S., please contact our International Sales department at 317-572-3993 or fax 317-572-4002.

For consumer information on foreign language translations, please contact our Customer Service department at 1-800-434-3422, fax 317-572-4002, or e-mail rights@idgbooks.com.

For information on licensing foreign or domestic rights, please phone +1-650-653-7098.

For sales inquiries and special prices for bulk quantities, please contact our Order Services department at 800-434-3422 or write to the address above.

For information on using IDG Books Worldwide's books in the classroom or for ordering examination copies, please contact our Educational Sales department at 800-434-2086 or fax 317-572-4005.

For press review copies, author interviews, or other publicity information, please contact our Public Relations department at 650-653-7000 or fax 650-653-7500.

For authorization to photocopy items for corporate, personal, or educational use, please contact Copyright Clearance Center, 222 Rosewood Drive, Danvers, MA 01923, or fax 978-750-4470.

Screen shots displayed in this book are based on pre-released software and are subject to change.

LIMIT OF LIABILITY/DISCLAIMER OF WARRANTY: THE PUBLISHER AND AUTHOR HAVE USED THEIR BEST EFFORTS IN PREPARING THIS BOOK. THE PUBLISHER AND AUTHOR MAKE NO REPRESENTATIONS OR WARRANTIES WITH RESPECT TO THE ACCURACY OR COMPLETENESS OF THE CONTENTS OF THIS BOOK AND SPECIFICALLY DISCLAIM ANY IMPLIED WARRANTIES OF MERCHANTABILITY OR FITNESS FOR A PARTICULAR PURPOSE. THERE ARE NO WARRANTIES WHICH EXTEND BEYOND THE DESCRIPTIONS CONTAINED IN THIS PARAGRAPH. NO WARRANTY MAY BE CREATED OR EXTENDED BY SALES REPRESENTATIVES OR WRITTEN SALES MATERIALS. THE ACCURACY AND COMPLETENESS OF THE INFORMATION PROVIDED HEREIN AND THE OPINIONS STATED HEREIN ARE NOT GUARANTEED OR WARRANTED TO PRODUCE ANY PARTICULAR RESULTS, AND THE ADVICE AND STRATEGIES CONTAINED HEREIN MAY NOT BE SUITABLE FOR EVERY INDIVIDUAL. NEITHER THE PUBLISHER NOR AUTHOR SHALL BE LIABLE FOR ANY LOSS OF PROFIT OR ANY OTHER COMMERCIAL DAMAGES, INCLUDING BUT NOT LIMITED TO SPECIAL, INCIDENTAL, CONSEQUENTIAL, OR OTHER DAMAGES.

Trademark Acknowledgments

Dreamweaver is a registered trademark of Macromedia, Inc. The maranGraphics logo is a trademark of maranGraphics, Inc. The IDG Books Worldwide logo is a registered trademark under exclusive license to IDG Books Worldwide, Inc., from International Data Group, Inc. Visual, the Visual logo, Teach Yourself VISUALLY, Master VISUALLY, Simplified and related trade dress are registered trademarks or trademarks of IDG Books Worldwide, Inc., in the United States and other countries, and may not be used without written permission. All other trademarks are the property of their respective owners. IDG Books Worldwide, Inc. and maranGraphics, Inc. are not associated with any product or vendor mentioned in this book.

FOR PURPOSES OF ILLUSTRATING THE CONCEPTS AND TECHNIQUES DESCRIBED IN THIS BOOK, THE AUTHOR HAS CREATED VARIOUS NAMES, COMPANY NAMES, MAILING ADDRESSES, E-MAIL ADDRESSES AND PHONE NUMBERS, ALL OF WHICH ARE FICTITIOUS. ANY RESEMBLANCE OF THESE FICTITIOUS NAMES, COMPANY NAMES, MAILING ADDRESSES, E-MAIL ADDRESSES AND PHONE NUMBERS TO ANY ACTUAL PERSON, COMPANY AND/OR ORGANIZATION IS UNINTENTIONAL AND PURELY COINCIDENTAL.

Permissions

Sunkist

The Sunkist home page is reprinted with sale purpose for use in Teach Yourself VISUALLY Dreamweaver.

maranGraphics

Certain of the Illustrations are Copyright 1992-2000 maranGraphics Inc., and are used with maranGraphics' permission.

is a registered trademark under exclusive license to IDG Books Worldwide, Inc. from International Data Group, Inc.

U.S. Corporate Sales

Contact maranGraphics at (800) 469-6616 or Fax (905) 890-9434.

U.S. Trade Sales

Contact IDG Books at (800) 434-3422 or (650) 655-3000.

ABOUT IDG BOOKS WORLDWIDE

Welcome to the world of IDG Books Worldwide.

IDG Books Worldwide, Inc., is a subsidiary of International Data Group, the world's largest publisher of computer-related information and the leading global provider of information services on information technology. IDG was founded more than 30 years ago by Patrick J. McGovern and now employs more than 9,000 people worldwide. IDG publishes more than 290 computer publications in over 75 countries. More than 90 million people read one or more IDG publications each month.

Launched in 1990, IDG Books Worldwide is today the #1 publisher of best-selling computer books in the United States. We are proud to have received eight awards from the Computer Press Association in recognition of editorial excellence and three from Computer Currents' First Annual Readers' Choice Awards. Our best-selling *...For Dummies®* series has more than 50 million copies in print with translations in 31 languages. IDG Books Worldwide, through a joint venture with IDG's Hi-Tech Beijing, became the first U.S. publisher to publish a computer book in the People's Republic of China. In record time, IDG Books Worldwide has become the first choice for millions of readers around the world who want to learn how to better manage their businesses.

Our mission is simple: Every one of our books is designed to bring extra value and skill-building instructions to the reader. Our books are written by experts who understand and care about our readers. The knowledge base of our editorial staff comes from years of experience in publishing, education, and journalism — experience we use to produce books to carry us into the new millennium. In short, we care about books, so we attract the best people. We devote special attention to details such as audience, interior design, use of icons, and illustrations. And because we use an efficient process of authoring, editing, and desktop publishing our books electronically, we can spend more time ensuring superior content and less time on the technicalities of making books.

You can count on our commitment to deliver high-quality books at competitive prices on topics you want to read about. At IDG Books Worldwide, we continue in the IDG tradition of delivering quality for more than 30 years. You'll find no better book on a subject than one from IDG Books Worldwide.

John Kilcullen
Chairman and CEO
IDG Books Worldwide, Inc.

Eighth Annual Computer Press Awards 1992

Ninth Annual Computer Press Awards 1993

Tenth Annual Computer Press Awards 1994

Eleventh Annual Computer Press Awards 1995

IDG is the world's leading IT media, research and exposition company. Founded in 1964, IDG had 1997 revenues of $2.05 billion and has more than 9,000 employees worldwide. IDG offers the widest range of media options that reach IT buyers in 75 countries representing 95% of worldwide IT spending. IDG's diverse product and services portfolio spans six key areas including print publishing, online publishing, expositions and conferences, market research, education and training, and global marketing services. More than 90 million people read one or more of IDG's 290 magazines and newspapers, including IDG's leading global brands — Computerworld, PC World, Network World, Macworld and the Channel World family of publications. IDG Books Worldwide is one of the fastest-growing computer book publishers in the world, with more than 700 titles in 36 languages. The "...For Dummies®" series alone has more than 50 million copies in print. IDG offers online users the largest network of technology-specific Web sites around the world through IDG.net (http://www.idg.net), which comprises more than 225 targeted Web sites in 55 countries worldwide. International Data Corporation (IDC) is the world's largest provider of information technology data, analysis and consulting, with research centers in over 41 countries and more than 400 research analysts worldwide. IDG World Expo is a leading producer of more than 168 globally branded conferences and expositions in 35 countries including E3 (Electronic Entertainment Expo), Macworld Expo, ComNet, Windows World Expo, ICE (Internet Commerce Expo), Agenda, DEMO, and Spotlight. IDG's training subsidiary, ExecuTrain, is the world's largest computer training company, with more than 230 locations worldwide and 785 training courses. IDG Marketing Services helps industry-leading IT companies build international brand recognition by developing global integrated marketing programs via IDG's print, online and exposition products worldwide. Further information about the company can be found at www.idg.com. 1/26/00

maranGraphics is a family-run business
located near Toronto, Canada.

At **maranGraphics**, we believe in producing great computer books — one book at a time.

maranGraphics has been producing high-technology products for over 25 years, which enables us to offer the computer book community a unique communication process.

Our computer books use an integrated communication process, which is very different from the approach used in other computer books. Each spread is, in essence, a flow chart — the text and screen shots are totally incorporated into the layout of the spread. Introductory text and helpful tips complete the learning experience.

maranGraphics' approach encourages the left and right sides of the brain to work together —resulting in faster orientation and greater memory retention.

Above all, we are very proud of the handcrafted nature of our books. Our carefully-chosen writers are experts in their fields, and spend countless hours researching and organizing the content for each topic. Our artists rebuild every screen shot to provide the best clarity possible, making our screen shots the most precise and easiest to read in the industry. We strive for perfection, and believe that the time spent handcrafting each element results in the best computer books money can buy.

Thank you for purchasing this book. We hope you enjoy it!

Sincerely,

Robert Maran
President
maranGraphics
Rob@maran.com
www.maran.com
www.idgbooks.com/visual

CREDITS

Acquisitions, Editorial, and Media Development

Project Editor
Maureen Spears

Acquisitions Editor
Martine Edwards

Associate Project Coordinator
Lindsay Sandman

Copy Editors
Tim Borek, Christine Berman

Proof Editor
Teresa Artman

Technical Editor
Yolanda Burrell

Editorial Manager
Mary Corder

Media Development Manager
Heather Heath Dismore

Editorial Assistant:
Sarah Shupert

Production

Book Design
maranGraphics™

Project Coordinator
Valery Bourke

Layout
Joe Bucki, Barry Offringa, Kathie Schutte

Editorial Graphics Production:
Ronda David-Burroughs, Craig Dearing, Dave Gregory, Mark Harris, Jill Johnson

Proofreaders:
Laura Albert, Nancy L. Reinhardt, Marianne Santy

Indexer:
York Production Services, Inc.

Special Help:
Mary Corder, Martine Edwards, Clint Lahnen, Kyle Looper, Darren Meiss, Rev Mengle, Shelley Norris, Ryan Roberts, Lindsay Sandman, Brent Savage

ACKNOWLEDGMENTS

General and Administrative

IDG Books Worldwide, Inc.: John Kilcullen, CEO

IDG Books Technology Publishing Group: Richard Swadley, Senior Vice President and Publisher; Walter R. Bruce III, Vice President and Publisher; Joseph Wikert, Vice President and Publisher; Mary Bednarek, Vice President and Director, Product Development; Andy Cummings, Publishing Director, General User Group; Mary C. Corder, Editorial Director; Barry Pruett, Publishing Director

IDG Books Consumer Publishing Group: Roland Elgey, Senior Vice President and Publisher; Kathleen A. Welton, Vice President and Publisher; Kevin Thornton, Acquisitions Manager; Kristin A. Cocks, Editorial Director

IDG Books Internet Publishing Group: Brenda McLaughlin, Senior Vice President and Publisher; Sofia Marchant, Online Marketing Manager

IDG Books Production for Branded Press: Debbie Stailey, Director of Production; Cindy L. Phipps, Manager of Project Coordination, Production Proofreading, and Indexing; Tony Augsburger, Manager of Prepress, Reprints, and Systems; Shelley Lea, Supervisor of Graphics and Design; Debbie J. Gates, Production Systems Specialist; Robert Springer, Supervisor of Proofreading; Trudy Coler, Page Layout Manager; Kathie Schutte, Senior Page Layout Supervisor; Janet Seib, Page Layout Supervisor; Michael Sullivan, Production Supervisor

Packaging and Book Design: Patty Page, Manager, Promotions Marketing

The publisher would like to give special thanks to Patrick J. McGovern, without whom this book would not have been possible.

ABOUT THE AUTHOR

Mike Wooldridge started his career in online publishing by putting up a personal Web site (www.thatguy.com), and hopes that this book helps others do the same. (He's still amazed at what one person can do with a computer, Web editor, and dial-up Internet account.)
Mike spent five years as an independent Web developer, building sites out of a spare bedroom in his pajamas. Nowadays he gets dressed and goes to work as the Director of Web Content at Namesecure, a domain name registrar. He also teaches Web classes at UC Berkeley Extension and writes about Web technology for online and print publications such as CNET and Macworld.

AUTHOR'S ACKNOWLEDGEMENTS

At IDG, I want to thank my Developmental Editor, Martine Edwards, for giving me the opportunity to write my first book; Project Editor Maureen Spears for her hard work, understanding, and adeptness under a tight schedule; and Copy Editor Tim Borek, with whom I never spoke, but whose careful work I really appreciated. And thanks to the all of the other folks in Indianapolis who pitched in to make this book happen, including: Brent Savage, Clint Lahnen, Shelley Norris, Craig Dearing, Jill Johnson, Mark Harris, Ronda David-Burroughs, Ryan Roberts, and Sarah Shupert.

AUTHOR DEDICATION

I'm also grateful to my book-writing friend Asha Dornfest for her advice and encouragement.

I dedicate this book to Linda, the loving partner in all of my life's projects; Griffin (www.thatkid.com), who was born about the time I started writing this book; and my parents, who have supported me in all my pursuits.

TABLE OF CONTENTS

Chapter 1

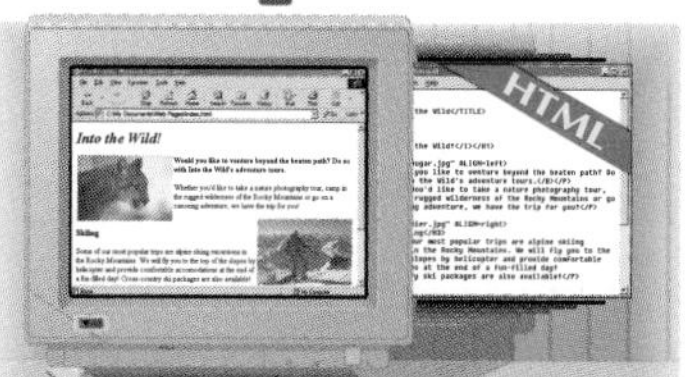

GETTING STARTED

Chapter 2

DREAMWEAVER BASICS

Chapter 3

HTML BASICS

Chapter 4

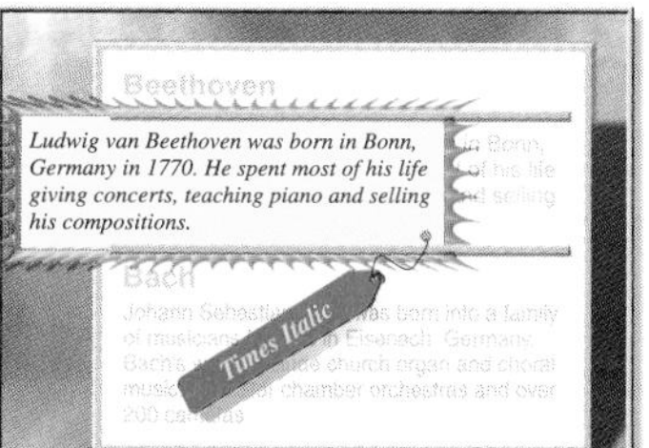

FORMATTING TEXT

Chapter 5

WORKING WITH IMAGES

Chapter 6

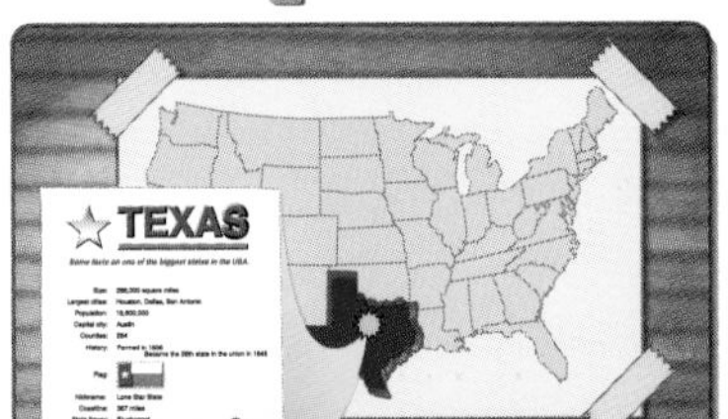

CREATING HYPERLINKS

Chapter 7

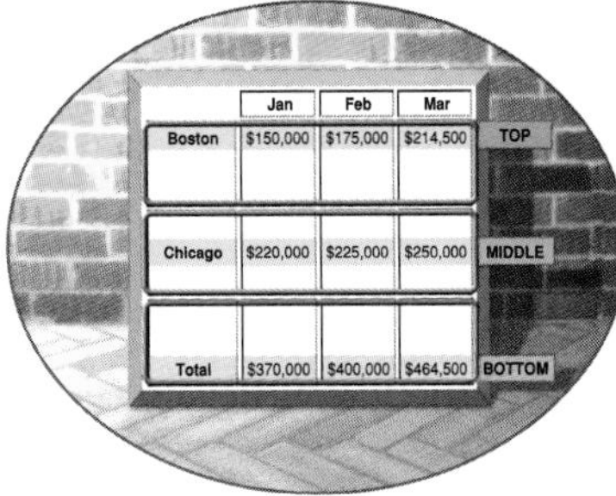

CREATING TABLES

Chapter 8

CREATING FORMS

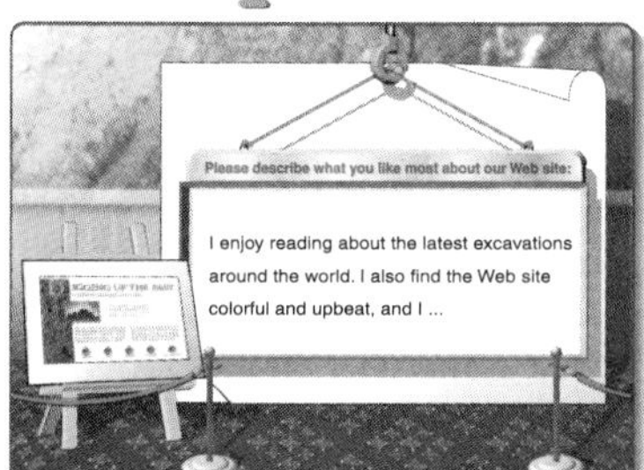
Please describe what you like most about our Web site:
I enjoy reading about the latest excavations around the world. I also find the Web site colorful and upbeat, and I ...

Chapter 9

DESIGNING WITH FRAMES

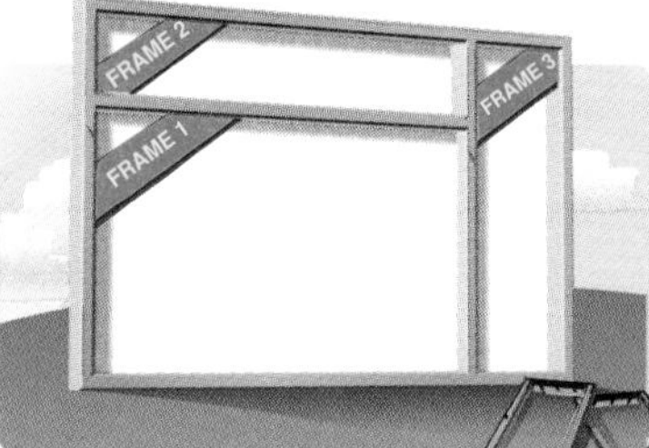
FRAME 2
FRAME 3
FRAME 1

Chapter 10 USING LIBRARIES AND TEMPLATES

Chapter 11 IMPLEMENTING STYLE SHEETS

Chapter 12

IMPLEMENTING BEHAVIOR

Chapter 13

IMPLEMENTING TIMELINES

Chapter 14

PUBLISHING YOUR WEB SITE

Faldo takes shot at James
Sunkist
Online Sunshine

CHAPTER 1

Getting Started

Are you thinking about creating a Web site? This chapter will help you get started by introducing you to Dreamweaver and the Web.

INTRODUCTION TO THE WORLD WIDE WEB

You can use Dreamweaver to create and publish Web pages on the World Wide Web.

WHAT IS THE WORLD WIDE WEB?

The World Wide Web (or "Web") is a global collection of documents you can access by using a Web browser.

Web pages are connected to one another by clickable hyperlinks.

WHAT IS DREAMWEAVER?

Dreamweaver is a program that enables you to build and create Web pages that feature text, images, and multimedia, and lets you transfer the finished files to a Web server.

WHAT IS HTML?

HTML, or Hypertext Markup Language, is the formatting language that creates Web pages. You can use Dreamweaver without knowing HTML because Dreamweaver writes the HTML for you behind the scenes.

WHAT IS A WEB BROWSER?

A Web browser is a program that interprets HTML and enables you to view files published on the Web. Two popular Web browsers are Microsoft Internet Explorer and Netscape Navigator.

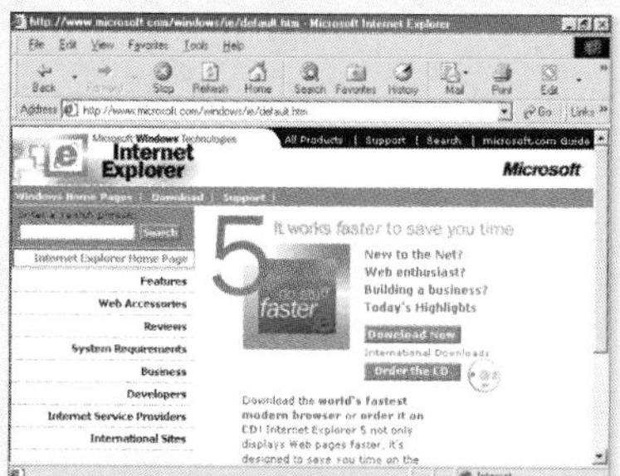

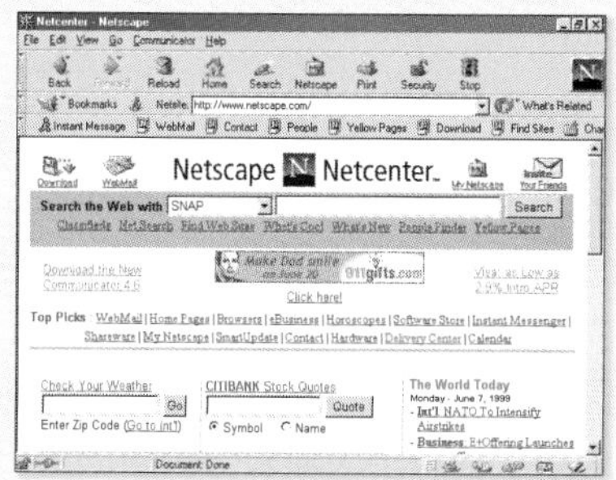

WHAT IS A WEB SERVER?

A Web server is an Internet-connected computer that transfers Web page information. Each Web page that you view on the World Wide Web is "served up" by a Web server.

WHAT IS A WEB SITE?

A Web site is a collection of linked Web pages stored on a Web server. The pages of a good Web site are intuitively organized and have a common theme.

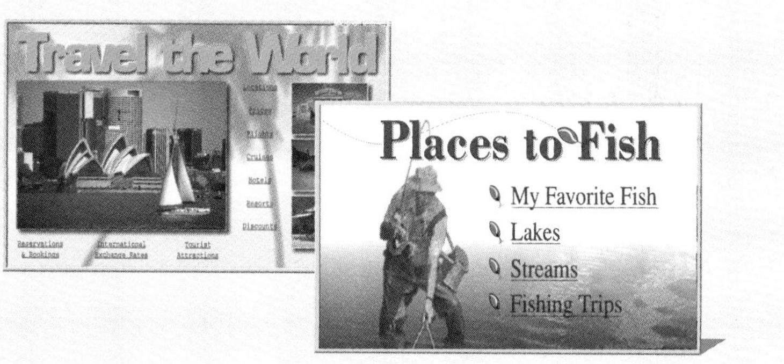

PARTS OF A WEB PAGE

You can communicate your message on the Web in a variety of ways. The following are some of the common elements found on Web pages.

TEXT

Text is the simplest type of content you can publish on the Web. Dreamweaver lets you change the size, color, and font of Web-page text and organize it into paragraphs and headings.

IMAGES

You can save photographs, drawings, and logos as image files by using a program known as an image editor. You can then place the images on your Web pages with Dreamweaver.

HYPERLINKS

Often simply called "links," a hyperlink is text or an image that is associated with another file on the Web. You can access the other file by clicking the hyperlink. (Hyperlinks usually link to other Web pages, but they can also link to other locations on the same page or to other types of files.)

TABLES

Tables organize information in columns and rows. Dreamweaver's commands give you an easy way to create complex tables.

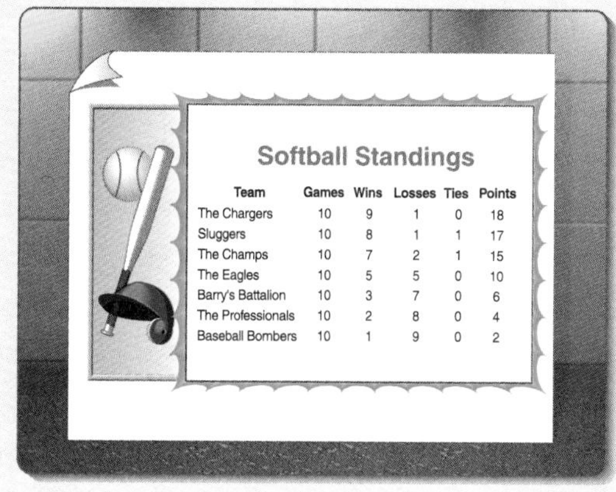

Softball Standings

Team	Games	Wins	Losses	Ties	Points
The Chargers	10	9	1	0	18
Sluggers	10	8	1	1	17
The Champs	10	7	2	1	15
The Eagles	10	5	5	0	10
Barry's Battalion	10	3	7	0	6
The Professionals	10	2	8	0	4
Baseball Bombers	10	1	9	0	2

FORMS

Forms enable your site's visitors to send you information. Dreamweaver lets you create forms that include text fields, drop-down menus, radio buttons, and other elements.

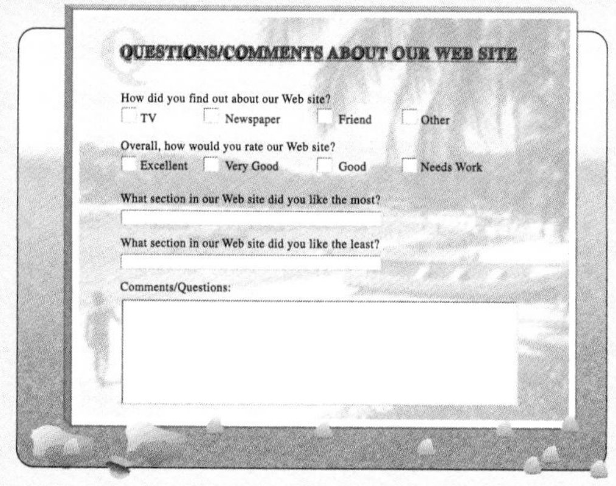

QUESTIONS/COMMENTS ABOUT OUR WEB SITE

How did you find out about our Web site?

☐ TV ☐ Newspaper ☐ Friend ☐ Other

Overall, how would you rate our Web site?

☐ Excellent ☐ Very Good ☐ Good ☐ Needs Work

What section in our Web site did you like the most?

What section in our Web site did you like the least?

Comments/Questions:

FRAMES

Frames enable you to divide a browser window into multiple panes and load a different Web page into each pane. Dreamweaver offers visual tools for building frame-based Web sites.

PLAN YOUR WEB SITE

Carefully planning your site before you start to build it can help you use Dreamweaver more efficiently.

ORGANIZE YOUR IDEAS

Build your site on paper before you start building it in Dreamweaver. Sketching out a site map, with rectangles representing Web pages and arrows representing hyperlinks, can help you visualize the size and scope of your project.

GATHER YOUR CONTENT

After you decide what types of Web pages you want to create, you must generate content that will appear on them. This process can involve writing text, shooting and scanning photos, and designing graphics. It can also involve producing multimedia content such as audio and video files.

DEFINE YOUR AUDIENCE

Carefully defining your audience can help you decide what kind of content to offer on your Web site. Some advanced Dreamweaver features — such as cascading style sheets and layers — can only be viewed using the most recent versions of Web browsers. Knowing how technologically advanced your audience is can help you decide whether to include more advanced features on your pages.

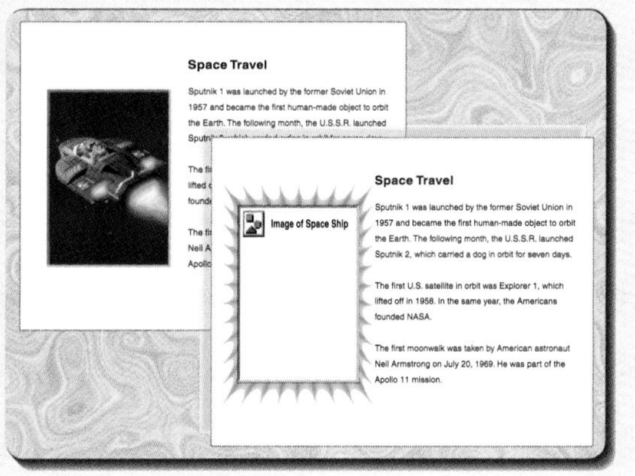

HOST YOUR FINISHED WEB SITE

For your finished site to be accessible on the Web, it needs to be stored on a Web server. This is known as hosting your site. Most people have their Web sites hosted on a Web server at a commercial *Internet service provider* (ISP) or at their company.

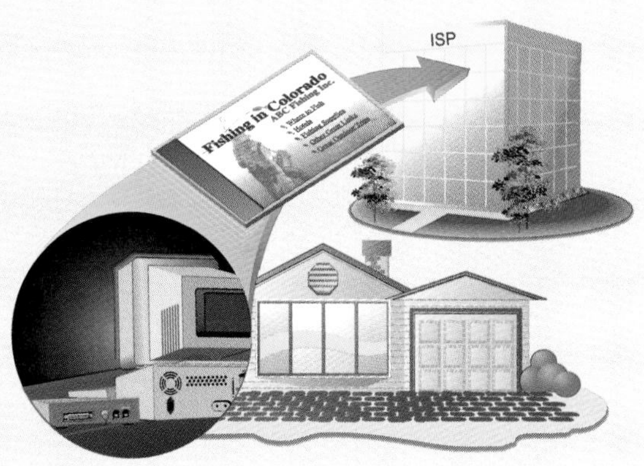

You build Web pages in Dreamweaver on a PC using various windows, palettes, and inspectors.

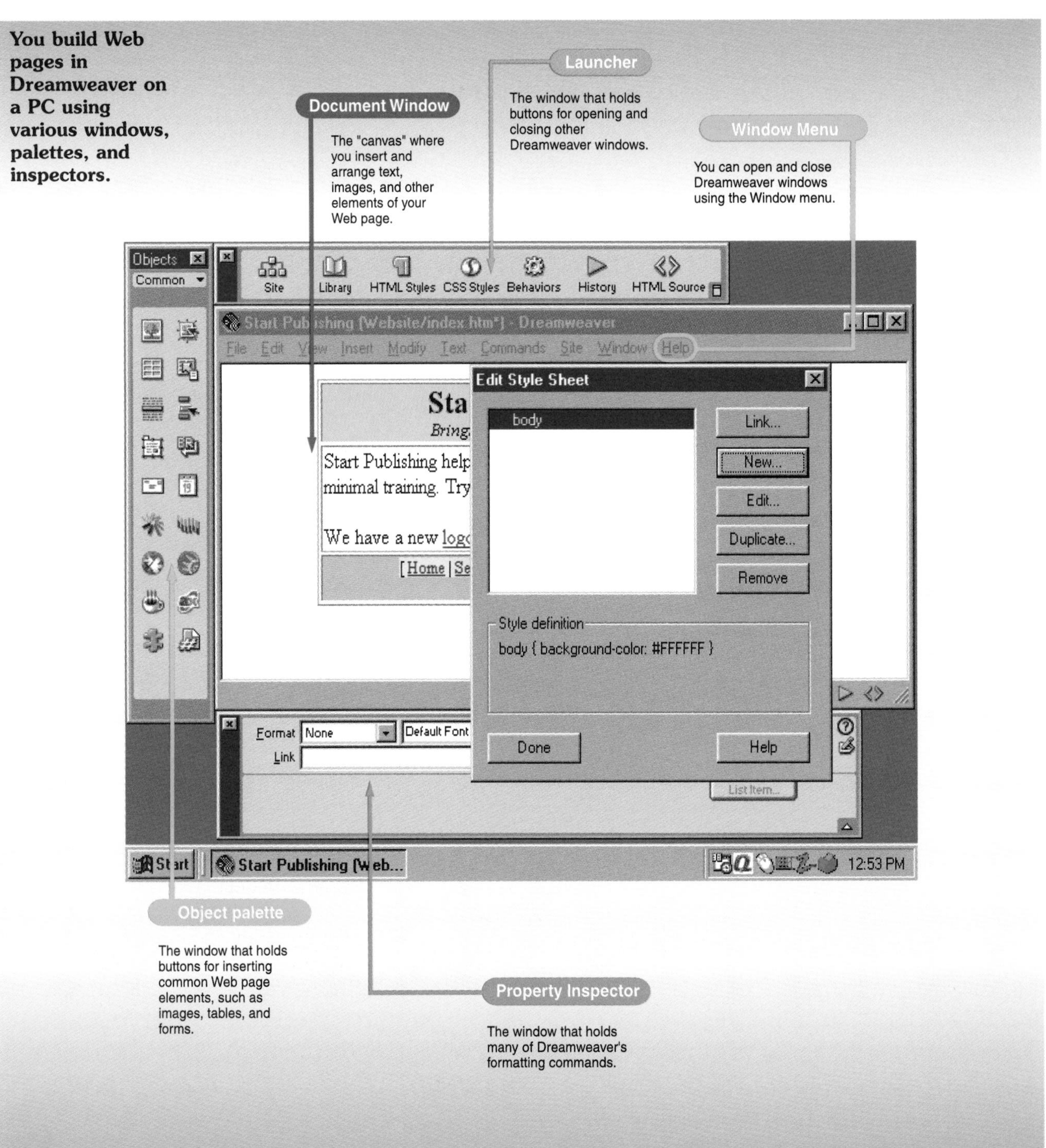
Document Window
The "canvas" where you insert and arrange text, images, and other elements of your Web page.
Launcher
The window that holds buttons for opening and closing other Dreamweaver windows.
Window Menu
You can open and close Dreamweaver windows using the Window menu.
Object palette
The window that holds buttons for inserting common Web page elements, such as images, tables, and forms.
Property Inspector
The window that holds many of Dreamweaver's formatting commands.
Objects
Common
Site
Library
HTML Styles
CSS Styles
Behaviors
History
HTML Source
Start Publishing (Website/index.htm*) - Dreamweaver
File Edit View Insert Modify Text Commands Site Window Help
Edit Style Sheet
body
Link...
New...
Edit...
Duplicate...
Remove
Style definition
body { background-color: #FFFFFF }
Done
Help
Start Publishing help
minimal training. Try
We have a new logo
[Home | Se
Format None
Default Font
Link
List Item...
Start
Start Publishing (Web...
12:53 PM

THE DREAMWEAVER INTERFACE ON A MACINTOSH

You build Web pages in Dreamweaver on a Macintosh using various windows, palettes, and inspectors.

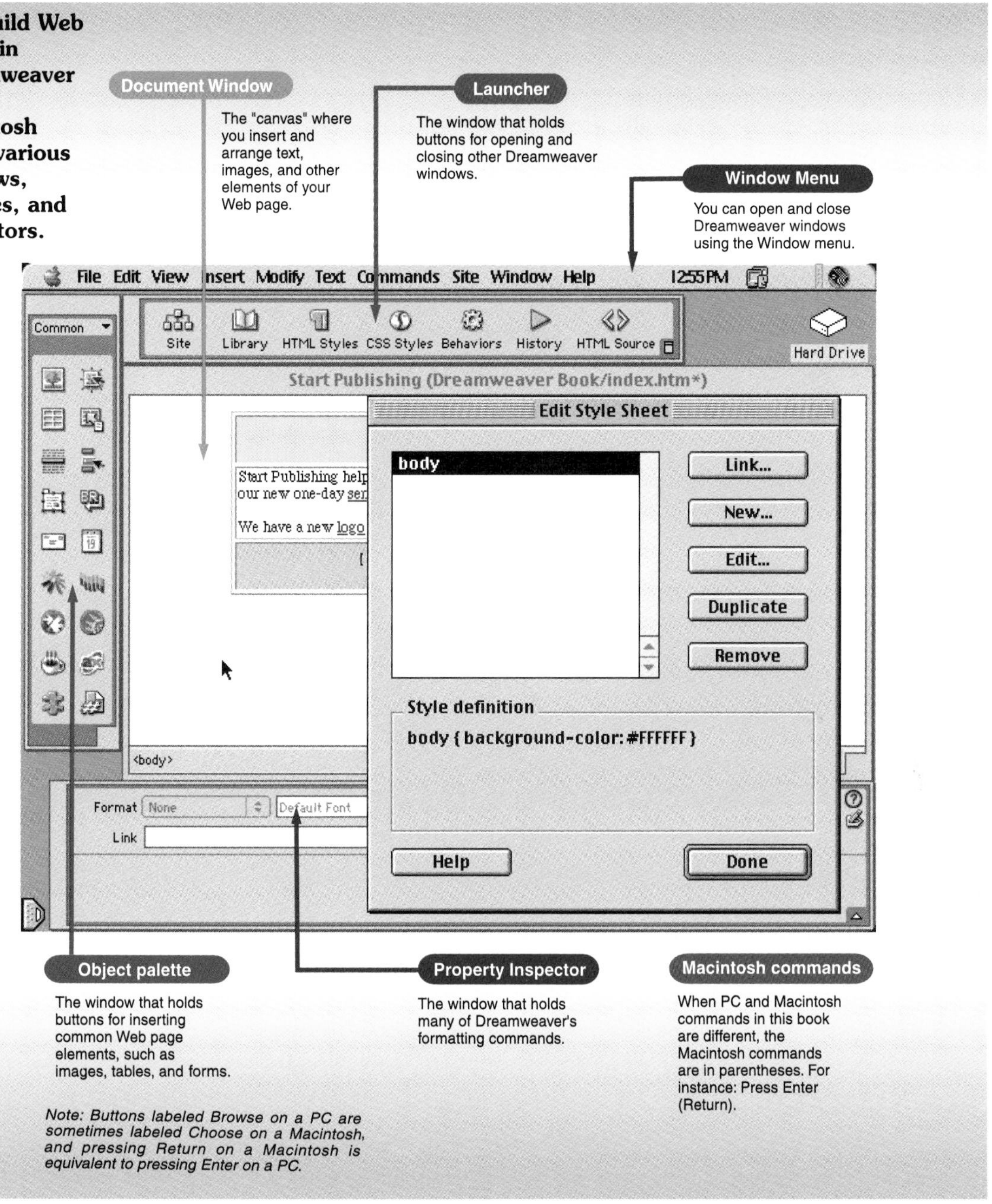

Document Window

The "canvas" where you insert and arrange text, images, and other elements of your Web page.

Launcher

The window that holds buttons for opening and closing other Dreamweaver windows.

Window Menu

You can open and close Dreamweaver windows using the Window menu.

Object palette

The window that holds buttons for inserting common Web page elements, such as images, tables, and forms.

Property Inspector

The window that holds many of Dreamweaver's formatting commands.

Macintosh commands

When PC and Macintosh commands in this book are different, the Macintosh commands are in parentheses. For instance: Press Enter (Return).

Note: Buttons labeled Browse on a PC are sometimes labeled Choose on a Macintosh, and pressing Return on a Macintosh is equivalent to pressing Enter on a PC.

START DREAMWEAVER ON A PC

You can start Dreamweaver on a PC and begin building documents that you can publish on the Web.

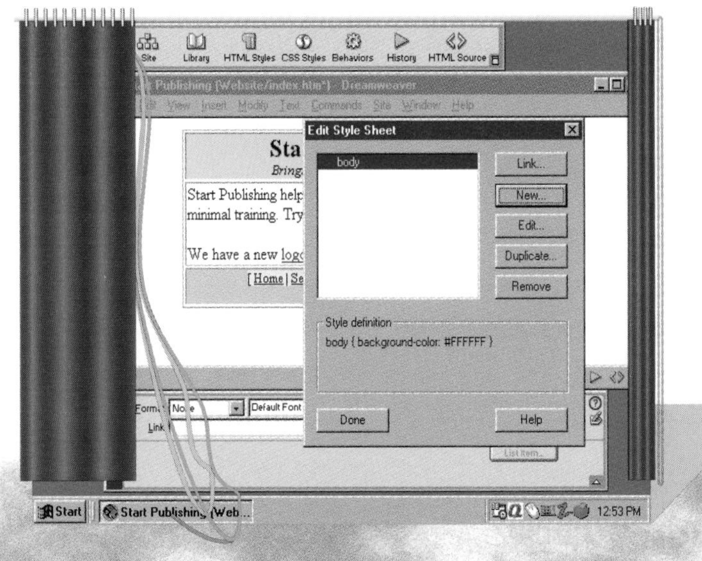

START DREAMWEAVER ON A PC

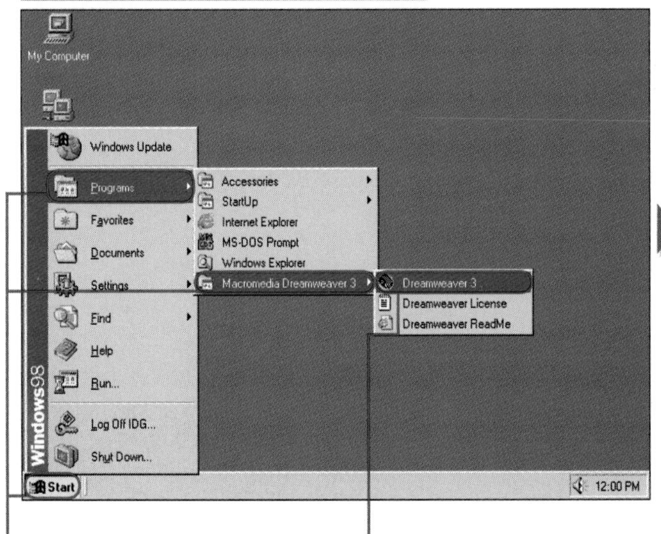

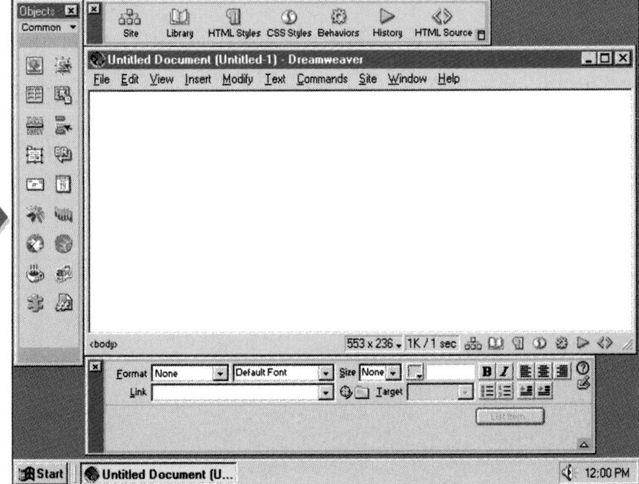

1 Click **Start**.

2 Click **Programs**.

3 Click **Macromedia Dreamweaver 3**.

4 Click **Dreamweaver 3**.

Note: Your path to the Dreamweaver application may be different, depending on how you installed your software.

■ Dreamweaver launches an untitled Web page in a Document window.

START DREAMWEAVER ON A MACINTOSH

You can start Dreamweaver on a Macintosh and begin building documents that you can publish on the Web.

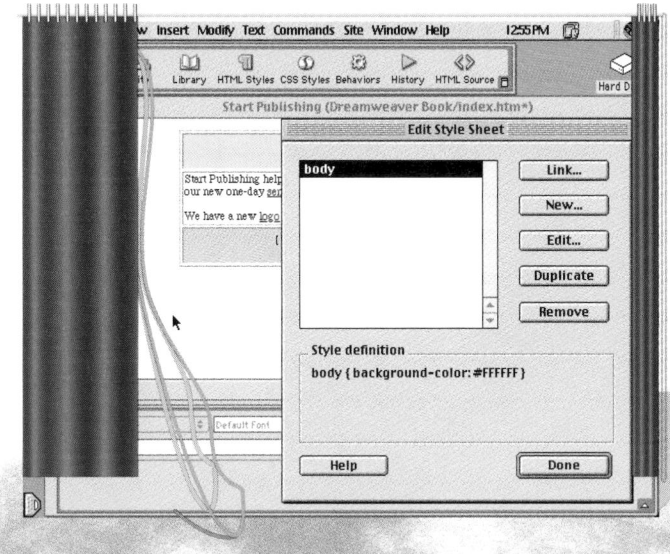

START DREAMWEAVER ON A MACINTOSH

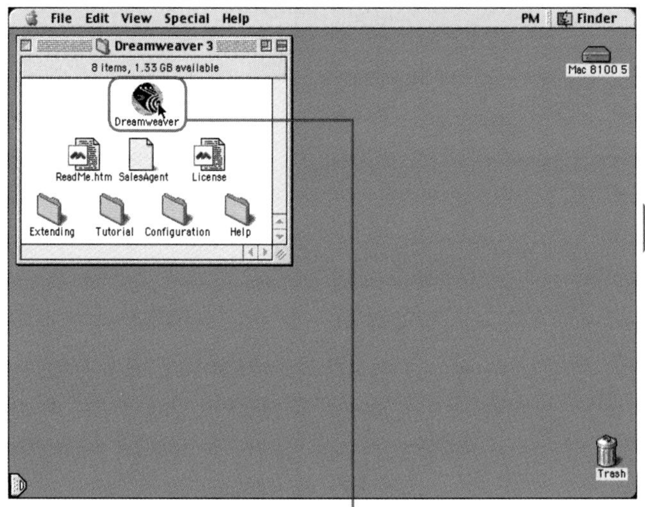

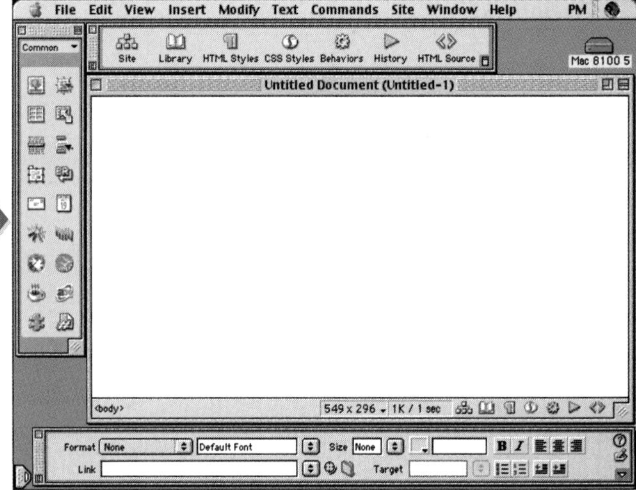

1 Open the Dreamweaver 3 folder on your hard drive.

2 Double-click the Dreamweaver icon.

■ Dreamweaver launches an untitled Web page in a Document window.

GET HELP

You can use the help tools built into Dreamweaver to get answers to your questions.

GET HELP

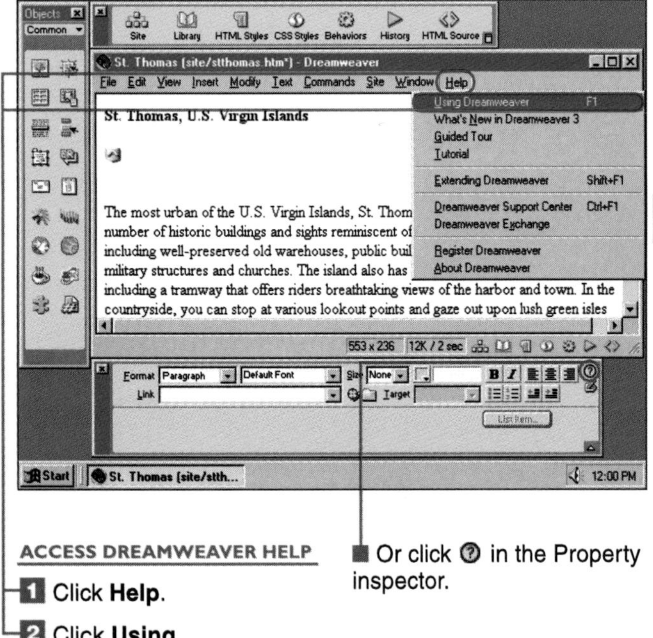

ACCESS DREAMWEAVER HELP

1 Click **Help**.

2 Click **Using Dreamweaver**.

■ Or click ⓘ in the Property inspector.

■ Dreamweaver opens the program's help pages in a Web browser.

3 Click a topic in the left frame of the browser window.

Are there different ways of getting the same thing done in Dreamweaver?

Often times, yes. For example, you may be able to access a command one way through a Dreamweaver menu, another way through the Object palette or Property inspector, and yet another way by right-clicking (control-clicking) an object with the mouse.

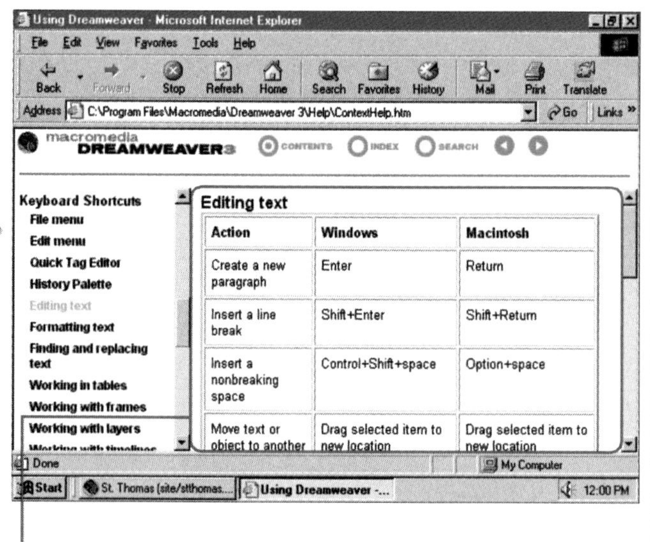

■ Dreamweaver opens up information on the topic in the right frame of the browser window.

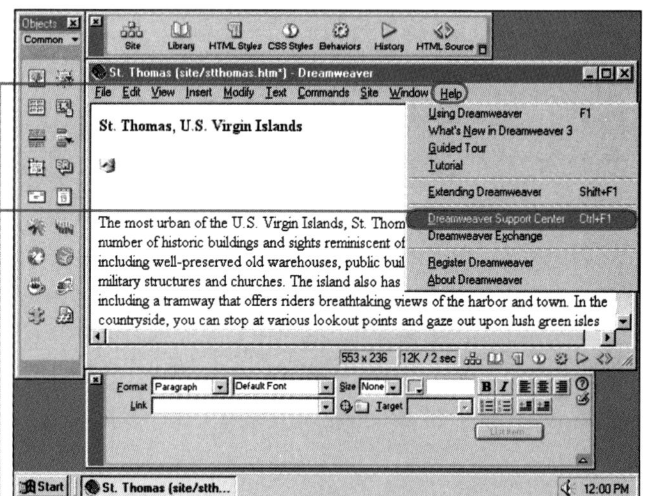

ACCESS DREAMWEAVER HELP ONLINE

1 To access Macromedia's online support site, click **Help**.

2 Click **Dreamweaver Support Center**.

■ The Support Center offers tips on Dreamweaver use, downloadable add-ons, bug fixes, and links to discussion groups.

BIRD WATCHERS'
HOME PAGE
The page dedicated to people who love to watch birds!
Bird watching is a fun and rewarding activity for any nature enthusiast.
There are thousands of types of birds across the United States and bird watching opportunities exist virtually everywhere.
There are a few items that make bird watching much easier and more enjoyable.
Items to Bring Bird Watching:
• A good pair of binoculars allow you to get a better view of the bird's colors and make identification easier.
• A field guide will tell you exactly what type of bird you are watching and provide you with in
about the bird.
• A camera allows you
home a permanent reminder of that rare bird.

CHAPTER 2

Dreamweaver Basics

Are you ready to begin creating Web pages? This chapter will familiarize you with Dreamweaver's Web-building tools.

ABOUT THE DOCUMENT WINDOW

The Document window is the main Dreamweaver window where you can create and edit your Web pages.

ABOUT THE DOCUMENT WINDOW

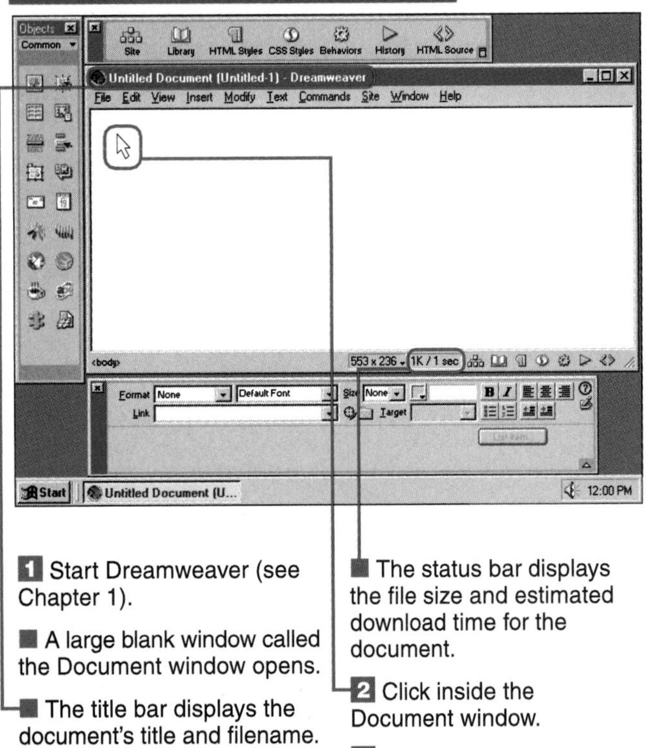

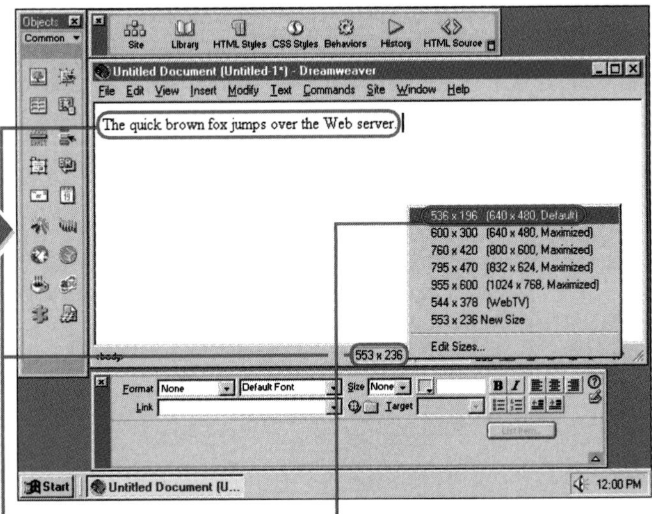

1 Start Dreamweaver (see Chapter 1).

■ A large blank window called the Document window opens.

■ The title bar displays the document's title and filename.

■ The status bar displays the file size and estimated download time for the document.

2 Click inside the Document window.

3 Type some text.

■ The text appears in the Document window approximately as it would when opened in a Web browser.

4 Click the Document window size menu.

■ The menu lists preset sizes that mimick the dimensions of Web browser windows at common monitor settings.

5 Select a window size.

What is WYSIWYG?

WYSIWYG (pronounced wizzy-wig) stands for "**W**hat **Y**ou **S**ee **I**s **W**hat **Y**ou **G**et." Because you build Web pages visually in the Document window and see the content approximately as it will appear in a Web browser, Dreamweaver is known as a WYSIWYG Web editor. (This is in contrast to text-based Web editors, which let you create Web pages by writing HTML code.)

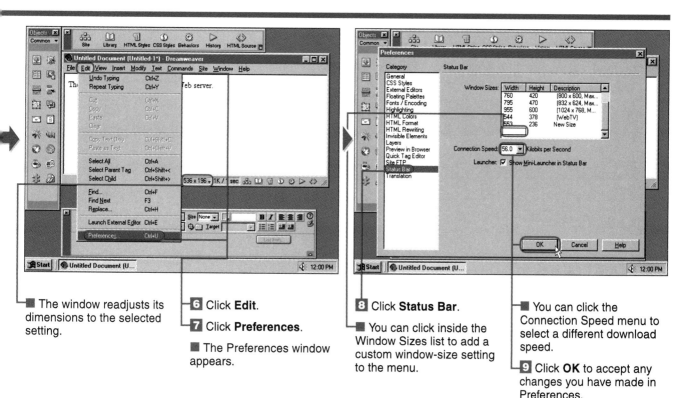

■ The window readjusts its dimensions to the selected setting.

6 Click **Edit**.

7 Click **Preferences**.

■ The Preferences window appears.

8 Click **Status Bar**.

■ You can click inside the Window Sizes list to add a custom window-size setting to the menu.

■ You can click the Connection Speed menu to select a different download speed.

9 Click **OK** to accept any changes you have made in Preferences.

USING THE PROPERTY INSPECTOR

You can format content in the Document window by using the Property inspector.

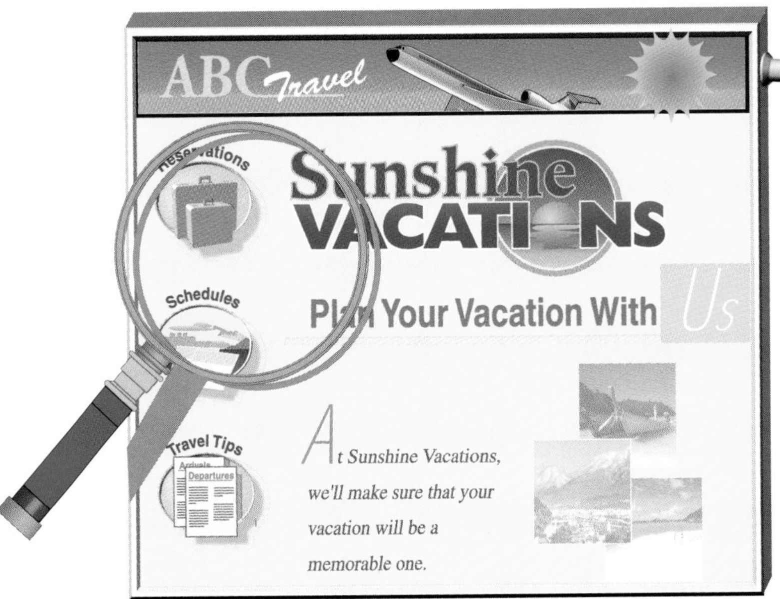

USING THE PROPERTY INSPECTOR

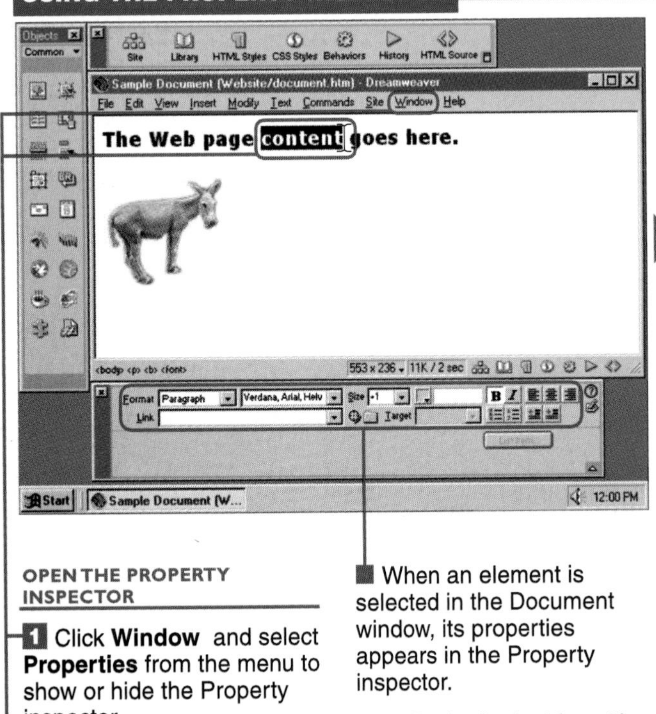

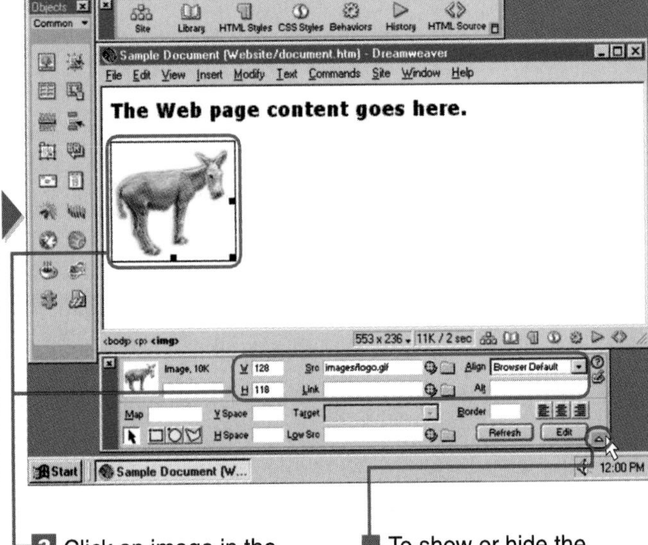

OPEN THE PROPERTY INSPECTOR

1 Click **Window** and select **Properties** from the menu to show or hide the Property inspector.

2 Drag the cursor to select some text.

■ When an element is selected in the Document window, its properties appears in the Property inspector.

Note: For details about formatting text, see Chapter 4.

3 Click an image in the Document window.

■ Image properties, such as image dimensions, filename, and alignment, will appear.

■ To show or hide the lower half of the Property inspector, click ▲.

Note: For details about formatting images, see Chapter 5.

USING THE OBJECT PALETTE

The Object palette allows you to add objects such as images and special characters to a Web page.

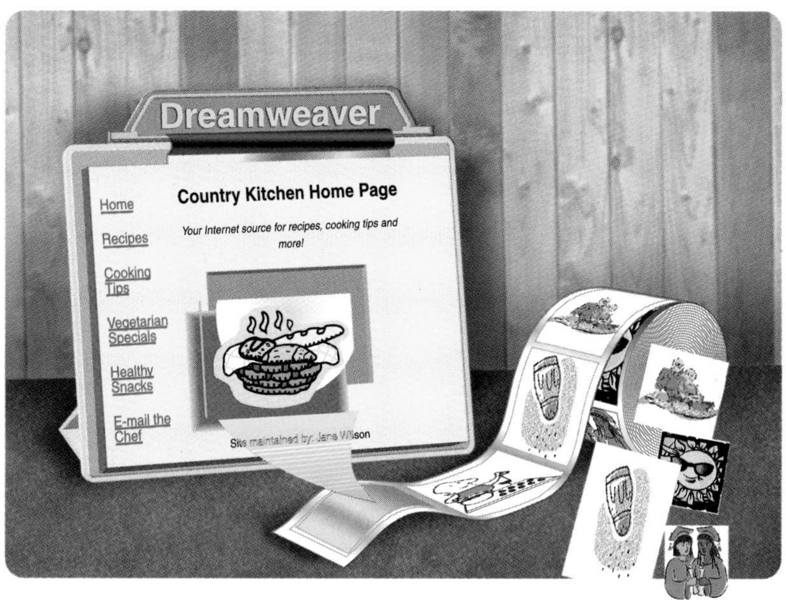

USING THE OBJECT PALETTE

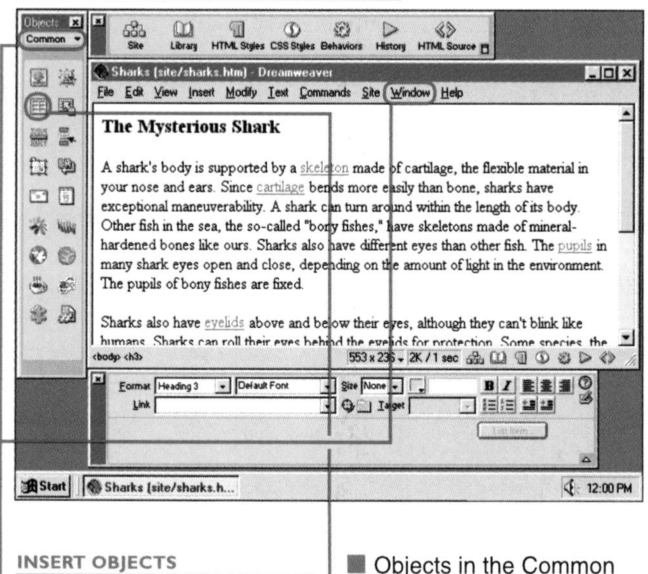

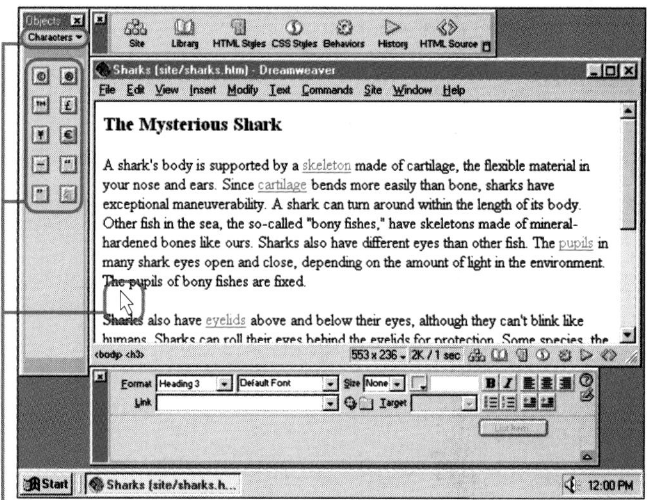

INSERT OBJECTS

1 Click **Window⇨Objects** to show or hide the Object palette.

2 Click a set of objects from the menu.

■ Objects in the Common set include images, tables, and layers.

3 Click inside the Document window.

4 Click the icon of the object you want to select.

INSERT SPECIAL CHARACTERS

1 Click ▼ and select **Characters** from the palette.

2 Click inside the Document window.

3 Click the special character that you want to insert.

■ You can insert a copyright symbol [©], trademark symbol [™], em dash [–], and other characters.

■ Other menu settings allow you to add form objects, frame objects, <head> tag objects, and invisible objects.

USING THE LAUNCHER

Dreamweaver's Launcher window lets you open and close windows, palettes, and inspectors with a single click. It saves you from constantly opening the Window menu and selecting a command.

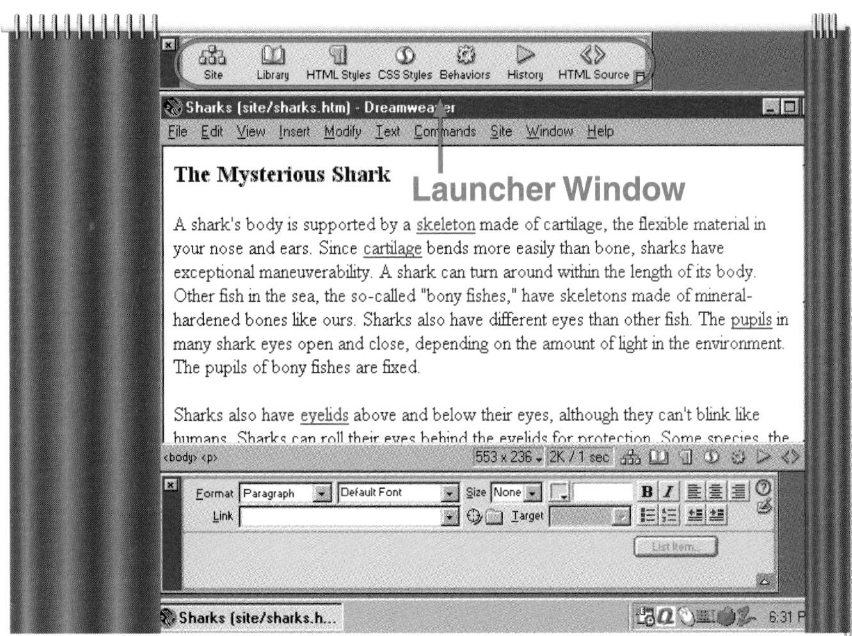

USING THE LAUNCHER

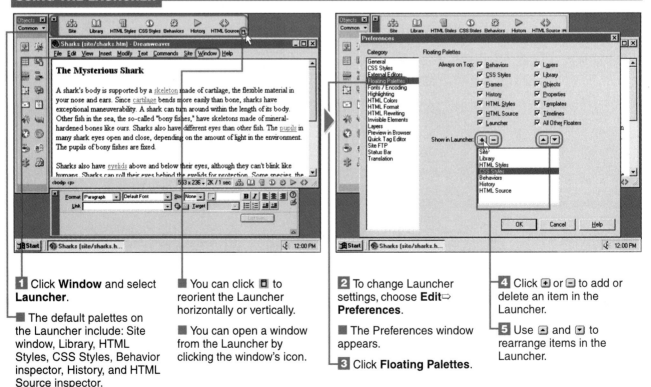

1 Click **Window** and select **Launcher**.

■ The default palettes on the Launcher include: Site window, Library, HTML Styles, CSS Styles, Behavior inspector, History, and HTML Source inspector.

■ You can click ⊡ to reorient the Launcher horizontally or vertically.

■ You can open a window from the Launcher by clicking the window's icon.

2 To change Launcher settings, choose **Edit⇨ Preferences**.

■ The Preferences window appears.

3 Click **Floating Palettes**.

4 Click ⊞ or ⊟ to add or delete an item in the Launcher.

5 Use ▲ and ▼ to rearrange items in the Launcher.

USING THE HISTORY PALETTE

Dreamweaver allows you to correct errors with the History Palette. With it, you can undo multiple commands at once.

USING THE HISTORY PALETTE

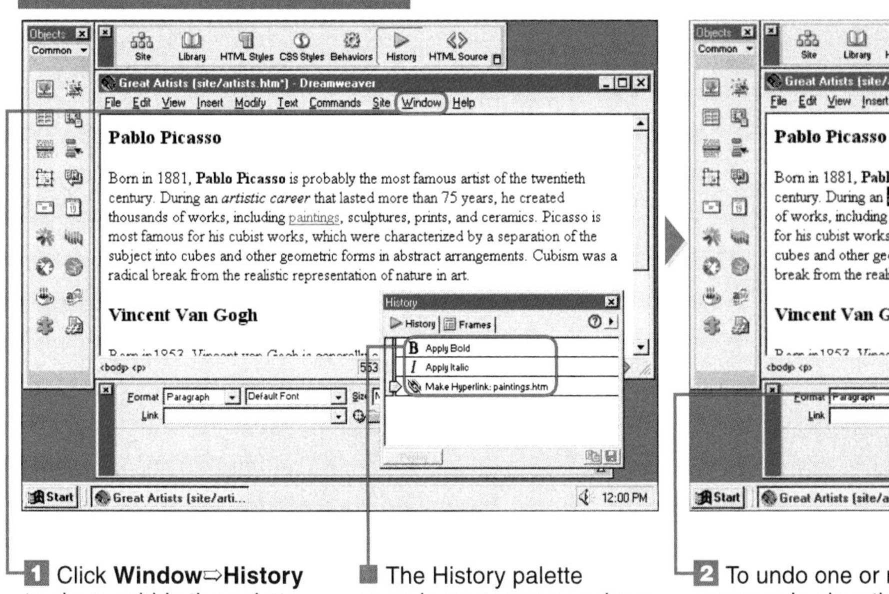

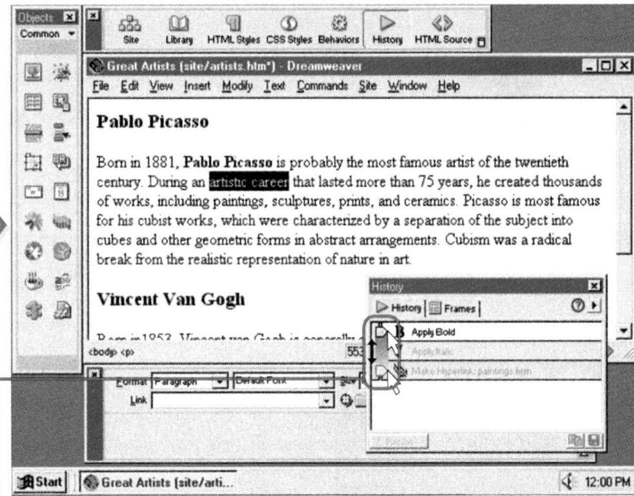

1 Click **Window⇨History** to show or hide the palette.

■ The History palette records every command you perform in Dreamweaver.

2 To undo one or more commands, drag the History palette's slider upward.

3 To redo the commands, drag the slider downward

CREATE AND APPLY A CUSTOM COMMAND

The History palette allows you to create custom commands by combining a string of single commands. This lets you make complex changes to content with one click.

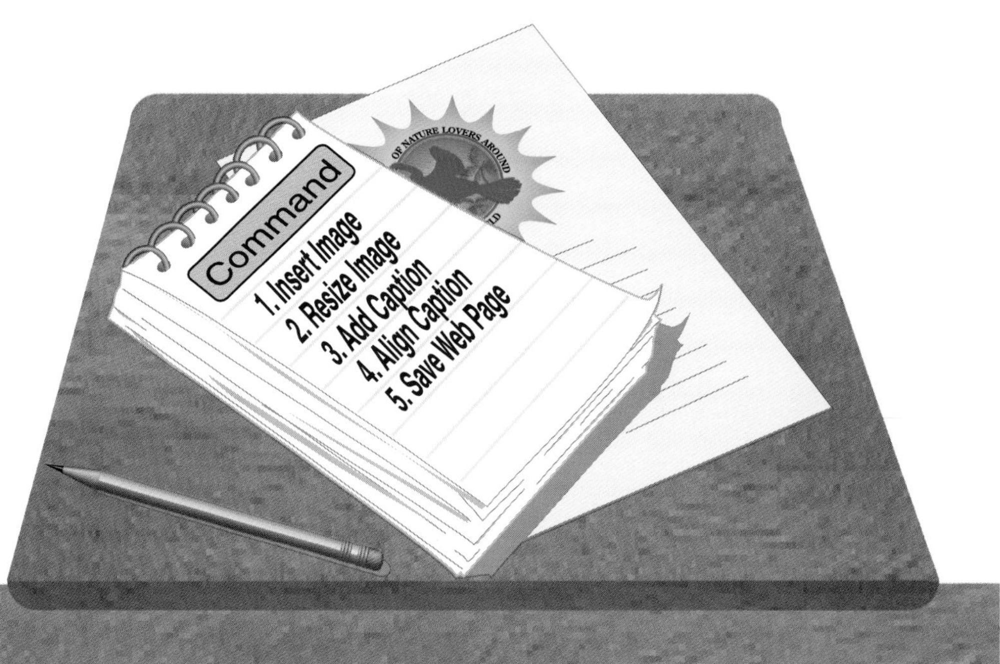

CREATE AND APPLY A CUSTOM COMMAND

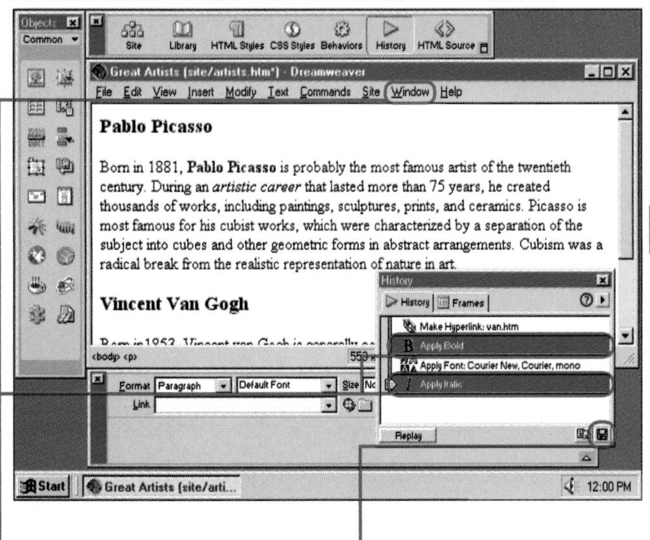

1. Click **Window⇨History** to open the History palette.
2. Ctrl-click (shift-click on the Mac) to select the commands you want to combine into a single command.
3. Click 🖫 to save the new command.

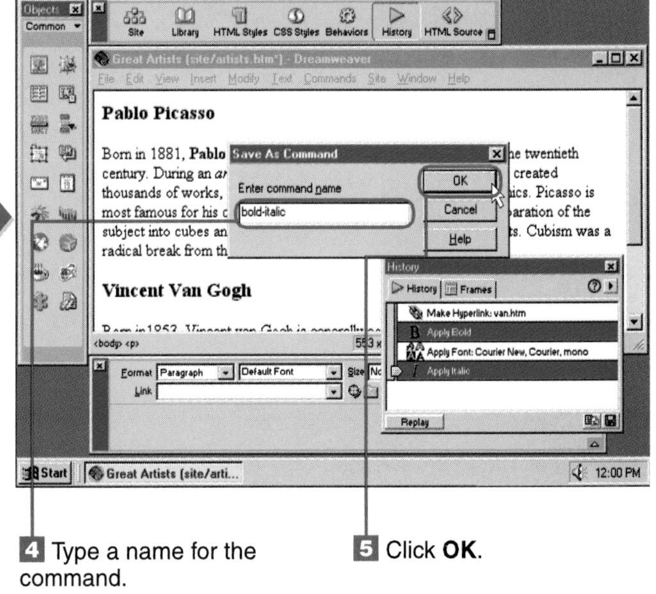

4. Type a name for the command.
5. Click **OK**.

How do I change the name of a custom command?

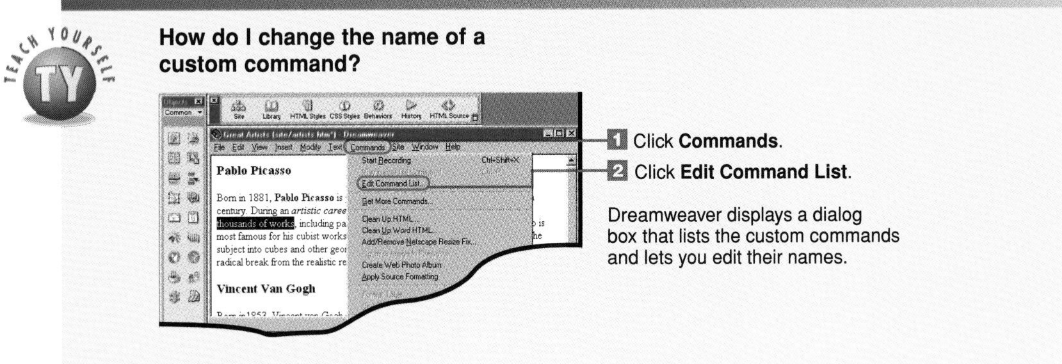

1 Click **Commands**.

2 Click **Edit Command List**.

Dreamweaver displays a dialog box that lists the custom commands and lets you edit their names.

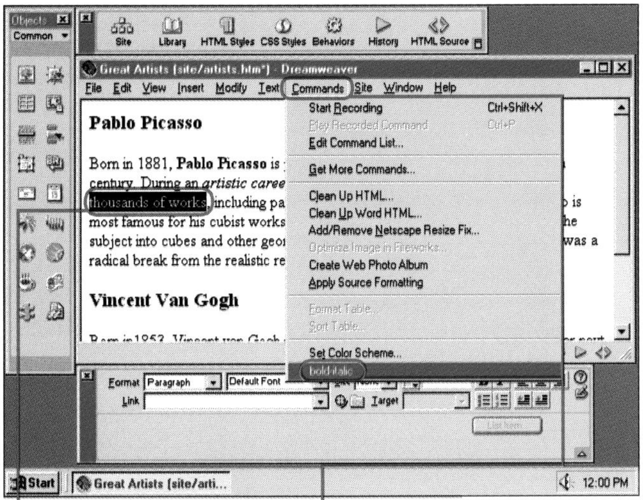

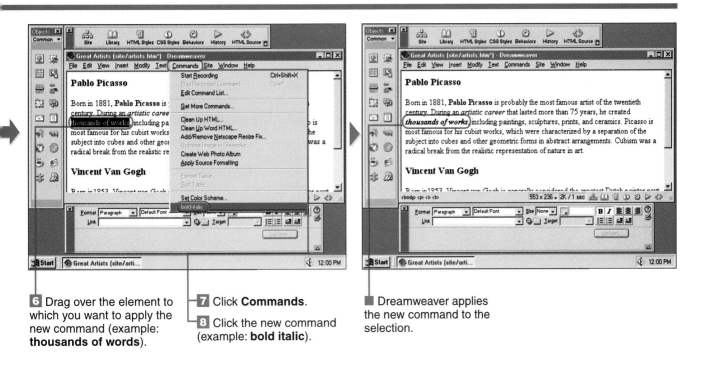

6 Drag over the element to which you want to apply the new command (example: **thousands of words**).

7 Click **Commands**.

8 Click the new command (example: **bold italic**).

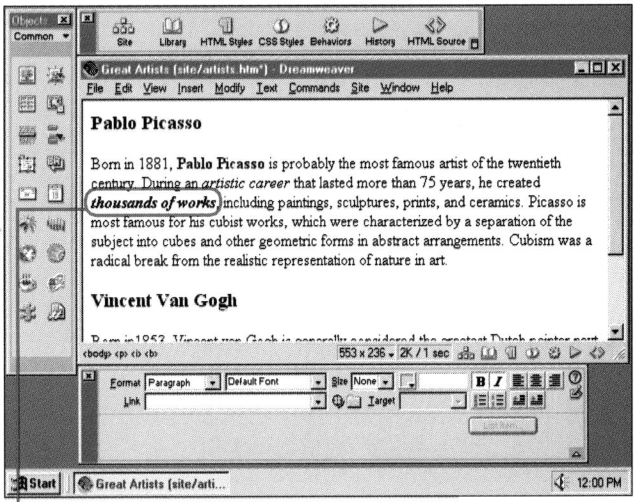

■ Dreamweaver applies the new command to the selection.

SET UP A LOCAL SITE

Set up your new Web site by naming it, and specify where on your computer you will store its files.

Before you start creating Web pages, you need to define a local site for your Web site so that Dreamweaver knows where to store certain files.

SET UP A LOCAL SITE

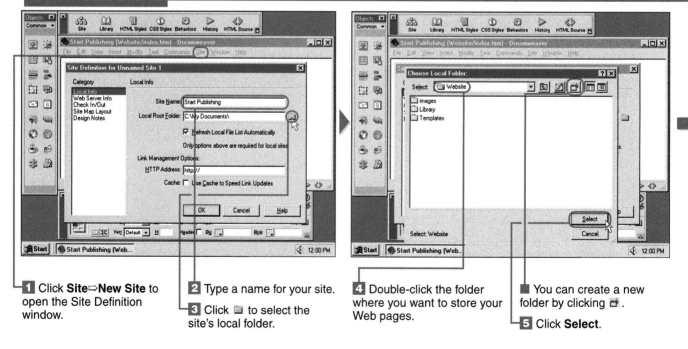

1 Click **Site⇨New Site** to open the Site Definition window.

2 Type a name for your site.

3 Click 🗀 to select the site's local folder.

4 Double-click the folder where you want to store your Web pages.

■ You can create a new folder by clicking 🗀.

5 Click **Select**.

Why is it important to keep all my Web site's files in a single folder on my computer?

If you do not organize your site files on the Web server the same way they appear on your local computer, hyperlinks will not work and images will not display properly. Keeping everything in the same folder enables you to easily transfer your site files to the Web server without changing their organization.

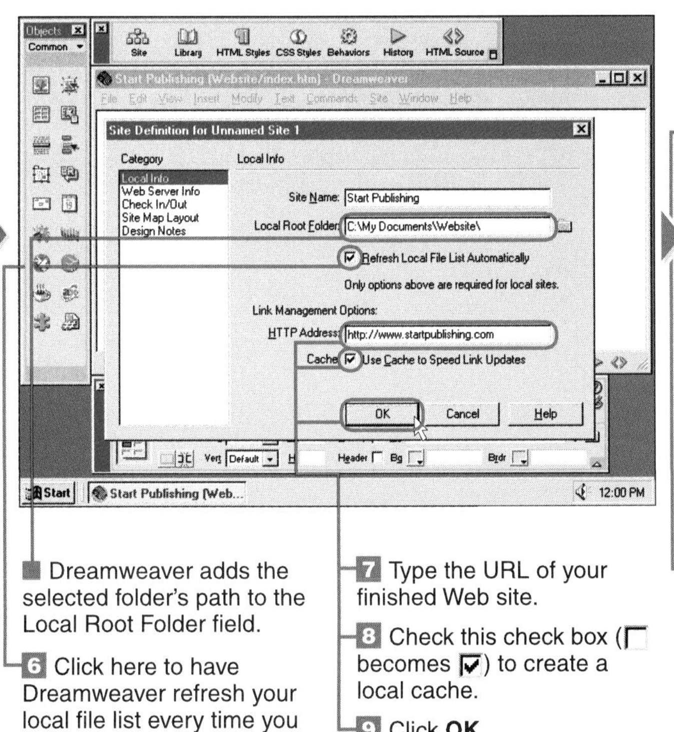

■ Dreamweaver adds the selected folder's path to the Local Root Folder field.

6 Click here to have Dreamweaver refresh your local file list every time you download (☐ becomes ☑.)

7 Type the URL of your finished Web site.

8 Check this check box (☐ becomes ☑) to create a local cache.

9 Click **OK**.

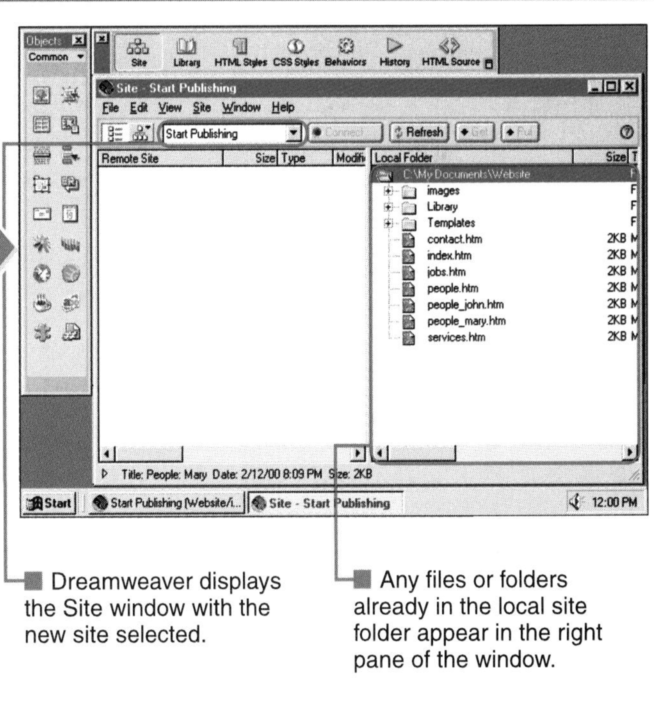

■ Dreamweaver displays the Site window with the new site selected.

■ Any files or folders already in the local site folder appear in the right pane of the window.

OPEN A WEB PAGE

You can open a Web page in Dreamweaver to add to and edit its content.

Note: *To open a Web page based on a template, see Chapter 10.*

OPEN A WEB PAGE

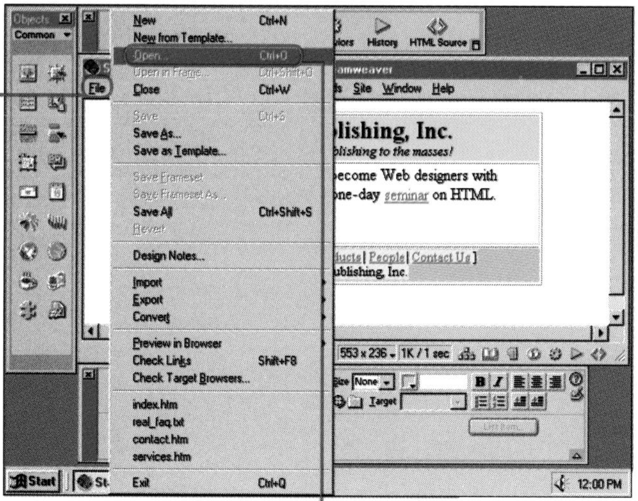

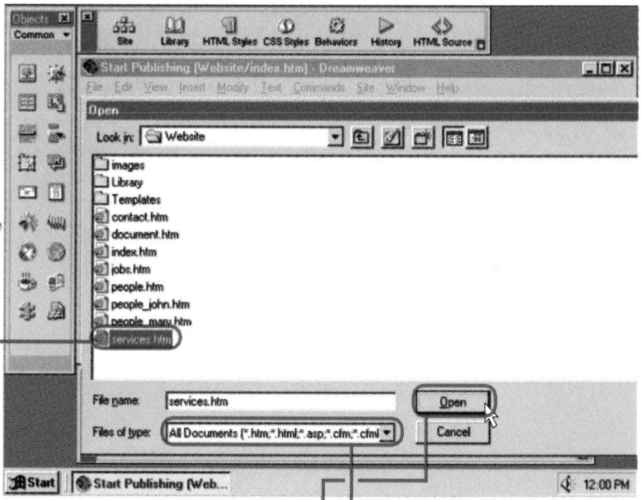

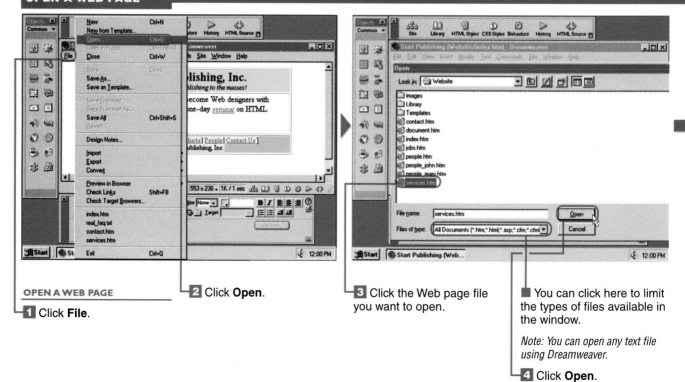

OPEN A WEB PAGE

1 Click **File**.

2 Click **Open**.

3 Click the Web page file you want to open.

■ You can click here to limit the types of files available in the window.

Note: You can open any text file using Dreamweaver.

4 Click **Open**.

Can I open Web pages created in other HTML editors?

Yes. Dreamweaver can open any HTML file, no matter where it was created.

It can also open non-HTML text files. However, the layout of such pages may look haphazard in Dreamweaver because they do not include HTML formatting.

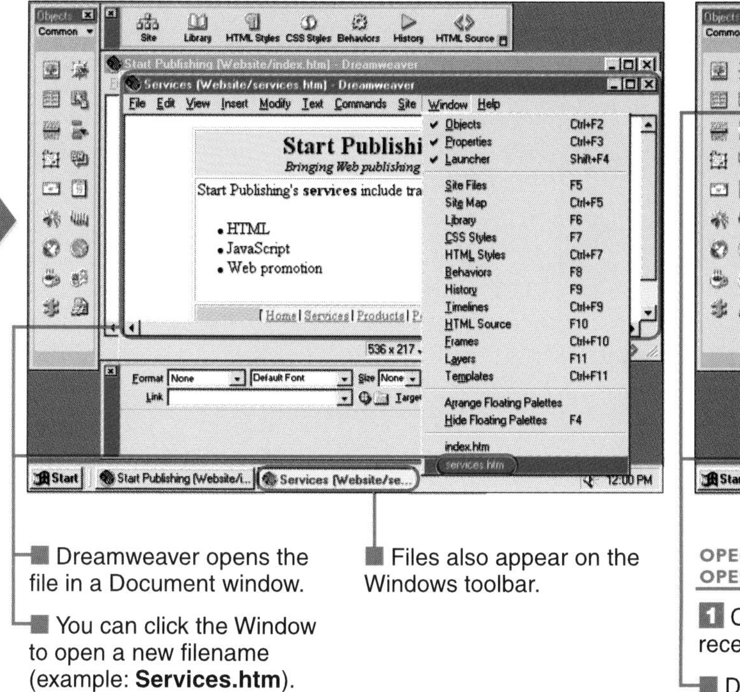

■ Dreamweaver opens the file in a Document window.

■ You can click the Window to open a new filename (example: **Services.htm**).

■ Files also appear on the Windows toolbar.

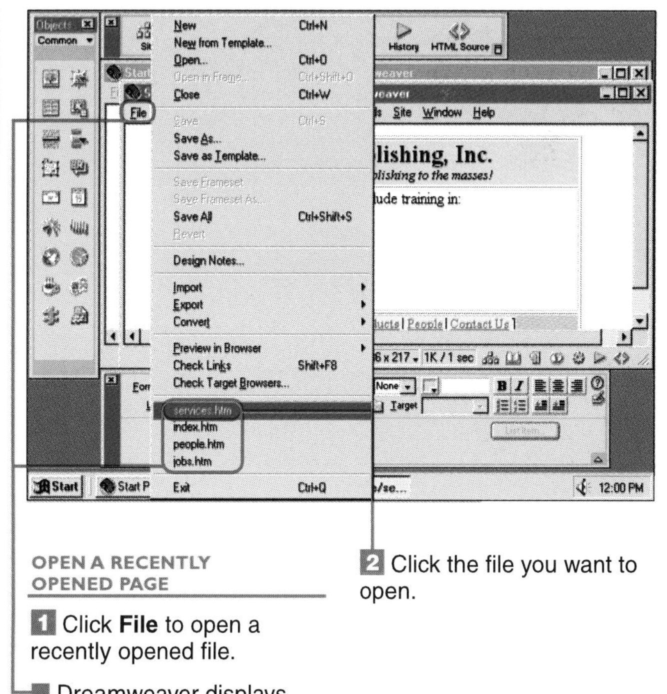

OPEN A RECENTLY OPENED PAGE

1 Click **File** to open a recently opened file.

■ Dreamweaver displays the last four files opened.

2 Click the file you want to open.

CREATE A NEW WEB PAGE

You can create a new, empty Web page in Dreamweaver.

CREATE A NEW WEB PAGE

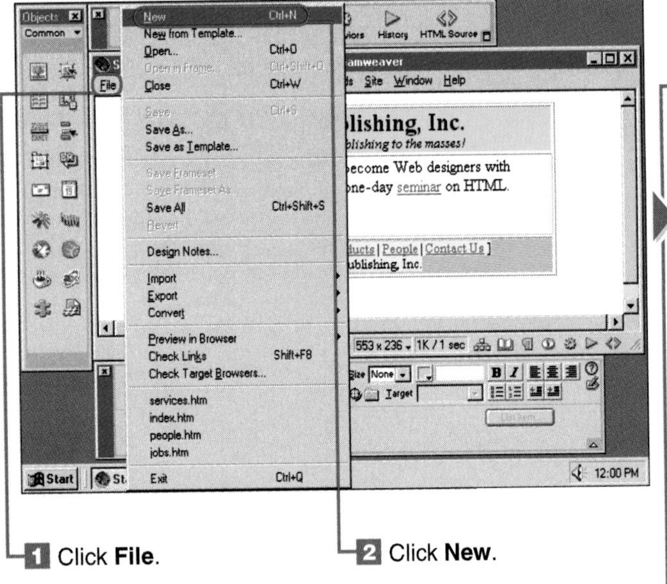

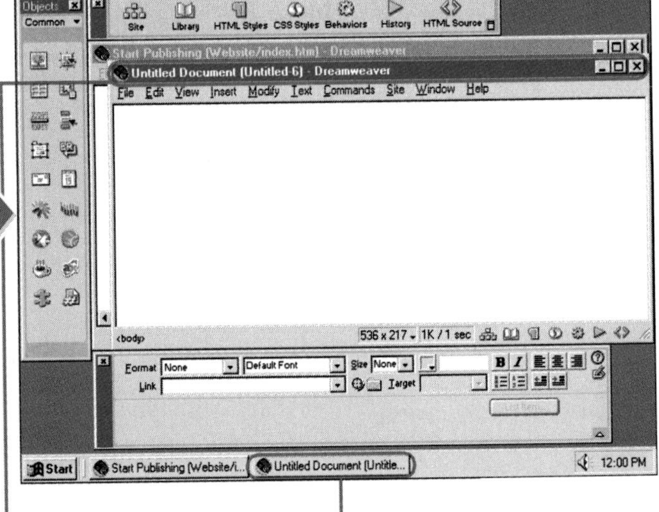

1 Click **File**.

2 Click **New**.

■ Dreamweaver opens an empty Document window.

■ The page name and filename are untitled until you save the page.

■ The file appears on the Windows tool bar.

Note: To save a page, see the section, "Save a Web Page."

ADD A TITLE TO A WEB PAGE

You can add a title to your Web page. This title appears in the browsers title bar when you view the page. Adding a title to your page allows it to be identified by viewers and search engines.

ADD A TITLE TO A WEB PAGE

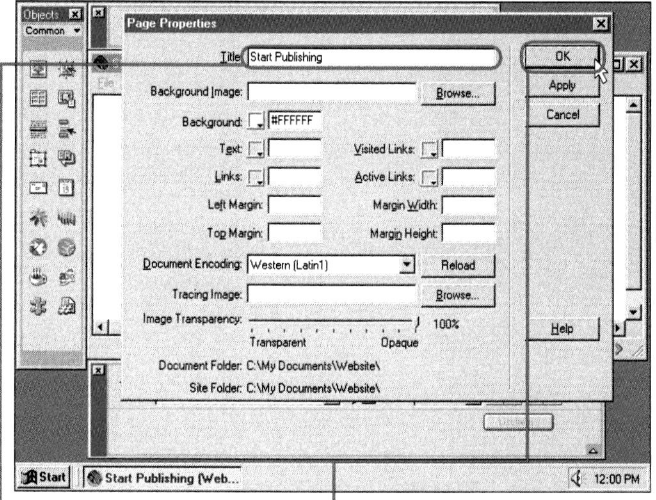

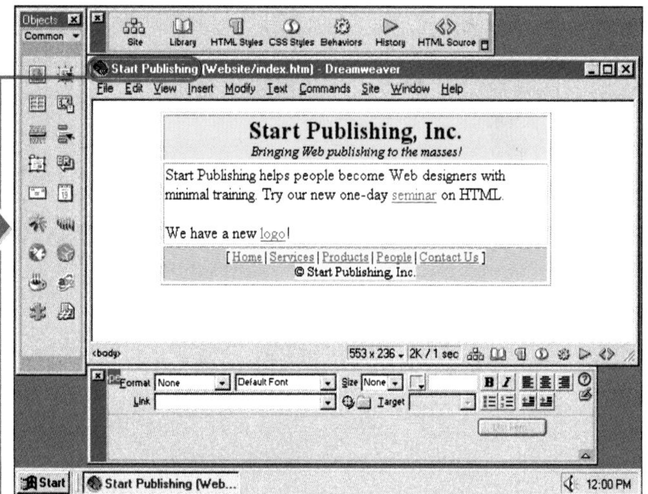

1 Choose **Modify⇨Page Properties** to open the Page Properties dialog box.

2 Type a descriptive title for your Web page.

Note: Search engines look at a Web page's title when they index it. The page title also appears in Favorite and Bookmark lists in Web browsers.

3 Click **OK**.

■ Dreamweaver places the new title in the title bar of the Document window.

SAVE A WEB PAGE

Saving your work frequently prevents data loss due to power outages or system failures.

SAVE A WEB PAGE

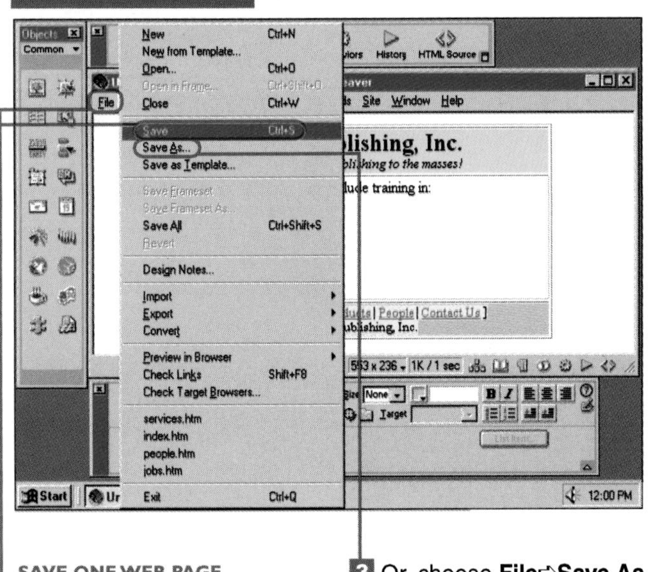

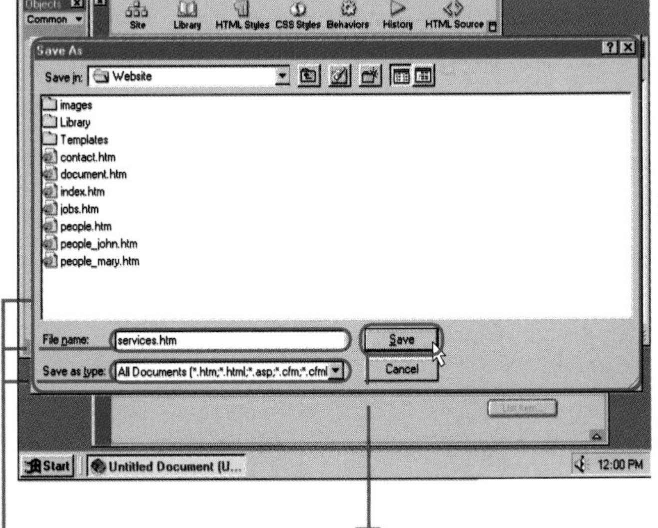

SAVE ONE WEB PAGE

1 Click **File**.

2 Click **Save**.

Note: You can also click **Save As** *to save a file with a new name.*

3 Or, choose **File⇨Save As** to save an existing file with a new filename.

Note: If you are saving the file for the first time or changing the name, the **Save As** *dialog box appears.*

WORK IN THE SAVE AS DIALOG BOX

1 Type a filename for the page.

■ Web pages are HTML files and must have their filenames end in .htm (PC default) or .html (Macintosh default).

2 Click **Save**.

How should I store the files for my Web site on my computer?

You should save all the files for your Web site in one folder on your computer. This makes things easier when you hyperlink between files or transfer the site to a Web server.

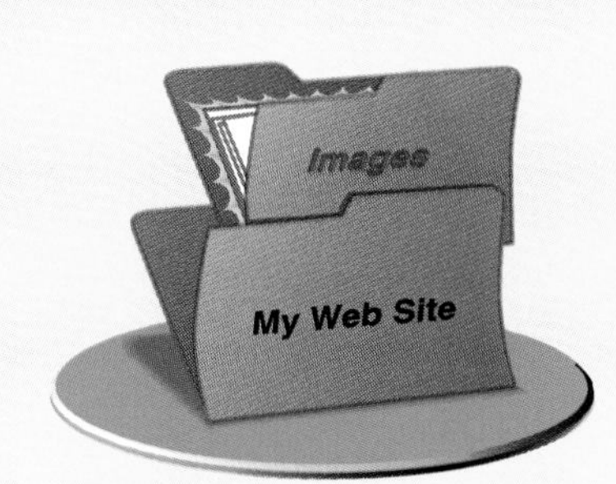

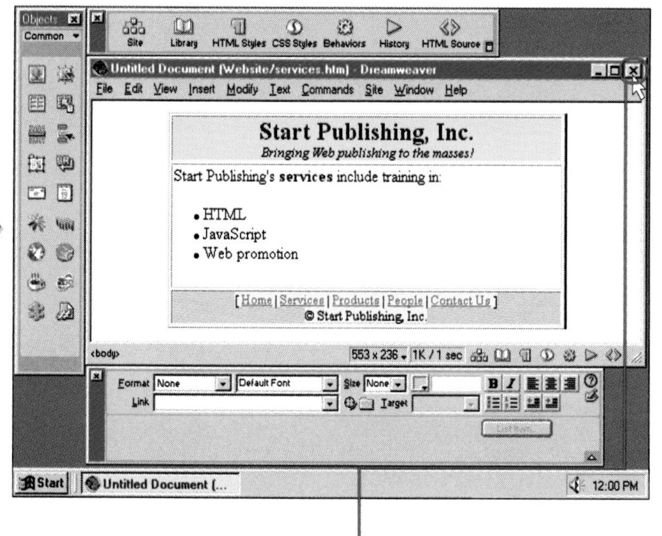

■ Dreamweaver saves the file and returns you to the Document window.

■ Click ☒ to close the page.

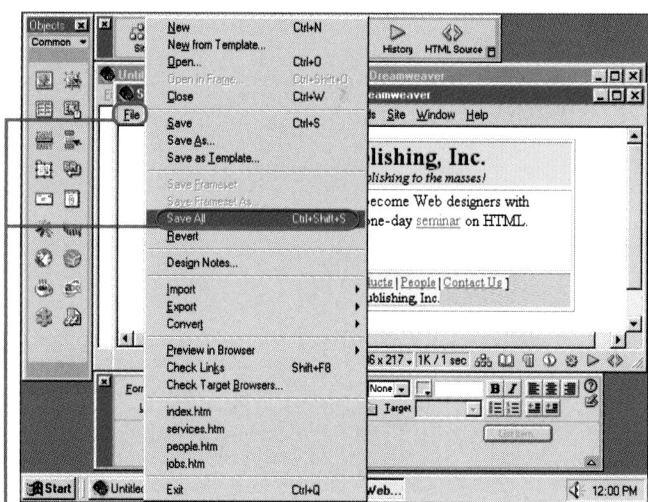

SAVE ALL OPEN WEB PAGES AT ONCE

1 Click **File**.

2 Click **Save All**.

■ Dreamweaver prompts you for any filenames that need to be specified.

PREVIEW A WEB PAGE IN A BROWSER

You can see how your page will really look online by viewing the page in a Web browser.

Viewing pages in a Web browser enables you to test features that do not appear in Dreamweaver's Document window, such as Behaviors and certain Style Sheet effects.

PREVIEW A WEB PAGE IN A BROWSER

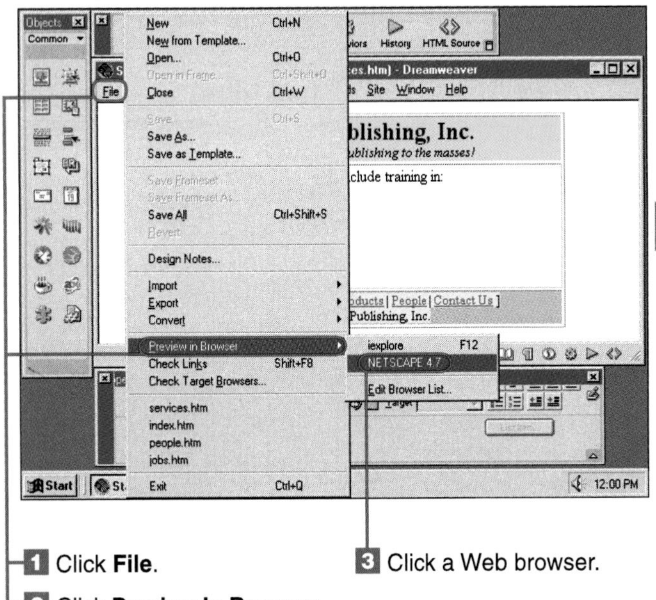

1 Click **File**.

2 Click **Preview In Browser**.

3 Click a Web browser.

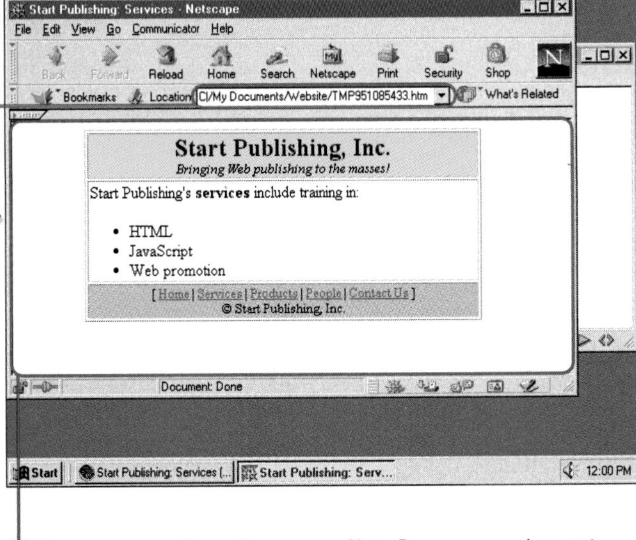

■ Dreamweaver launches the Web browser and opens the page inside it.

■ The file is given a temporary filename for viewing in the browser.

Note: Dreamweaver does not come with Web browser software.

SET PREFERENCES

You can easily change the default behavior of Dreamweaver in the Preferences window.

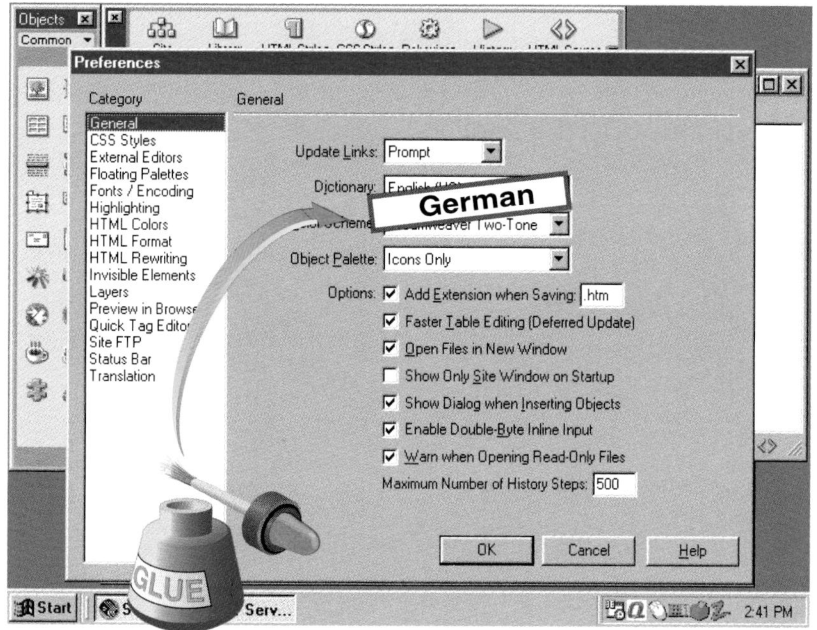

Preferences let you change the appearance of Dreamweaver's user interface. You can also change the way Dreamweaver writes HTML and generates features such as layers and style sheets.

SET PREFERENCES

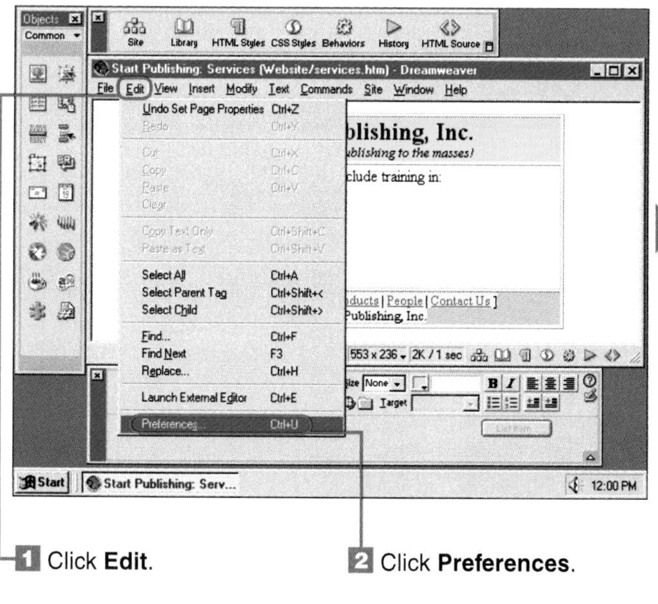

1 Click **Edit**.

2 Click **Preferences**.

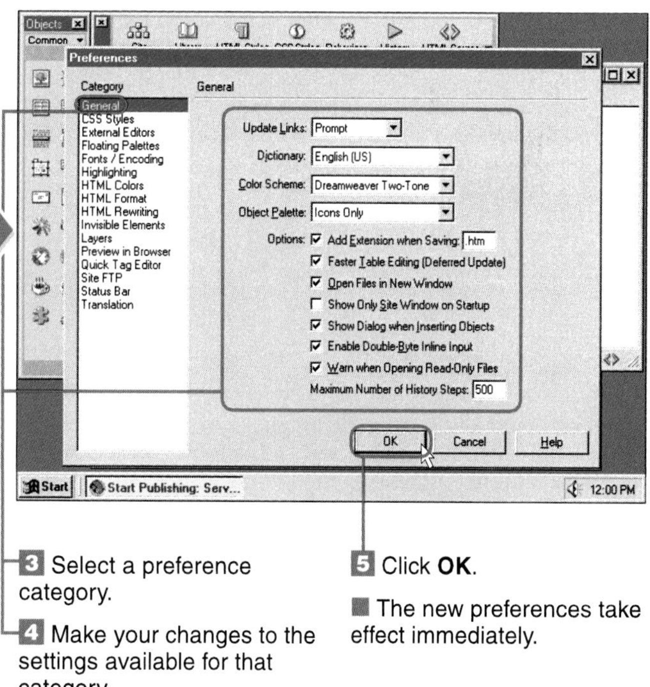

3 Select a preference category.

4 Make your changes to the settings available for that category.

5 Click **OK**.

■ The new preferences take effect immediately.

Into the Wild!
Would you like to venture beyond the beaten path? Do so with Into the Wild's adventure tours.
Whether you'd like to take a nature photography tour, camp in the rugged wilderness of the Rocky Mountains or go on a canoeing adventure, we have the trip for you!
Skiing
Some of our most popular trips are alpine skiing excursions in the Rocky Mountains. We will fly you to the top of the slopes by helicopter and provide comfortable accomodations at the end of a fun-filled day! Cross-country ski packages are also available!
Notepad
rch Help
HTML
the Wild</TITLE>
the Wild!</I></H1>
ougar.jpg" ALIGN=left>
you like to venture beyond the beaten path? Do
o the Wild's adventure tours.</B></P>
you'd like to take a nature photography tour,
rugged wilderness of the Rocky Mountains or go
ng adventure, we have the trip for you!</P>
kier.jpg" ALIGN=right>
ing</H3>
our most popular trips are alpine skiing
in the Rocky Mountains. We will fly you to the
slopes by helicopter and provide comfortable
ns at the end of a fun-filled day!
ry ski packages are also available!</P>

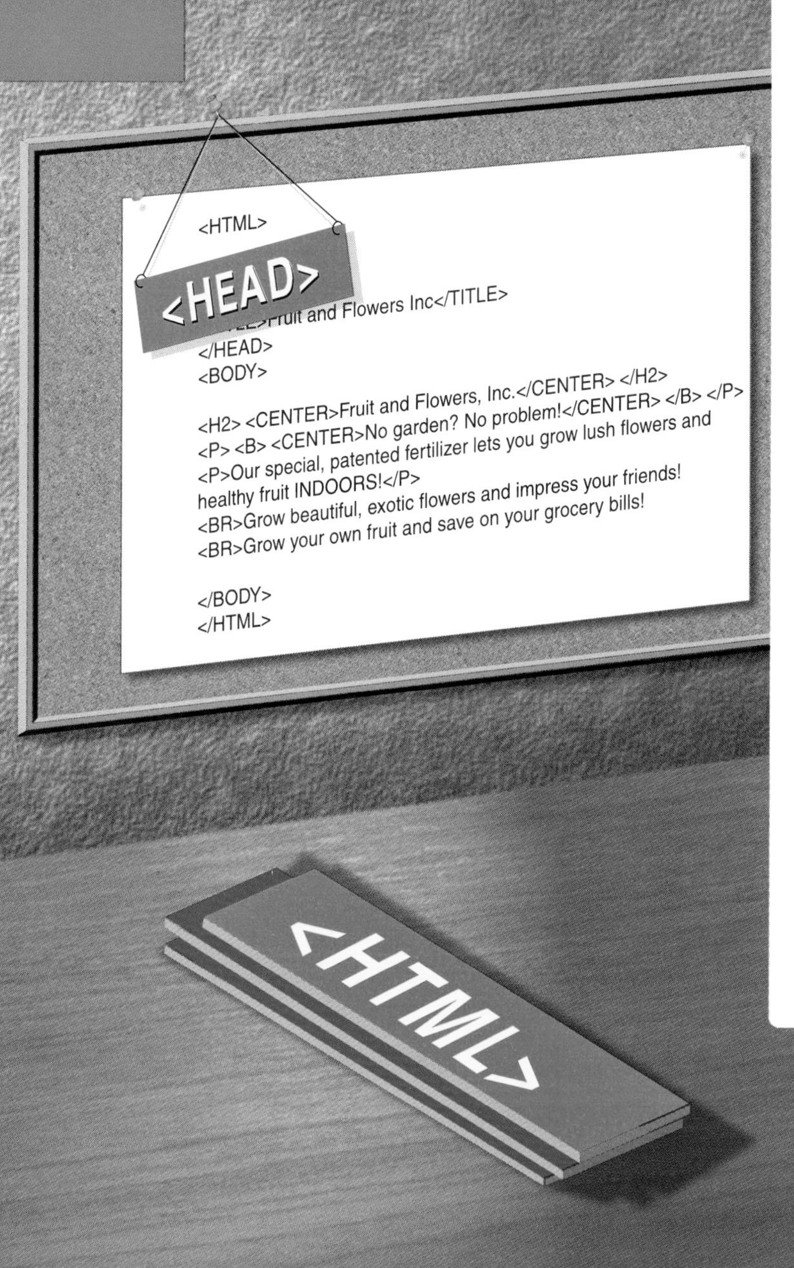
<HTML>
<HEAD>
Fruit and Flowers Inc</TITLE>
</HEAD>
<BODY>
<H2> <CENTER>Fruit and Flowers, Inc.</CENTER> </H2>
<P> <B> <CENTER>No garden? No problem!</CENTER> </B> </P>
<P>Our special, patented fertilizer lets you grow lush flowers and
healthy fruit INDOORS!</P>

Grow beautiful, exotic flowers and impress your friends!

Grow your own fruit and save on your grocery bills!
</BODY>
</HTML>
<HTML>

CHAPTER 3

HTML Basics

Dreamweaver helps you build Web pages by writing HTML. This chapter will introduce you to the important features of this language.

You can create Web pages with HTML.

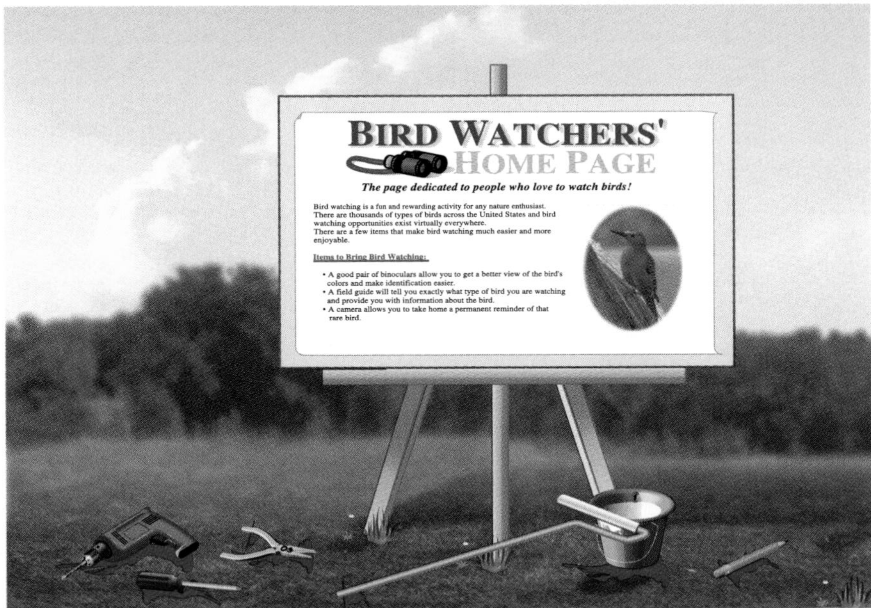

HTML

Hypertext Markup Language, or HTML, is the formatting language that you use to create Web pages. When you open a Web page in a browser, its HTML code tells the browser how to display the text, images, and other content on the page.

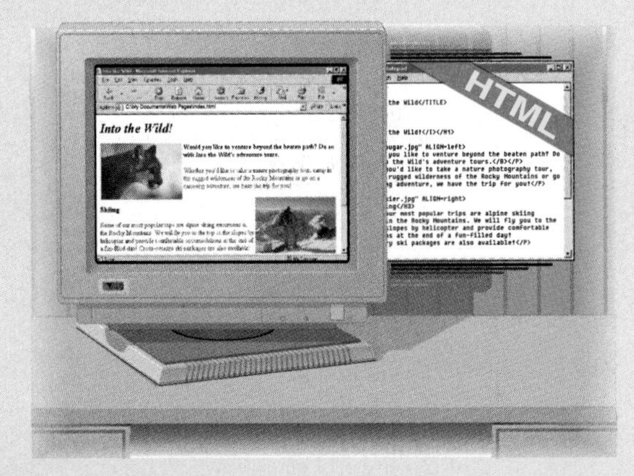

HTML TAGS

The basic unit of HTML is a *tag.* You can recognize HTML tags by their angle brackets:

```
<p>Today the weather was <b>nice</b>.<br>
Tomorrow it may <i>rain</i>.</p>
```

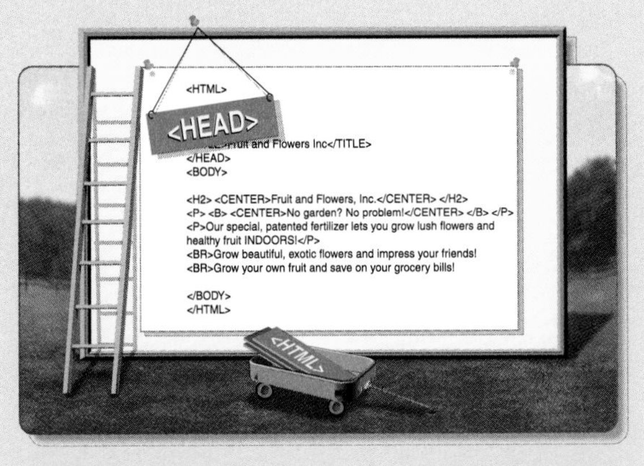

HOW TAGS WORK

Some HTML tags work in twos — opening and closing tags surround content in a document and control the formatting of the content (for instance, <b> tags cause text to be bold). Closing tags are distinguished by a forward slash (/). Other tags can stand alone (for instance, the <br> tag adds a line break). HTML tags are not case sensitive — they can be uppercase, lowercase, or mixed case.

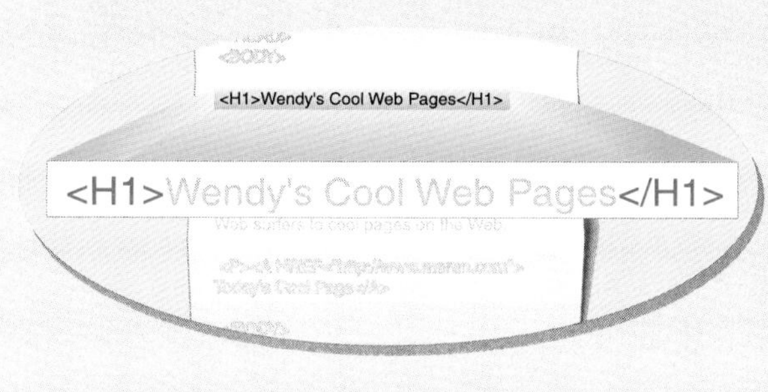

HTML DOCUMENTS

Because HTML documents are plain text files, you can open and edit them with any text editor. But writing HTML by hand can be a slow, tedious process, especially when creating advanced HTML elements such as tables, forms, and frames.

CREATE WEB PAGES WITHOUT KNOWING CODE

Dreamweaver streamlines the process of creating Web pages by giving you an easy-to-use, visual interface with which to generate HTML. You specify formatting with menu commands and button clicks, and Dreamweaver takes care of writing the HTML code behind the scenes. When you build a Web page in the Document window, you see your page as it will eventually appear in a Web browser, instead of as HTML code.

DIRECT ACCESS TO THE CODE

Dreamweaver gives you direct access to the raw HTML code. This can be an advantage for people who know HTML and want to do some formatting of their page by typing tags. The HTML Source inspector and QuickTag Editor in Dreamweaver enable you to edit your page by adding HTML tags manually.

STRUCTURAL TAGS

You define the basic structure of every HTML document with several tags. To view a page's HTML, click the HTML Source icon in the Launcher.

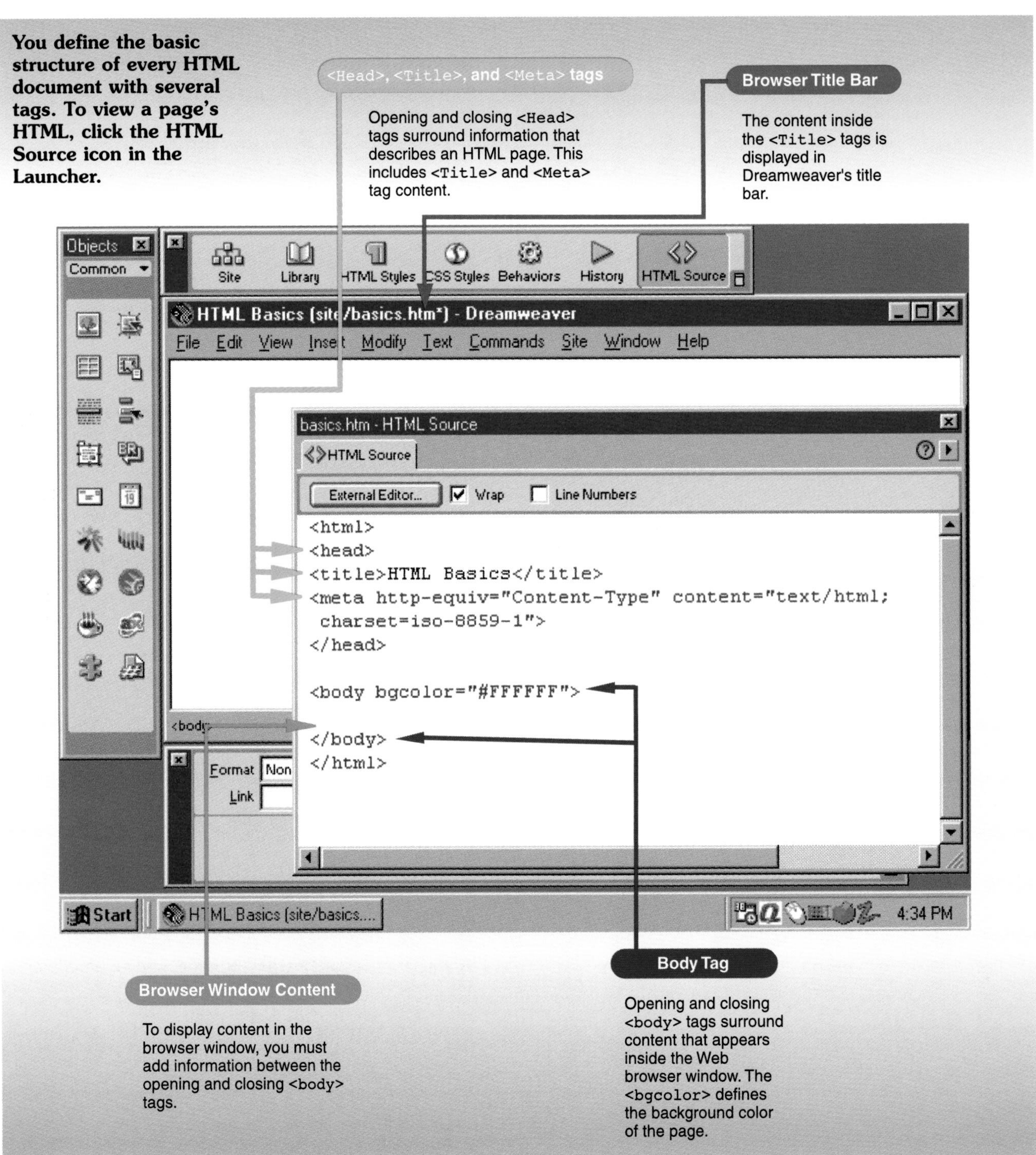

<Head>, <Title>, and <Meta> tags
Opening and closing <Head> tags surround information that describes an HTML page. This includes <Title> and <Meta> tag content.
Browser Title Bar
The content inside the <Title> tags is displayed in Dreamweaver's title bar.
Objects
Common
Site
Library
HTML Styles
CSS Styles
Behaviors
History
HTML Source
HTML Basics (site/basics.htm*) - Dreamweaver
File Edit View Insert Modify Text Commands Site Window Help
basics.htm - HTML Source
HTML Source
External Editor...
Wrap
Line Numbers
<html>
<head>
<title>HTML Basics</title>
<meta http-equiv="Content-Type" content="text/html; charset=iso-8859-1">
</head>
<body bgcolor="#FFFFFF">
</body>
</html>
<body>
Format
Link
Start
HTML Basics (site/basics....
4:34 PM
Browser Window Content
To display content in the browser window, you must add information between the opening and closing <body> tags.
Body Tag
Opening and closing <body> tags surround content that appears inside the Web browser window. The <bgcolor> defines the background color of the page.

BLOCK-FORMATTING TAGS

You organize information in your Web page with block-formatting tags. To view a page's HTML, click the HTML Source icon in the Launcher.

View of HTML Code

<h> Tag

An <h> tag defines information as a heading. There are six levels of headings, <h1> (the largest) through <h6> (the smallest).

, <ol>, and <pre> Tags

Other block-formatting tags include
 (line break), <ol> (ordered list), and <pre> (preformatted text).

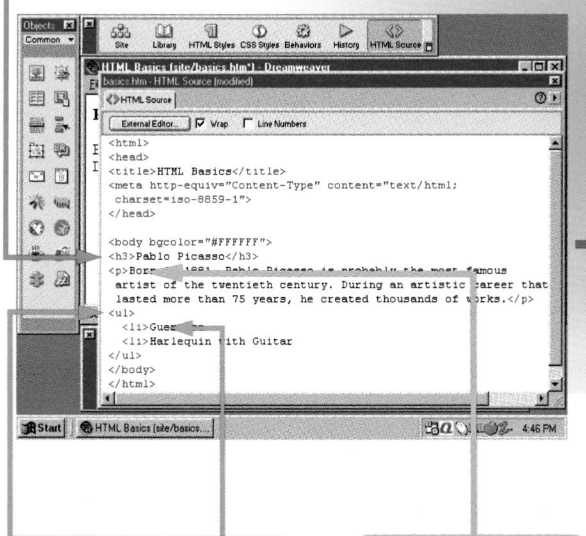

<ul> and <li> Tags

The <ul> tag defines an unordered list. Each list item is defined with the <li> tag.

<p> Tag

The <p> tag defines information as a paragraph.

Web Page View

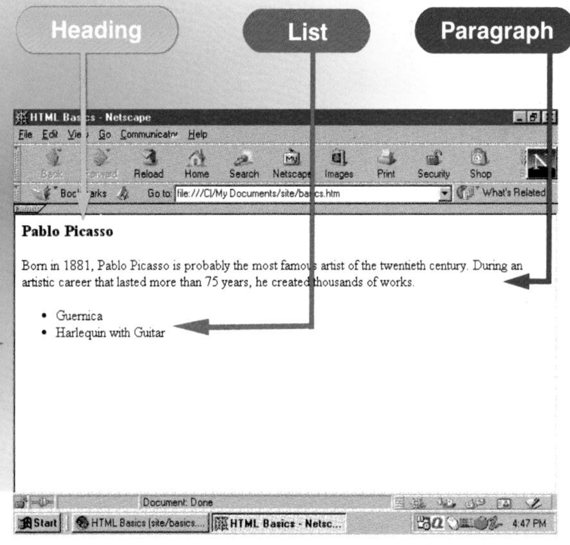

Heading, Paragraph, and Unordered List

This page has a heading, a paragraph, and an unordered list.

TEXT-FORMATTING TAGS

You can format the style of sentences, words, and characters with text-formatting tags. To view a page's HTML, click the HTML Source icon in the Launcher.

<font> Tag

The <font> tag controls various characteristics of the text on a Web page.

size Attribute

The size attribute goes inside the <font> tag and changes the size of text.

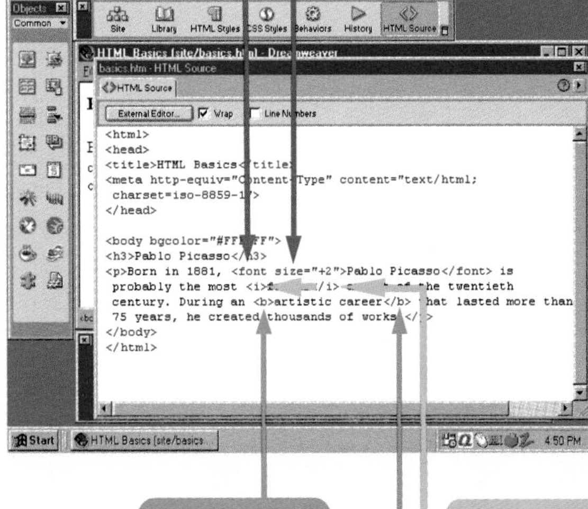

<b> Tag

The <b> tag defines the text as bold.

<i> Tag

The <i> tag defines text as italic.

face and color Attributes

Other font attributes include face and color, which modify the font face and color of text.

Web Page View

Bold Text

Font Size

Italic Text

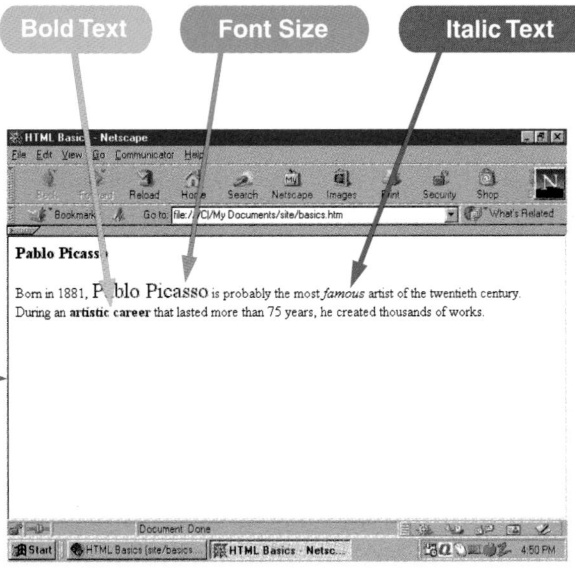

Font Size, Bold Text, and Italic Text

This paragraph has text with a different font size, as well as bold and italic text.

THE IMAGE TAG

The <img> tag lets you add an image to your page. To view a page's HTML, click the HTML Source icon in the Launcher.

View of HTML code

align Attribute

The align attribute aligns the image to one side of the page and causes content that follows to wrap around it.

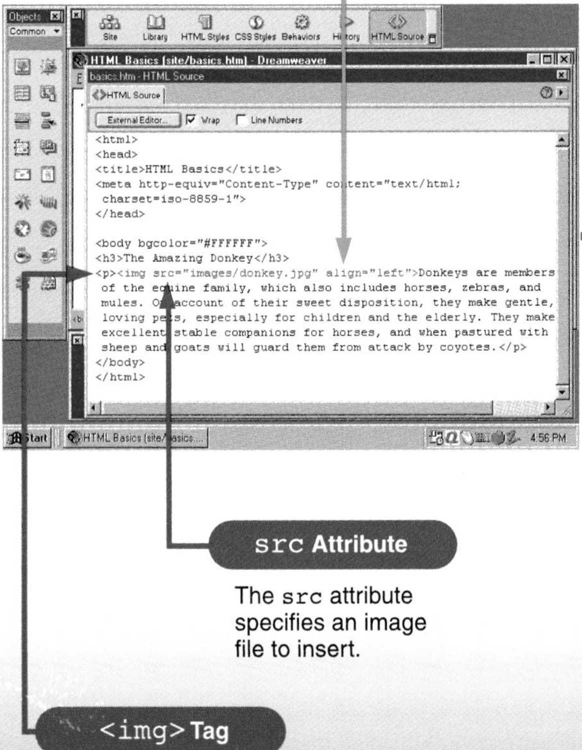

src Attribute

The src attribute specifies an image file to insert.

<img> Tag

The <img> tag inserts an image into a page.

Web Page View

Text

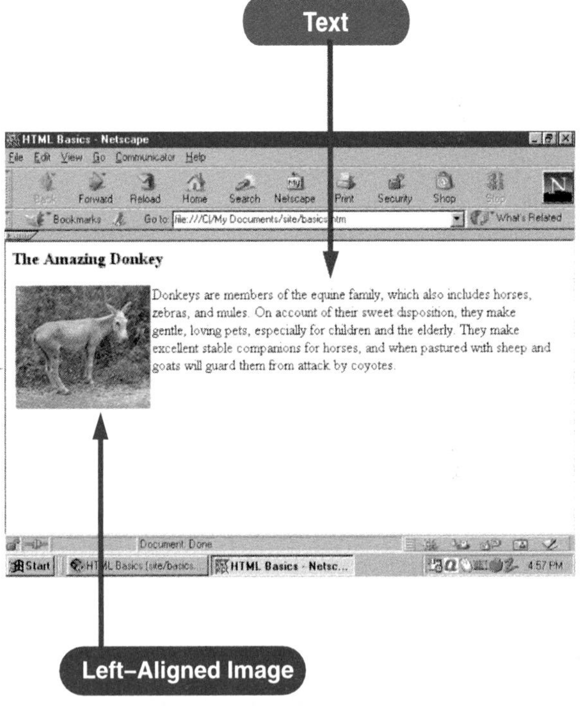

Left-Aligned Image

Image Alignment and Text Wrapping

This page has a left-aligned image. The text that follows it wraps to the right of the image.

You can create hyperlinks with the <a> tag. To view a page's HTML, click the HTML Source icon in the Launcher.

View of HTML code

<a> Tag

The <a> tag creates a hyperlink. It can surround text or an image.

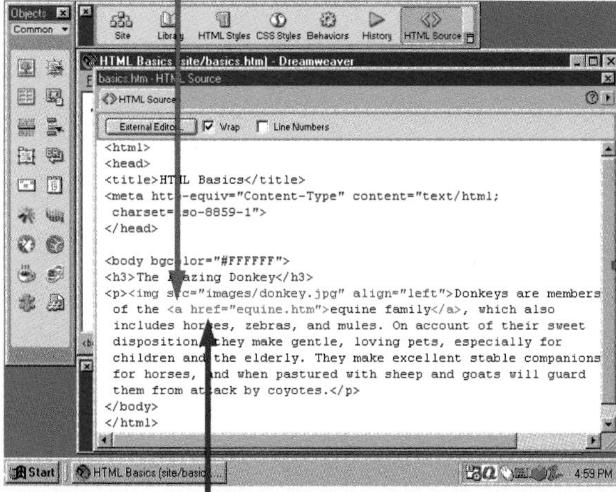

href Attribute

The `href` attribute defines the hyperlink destination.

Web Page View

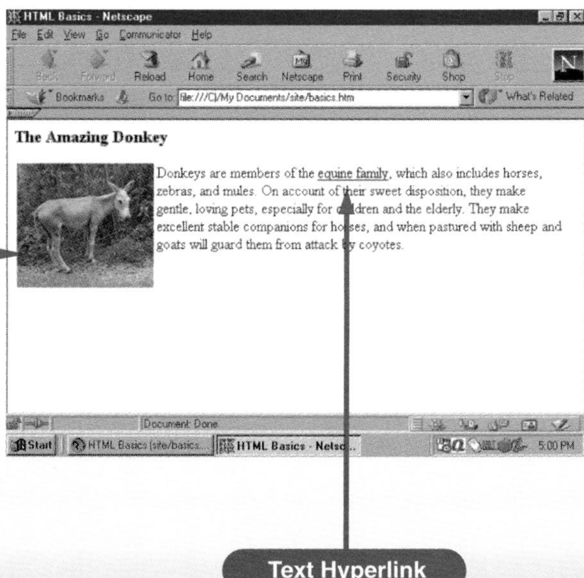

Text Hyperlink

The paragraph displays a text hyperlink. Clicking the underlined words takes the viewer to a file that further explains the text.

ADVANCED FEATURES

You can add advanced features, such as tables and forms to your Web page using HTML.

Other Advanced HTML features include frames and layers. To view a page's HTML, click the HTML Source icon in the Launcher.

View of HTML Code

<Form> Tags

You can create forms with the <form> tag. The <input> tags define places in the form where the user enters information.

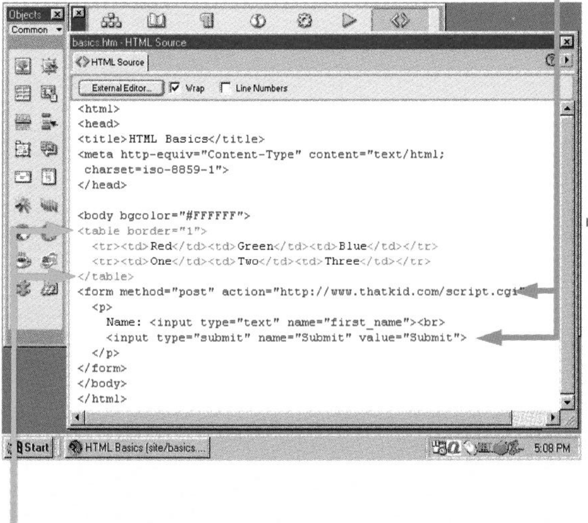

Table Tags

You can create tables with the <table> tag. The <tr> and <td> tags define a table's rows and columns.

Web Page View

Table Formatting

The table has three columns and two rows (for more about tables, see Chapter 7).

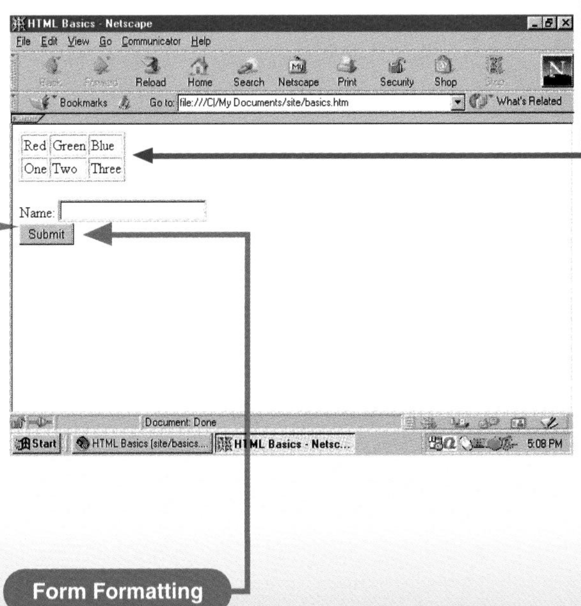

Form Formatting

The form has a text field for entering information. The button allows the user to send the form information to the Web server (for more about forms, see Chapter 8).

You can view and edit the HTML of a Web page directly in the HTML Source inspector, which is useful when you want to create or modify something at the code level.

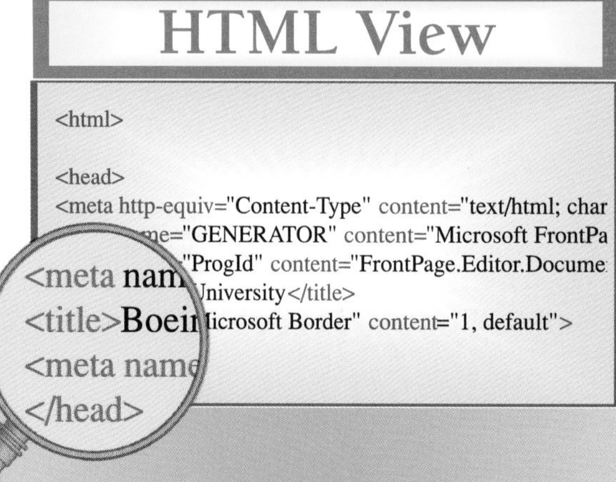

You can also use the Quick Tag Editor to rapidly add or edit a single HTML tag (see the section "Using the Quick Tag Editor" in this chapter).

USING THE HTML SOURCE INSPECTOR

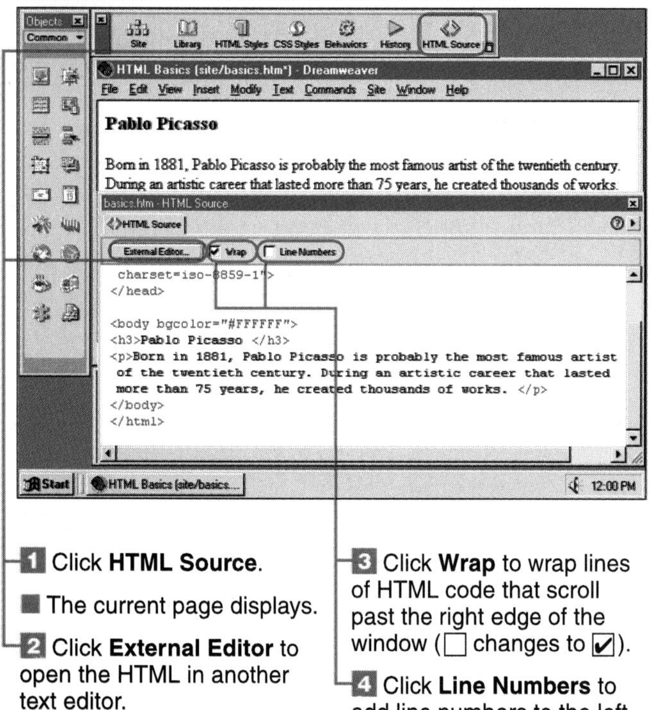

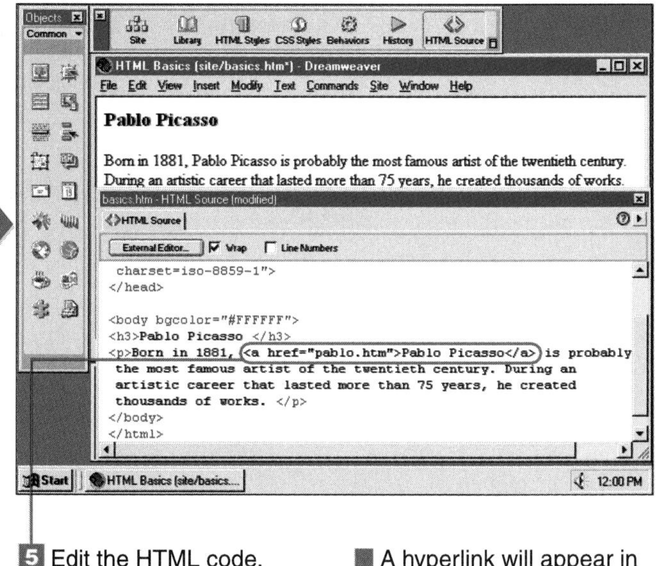

1 Click **HTML Source**.

■ The current page displays.

2 Click **External Editor** to open the HTML in another text editor.

3 Click **Wrap** to wrap lines of HTML code that scroll past the right edge of the window (☐ changes to ☑).

4 Click **Line Numbers** to add line numbers to the left side of the window.

5 Edit the HTML code.

■ A hyperlink will appear in the paragraph.

Does a Web page coded by hand in the HTML Source inspector look different from a page coded using Dreamweaver commands?

No, there is no difference. As long as the manually written HTML is valid, it produces the same results in a Web browser as the HTML that Dreamweaver generates.

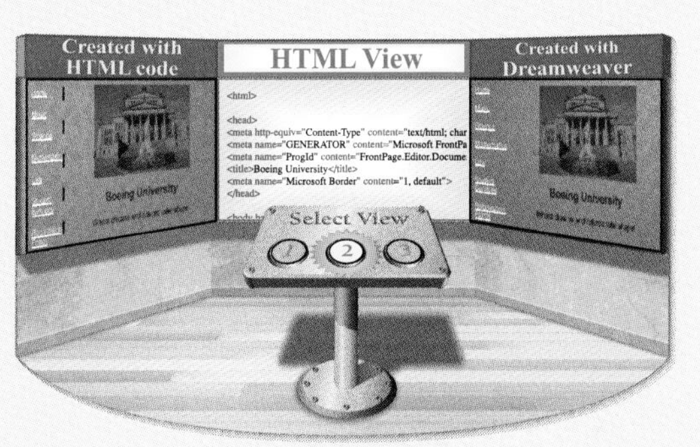

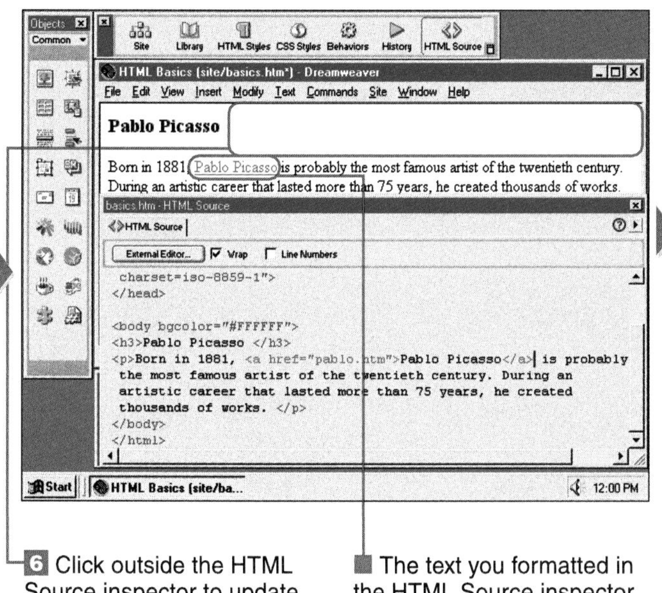

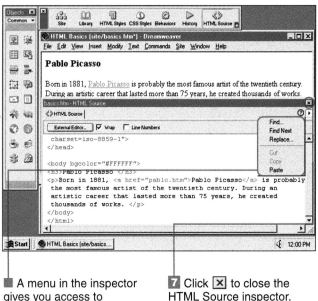

6 Click outside the HTML Source inspector to update the current document.

■ The text you formatted in the HTML Source inspector becomes a hyperlink.

■ A menu in the inspector gives you access to frequently used commands. (For details on using the Find and Replace commands, see Chapter 13).

7 Click ☒ to close the HTML Source inspector.

USING THE QUICK TAG EDITOR

You can quickly add or edit an HTML tag with the Quick Tag Editor, which saves you from switching between the Document window and the HTML Source inspector.

For large-scale editing of a page's HTML code, use the HTML Source inspector (see the section "Using the HTML Source Inspector").

USING THE QUICK TAG EDITOR

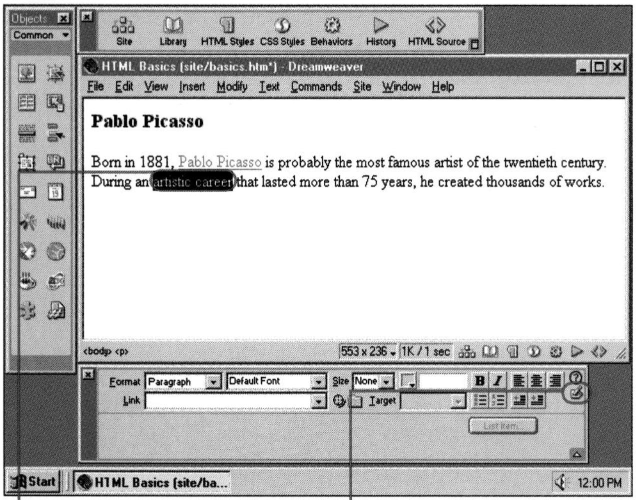

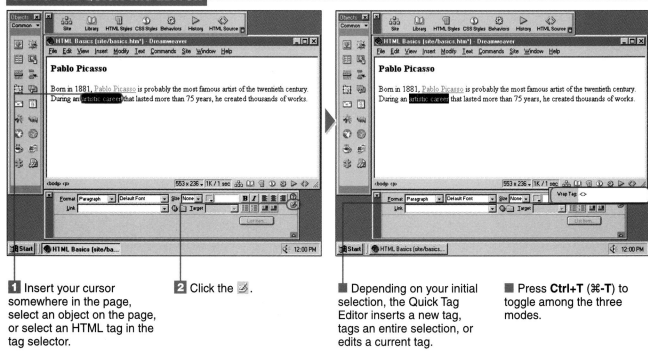

1 Insert your cursor somewhere in the page, select an object on the page, or select an HTML tag in the tag selector.

2 Click the .

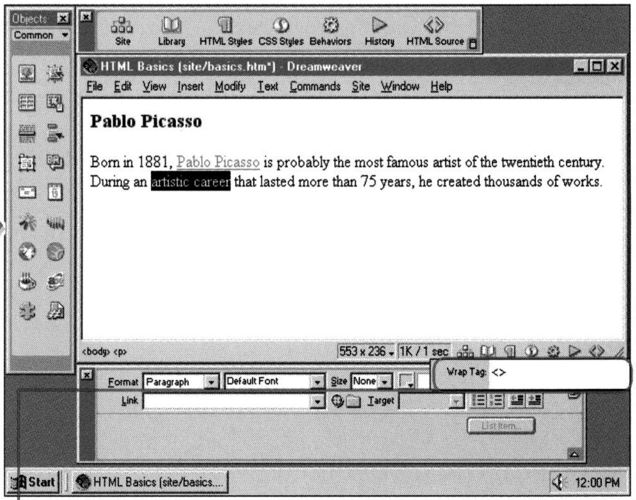

■ Depending on your initial selection, the Quick Tag Editor inserts a new tag, tags an entire selection, or edits a current tag.

■ Press **Ctrl+T** (**⌘-T**) to toggle among the three modes.

Does Dreamweaver fix invalid HTML?

By default, Dreamweaver rewrites some instances of invalid HTML. When you open an HTML document, Dreamweaver rewrites tags that are not nested properly, closes tags that are not allowed to remain open, and removes extra closing tags. If Dreamweaver does not recognize a tag, it highlights it in yellow and displays it in the Document window (but will not remove it). You can change this behavior by clicking **Edit**, clicking **Preferences,** and then selecting **HTML Rewriting**.

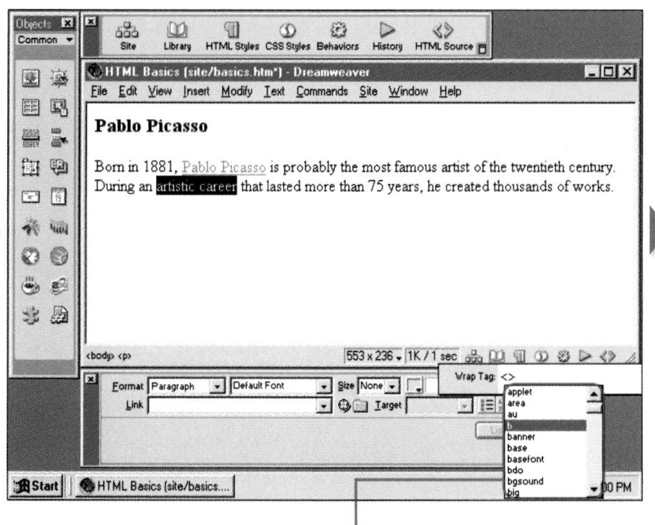

■ If you pause in the insert or wrap modes, a menu displays. You can select an HTML tag by using the ▲ and ▼ keys.

3 Select the desired item from the menu.

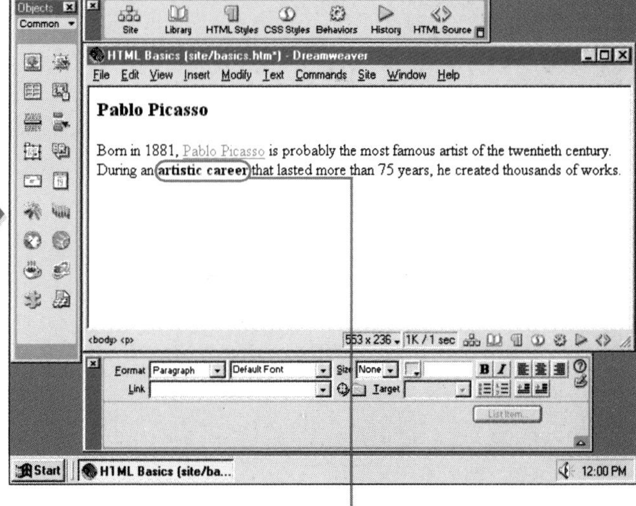

4 Apply a change by pressing **Enter** (**Return**).

■ The selection is tagged and bolded.

■ To exit without applying changes, press **Esc**.

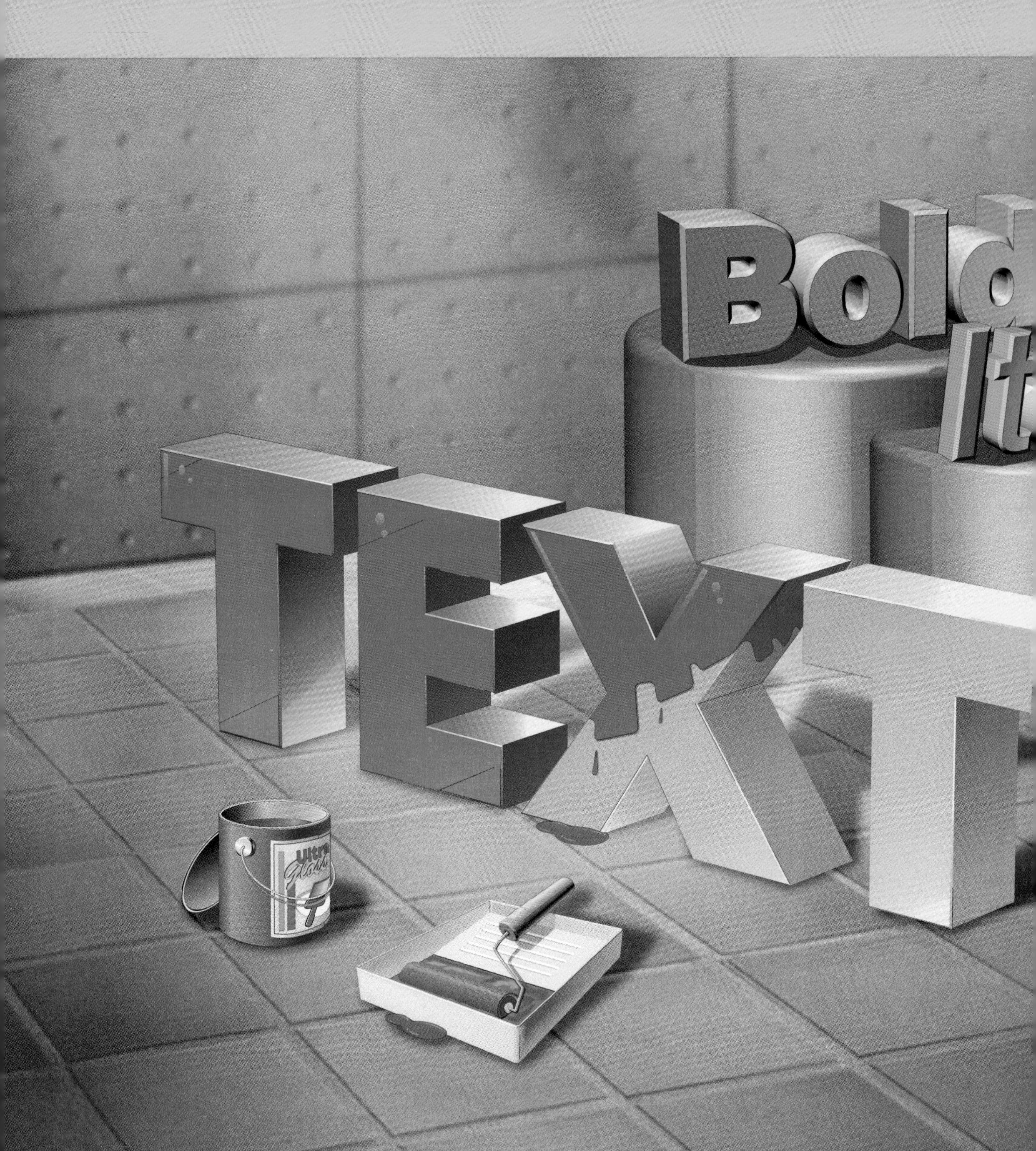
Bold
TEXT

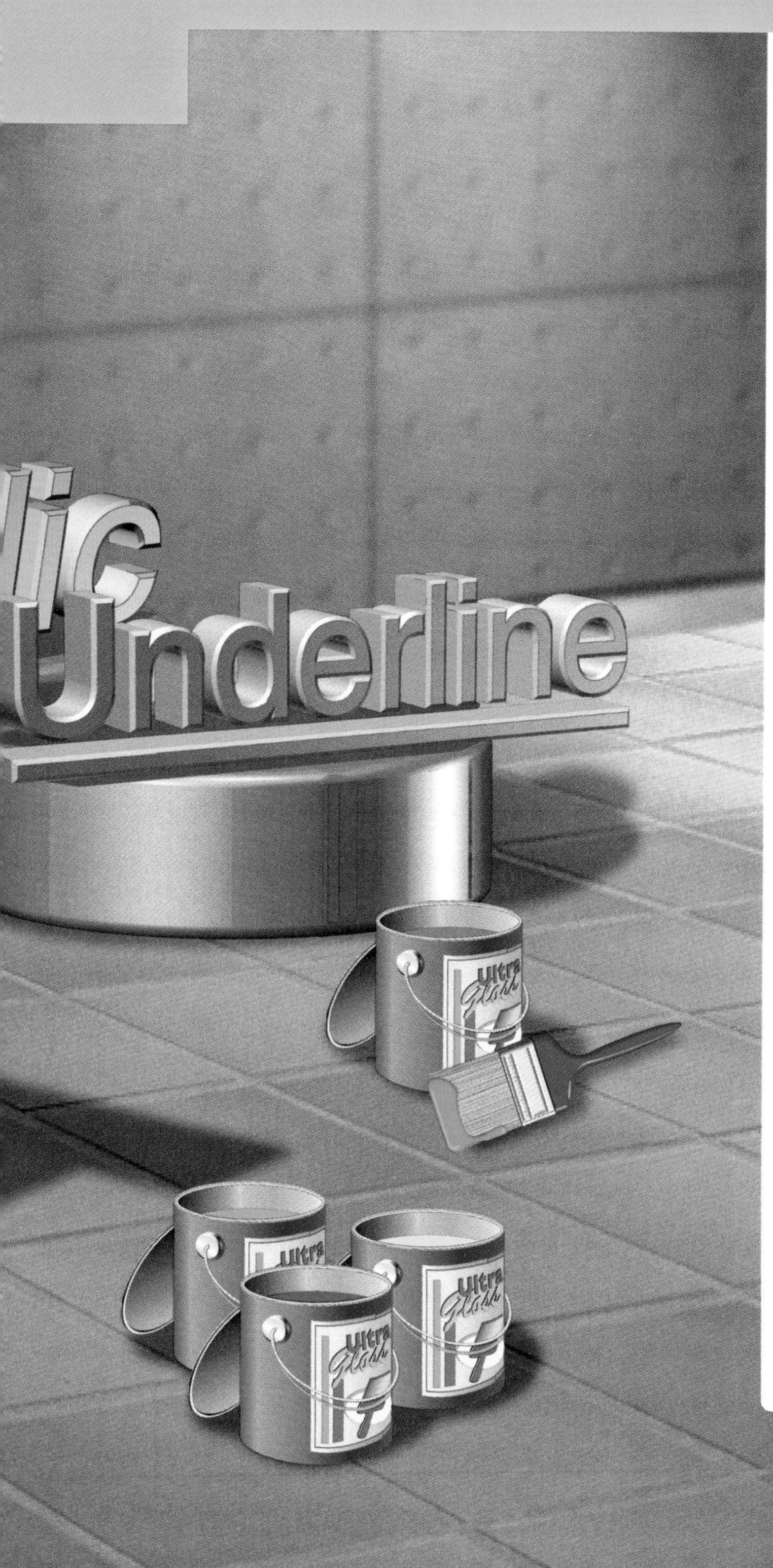

Formatting Text

Would you like to add text to your Web pages? This chapter shows you how to create paragraphs, bulleted lists, stylized text, and more.

CREATE PARAGRAPHS

You can create and align paragraphs on your Web page.

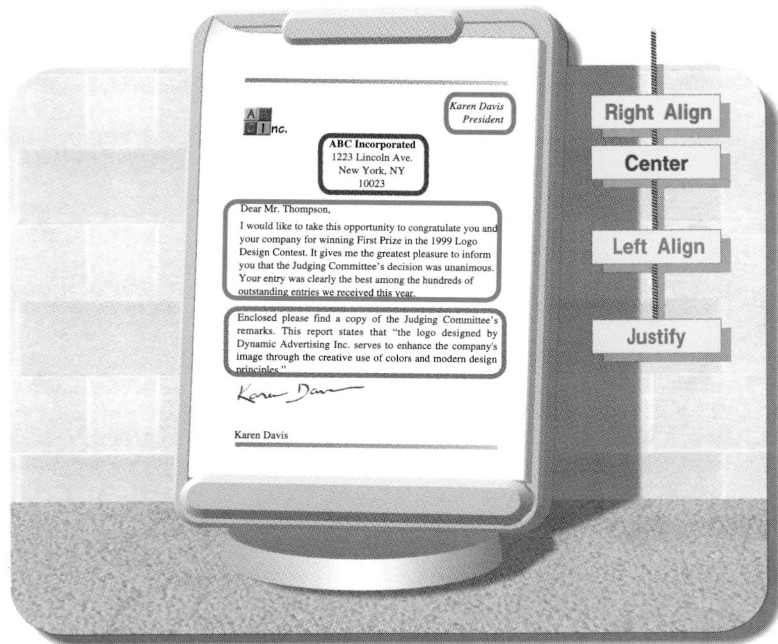

CREATE PARAGRAPHS

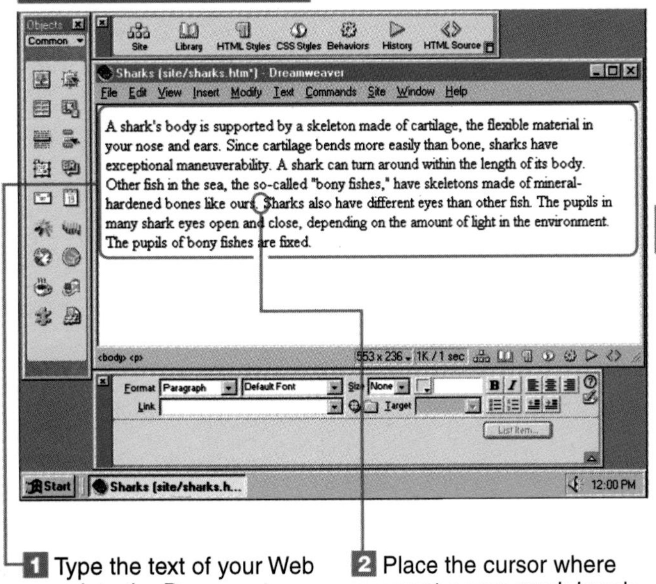

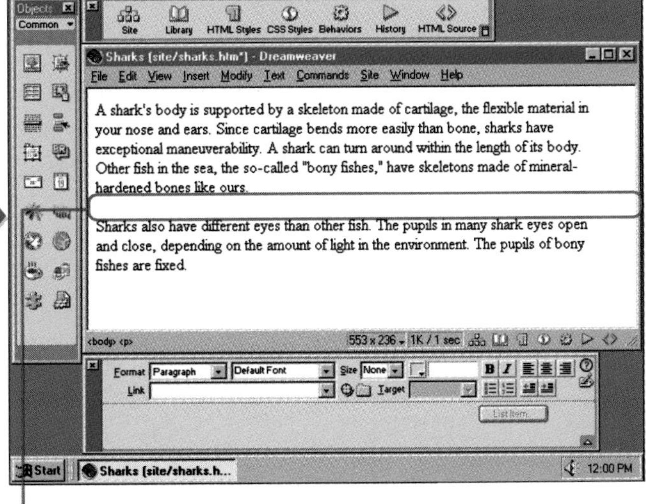

1 Type the text of your Web page into the Document window.

2 Place the cursor where you want a paragraph break.

3 Press **Enter** (**Return**).

■ A blank line appears between the blocks of text, separating them into paragraphs.

What controls the width of the paragraphs on my Web page?

The width of your paragraphs depends on the width of the Web browser window. When a user changes the size of the browser window, the widths of the paragraphs also change. That way, the user always sees all the text of the paragraphs.

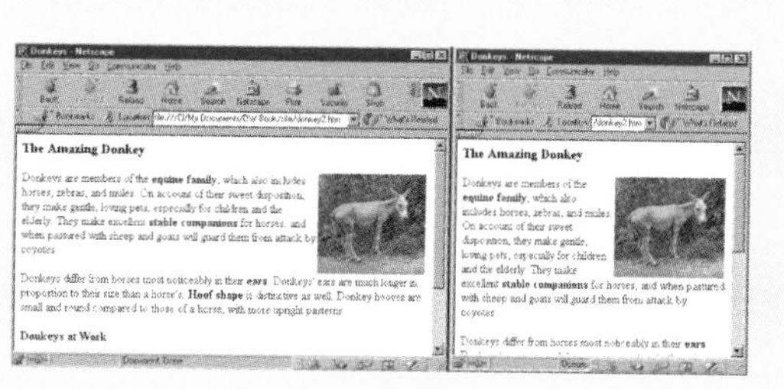

ALIGNING A PARAGRAPH

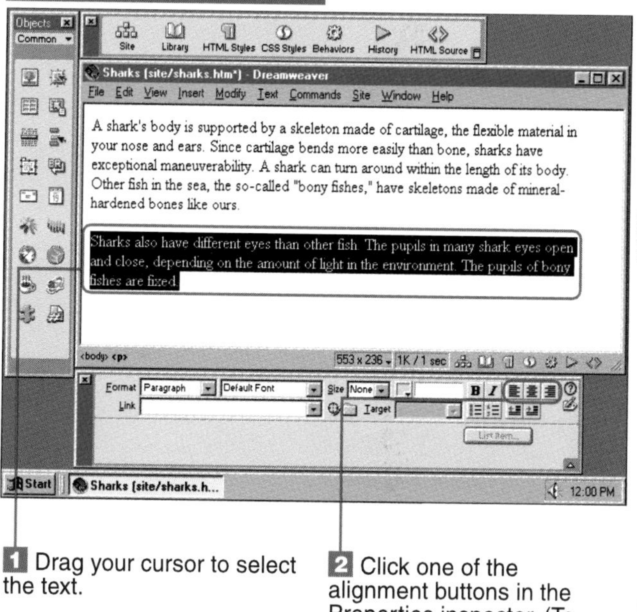

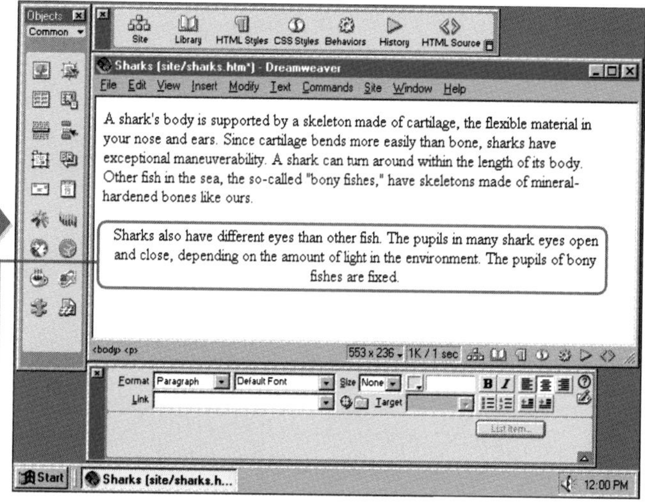

1 Drag your cursor to select the text.

2 Click one of the alignment buttons in the Properties inspector. (To right-align, click ▤. To center align, click ▤. To left-align, click ▤.)

■ Left alignment is the default.

■ In this example, the paragraph is center-aligned. To left-align, click ▤.

CREATE A HEADING

You can add headings to structure the text on your Web page hierarchically with titles and subtitles. You can also align your heading text.

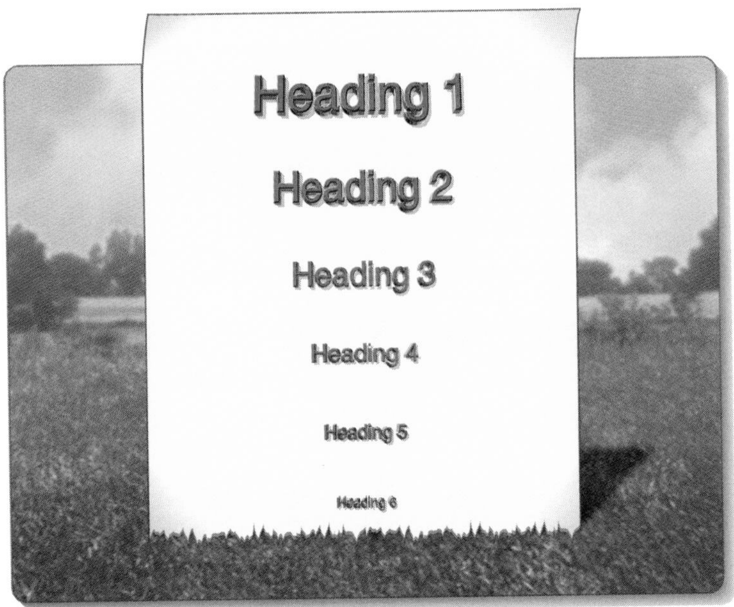

CREATE A HEADING

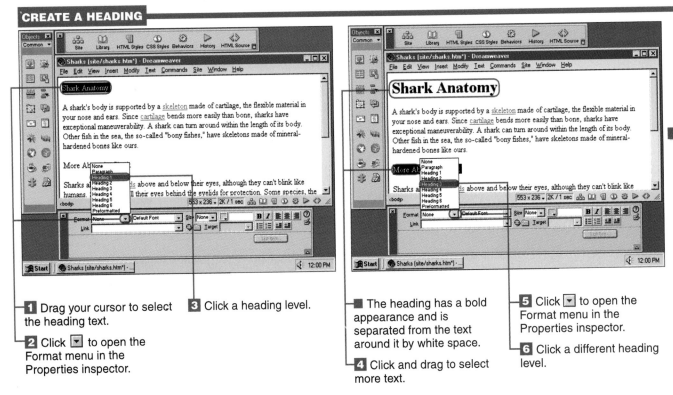

1 Drag your cursor to select the heading text.

2 Click ▾ to open the Format menu in the Properties inspector.

3 Click a heading level.

■ The heading has a bold appearance and is separated from the text around it by white space.

4 Click and drag to select more text.

5 Click ▾ to open the Format menu in the Properties inspector.

6 Click a different heading level.

What heading levels should I use?

Headings 1, 2, and 3 are often used for titles and subtitles. Heading 4 is similar to a bold version of default text. Headings 5 and 6 are often used for copyright and disclaimer information in page footers.

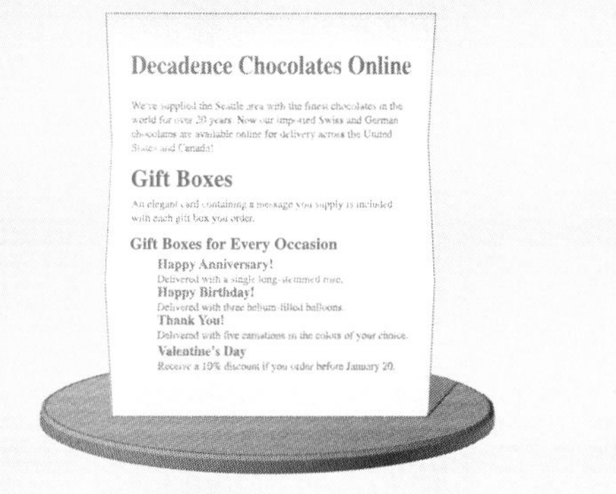

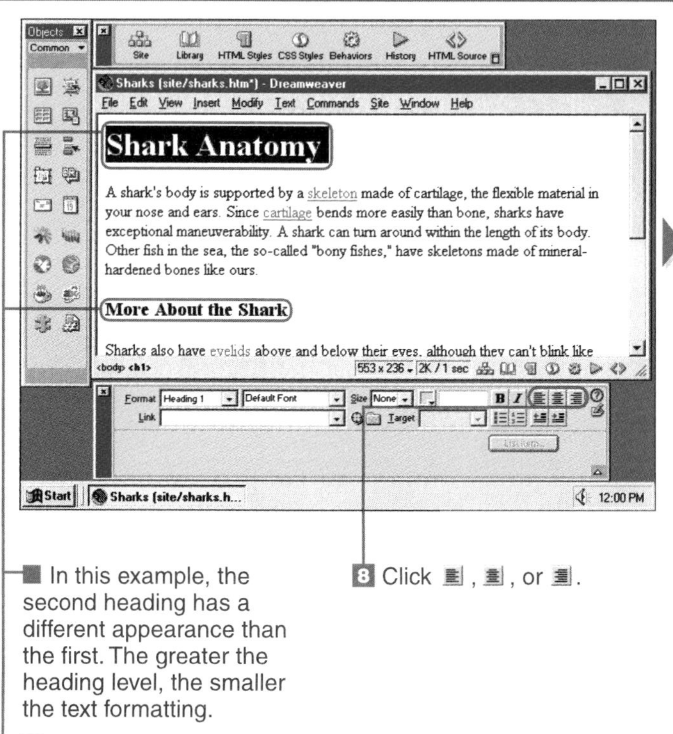

■ In this example, the second heading has a different appearance than the first. The greater the heading level, the smaller the text formatting.

7 Drag your cursor to select some heading text.

8 Click ≡, ≡, or ≡.

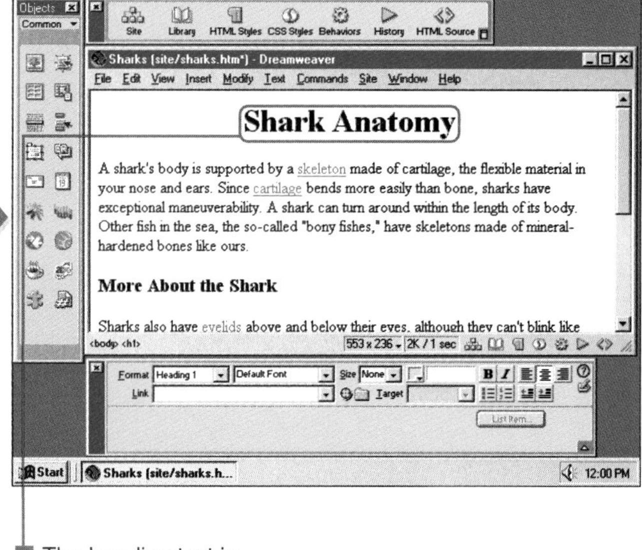

■ The heading text is aligned. In this example, the heading text is centered on the page.

Adding line breaks to your page allows you to keep adjacent lines of related text close together.

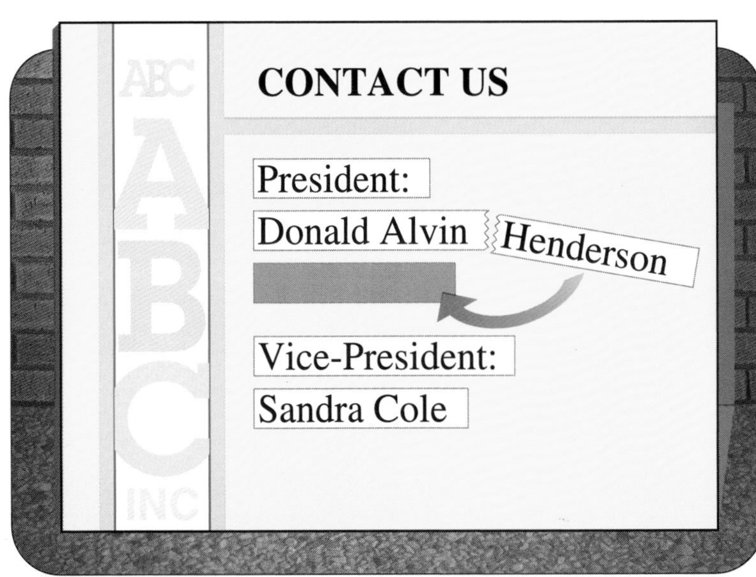

Line breaks are an alternative to paragraph breaks, which add more space between lines of text (see the section "Create Paragraphs").

CREATE LINE BREAKS

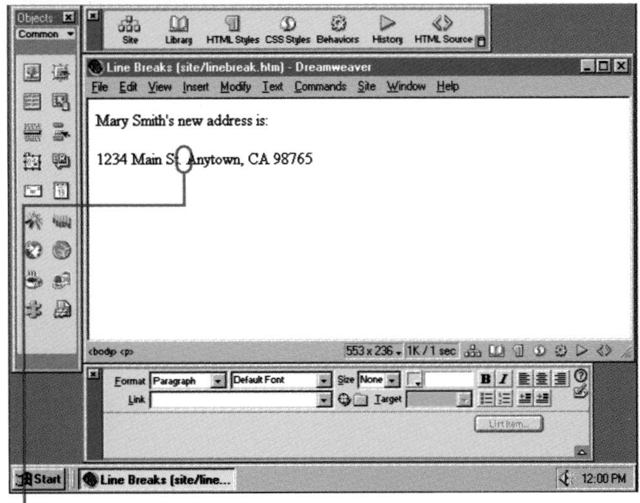

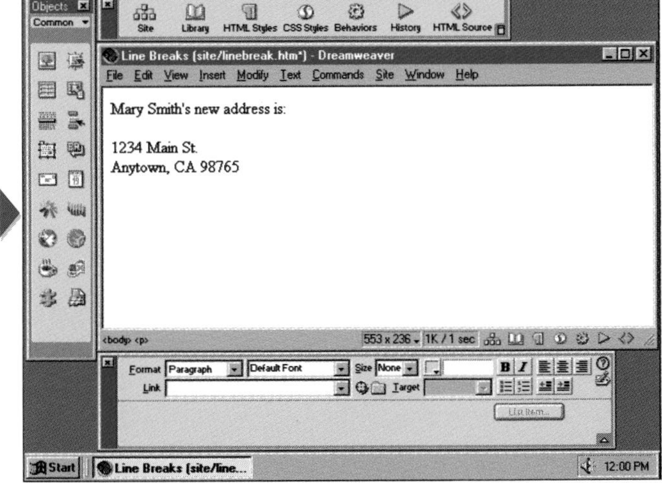

1 Place your cursor where you want the line to break.

2 Press **Shift+Enter** (**Shift+Return**).

■ This adds a line break.

Note: You can insert multiple line breaks to add more space between lines of text.

ADD EXTRA BLANK SPACE

Dreamweaver has a special command to insert more than one blank space between characters. In most cases, you can insert only one space between characters with the space bar (except when using preformatted text; see the section "Use Preformatted Text").

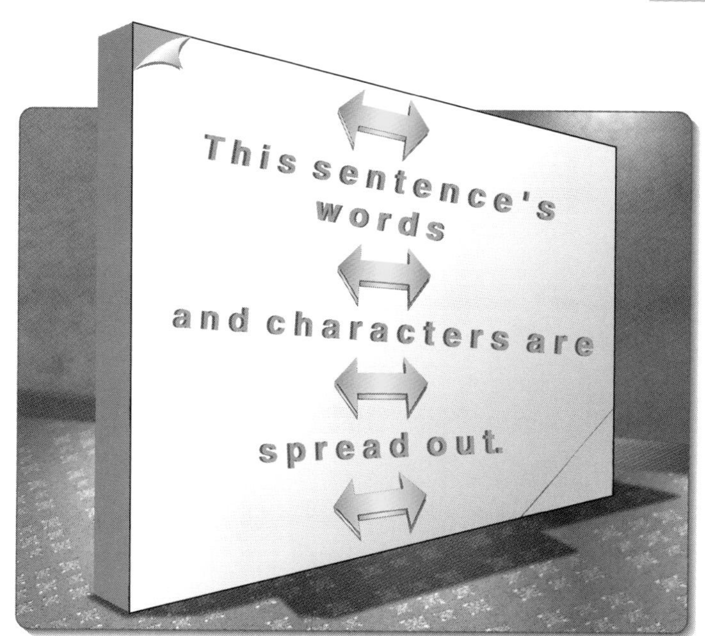

ADD EXTRA BLANK SPACE

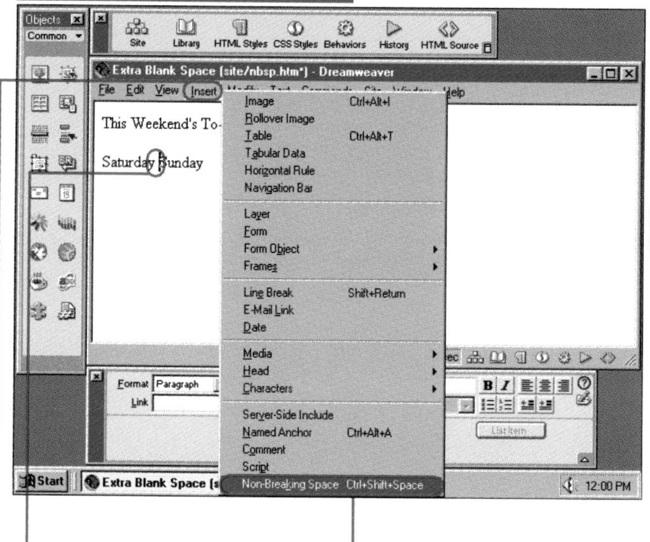

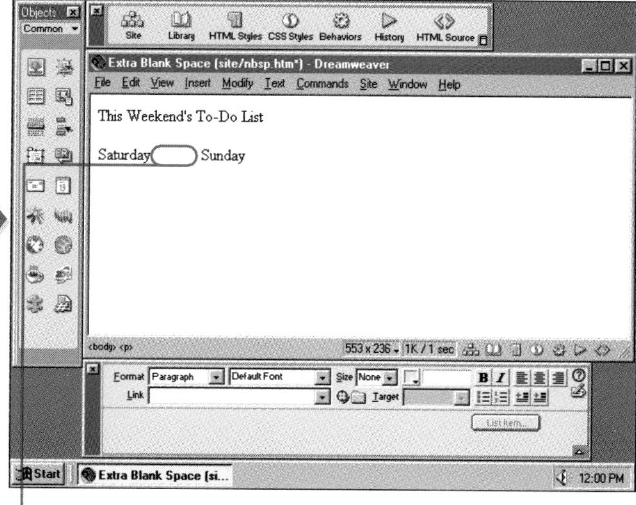

1 Place your cursor where you want to add an extra blank space.

2 Click **Insert**.

3 Click **Non-Breaking Space**.

Note: You can also add extra blank space by typing Ctl+Alt+Space (Shift+Cmd+Space).

■ In this example, there are 12 blank spaces between the words Saturday and Sunday.

CREATE UNORDERED LISTS

You can organize text items into unordered lists. Unordered lists have items that are indented and bulleted.

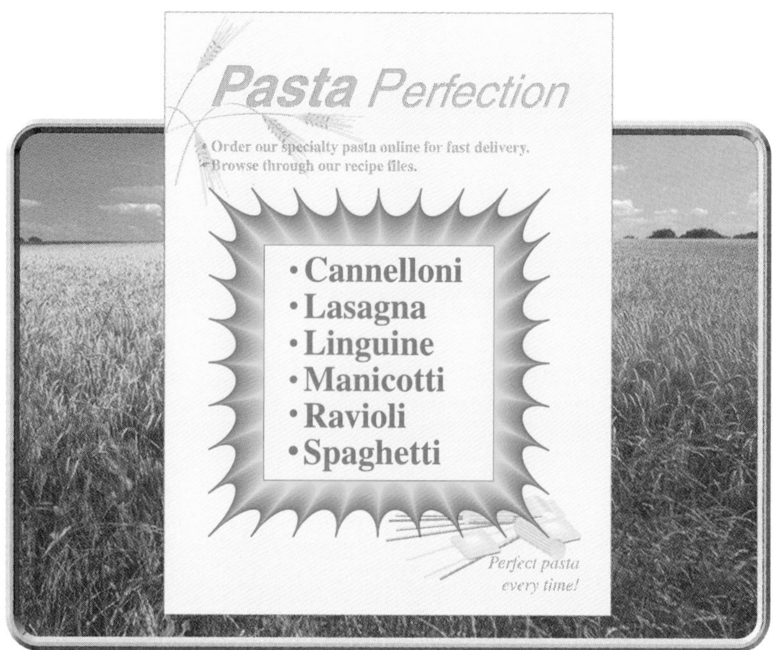

CREATE UNORDERED LISTS

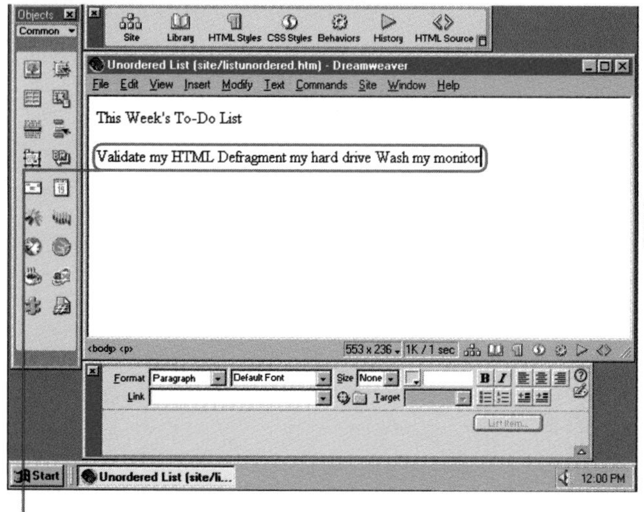

1 Type your list items into the Document window.

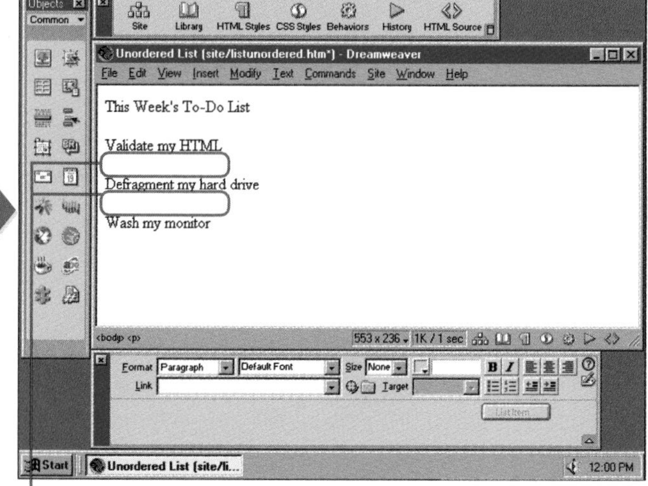

2 Make each item a separate paragraph by pressing **Enter** (**Return**) between the items.

Can I modify the appearance of my unordered lists?

You can modify the style of unordered lists by highlighting an item in the list and clicking **Text⇨List⇨Properties**. The dialog box enables you to select different bullet styles for your unordered list.

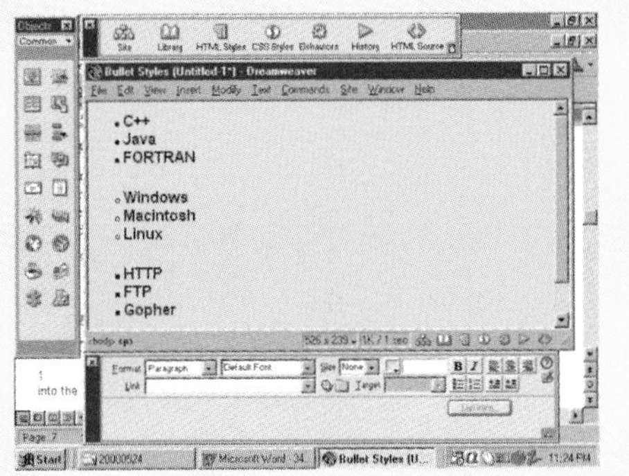

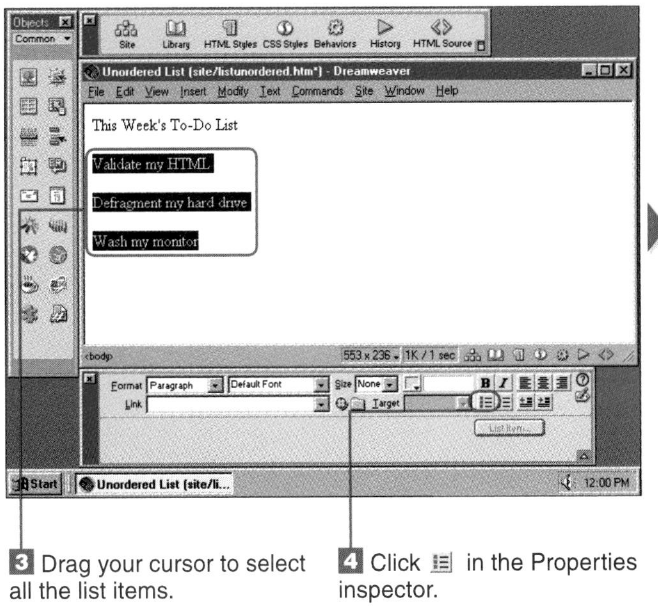

3 Drag your cursor to select all the list items.

4 Click ☰ in the Properties inspector.

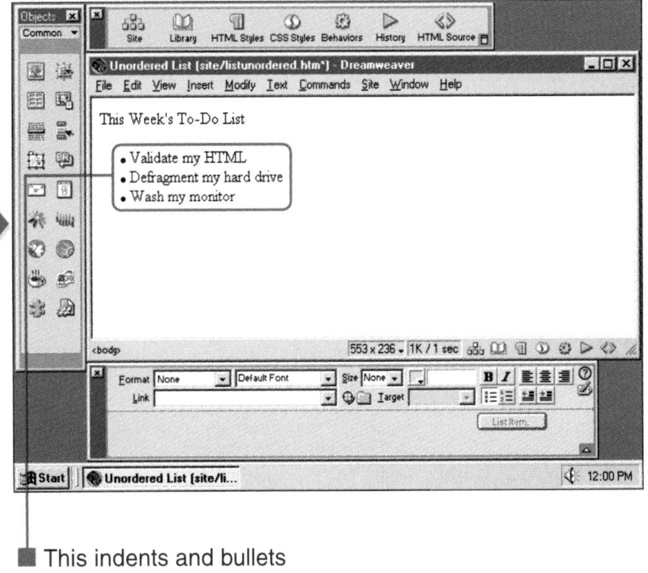

■ This indents and bullets the list items.

CREATE ORDERED LISTS

You can display step-by-step instructions on your Web page by organizing text items into an ordered list. Ordered lists have items that are indented and numbered.

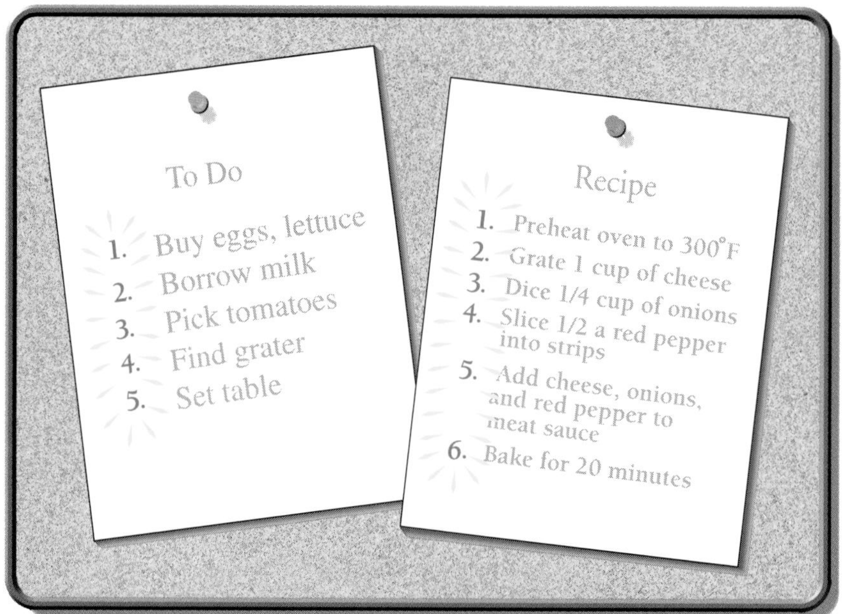

CREATE ORDERED LISTS

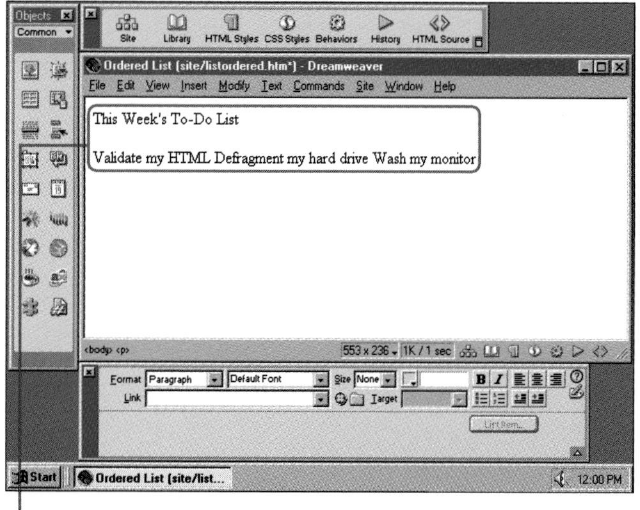

1 Type your list items into the Document window.

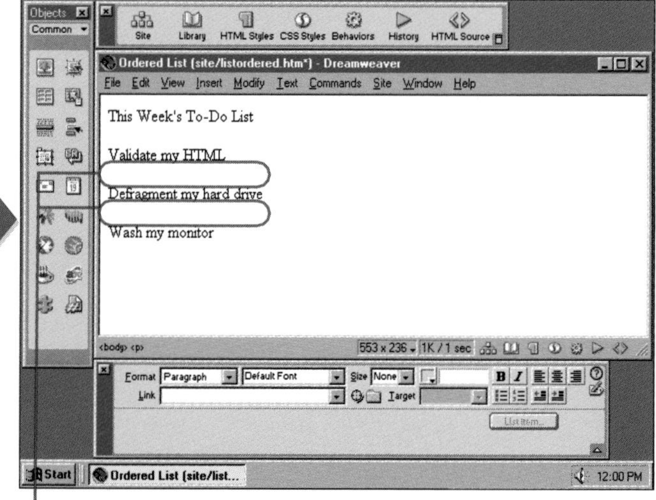

2 Make each item a separate paragraph by pressing **Enter** (**Return**) between the items.

Can I modify the appearance of my ordered lists?

You can modify the style of ordered lists by highlighting an item in the list and clicking **Text⇨List⇨Properties**. The dialog box that appears enables you to select different numbering schemes for your ordered list.

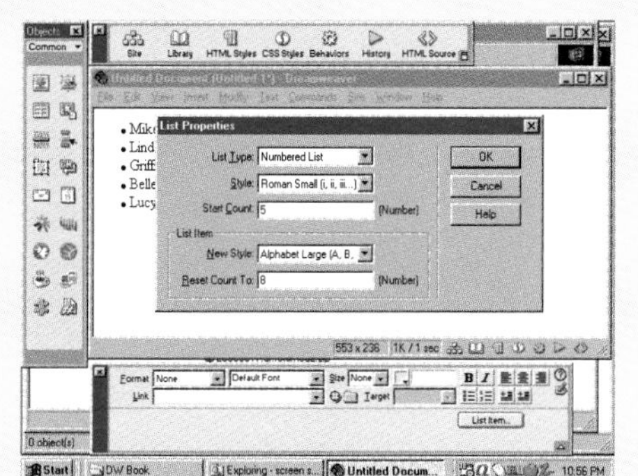

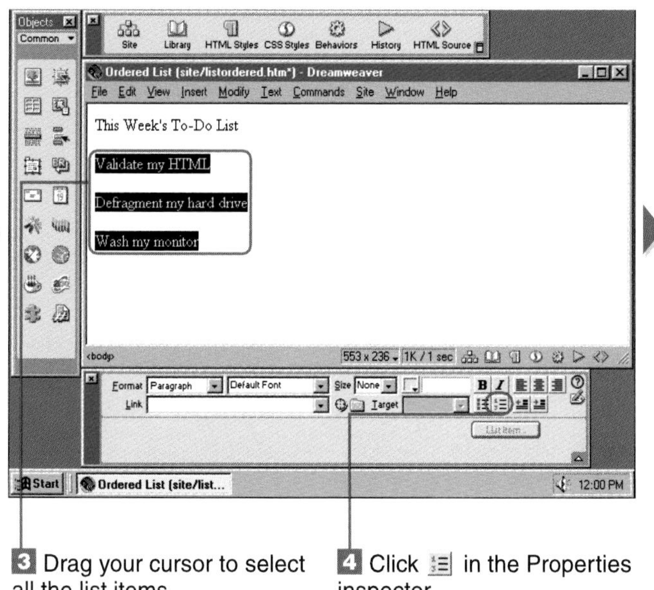

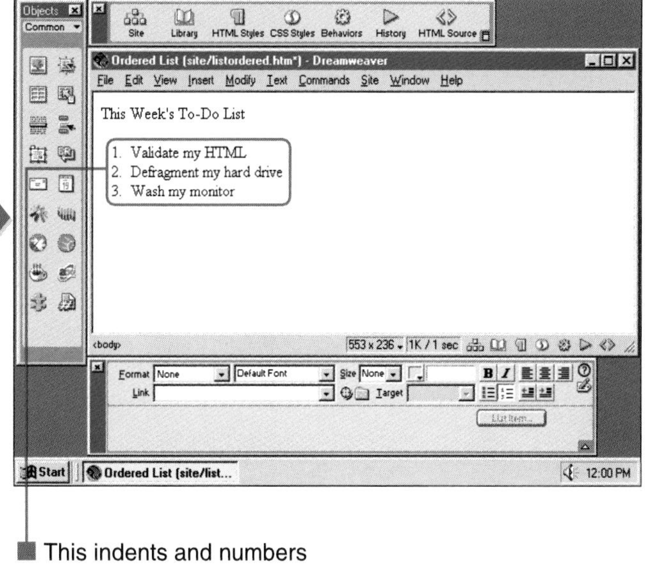

3 Drag your cursor to select all the list items.

4 Click ☰ in the Properties inspector.

■ This indents and numbers the list items.

INSERT SPECIAL CHARACTERS

You can insert special characters that do not appear on your keyboard.

INSERT CHARACTERS

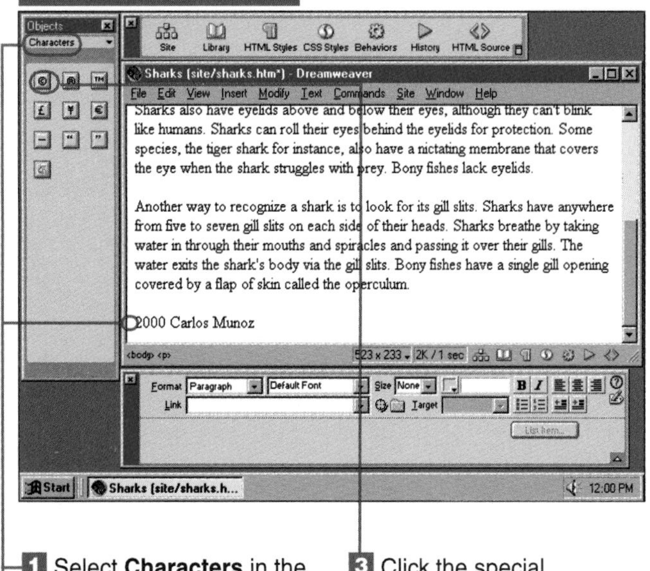

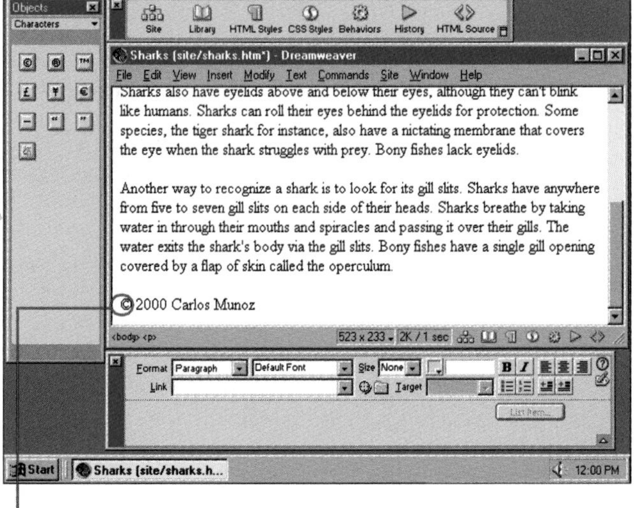

1 Select **Characters** in the Objects menu.

2 Place your cursor where you want to insert the special character.

3 Click the special character button in the Objects window.

■ The special character appears in your Web page text.

How do I include non-English-language text on my Web page?

Many European languages feature accented characters that do not appear on standard keyboards. You can insert many of these characters using the special characters tools described in this section.

Der Computer
gefällt mir

INSERT OTHER CHARACTERS

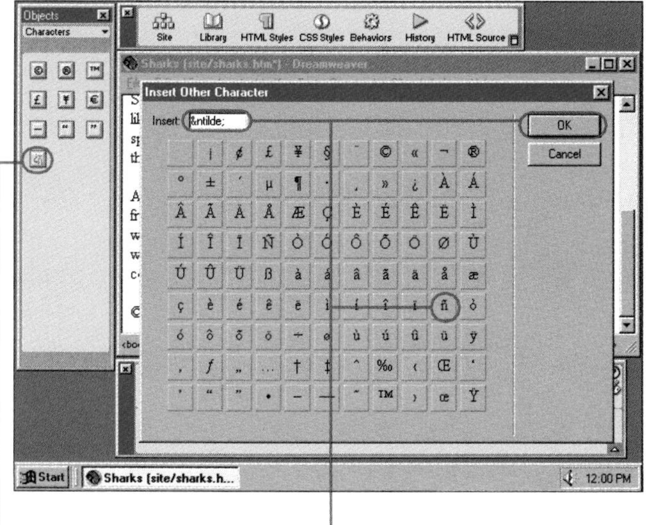

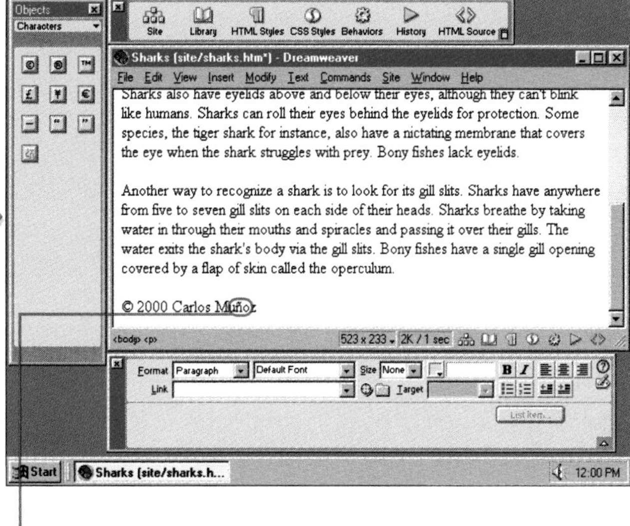

1 To access a wider variety of special characters, click [icon] in the Objects window.

2 Click the special character button.

■ The HTML code that defines the special character appears in the text field.

3 Click **OK**.

■ This inserts a special character into your Web page.

INDENT PARAGRAPHS

You can make selected paragraphs stand out from the rest of the text on your Web page by indenting them. Indents are often used for displaying quotations.

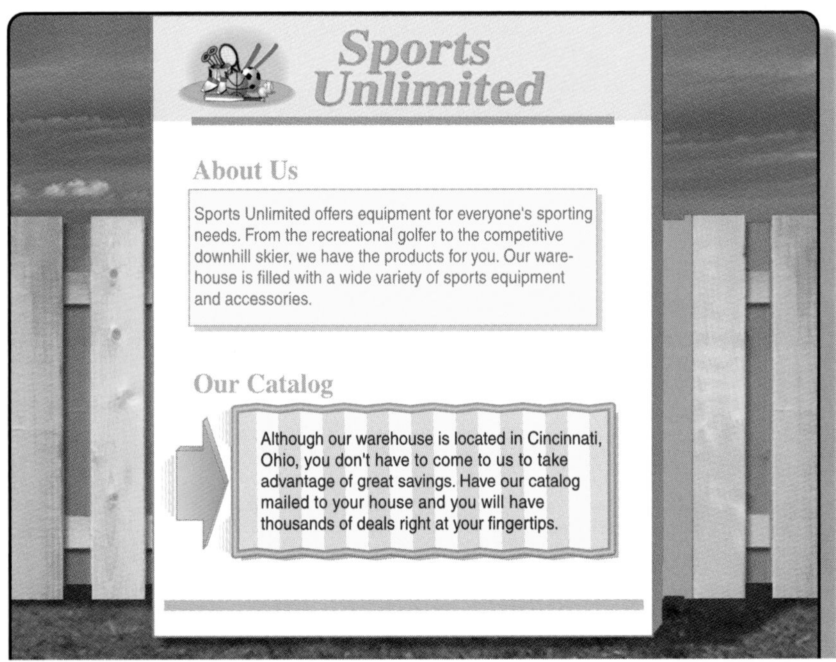

INDENT PARAGRAPHS

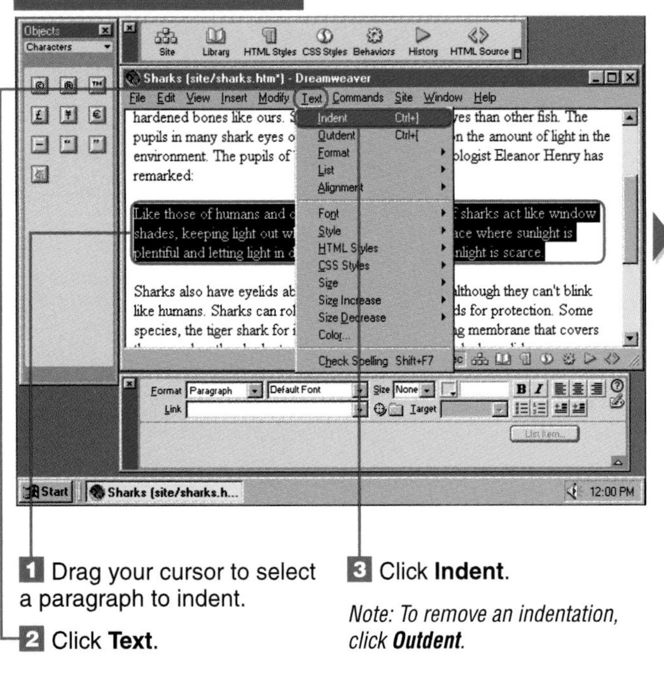

1 Drag your cursor to select a paragraph to indent.

2 Click **Text**.

3 Click **Indent**.

*Note: To remove an indentation, click **Outdent**.*

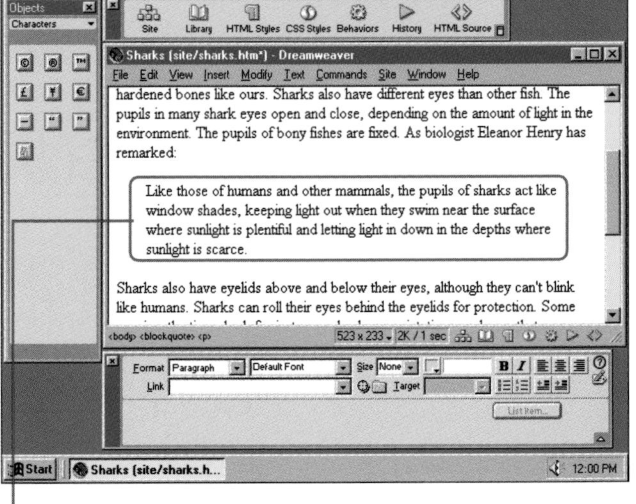

■ This adds space to both the left and right margins of the paragraph. You can repeat the steps to indent a paragraph further.

USING PREFORMATTED TEXT

Preformatting **text is a simple way to align columns of text on your Web page. After defining text as preformatted, you can add blank spaces and line breaks with the spacebar and Enter (Return) key, respectively.**

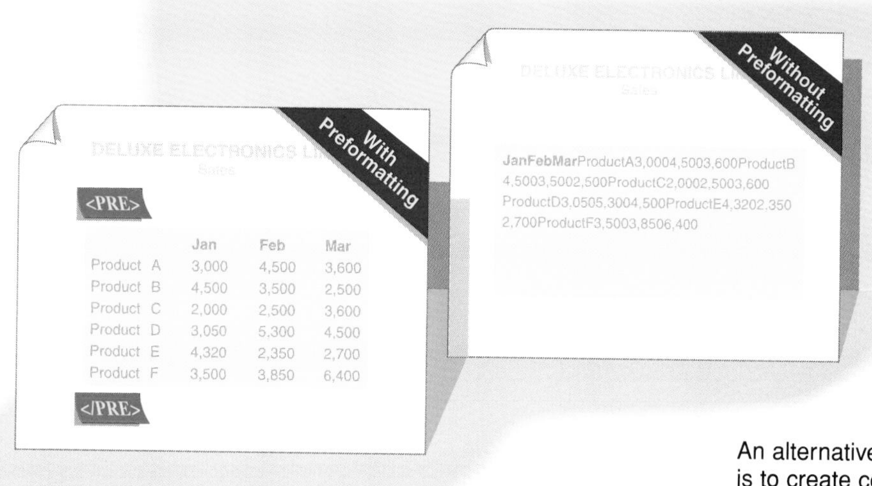

An alternative method is to create columns of text by using tables (see Chapter 7).

USING PREFORMATTED TEXT

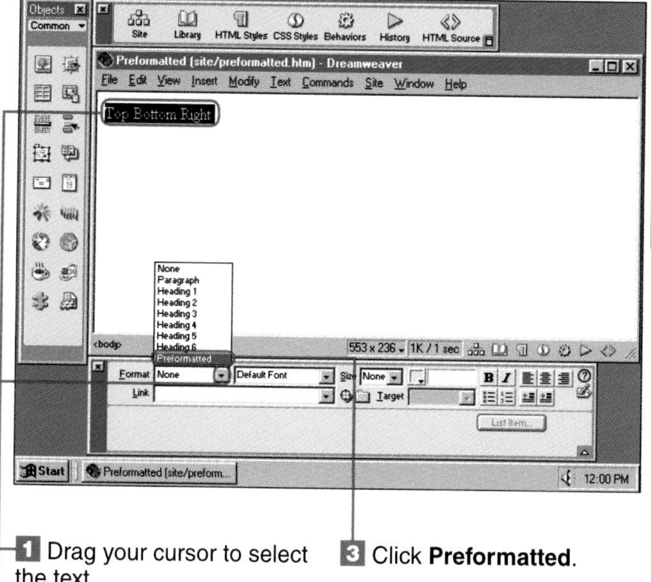

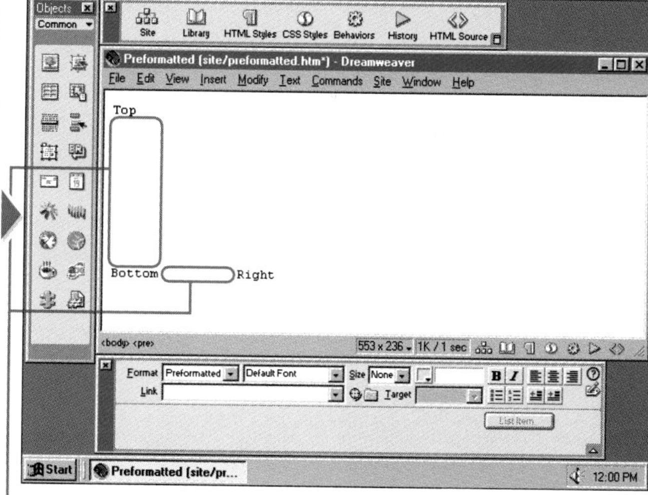

1 Drag your cursor to select the text.

2 Click ▾ to open the Format drop-down list in the Properties inspector.

3 Click **Preformatted**.

■ You can adjust vertical spacing in the text by pressing **Enter** (**Return**).

■ You can adjust horizontal spacing in the text by pressing the spacebar.

Note: Preformatted text is displayed in a monospace font. This makes it easier to align the information into columns.

CHANGE THE FONT

To add variety to or emphasize certain elements of your Web page, you can change the font of your text.

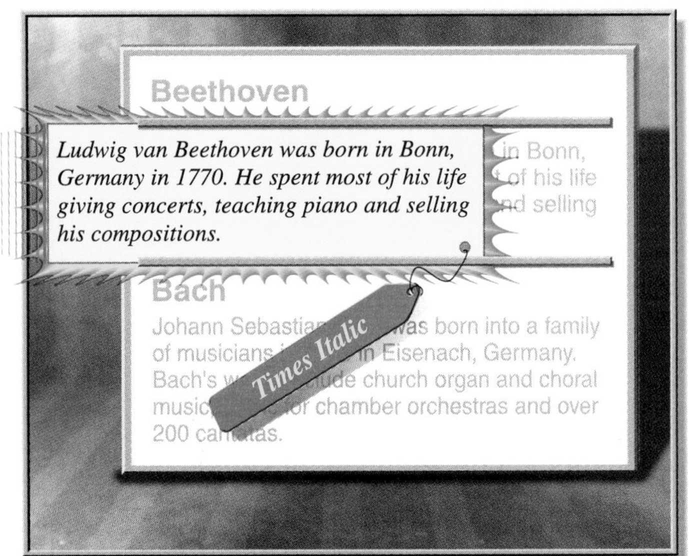

You can also customize the fonts on your Web pages by using Style Sheets (see Chapter 11).

CHANGE THE FONT

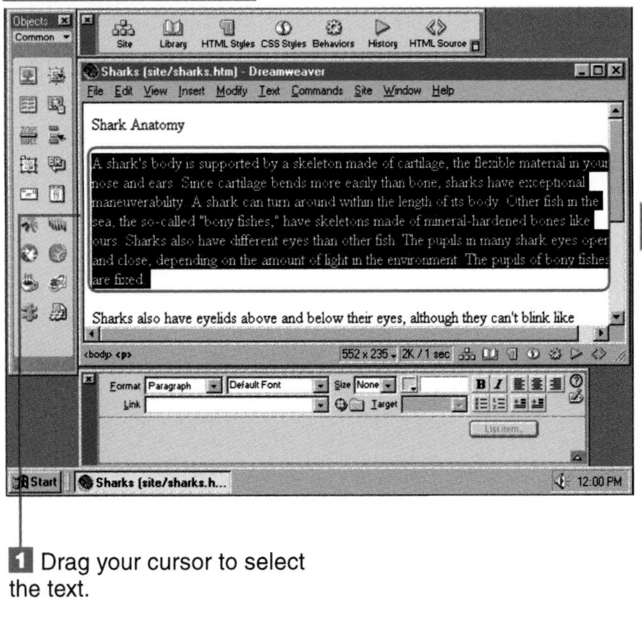

1 Drag your cursor to select the text.

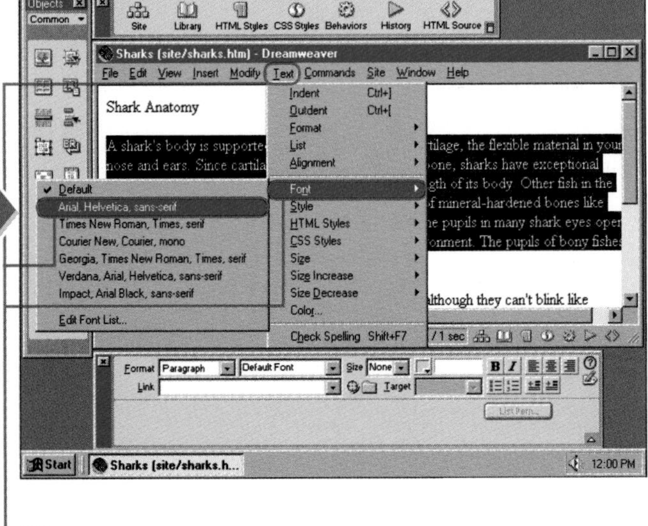

2 Click **Text**.

3 Click **Font**.

4 Click a list of fonts.

■ To be displayed correctly, a font must already be installed on the user's computer. A list specifies alternate styles if the user doesn't have certain fonts installed.

How are fonts categorized?

The two most common categories of fonts are *serif* fonts and *sans-serif* fonts. Serif fonts are distinguished by the decorations on the ends of their lines. Common serif fonts include Times New Roman, Palatino, and Garamond. Sans-serif fonts lack these decorations. Common sans-serif fonts include Arial, Verdana, and Helvetica. Long passages of text are easier to read in a serif font, while smaller texts read easier in a sans-serif font.

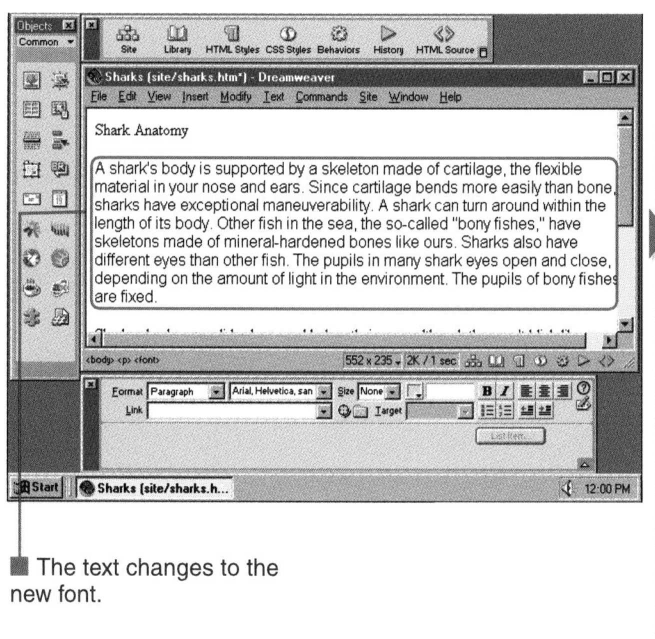

■ The text changes to the new font.

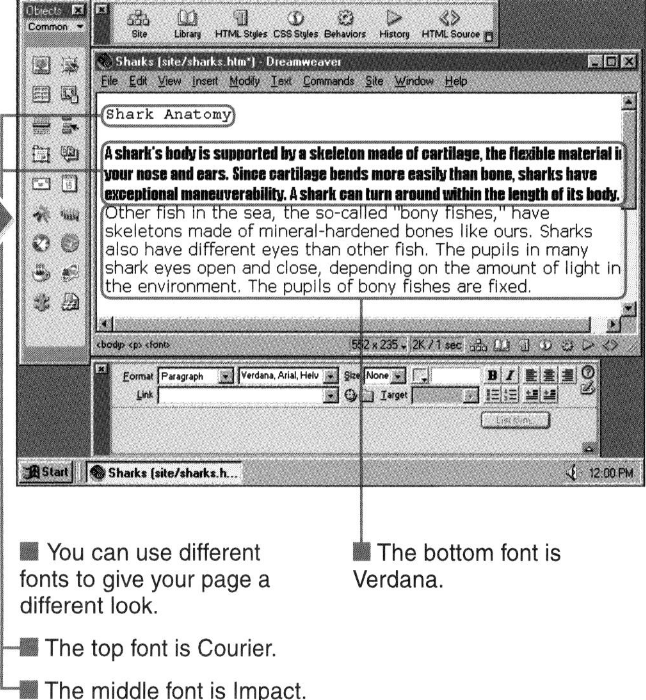

■ You can use different fonts to give your page a different look.

■ The top font is Courier.

■ The middle font is Impact.

■ The bottom font is Verdana.

CREATE BOLD OR ITALIC TEXT

You can emphasize text on your Web page with bold or italic styles.

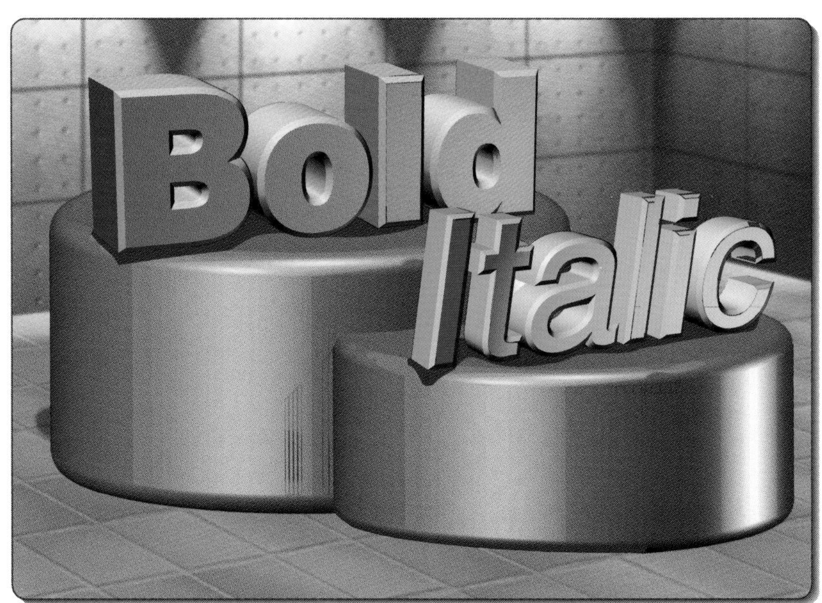

You can also control the style of text on your Web page using Style Sheets (see Chapter 11).

CREATE BOLD TEXT

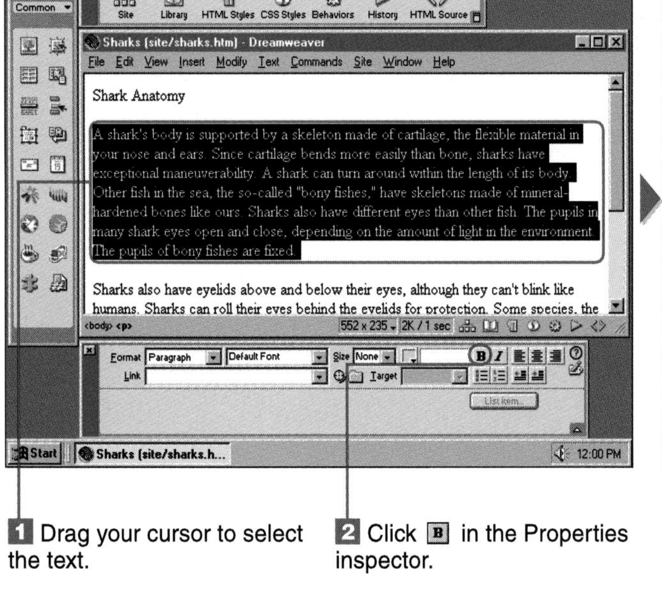

1 Drag your cursor to select the text.

2 Click **B** in the Properties inspector.

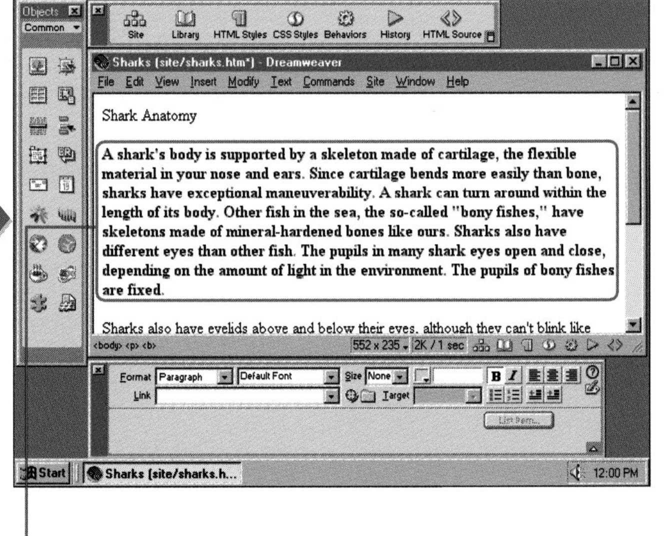

■ The text has a heavier weight.

What other kinds of styles are available besides bold and italic?

You can create other styles of text besides bold and italic using commands in the **Text⇨Style** menu. The styles include Underline, Strikethrough, and Teletype (typewriter style).

CREATE ITALIC TEXT

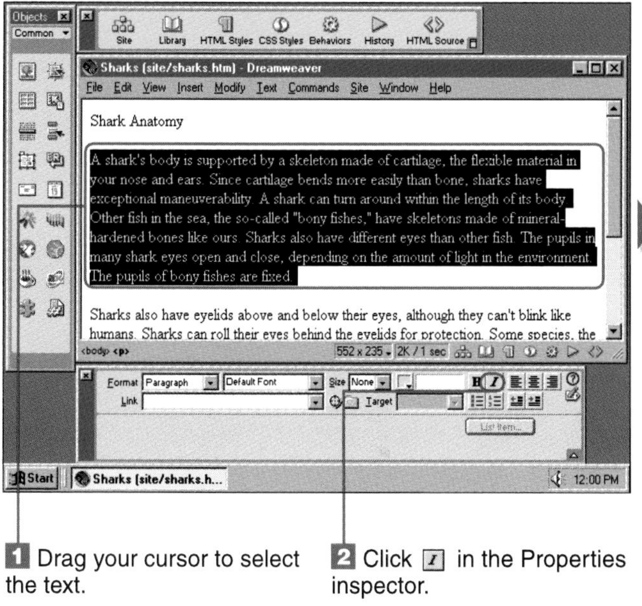

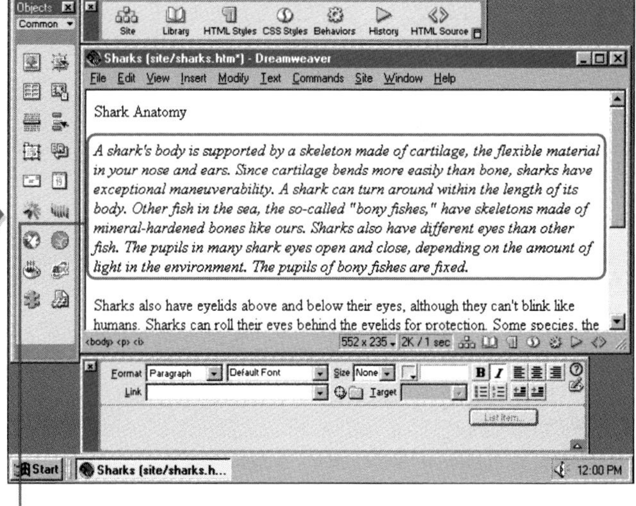

1 Drag your cursor to select the text.

2 Click [I] in the Properties inspector.

■ The selected text is italicized.

CHANGE FONT SIZE

You can emphasize or de-emphasize sections of text by changing the font size. Absolute font sizes on a Web page range from 1 to 7.

CHANGE THE ABSOLUTE TEXT SIZE

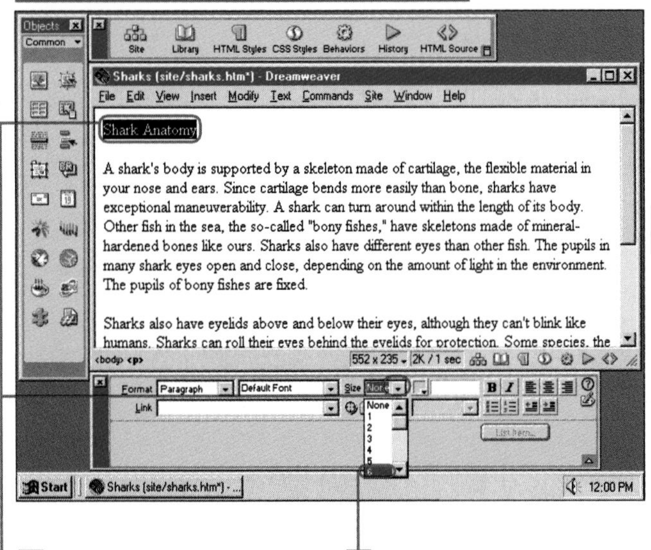

1 Drag your cursor to select the text.

2 Click ▾ to open the Size drop-down list in the Properties inspector.

3 Click an absolute size.

■ The default font size is 3.

■ The text changes size.

How can changing the size of text enhance my Web page?

You can experiment with the size of words to produce interesting headlines on your Web pages. You can also change the size of individual characters at the beginning of text passages for a traditional effect.

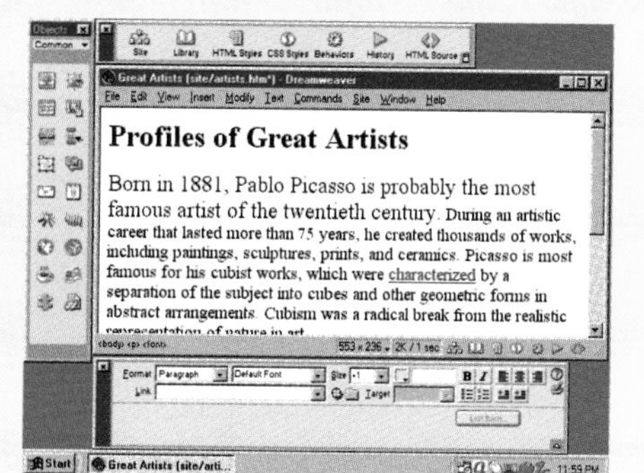

CHANGE THE RELATIVE TEXT SIZE

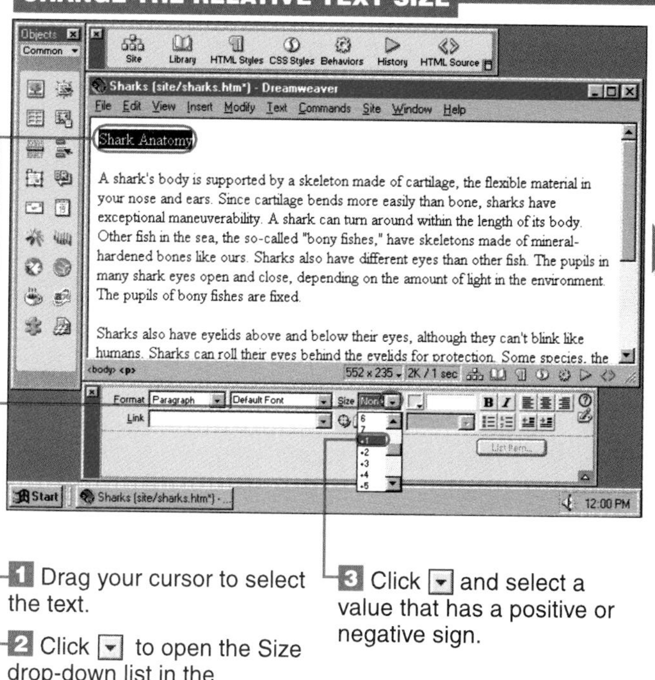

1 Drag your cursor to select the text.

2 Click ▼ to open the Size drop-down list in the Properties inspector.

3 Click ▼ and select a value that has a positive or negative sign.

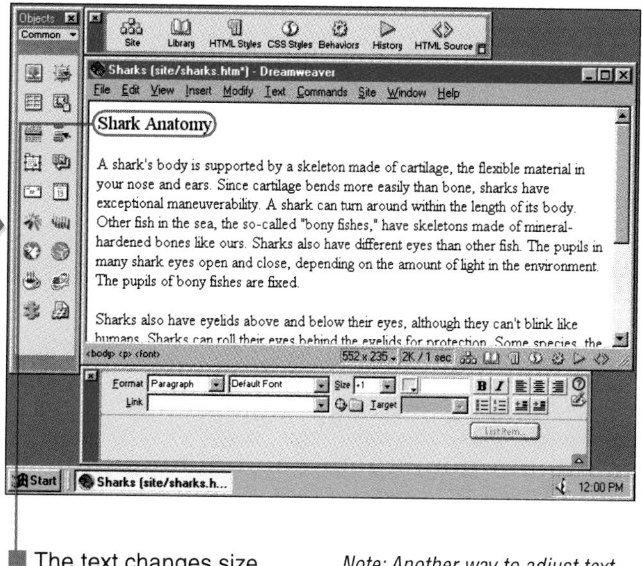

■ The text changes size.

Note: Another way to adjust text size is with heading formatting (see the section "Create a Heading").

CHANGE FONT COLOR

You can change the color of text on all or part of your Web page.

Make sure the color of your text contrasts with the background color of your Web page.

To adjust the background color of your Web page, see Chapter 5.

CHANGE THE COLOR OF ALL TEXT

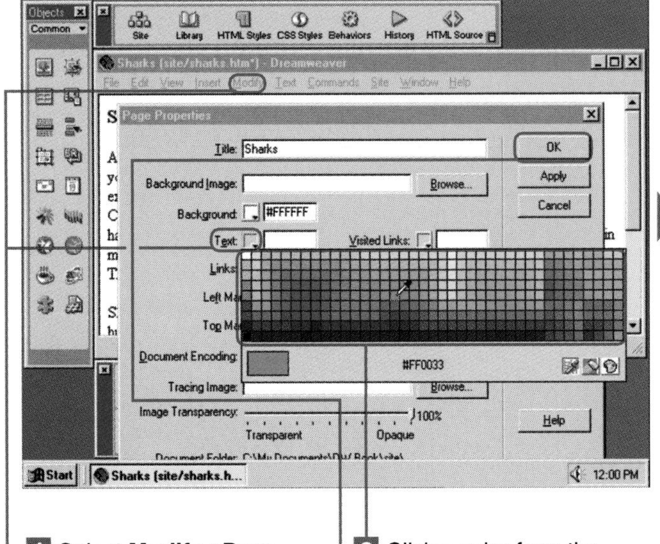

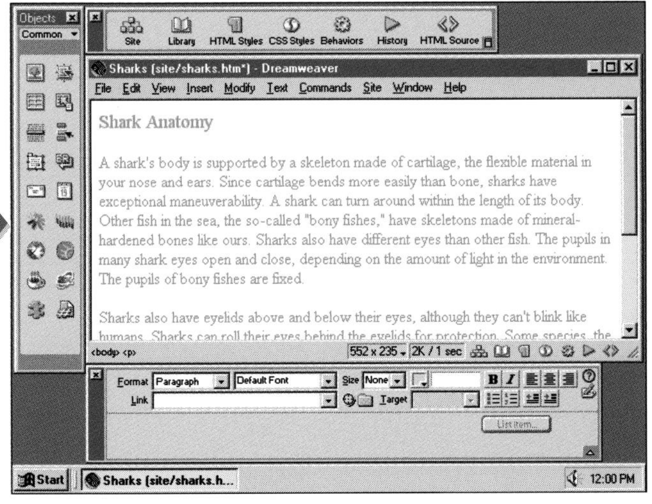

1 Select **Modify⇨Page Properties** to bring up the Page Properties dialog box.

2 Click the **Text** color swatch.

3 Click a color from the menu by using the eyedropper tool.

4 Click **OK**.

Note: The default color of text on a Web page is black.

■ All the text on your Web page displays in the new color.

What are the letter and number combinations that show up in Dreamweaver's color fields?

HTML represents colors using six-digit codes (called *hexadecimal codes*). Hex codes are preceded by a pound sign (#). Instead of ranging from 0 through 9, hex-code digits range from 0 through F, with A equal to 10, B equal to 11, and so on through F, which is equal to 15. The first two digits in a hex code specify the amount of red in the selected color, the second two digits specify the amount of green, and the third two digits specify the amount of blue.

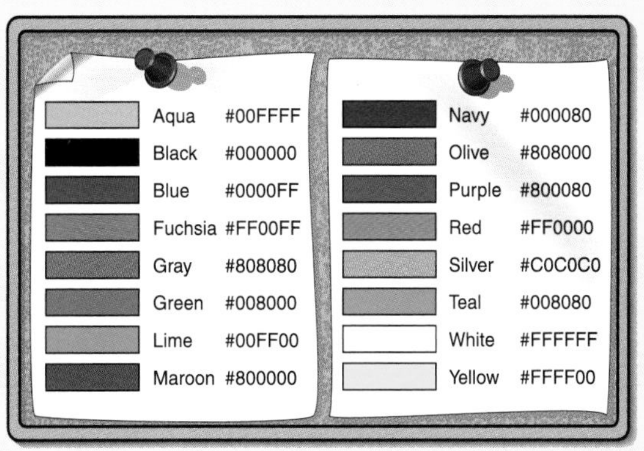

Color	Code	Color	Code
Aqua	#00FFFF	Navy	#000080
Black	#000000	Olive	#808000
Blue	#0000FF	Purple	#800080
Fuchsia	#FF00FF	Red	#FF0000
Gray	#808080	Silver	#C0C0C0
Green	#008000	Teal	#008080
Lime	#00FF00	White	#FFFFFF
Maroon	#800000	Yellow	#FFFF00

CHANGE THE COLOR OF SELECTED TEXT

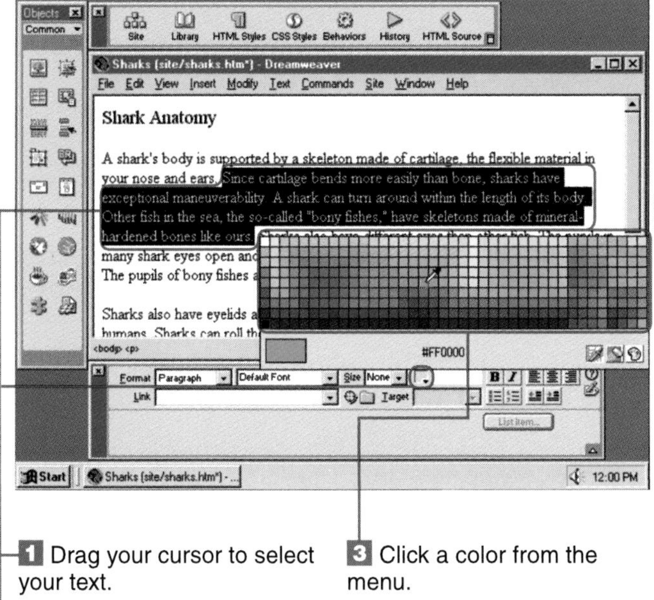

1 Drag your cursor to select your text.

2 Click the color swatch in the Properties inspector.

3 Click a color from the menu.

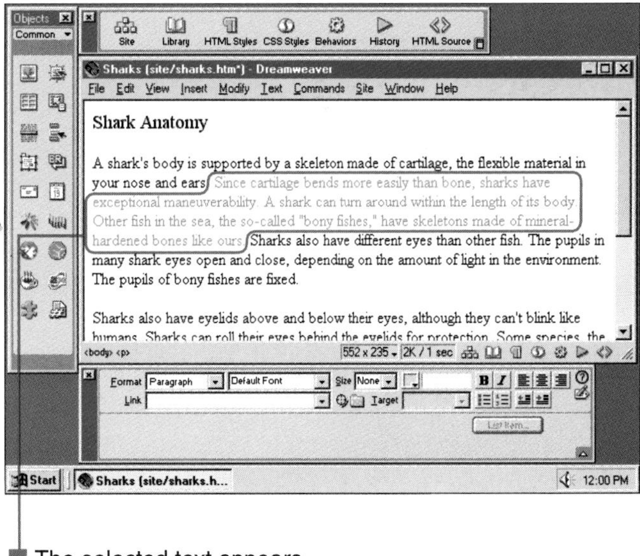

■ The selected text appears in the new color.

APPLY HTML STYLES

You can format text using the HTML Styles window, which allows you to apply complicated styles with a single click.

APPLY HTML STYLES

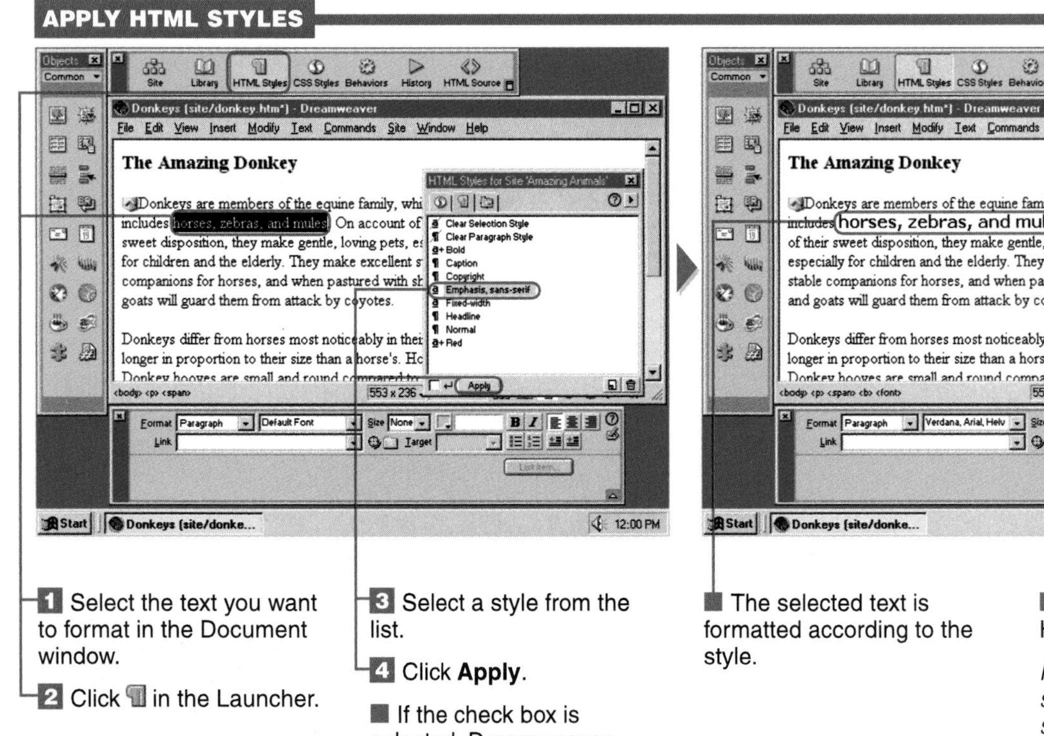

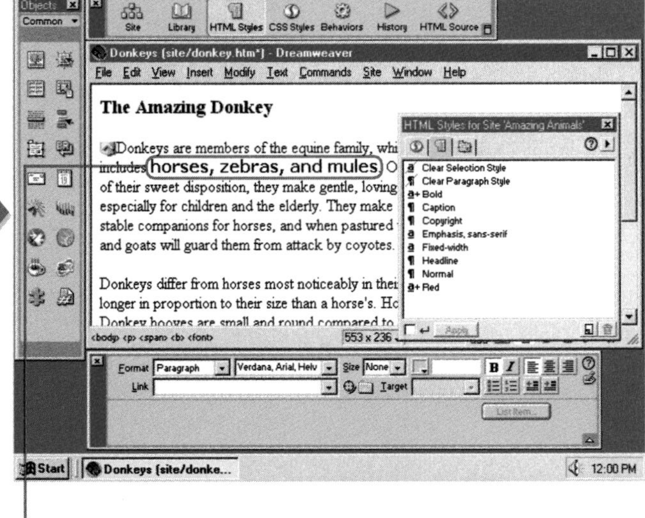

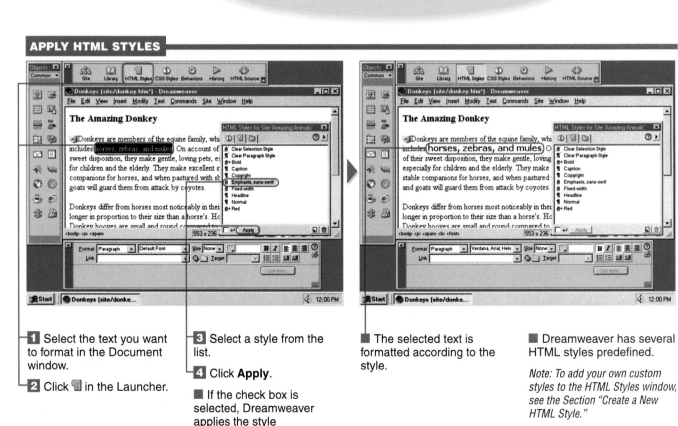

1. Select the text you want to format in the Document window.
2. Click the HTML Styles button in the Launcher.
3. Select a style from the list.
4. Click **Apply**.

■ If the check box is selected, Dreamweaver applies the style automatically.

■ The selected text is formatted according to the style.

■ Dreamweaver has several HTML styles predefined.

Note: To add your own custom styles to the HTML Styles window, see the Section "Create a New HTML Style."

CREATE A NEW HTML STYLE

Dreamweaver allows you to save time by creating complicated text styles and adding them to the HTML Styles window. From the window, you can apply the styles to content in your page quickly and easily.

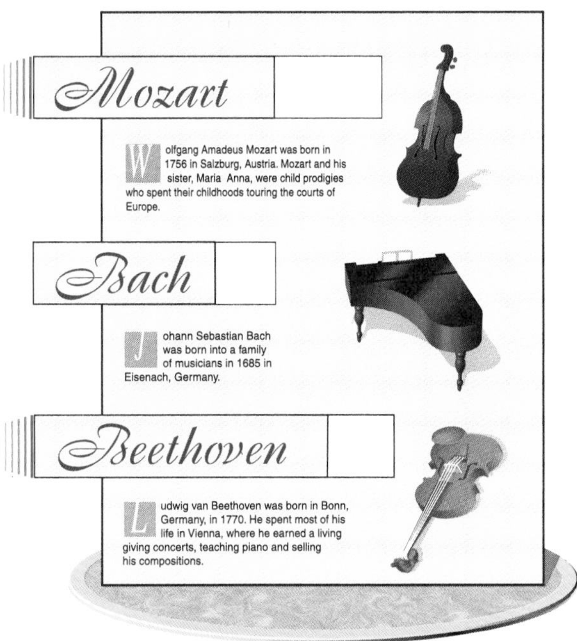

CREATE A NEW HTML STYLE

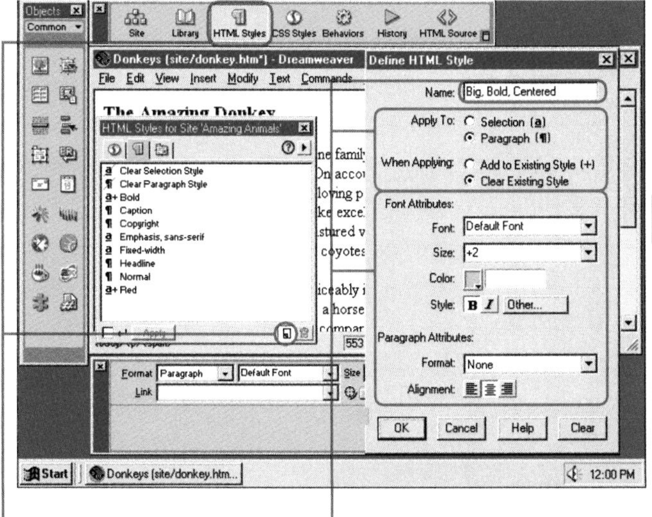

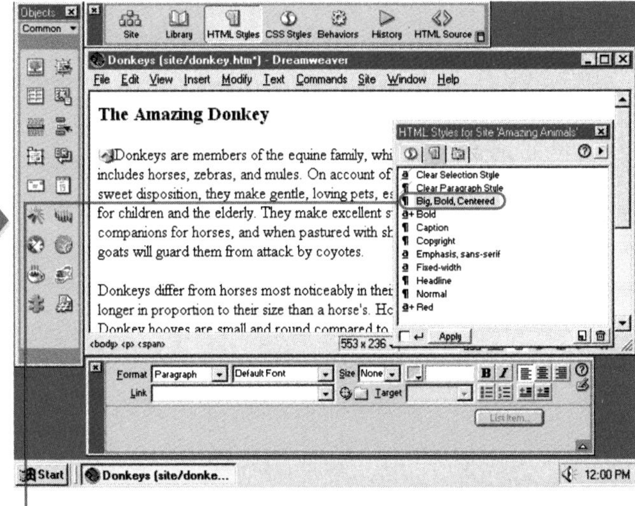

1 Click the **HTML Styles** icon in the Launcher.

■ The HTML Styles dialog box appears.

2 Click ◙.

■ The Define HTML Style dialog box appears.

3 Name the new style.

■ You can apply styles to a selected text or paragraph. You can apply new styles to any existing styles or clear old styles to add new ones.

4 Select the text formatting for your style.

■ The new style appears in the HTML Styles window.

Note: To apply a style from the HTML Styles window, see the section "Apply HTML Styles."

DIGGING UP THE PAST
A GUIDE TO ARCHAEOLOGICAL DIGS

Working with Images

Would you like to add scanned art, digital photos, and other types of images to your Web site? This chapter shows you how.

INSERT AN IMAGE

You can insert different types of images, including clip art, digital camera images, and scanned photos, into your Web page.

INSERT AN IMAGE

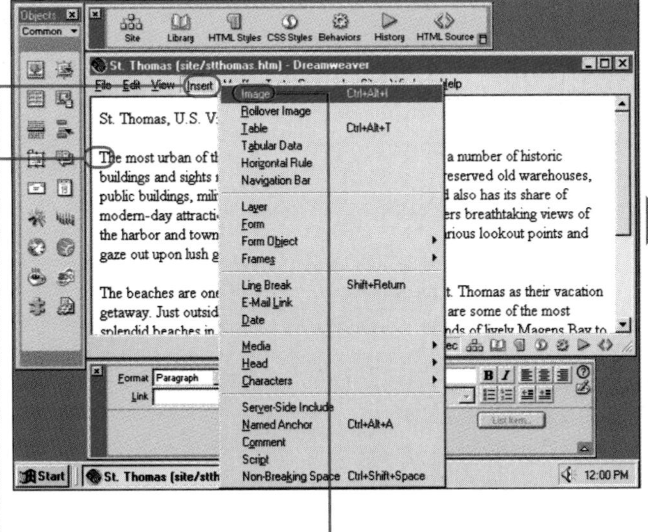

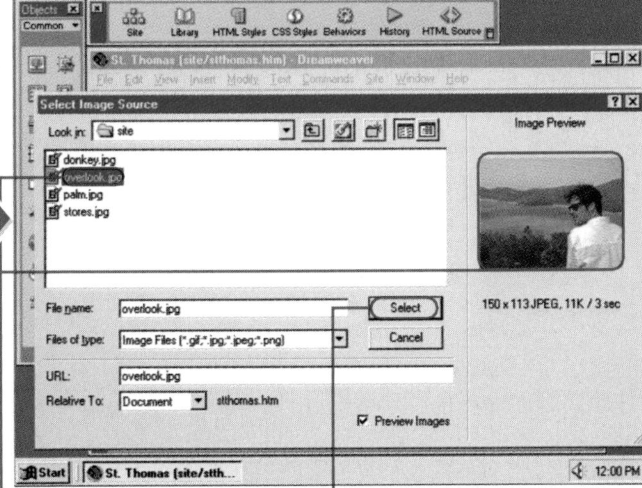

INSERT IMAGE

1 Place your cursor where you want to insert the image.

2 Click **Insert**.

3 Click **Image** to bring up the Select Image Source dialog box.

Note: You can also click the Image icon in the Objects window to insert an image.

4 From the list, click the image file you want to insert into your Web page.

■ A preview of the image appears.

Note: If you want to insert an image that exists at a Web address on the Internet, you can type the image's address into the URL field.

5 Click **Select**.

Where should I store images that I want to use on my Web pages?

You should store your images in the same directory as your HTML files. When your site consists of many files, consider keeping images in a subdirectory called "images." Keeping your HTML files and image files in the same directory ensures that your Web site works correctly when you transfer it to a live Web server.

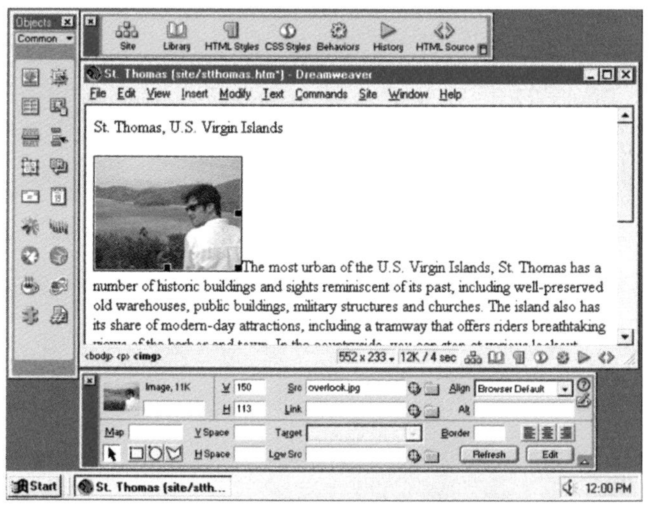

■ The image is inserted into the Web page.

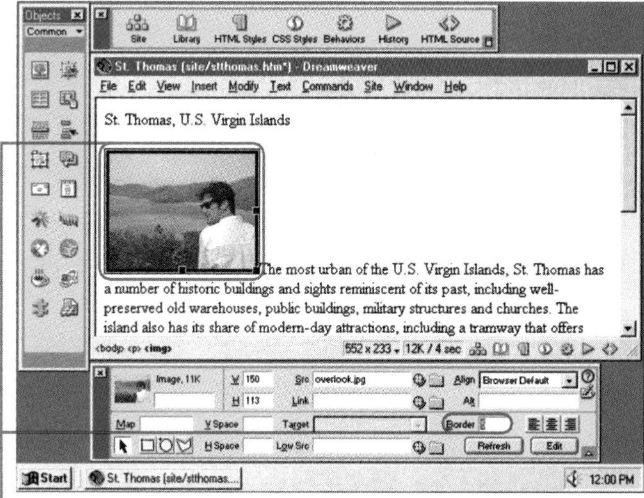

ADD A BORDER TO AN IMAGE

1 Click the image to select it.

2 Type the width (in pixels) into the Border field.

3 Press **Enter** (**Return**).

■ A border appears around the image. The color of the border is the same as the Web page's text.

Aligning an image to one side of a Web page allows you to wrap text around it. Wrapping text around images enables you to fit more information onto the screen and gives your Web pages a more professional look.

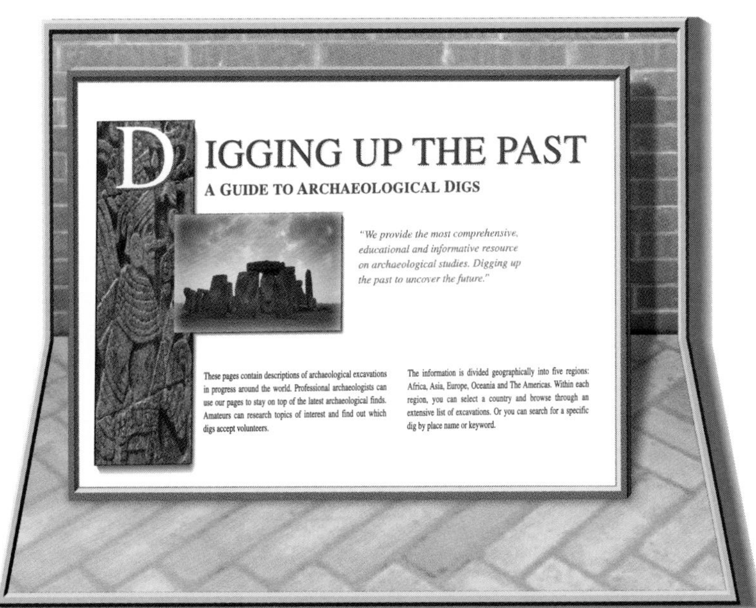

WRAP TEXT AROUND AN IMAGE

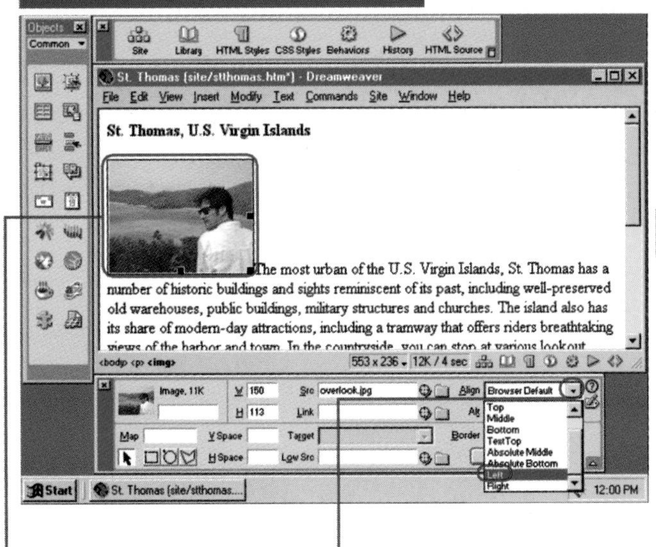

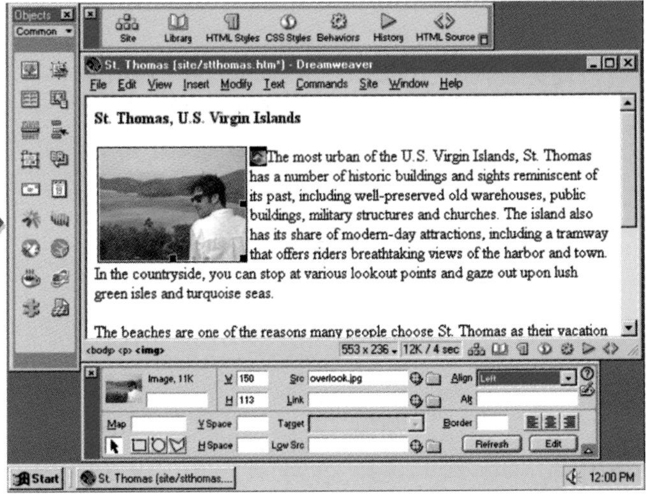

1 Click the image to select it.

Note: To insert an image, see the section "Insert an Image."

2 Click ▾ to open the Align drop-down menu.

3 Select the alignment for the image.

■ Text flows around the image according to your alignment selection.

■ In this example, text flows to the right of the left-aligned image.

How do I make text flow between two images?

Insert the two images one after the other before inserting the passage of text (to insert an image, see the Section "Insert an Image"). Align the first image to the left. Then align the second image to the right. When inserted the text flows down the middle of the Web page, between the two images.

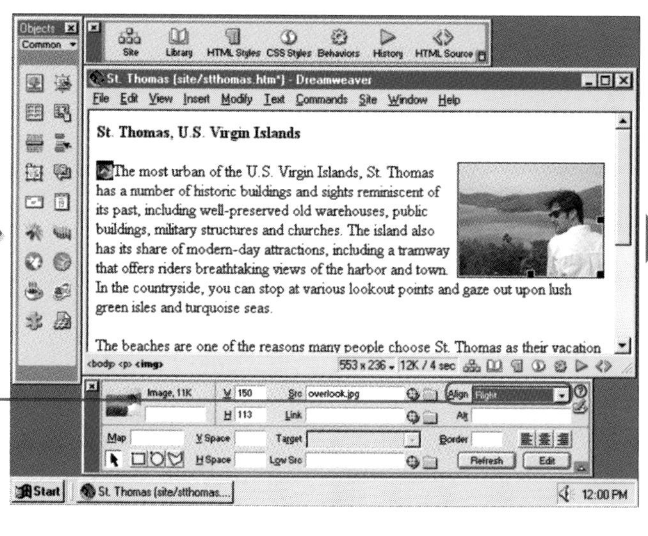

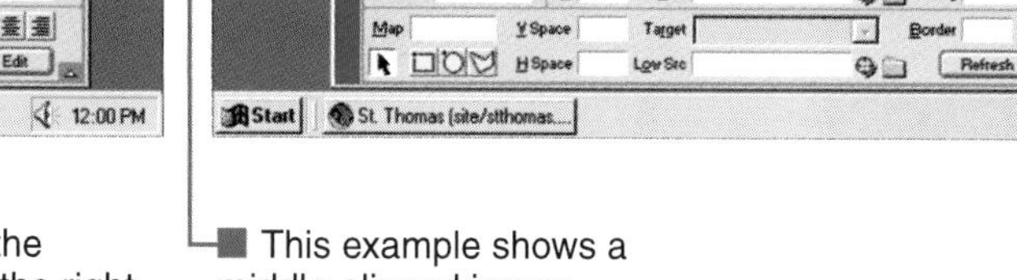

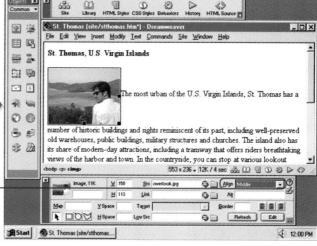

■ You can select other options from the Align drop-down list for different wrapping effects.

■ In this example, the image is aligned to the right.

■ This example shows a middle-aligned image.

CENTER AN IMAGE

Centering an image can give a photo or banner prominence on your page.

CENTER AN IMAGE

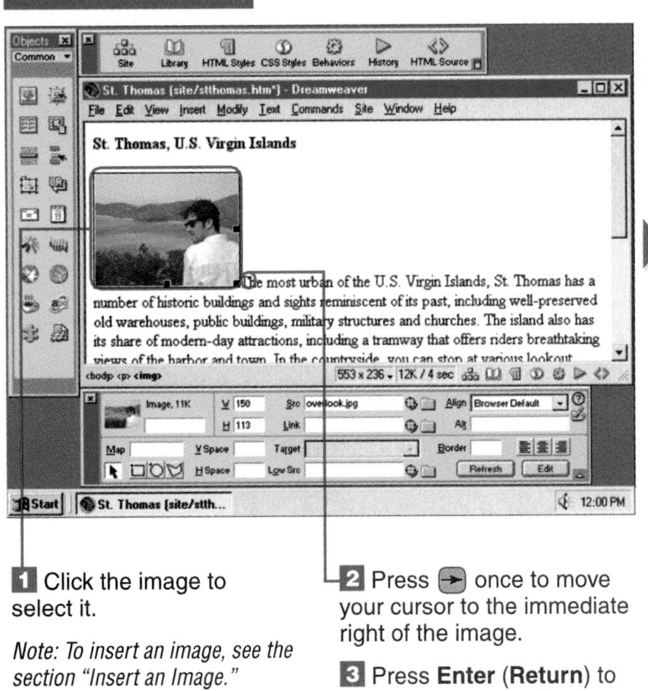

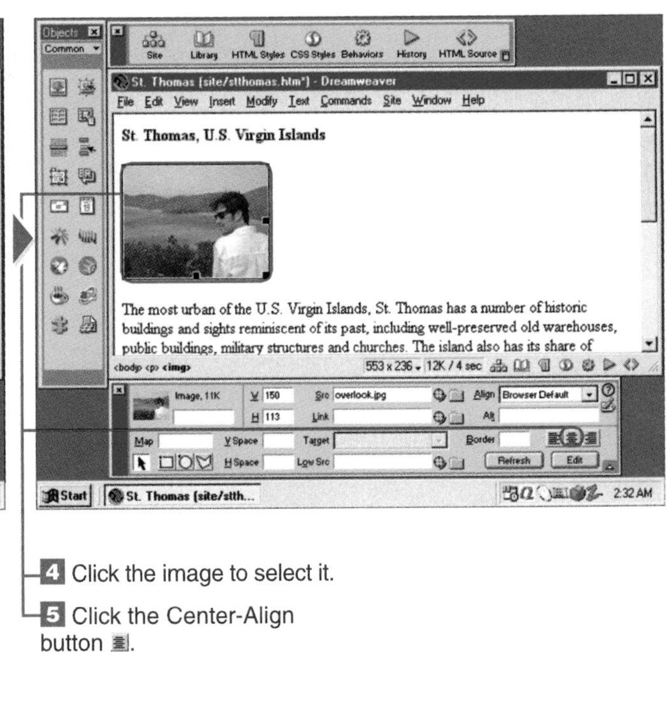

1 Click the image to select it.

Note: To insert an image, see the section "Insert an Image."

2 Press → once to move your cursor to the immediate right of the image.

3 Press **Enter** (**Return**) to place the image on its own line.

4 Click the image to select it.

5 Click the Center-Align button.

How can I use centered images to enhance my text?

You can center small icons to divide main sections of text in your Web page. These icons serve the same purpose as horizontal rules (see the Section, "Add a Horizontal Rule"), but can add a more sophisticated look to your pages.

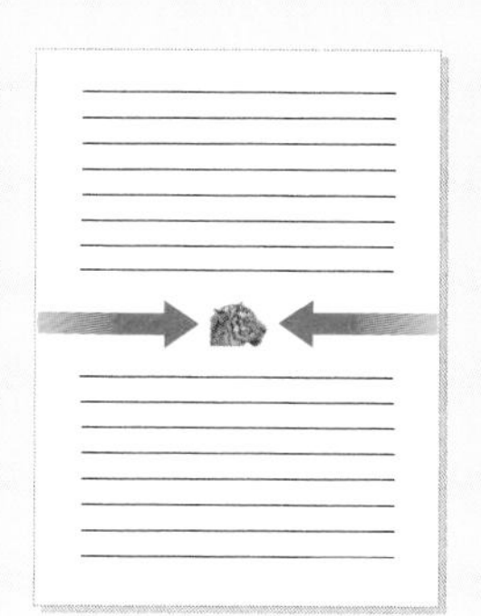

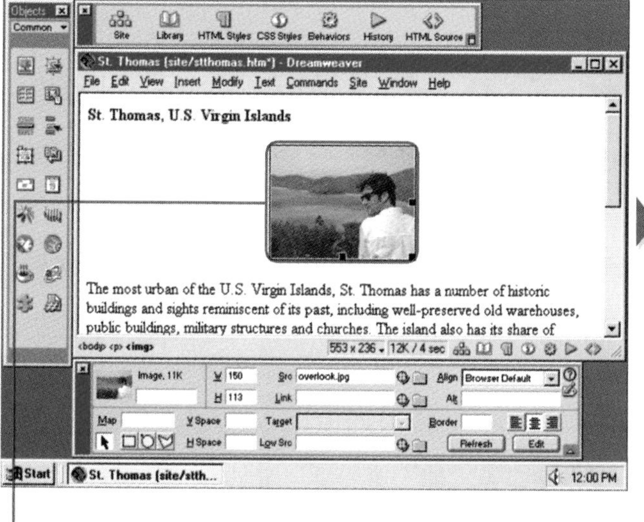

■ This centers the image.

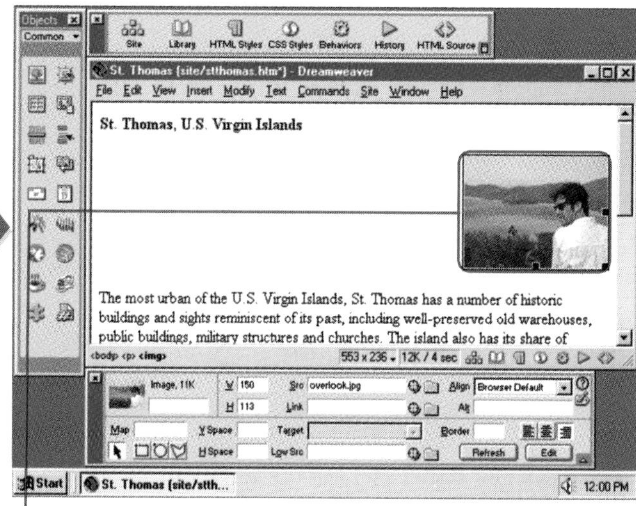

■ You can also align the image to right side of the page by clicking the Right-Align button in Step 5.

CHANGE THE SIZE OF AN IMAGE

Dreamweaver allows you to change an image's size in three ways. You can change the image's pixel dimensions, make the image a percentage of the browser window, or simply click and drag a corner of the image.

CHANGE THE SIZE OF AN IMAGE

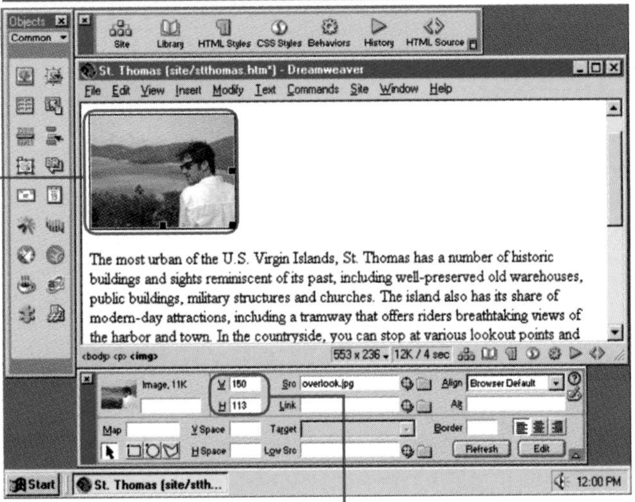

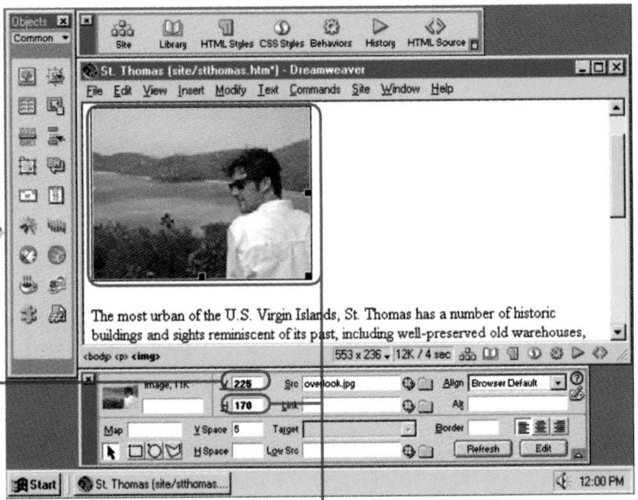

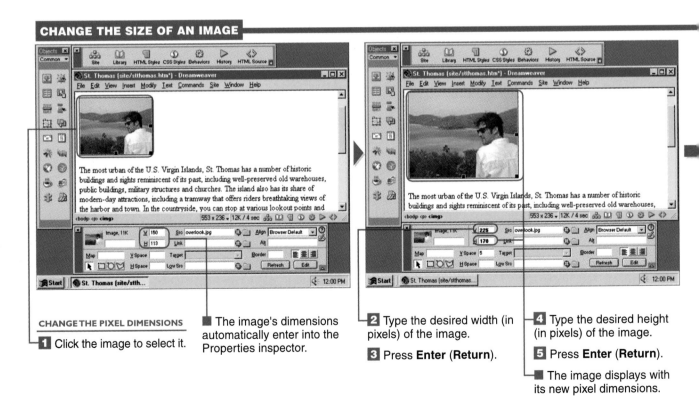

CHANGE THE PIXEL DIMENSIONS

1. Click the image to select it.

■ The image's dimensions automatically enter into the Properties inspector.

2. Type the desired width (in pixels) of the image.
3. Press **Enter** (**Return**).
4. Type the desired height (in pixels) of the image.
5. Press **Enter** (**Return**).

■ The image displays with its new pixel dimensions.

What is the best way to change the dimensions of a Web page image?

The best way to change the dimensions of a Web page image is with an image editor, which enables you to adjust its real height and width and save it as a new file. This maximizes the quality of the image.

Changing the dimensions of an image in Dreamweaver stretches or shrinks the original image to fit the new dimensions, but does not change the file's real dimensions. This can result in an image on a Web page that has reduced quality compared to the original.

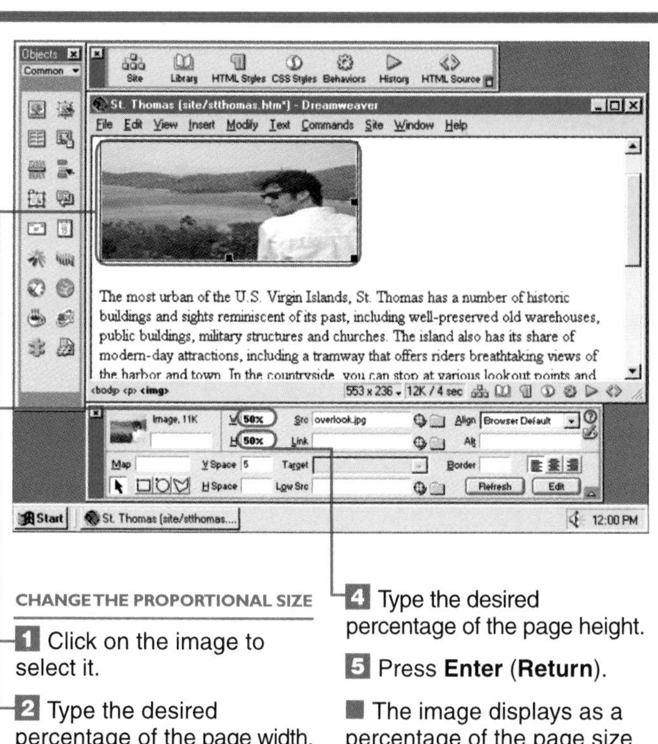

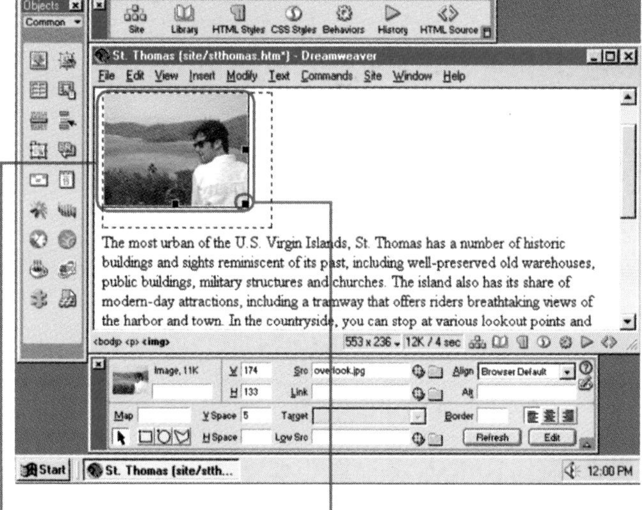

CHANGE THE PROPORTIONAL SIZE

1 Click on the image to select it.

2 Type the desired percentage of the page width.

3 Press **Enter** (**Return**).

4 Type the desired percentage of the page height.

5 Press **Enter** (**Return**).

■ The image displays as a percentage of the page size (not as a percentage of its original size).

CLICK AND DRAG THE IMAGE

1 Click on the image to select it.

2 Drag the handles at the edges of the image. To constrain proportions, hold down the Shift key as you drag a corner.

■ The image expands or contracts to its new dimensions.

Adding space around an image distinguishes it from the text and other images on your Web page.

ADD SPACE ABOVE AND BELOW AN IMAGE

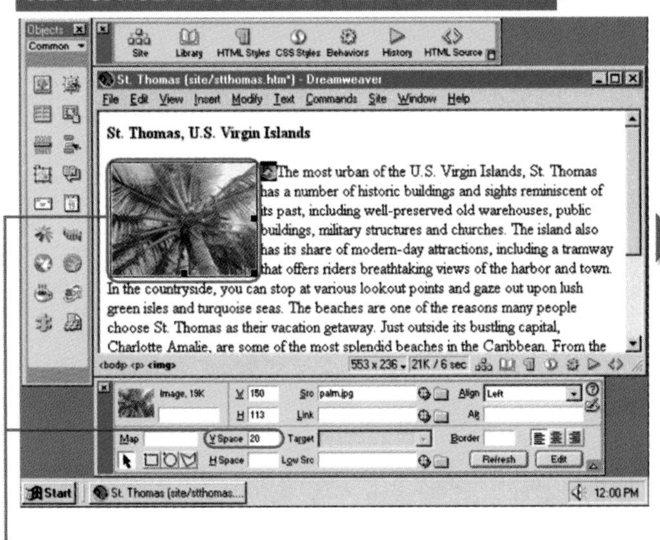

1 Click the image to select it.

2 Type the desired amount of space (in pixels).

3 Press **Enter** (**Return**).

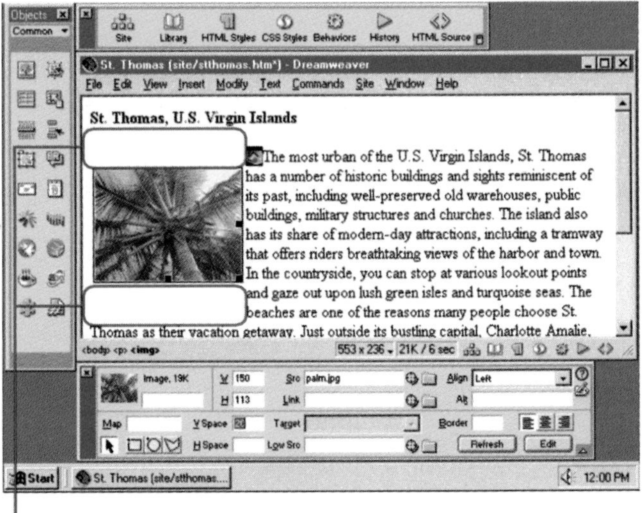

■ Extra space appears between the image and objects to the top and bottom of it.

Why should I add space around my images?

In many cases, adding space around your images enhances the appearance of your Web page. It makes text that wraps around images easier to read. It also keeps adjacent images from appearing as a single image.

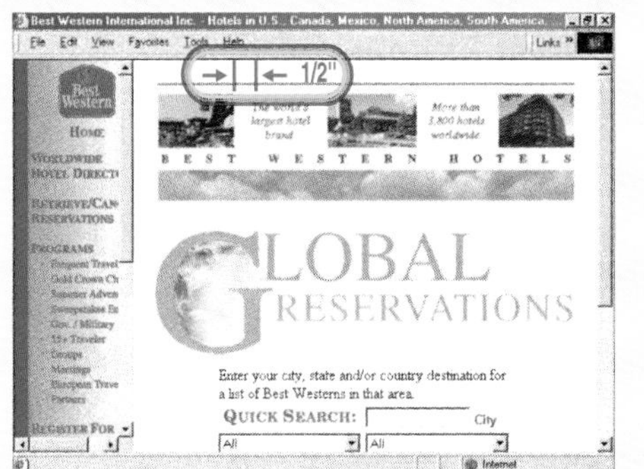

ADD SPACE TO THE LEFT AND RIGHT OF AN IMAGE

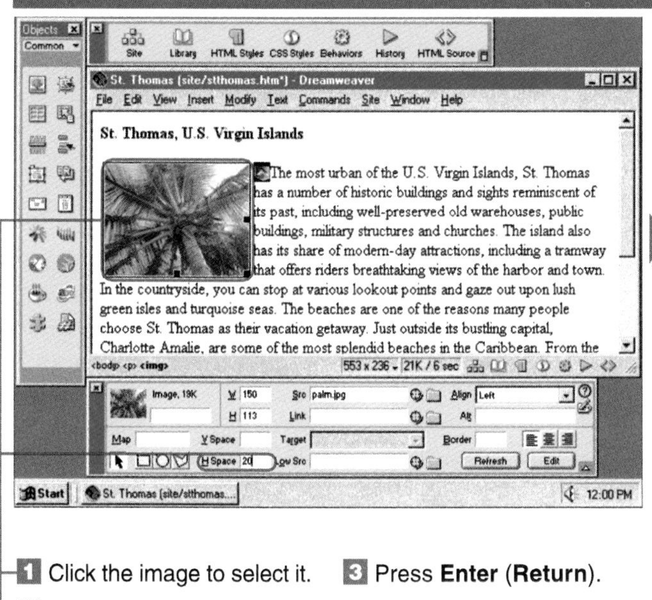

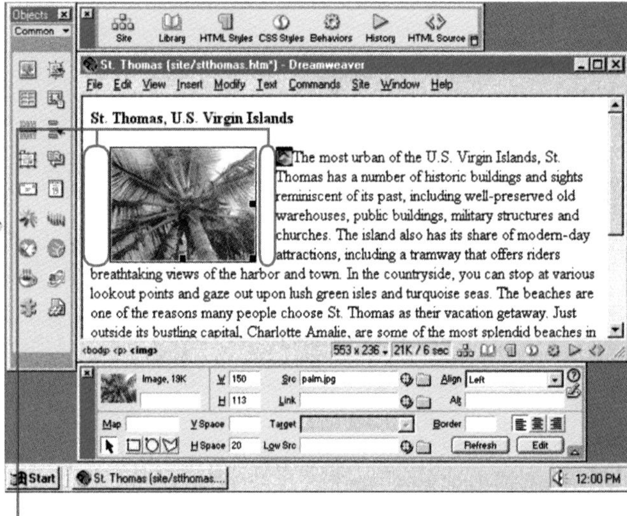

1 Click the image to select it.

2 Type the desired amount of space (in pixels).

3 Press **Enter** (**Return**).

■ Extra space appears between the image and objects to the left and right of it.

ADD A HORIZONTAL RULE

You can add a horizontal rule to your Web page to separate sections of content.

ADD A HORIZONTAL RULE

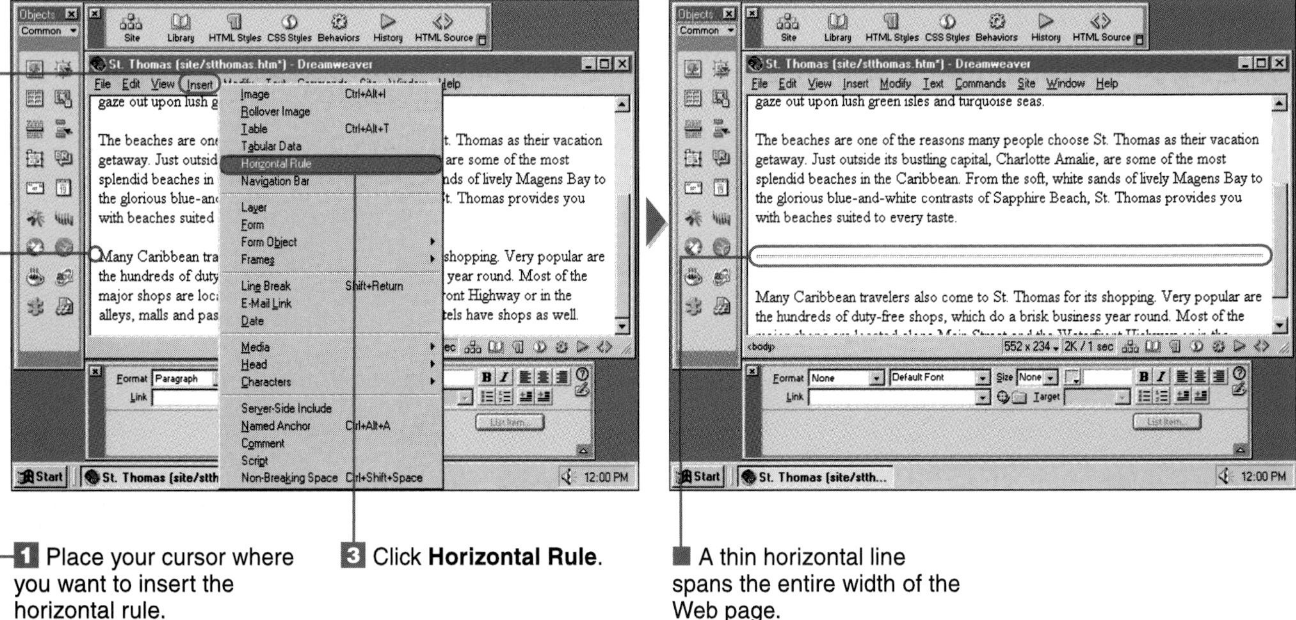

1 Place your cursor where you want to insert the horizontal rule.

2 Click **Insert**.

3 Click **Horizontal Rule**.

■ A thin horizontal line spans the entire width of the Web page.

Can I customize the color of my horizontal rule?

You can define the shading but not the color of your horizontal rule. However, creating your own colored horizontal graphics can serve the same purpose as a horizontal rule. You can create graphics in programs such as Adobe Photoshop and Macromedia Fireworks.

CUSTOMIZE YOUR HORIZONTAL RULE

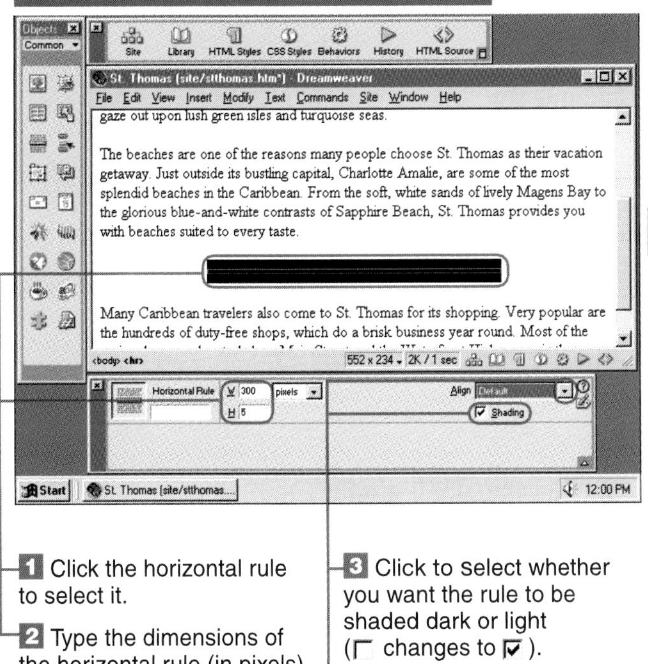

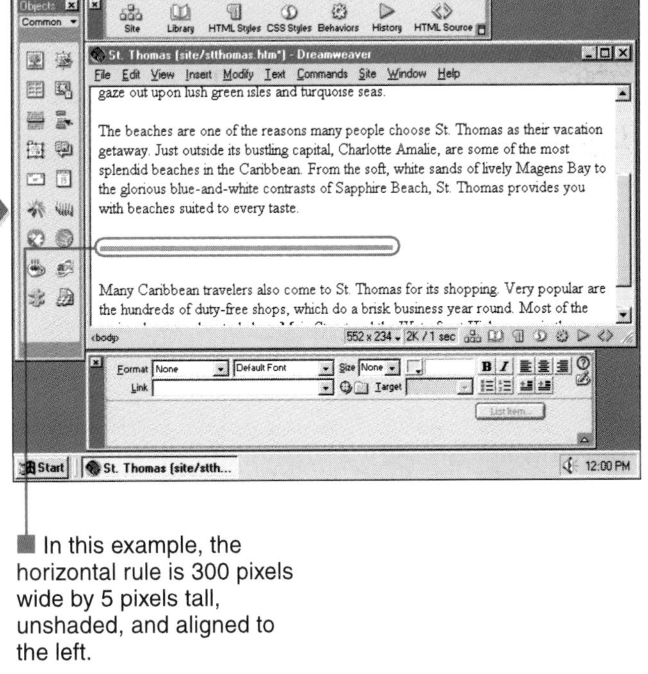

1 Click the horizontal rule to select it.

2 Type the dimensions of the horizontal rule (in pixels) in the W (width) and H (height) fields.

3 Click to select whether you want the rule to be shaded dark or light (☐ changes to ☑).

4 Click ▾ to choose the alignment.

■ In this example, the horizontal rule is 300 pixels wide by 5 pixels tall, unshaded, and aligned to the left.

ADD A BACKGROUND IMAGE

You can incorporate a background image to add texture to your Web page. Background images appear beneath any text or images on your page.

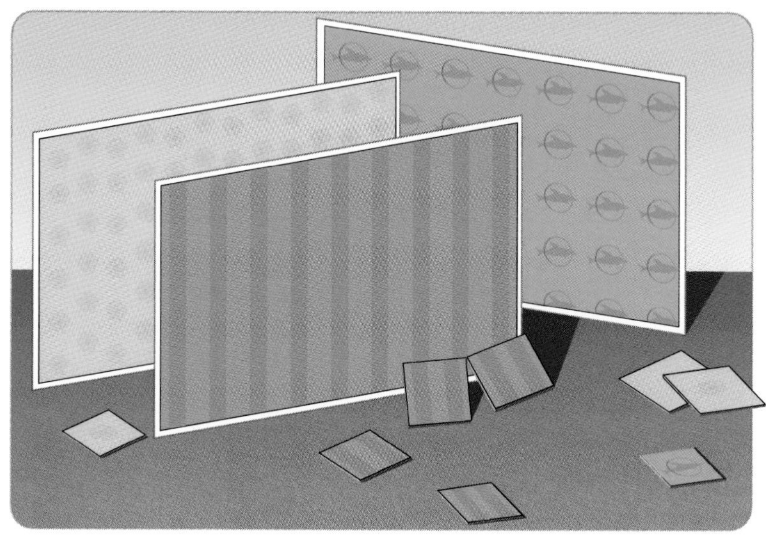

ADD A BACKGROUND IMAGE

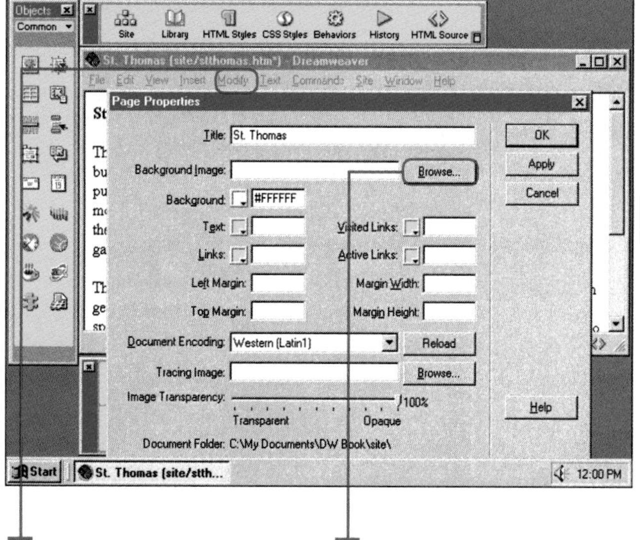

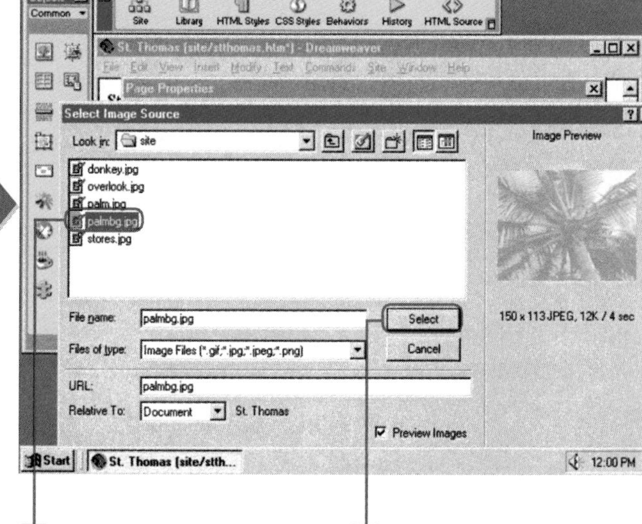

1 Click **Modify**.

2 Click **Page Properties** from the drop-down menu.

■ The Page Properties dialog box appears.

3 Click **Browse** to open the Select Image Source dialog box.

4 Select the background image that you want to insert from the list menu.

5 Click **Select**.

What types of images make good backgrounds?

Typically, images that don't clash with the text and other content in the foreground. You don't want your background image to overwhelm the rest of the page.

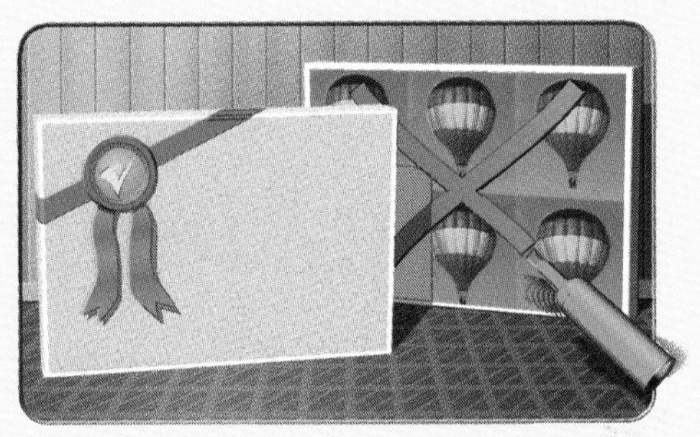

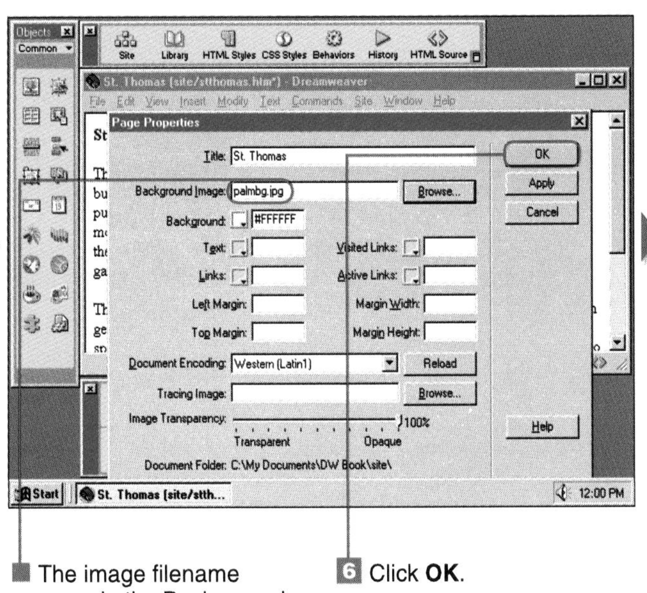

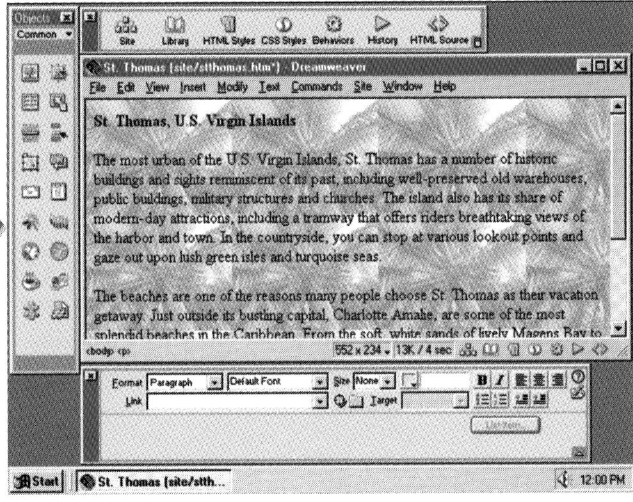

■ The image filename appears in the Background Image field.

6 Click **OK**.

■ The image appears as a background on the Web page. If necessary, the image tiles horizontally and vertically to fill the entire window.

CHANGE THE BACKGROUND COLOR

For variety, you can change the background color of your Web page.

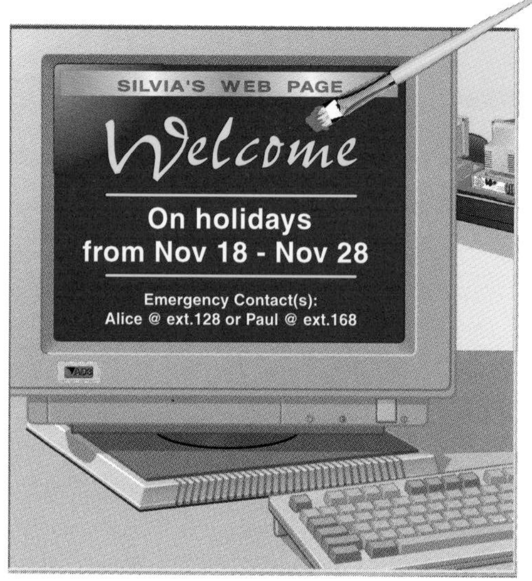

The default background color of Dreamweaver Web pages is white.

CHANGE THE BACKGROUND COLOR

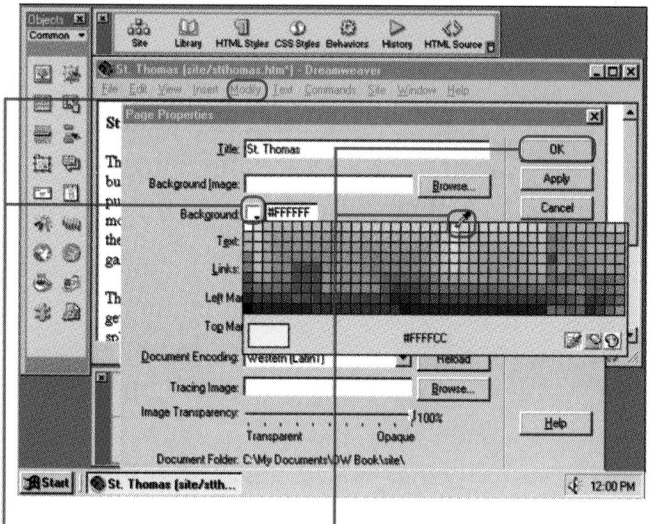

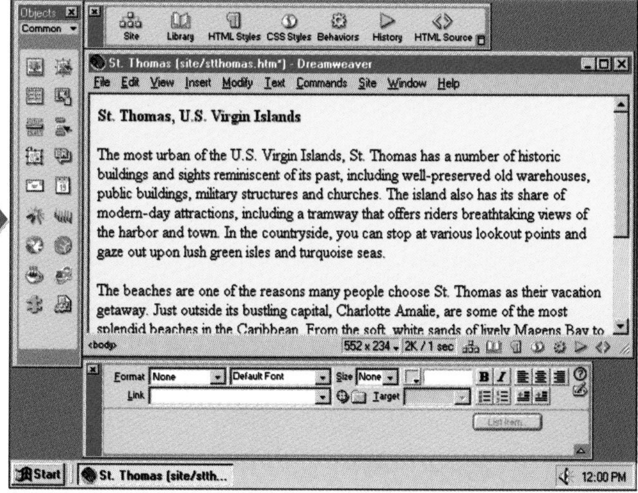

1 Select **Modify⇨Page Properties** to bring up the Page Properties dialog box.

2 Click the **Background** color swatch.

3 Click a color from the menu using the eyedropper tool.

4 Click **OK**.

■ The background of your Web page is now the new color.

ADD ALTERNATE TEXT

You can add alternate text for users to read when images does not appear. Some Web browsers cannot display images, and some users surf the Web with images turned off.

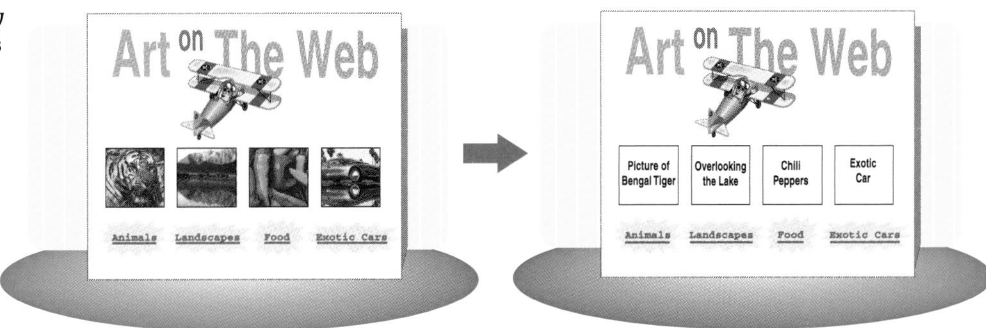

ADD ALTERNATE TEXT

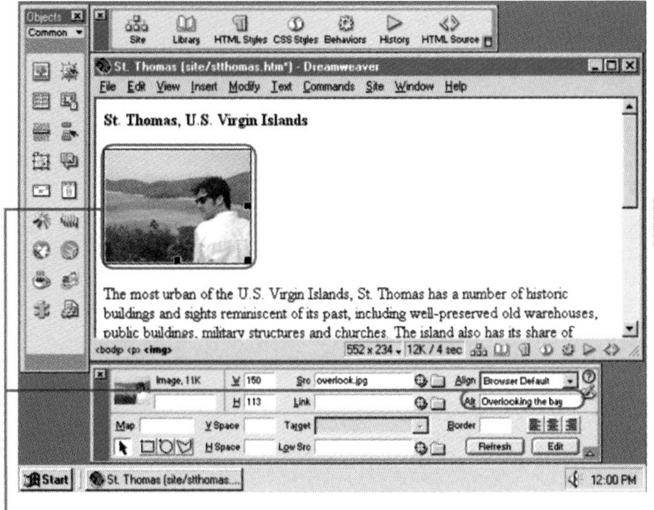

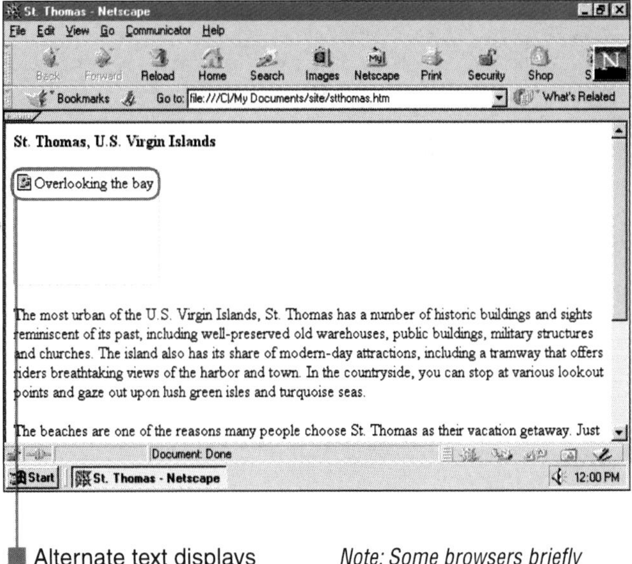

1 Click the image to select it.

2 Type the desired alternate text into the Alt field.

3 Press **Enter** (**Return**).

■ Alternate text displays when the image does not appear in the browser window.

Note: Some browsers briefly display alternative text when you hold your cursor over an image.

INSERT MULTIMEDIA

Inserting video clips and other multimedia can add life to your Web page.

INSERT MULTIMEDIA

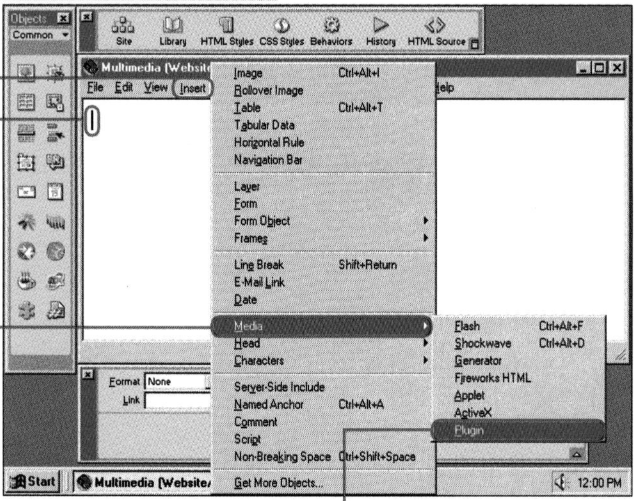

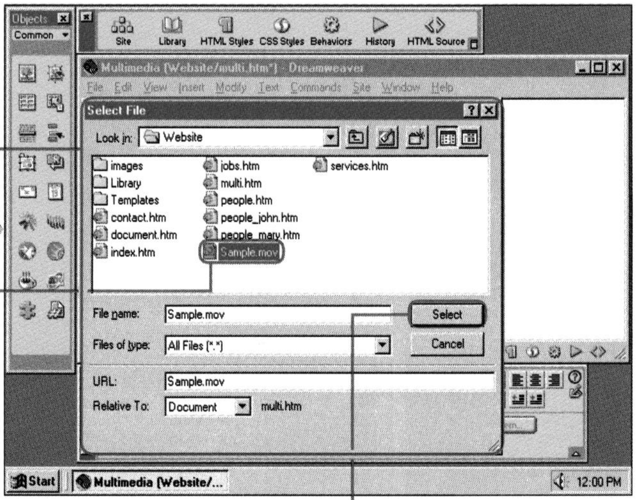

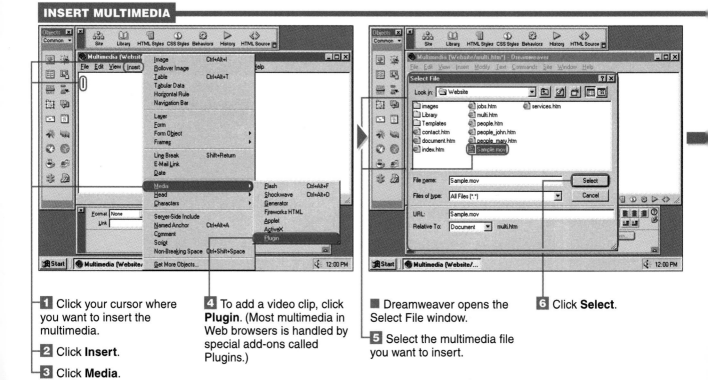

1 Click your cursor where you want to insert the multimedia.

2 Click **Insert**.

3 Click **Media**.

4 To add a video clip, click **Plugin**. (Most multimedia in Web browsers is handled by special add-ons called Plugins.)

■ Dreamweaver opens the Select File window.

5 Select the multimedia file you want to insert.

6 Click **Select**.

What should I consider when adding multimedia content to my site?

Adding video clips, sounds and interactive features such as Flash, can be an attractive way to jazz up a Web site. Remember that some users can not view such content because their browsers do not support it.

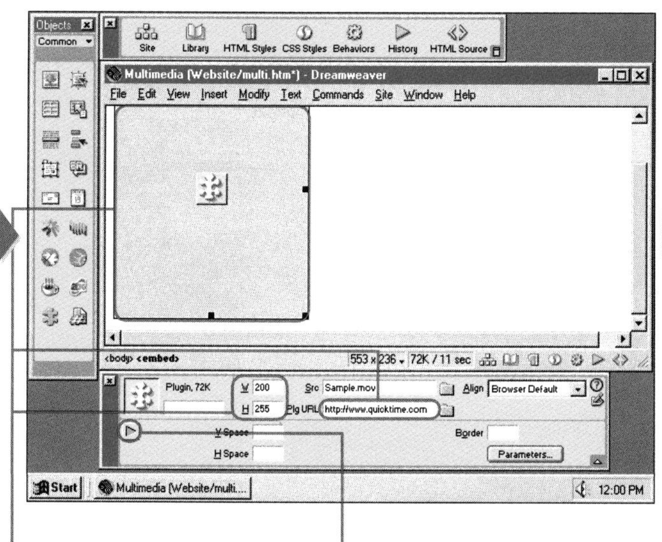

■ Dreamweaver inserts a plugin icon.

7 Type the dimensions of the file (in pixels).

8 Type the URL of the site where the user can download the plugin.

■ If the plugin is not installed on a user's browser, the browser will ask whether the user wants to visit the site to download it.

9 Click ▷ to test the multimedia file.

■ Some multimedia files, such as QuickTime movies, can be tested directly in the Dreamweaver Document window.

Science Today
Chapter 1 - Introduction to Our World
Chapter 2 - Nature Now and Then
Chapter 3 - Chemistry of the Environment
Chapter 4 - The Water Around Us
Chapter 5 - How Healthy Are We?
Chapter 6 - Solar Energy

Creating Hyperlinks

You can connect your pages to other pages on the Web with hyperlinks. Learn about adding links to your pages in this chapter.

HYPERLINK TO ANOTHER PAGE IN YOUR SITE

To allow readers to move from one area of your Web site to another, you can create a hyperlink.

HYPERLINK TO ANOTHER PAGE IN YOUR SITE

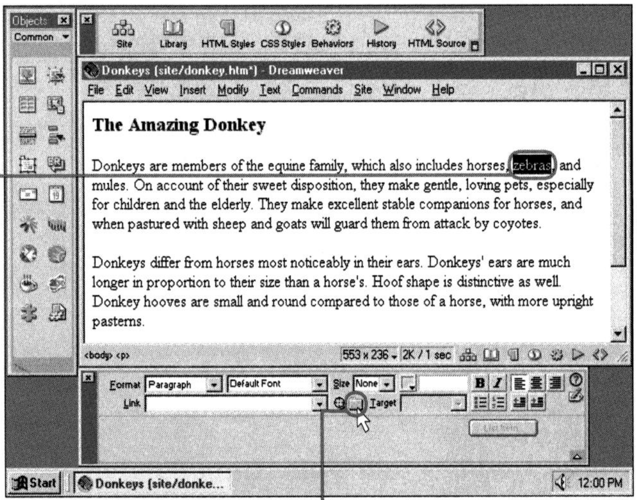

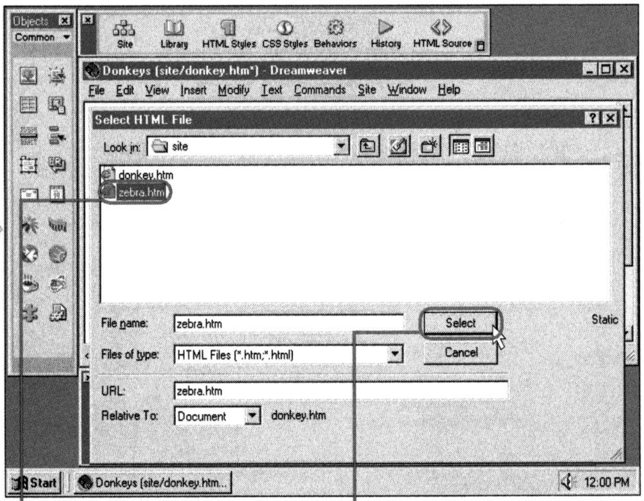

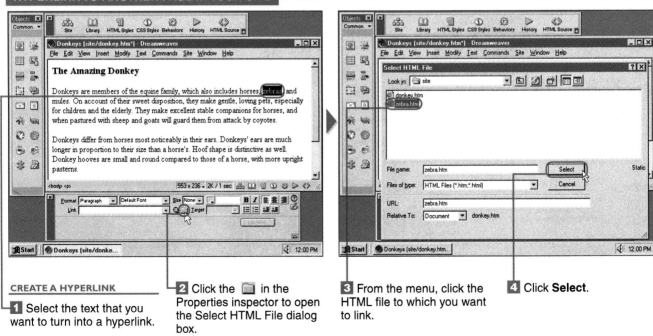

CREATE A HYPERLINK

1 Select the text that you want to turn into a hyperlink.

2 Click the 📁 in the Properties inspector to open the Select HTML File dialog box.

3 From the menu, click the HTML file to which you want to link.

4 Click **Select**.

How should I organize the files that make up my Web site?

Keep the files that make up your Web site in a single folder on your computer. This makes it easier to create links between them and ensures that all the links work correctly when you transfer the files to a live Web server (see Chapter 13).

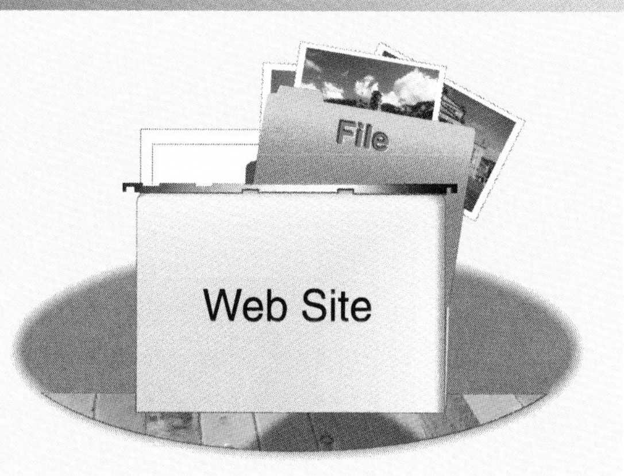

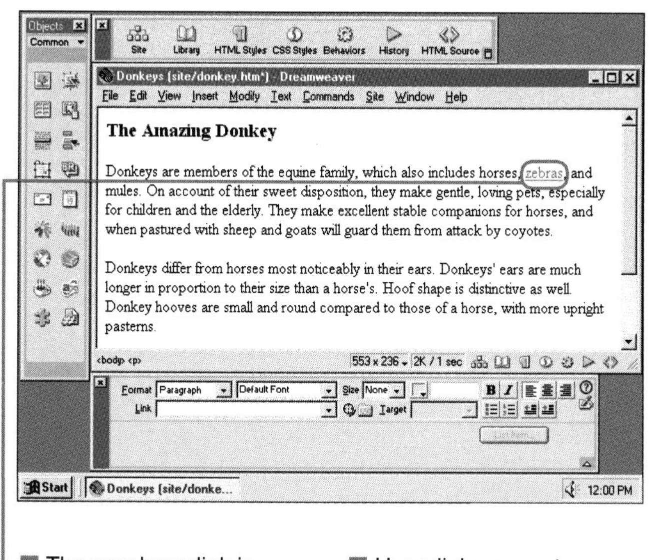

■ The new hyperlink is colored and underlined.

■ Hyperlinks are not clickable in the Document window. To test the link, open the file in a Web browser (see Chapter 2).

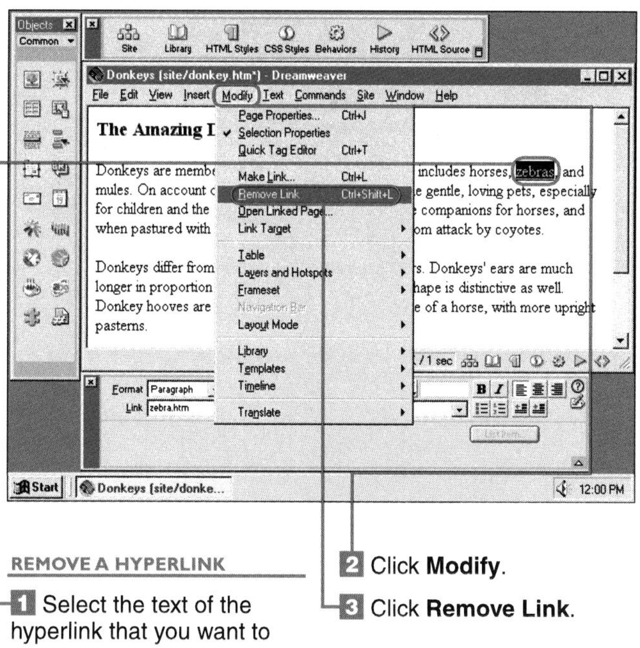

REMOVE A HYPERLINK

1 Select the text of the hyperlink that you want to remove.

2 Click **Modify**.

3 Click **Remove Link**.

You can give viewers access to additional information about topics by linking to other Web sites.

HYPERLINK TO ANOTHER WEB SITE

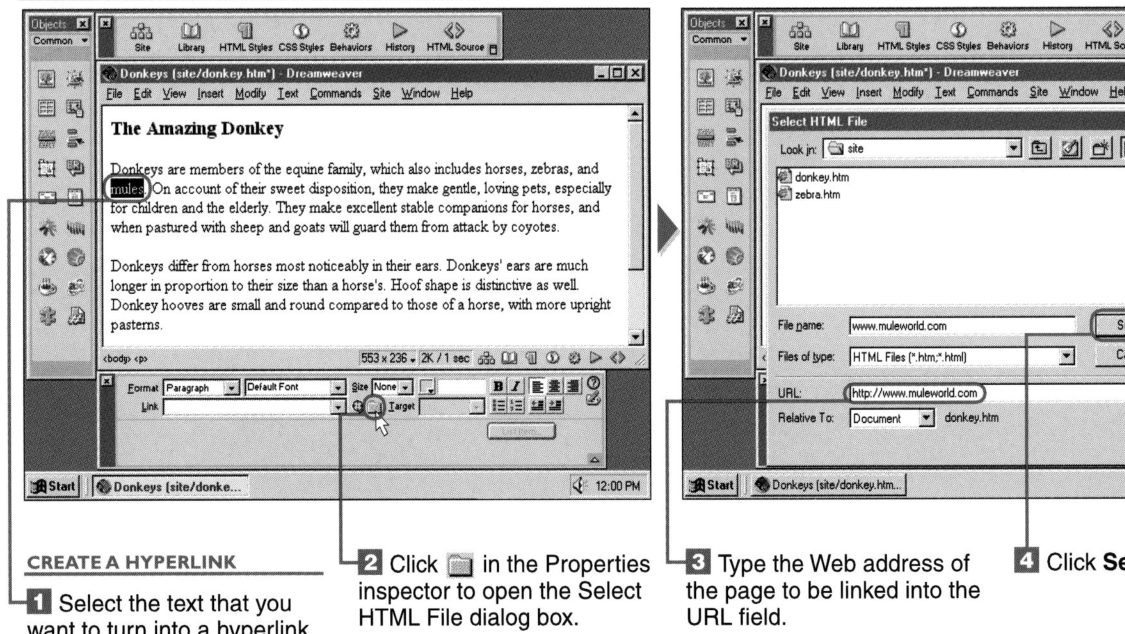

CREATE A HYPERLINK

1 Select the text that you want to turn into a hyperlink to another site.

2 Click ▭ in the Properties inspector to open the Select HTML File dialog box.

3 Type the Web address of the page to be linked into the URL field.

4 Click **Select**.

How do I make sure my links to other Web sites always work?

You have no control over the Web pages on other sites to which you have linked (unless you happen to maintain those Web sites, too). If you have linked to a Web page that is later renamed or taken offline, your viewer will receive an error message when they click on the link. Maintain your site by periodically testing your links.

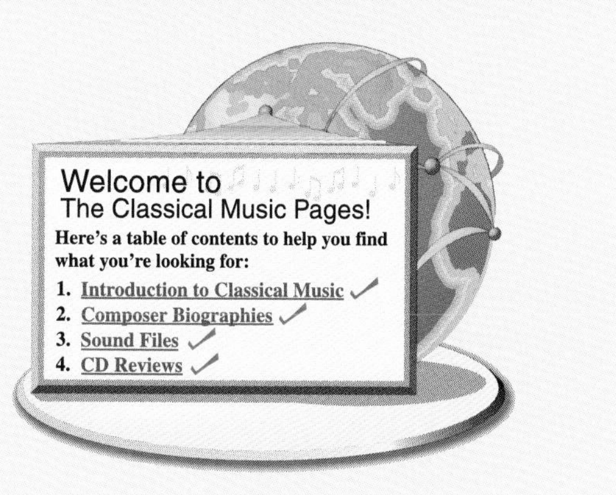

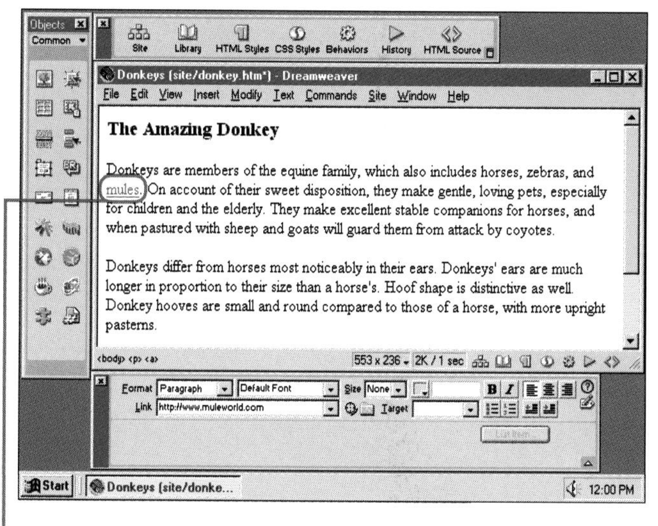

■ The new hyperlink appears colored and underlined.

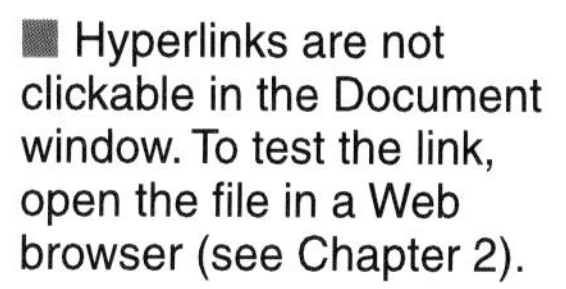

■ Hyperlinks are not clickable in the Document window. To test the link, open the file in a Web browser (see Chapter 2).

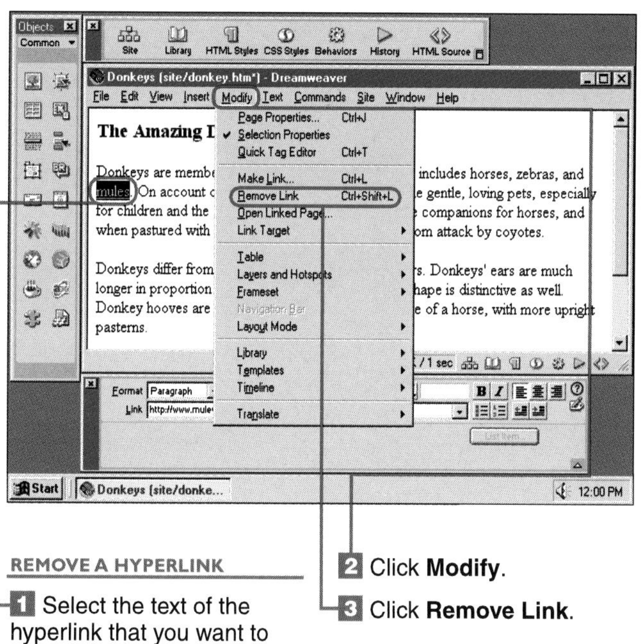

REMOVE A HYPERLINK

1 Select the text of the hyperlink that you want to remove.

2 Click **Modify**.

3 Click **Remove Link**.

An image hyperlink allows you to click an image to go to another Web page.

IMAGE HYPERLINKS

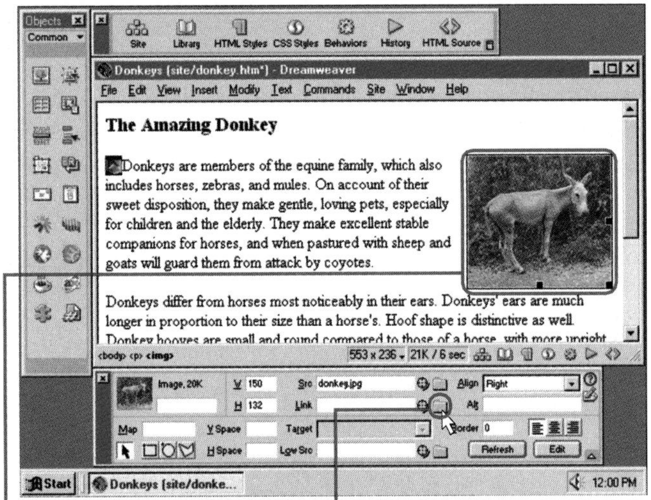

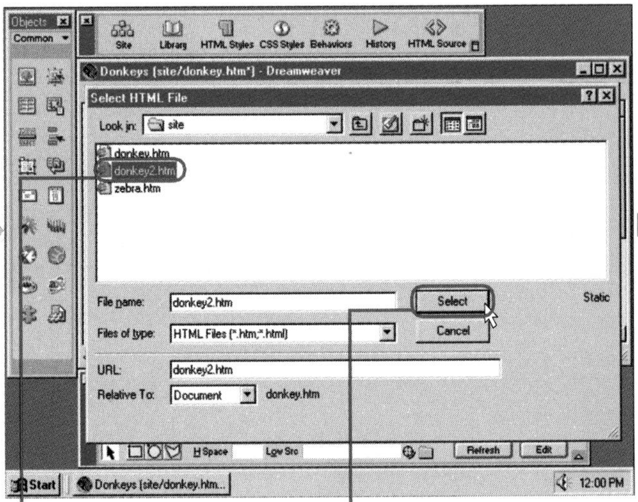

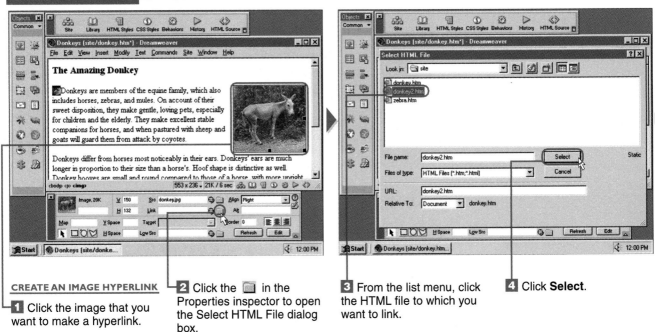

CREATE AN IMAGE HYPERLINK

1 Click the image that you want to make a hyperlink.

2 Click the ▭ in the Properties inspector to open the Select HTML File dialog box.

3 From the list menu, click the HTML file to which you want to link.

4 Click **Select**.

How do I create a navigation bar for my Web page?

Many Web sites include a set of hyperlinked buttons on the top, side, or bottom of each page. These buttons let viewers navigate to the main pages of the Web site. You can create these buttons using image-editing software such as Adobe Photoshop or Macromedia Fireworks. To insert images into your Web page, see Chapter 5.

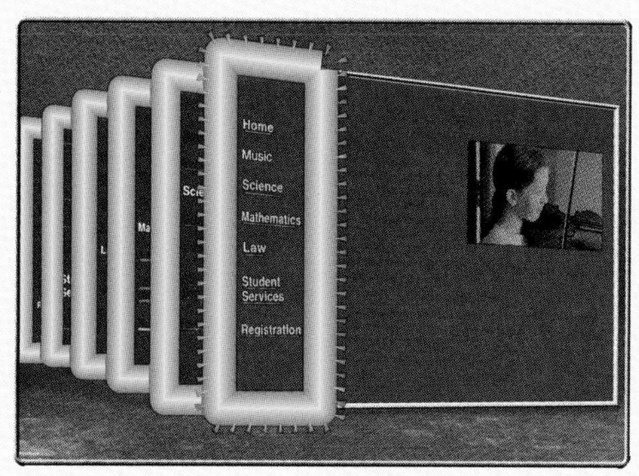

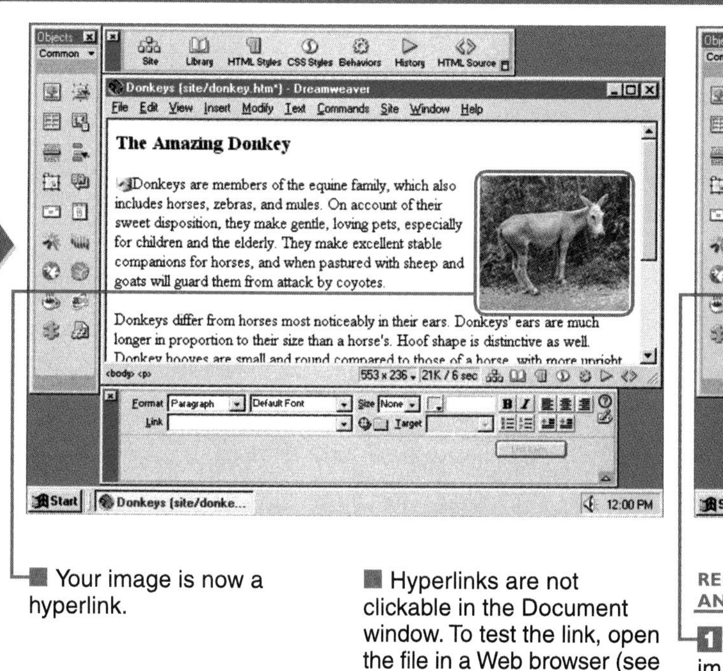

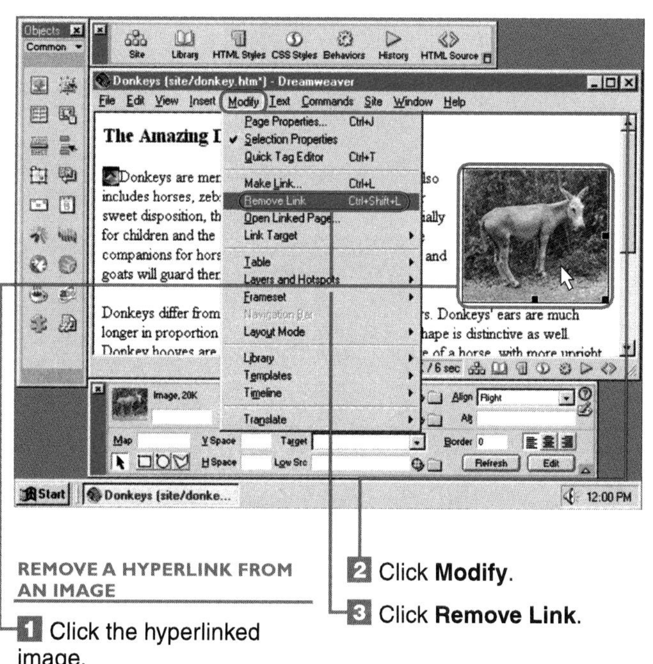

■ Your image is now a hyperlink.

■ Hyperlinks are not clickable in the Document window. To test the link, open the file in a Web browser (see Chapter 2).

REMOVE A HYPERLINK FROM AN IMAGE

1 Click the hyperlinked image.

2 Click **Modify**.

3 Click **Remove Link**.

HYPERLINK TO CONTENT ON THE SAME WEB PAGE

You can create a hyperlink to other content on the same Web page. The first step is creating a named anchor.

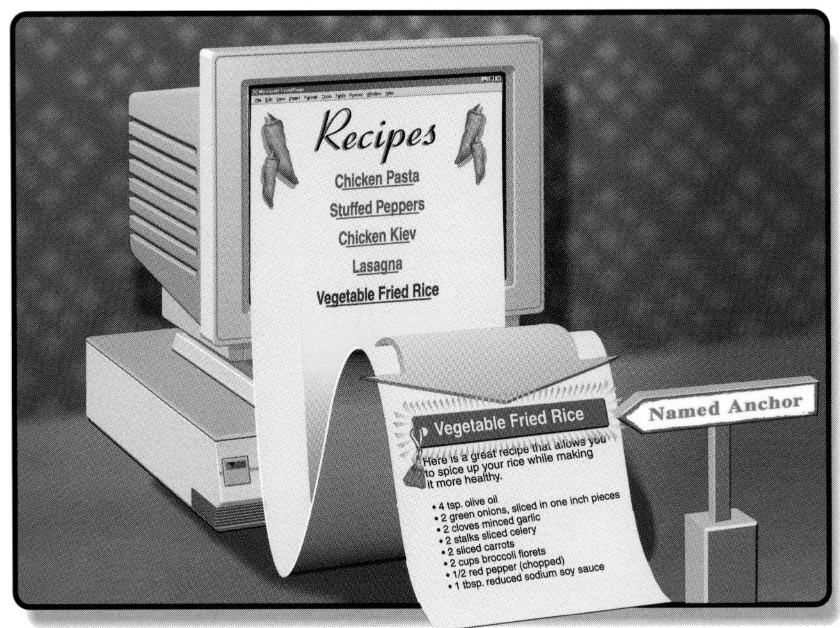

Same-page hyperlinks are useful when a page is very long.

CREATE A NAMED ANCHOR

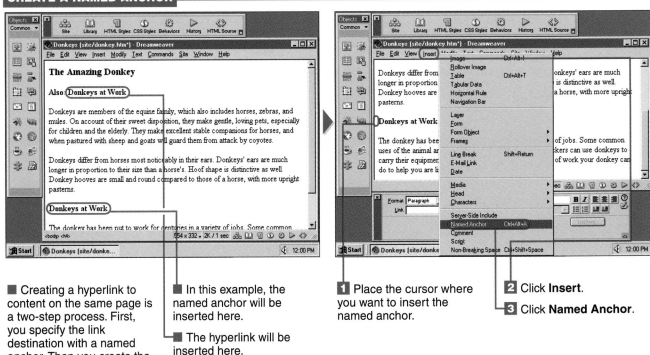

■ Creating a hyperlink to content on the same page is a two-step process. First, you specify the link destination with a named anchor. Then you create the hyperlink.

■ In this example, the named anchor will be inserted here.

■ The hyperlink will be inserted here.

1 Place the cursor where you want to insert the named anchor.

2 Click **Insert**.

3 Click **Named Anchor**.

How are same-page links useful?

If you have a Web page that is a glossary, same-page links let you link to different parts of the glossary from a hyperlink menu at the top.

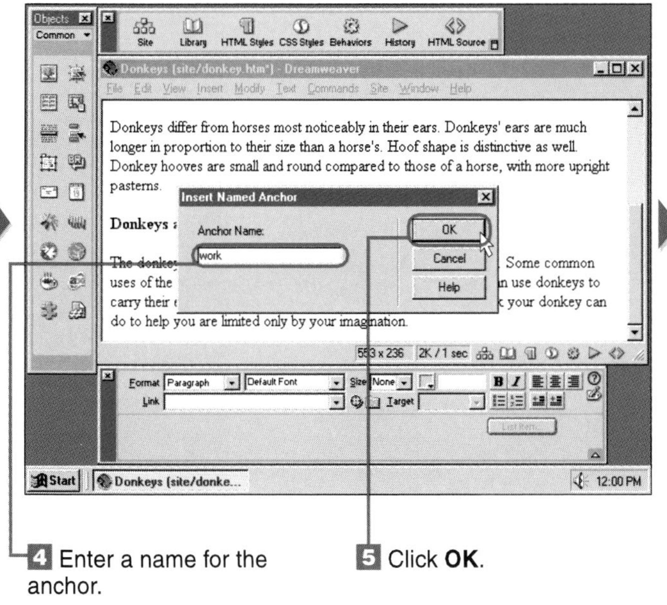

4 Enter a name for the anchor.

5 Click **OK**.

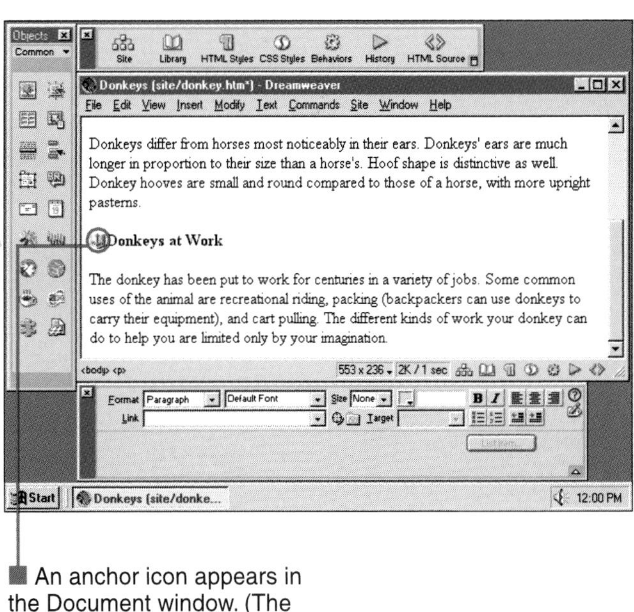

■ An anchor icon appears in the Document window. (The symbol does not appear in Web browsers when they load the page.)

CONTINUED

HYPERLINK TO CONTENT ON THE SAME WEB PAGE (CONTINUED)

The second step in linking to content on the same Web page is creating a hyperlink to the named anchor.

CREATE THE HYPERLINK

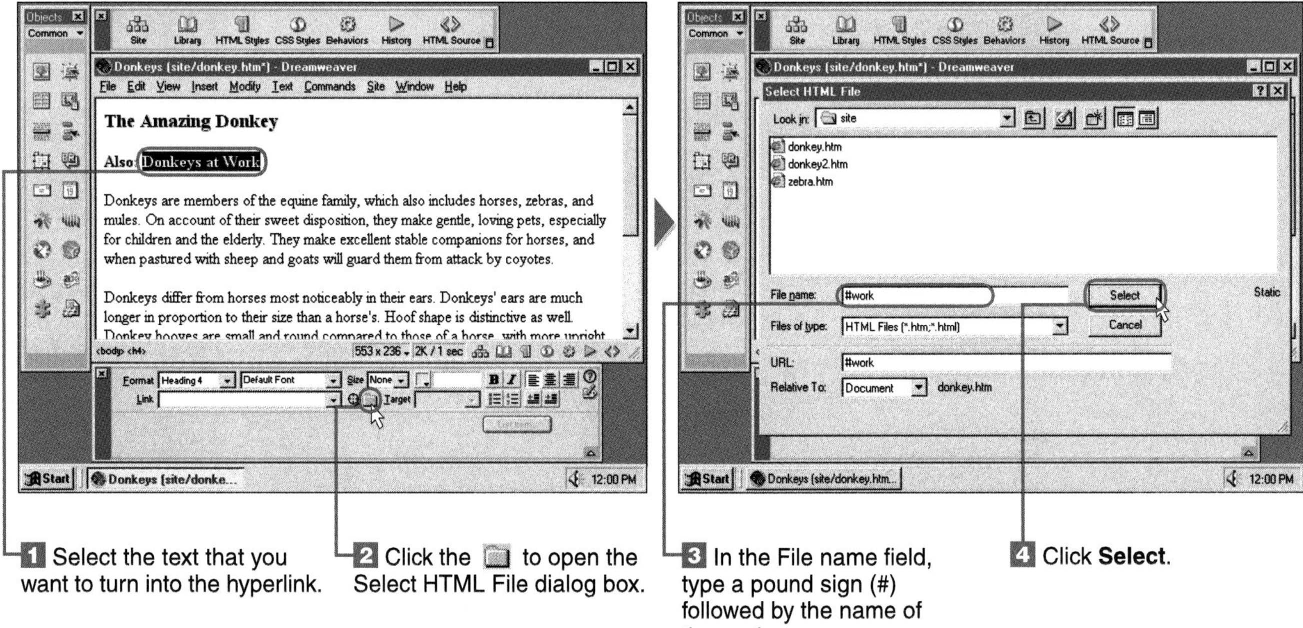

1 Select the text that you want to turn into the hyperlink.

2 Click the ▢ to open the Select HTML File dialog box.

3 In the File name field, type a pound sign (#) followed by the name of the anchor.

4 Click **Select**.

How can I create a link that leads to the top of the current Web page?

Every Web page has an implicit "top" anchor at the top of the page. To reference it, specify **#top** when you define a hyperlink's destination.

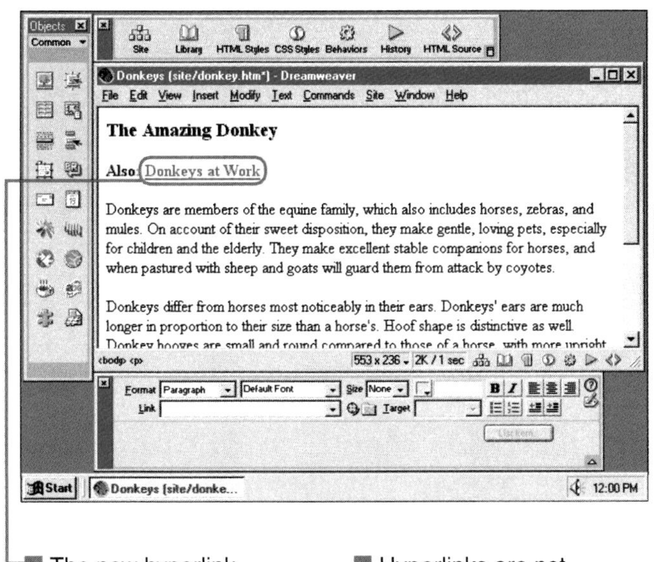

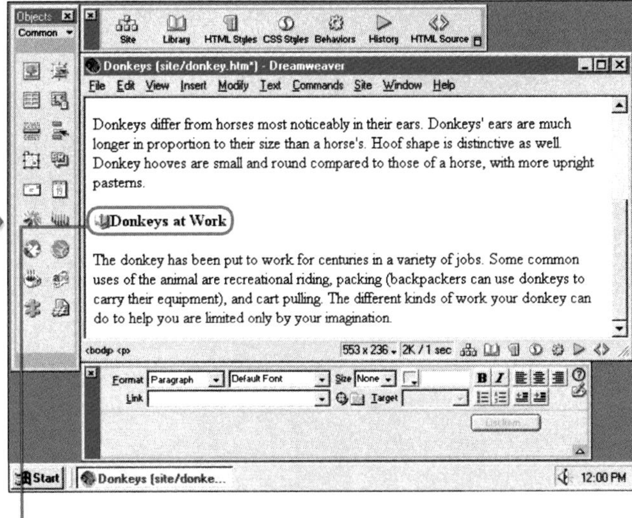

■ The new hyperlink appears colored and underlined.

■ Hyperlinks are not clickable in the Document window. To test the link, open the file in a Web browser (see Chapter 2).

■ Clicking the link in a Web browser takes the viewer to the named anchor.

HYPERLINK TO OTHER FILES

Hyperlinks do not have to lead just to other Web pages. You can link to other file types, such as image files, word processing documents, or multimedia files.

HYPERLINK TO OTHER FILES

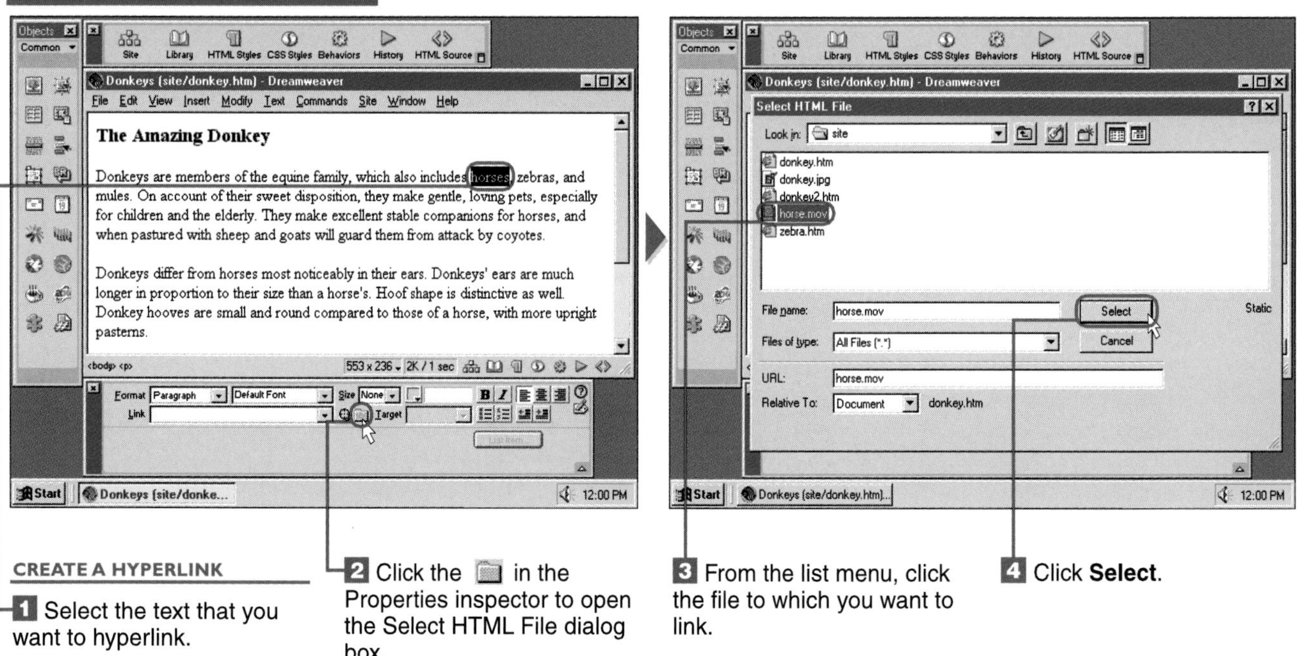

CREATE A HYPERLINK

1 Select the text that you want to hyperlink.

2 Click the (folder icon) in the Properties inspector to open the Select HTML File dialog box.

3 From the list menu, click the file to which you want to link.

4 Click **Select**.

How do users see files that are not HTML documents?

What users see when they click links to other types of files depends on how their Web browser is configured and what applications they have on their computer. For instance, if you link to a QuickTime movie, users will need to have QuickTime software installed on their computer to see the movie. If a user does not have the software installed, the browser will typically ask if the user wants to download the file and save it so they can view it later (after they have installed the correct software).

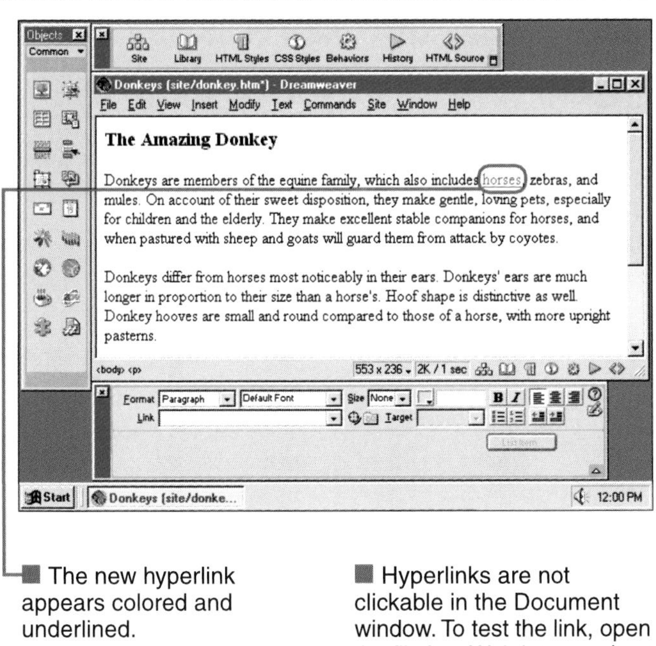

■ The new hyperlink appears colored and underlined.

■ Hyperlinks are not clickable in the Document window. To test the link, open the file in a Web browser (see Chapter 2).

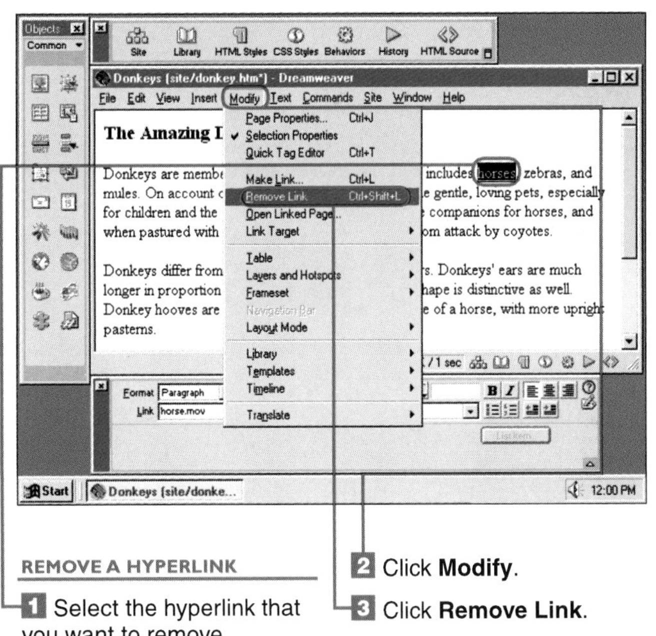

REMOVE A HYPERLINK

1 Select the hyperlink that you want to remove.

2 Click **Modify**.

3 Click **Remove Link**.

CREATE MULTIPLE HYPERLINKS WITHIN AN IMAGE

To add variety to your Web site, you can assign different hyperlinks to different parts of an image using the Dreamweaver image-mapping tools.

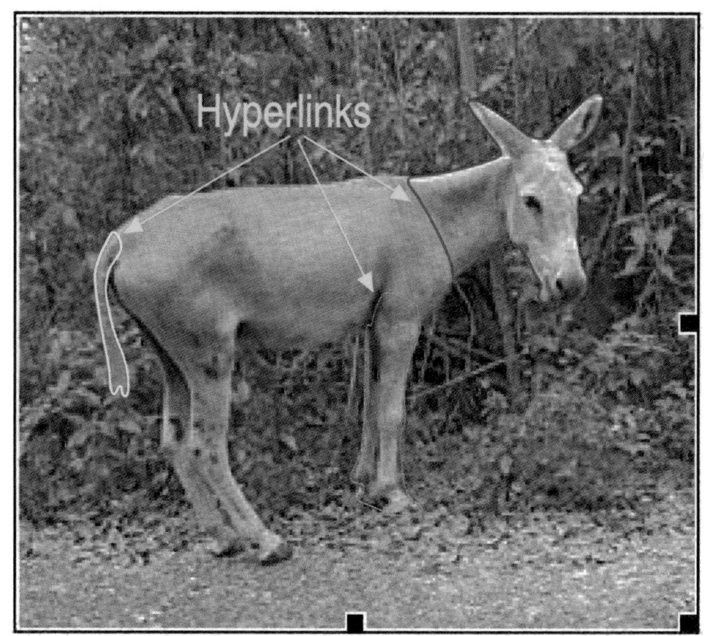

CREATE MULTIPLE HYPERLINKS WITHIN AN IMAGE

1 Click the image.

2 Type a descriptive name in the Map field in the Properties inspector. This serves as the name of the image map.

3 Click a drawing tool: ▭ for rectangular areas, ◯ for circular areas, or ▽ for polygons.

■ ▽ lets you create irregularly shaped areas by clicking the corner points one at a time.

4 Draw an area on the image using the selected tool.

5 Click the 📁 to bring up the Select HTML File dialog box.

How can I create an interactive map of United States with each state having a different hyperlink?

Create an image map. Use the polygon tool to define a shape for each state. Assign a different hyperlink to each shape.

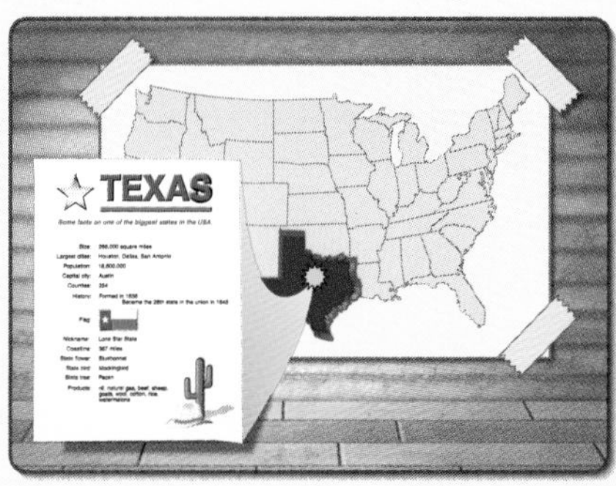

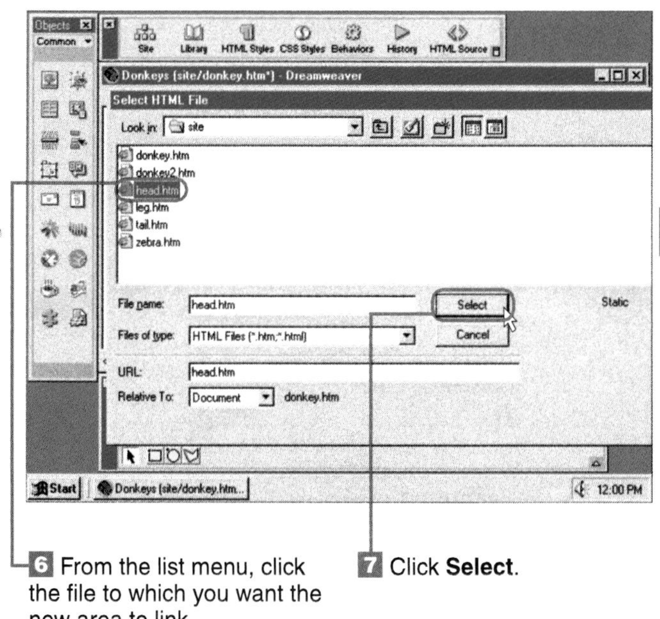

6 From the list menu, click the file to which you want the new area to link.

7 Click **Select**.

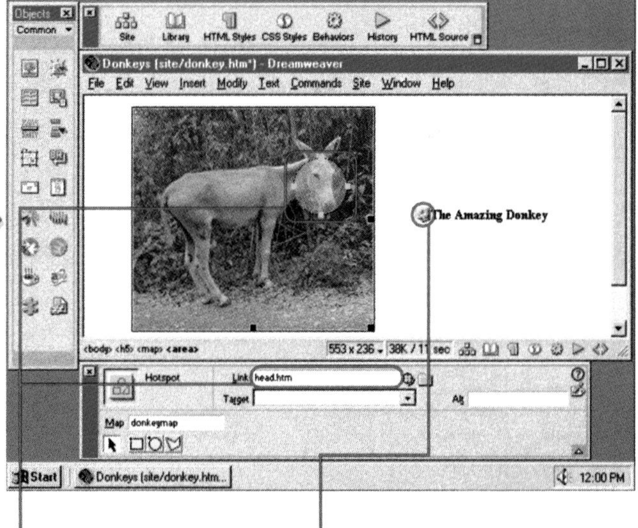

■ The area defined by the shape becomes a hyperlink to the selected file.

■ In this example, the head area links to head.htm.

■ Repeat Steps 3 through 7 to add more links to your image.

■ Image-map shapes do not appear when opened in a Web browser. To test the page in a browser, see Chapter 2.

CREATE A HYPERLINK THAT OPENS A NEW WINDOW

You can create a hyperlink that opens a new browser window when clicked. The hyperlinked destination opens in the new window.

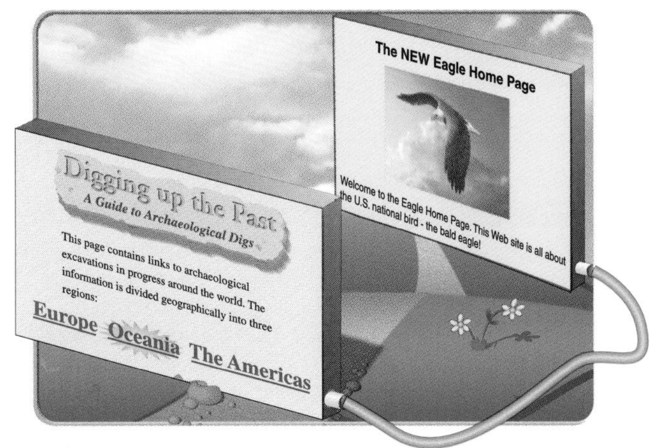

This lets you keep a previous Web page open on a viewer's computer.

CREATE A HYPERLINK THAT OPENS A NEW WINDOW

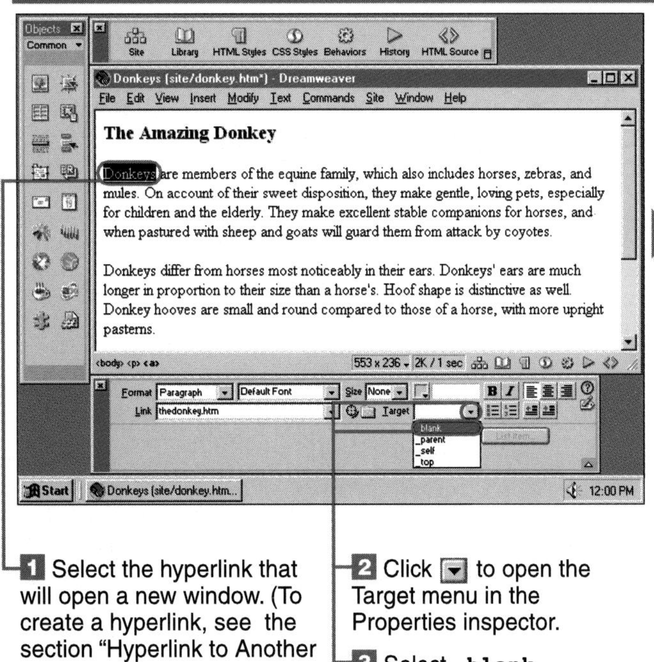

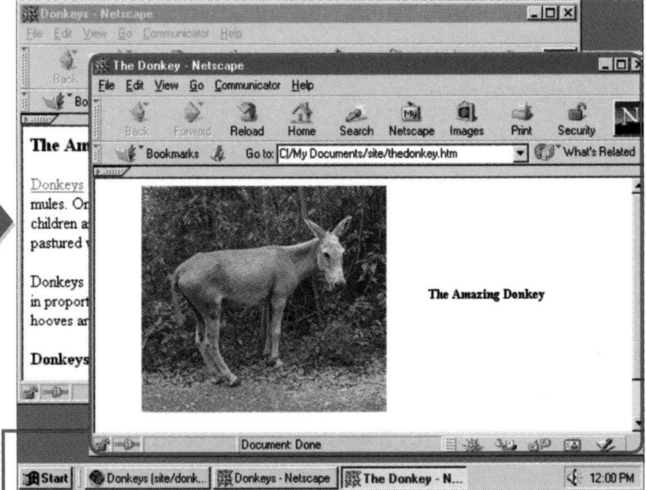

1 Select the hyperlink that will open a new window. (To create a hyperlink, see the section "Hyperlink to Another Web site.")

2 Click ▼ to open the Target menu in the Properties inspector.

3 Select `_blank`.

■ A new window opens when the hyperlink is clicked. The hyperlinked destination is displayed in the new window.

CHANGE THE COLOR OF HYPERLINKS

You can change the color of your links to make them match the visual style of your site.

CHANGE THE COLOR OF HYPERLINKS

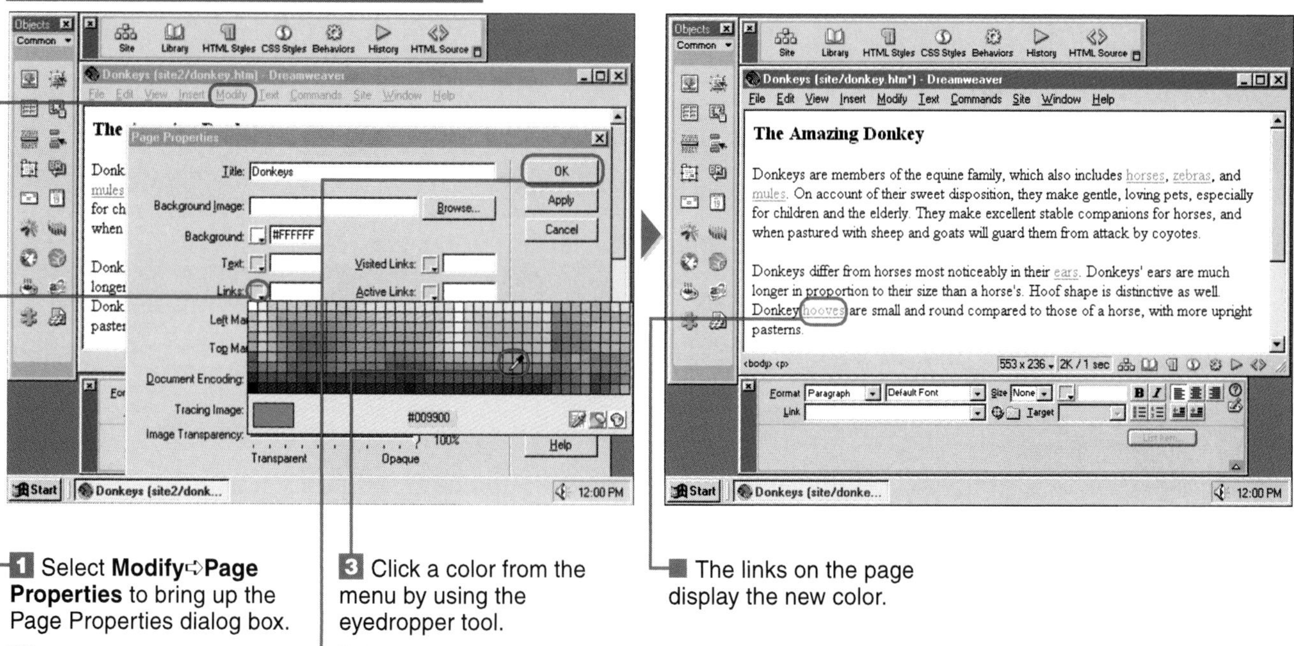

1. Select **Modify⇨Page Properties** to bring up the Page Properties dialog box.
2. Click the **Links** color swatch.
3. Click a color from the menu by using the eyedropper tool.
4. Click **OK**.

■ The links on the page display the new color.

CHANGE THE COLOR OF VISITED HYPERLINKS

You can change the color of *visited links* to make them match the visual style of your site. Visited links are links that a user has previously selected.

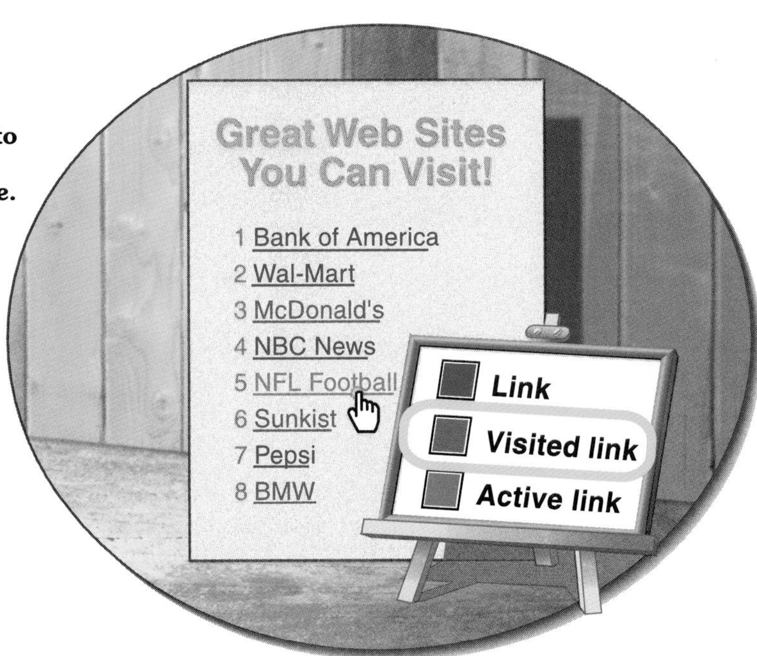

CHANGE THE COLOR OF VISITED HYPERLINKS

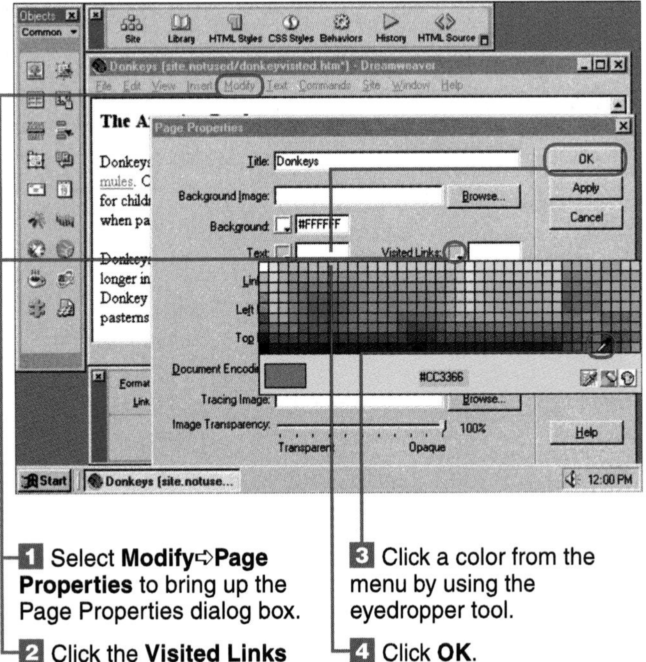

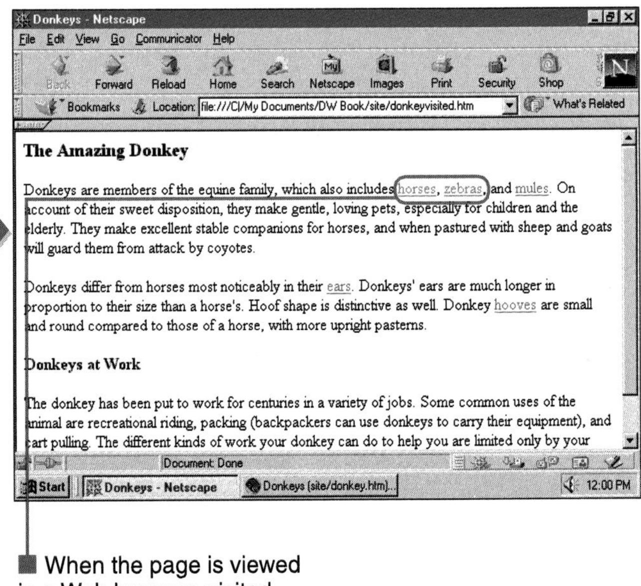

1 Select **Modify⇨Page Properties** to bring up the Page Properties dialog box.

2 Click the **Visited Links** color swatch.

3 Click a color from the menu by using the eyedropper tool.

4 Click **OK**.

■ When the page is viewed in a Web browser, visited links on the page display in the new color.

CHANGE THE COLOR OF ACTIVE HYPERLINKS

You can change the color of *active links* to make them match the visual style of your site. An active link is a link that the user is currently selecting.

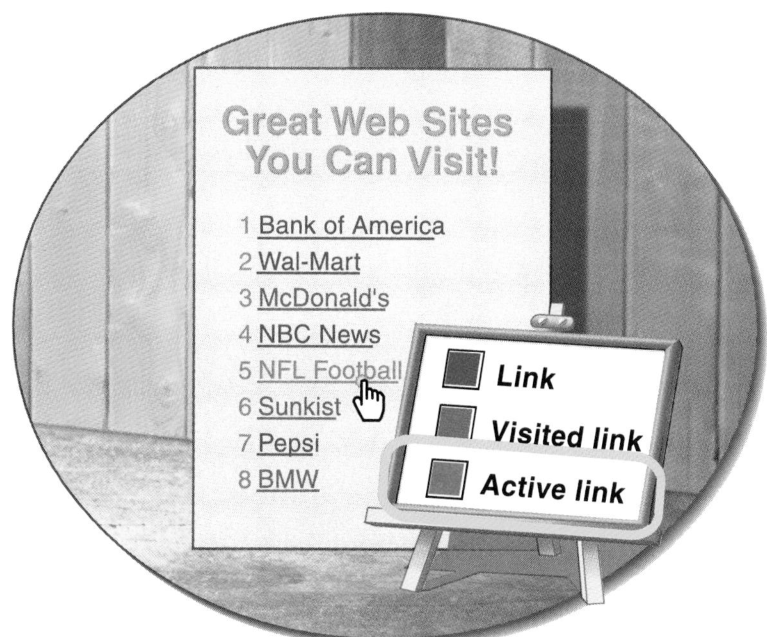

CHANGE THE COLOR OF ACTIVE HYPERLINKS

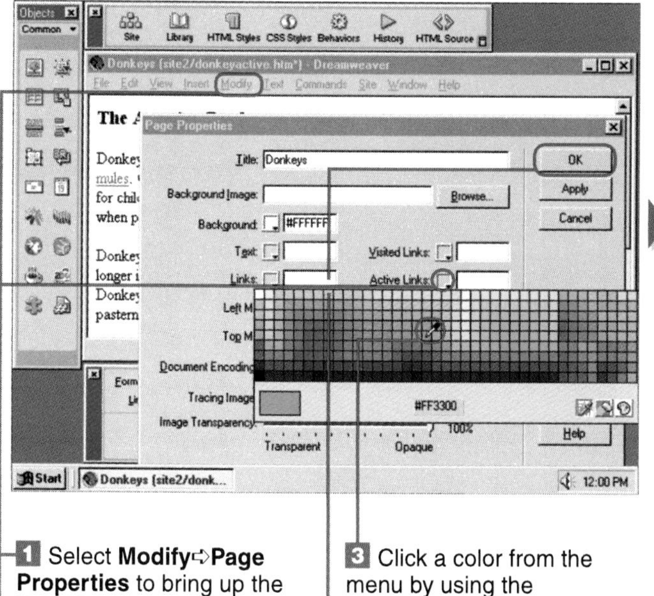

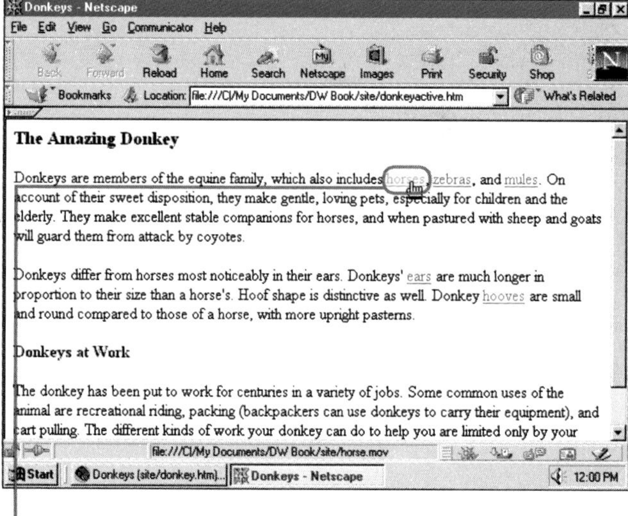

1 Select **Modify⇨Page Properties** to bring up the Page Properties dialog box.

2 Click the **Active Links** color swatch.

3 Click a color from the menu by using the eyedropper tool.

4 Click **OK**.

■ When the page is viewed in a Web browser, active links display in the new color.

CHECK HYPERLINKS

With Dreamweaver you can verify a Web page's links and determine if any are broken.

CHECK HYPERLINKS

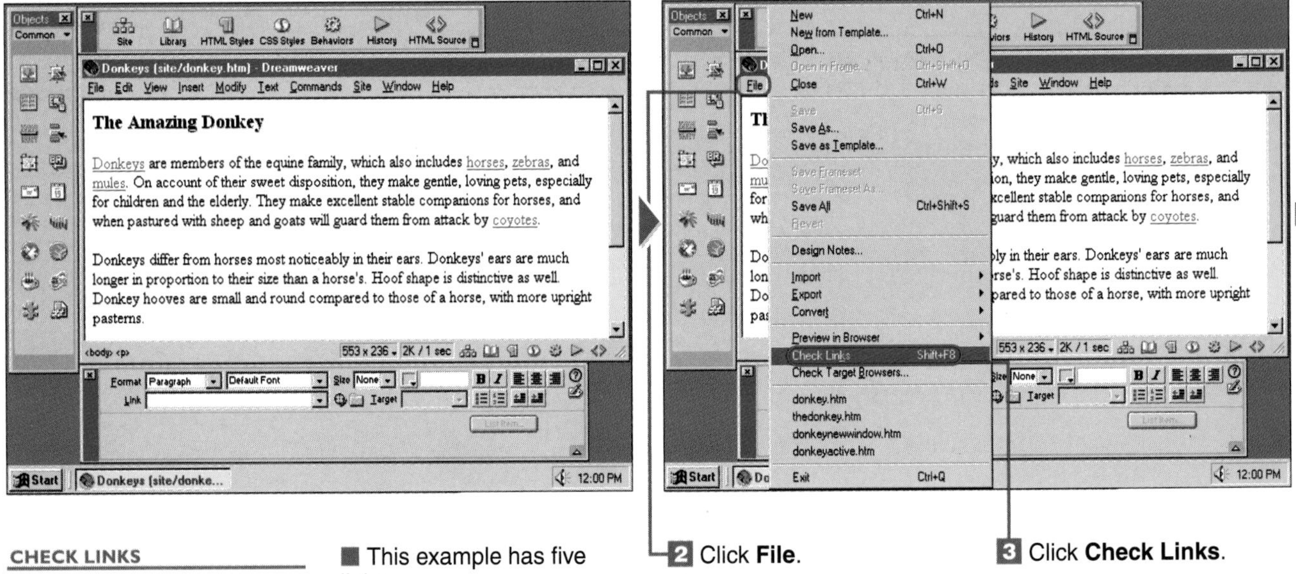

CHECK LINKS

1 Open your Web page (to open a Web page, see Chapter 2).

■ This example has five links.

2 Click **File**.

3 Click **Check Links**.

What can cause a hyperlink to break?

Hyperlinks can break if a filename is misspelled in a Web page's HTML or if the destination file that a hyperlink points to is renamed or deleted.

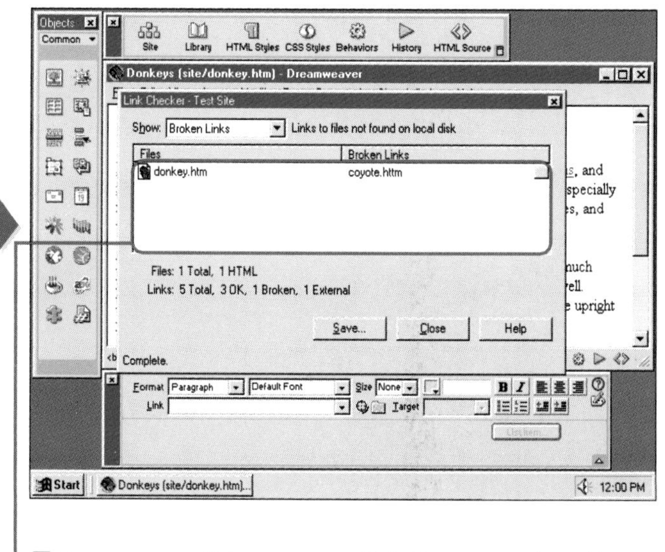

■ Dreamweaver lists any broken links it finds.

Note: Dreamweaver is unable to verify links to Web pages on external sites.

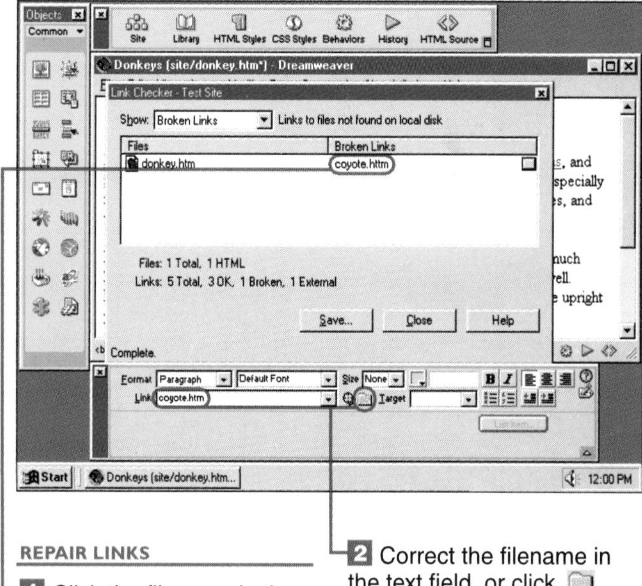

REPAIR LINKS

1 Click the filename in the list.

2 Correct the filename in the text field, or click 📁 to select a new hyperlink destination.

CREATE AN E-MAIL HYPERLINK

You can create hyperlinks that will launch an e-mail composition window.

CREATE AN E-MAIL HYPERLINK

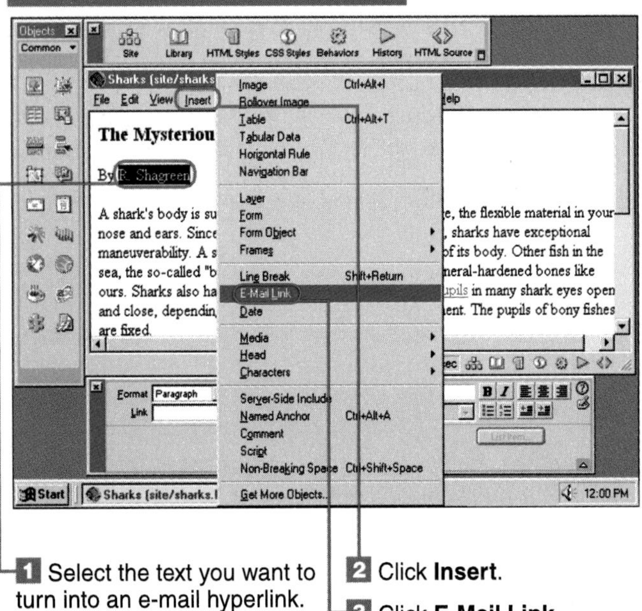

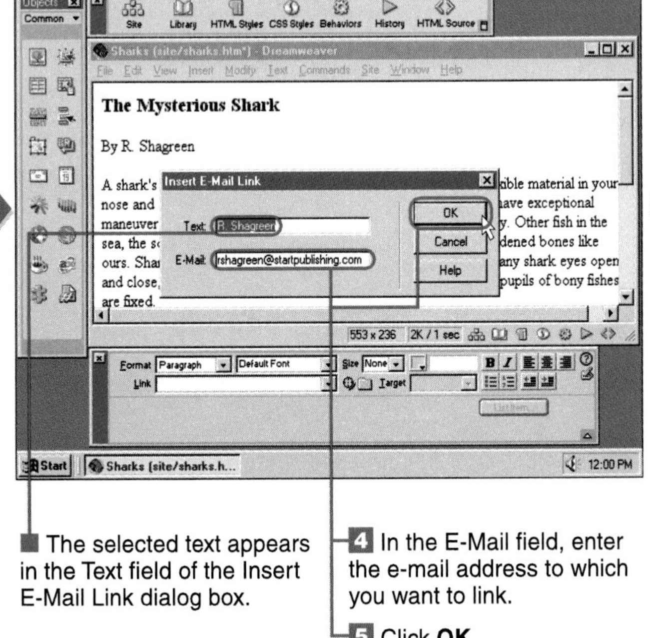

1 Select the text you want to turn into an e-mail hyperlink.

■ You can also turn an image into an e-mail hyperlink by selecting it.

2 Click **Insert**.

3 Click **E-Mail Link**.

■ The selected text appears in the Text field of the Insert E-Mail Link dialog box.

4 In the E-Mail field, enter the e-mail address to which you want to link.

5 Click **OK**.

Why are e-mail hyperlinks useful?

E-mail hyperlinks allow users to send information to you without using forms, which are more time consuming to create. However, these links will not work with Web browsers that lack e-mail capability.

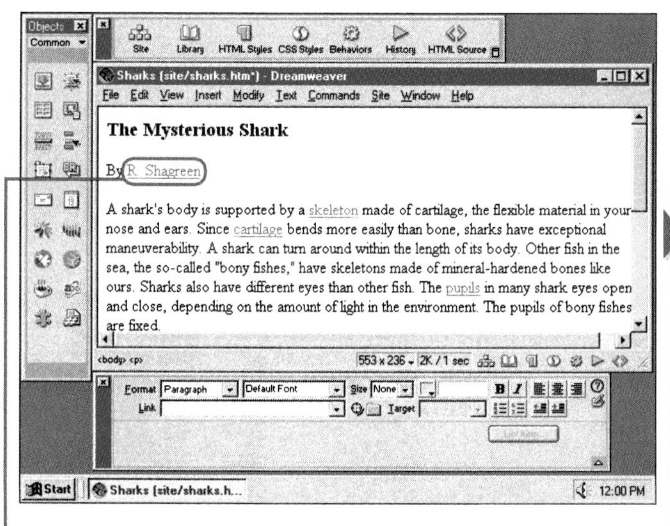

■ The new hyperlink is colored and underlined.

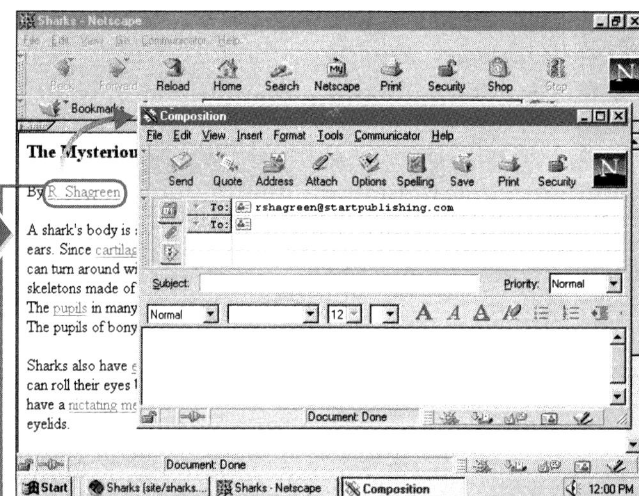

■ In Web browsers that support e-mail, clicking the hyperlink launches an e-mail composition window. The To: field automatically fills with the e-mail address you specified in Step 4.

■ If the browser does not have e-mail capability, clicking the link has no effect.

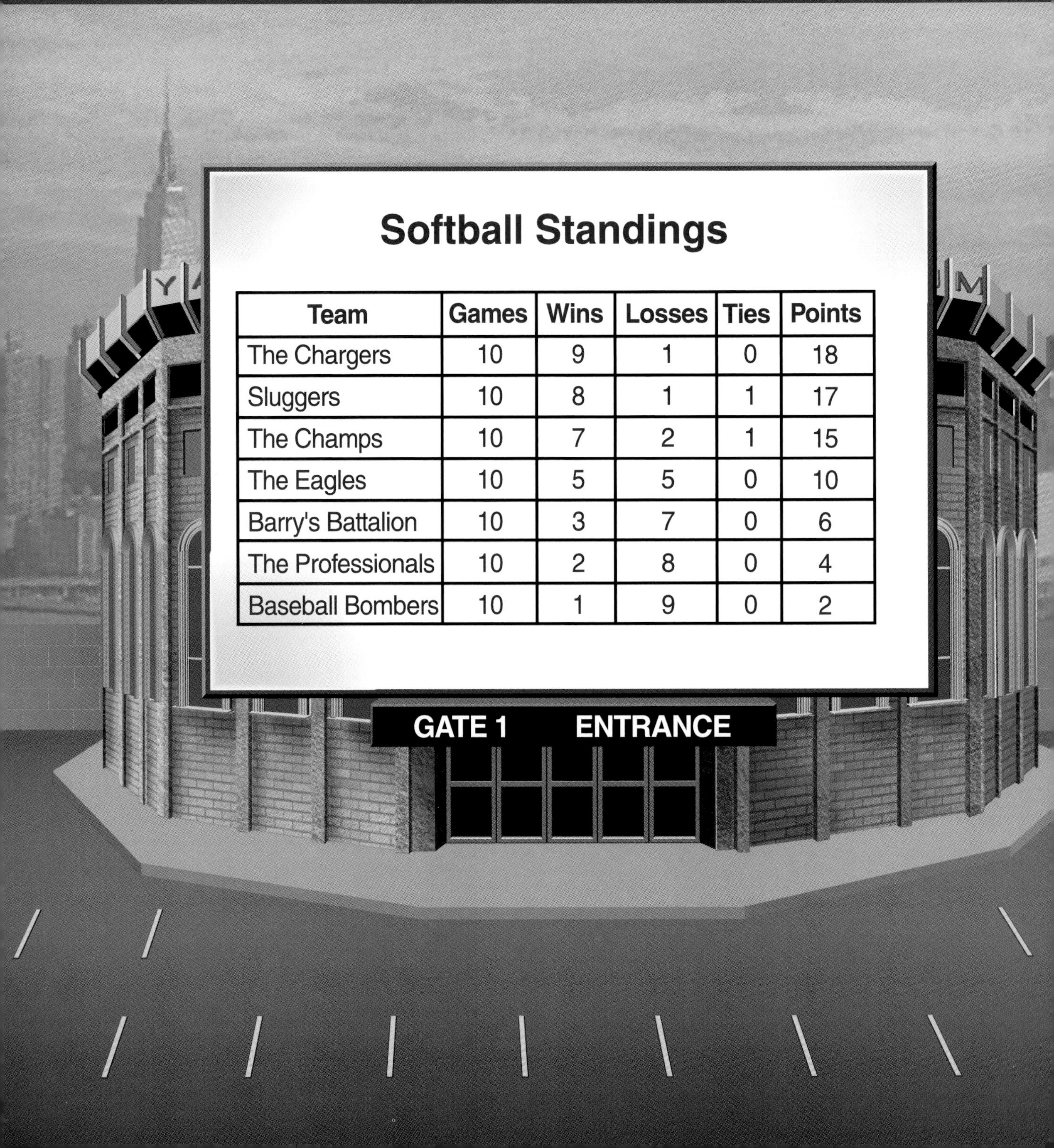

Softball Standings

Team	Games	Wins	Losses	Ties	Points
The Chargers	10	9	1	0	18
Sluggers	10	8	1	1	17
The Champs	10	7	2	1	15
The Eagles	10	5	5	0	10
Barry's Battalion	10	3	7	0	6
The Professionals	10	2	8	0	4
Baseball Bombers	10	1	9	0	2

GATE 1 ENTRANCE

CHAPTER 7

Creating Tables

Tables let you organize text, images, and other information in rows and columns on your Web pages. This chapter shows you how to build tables.

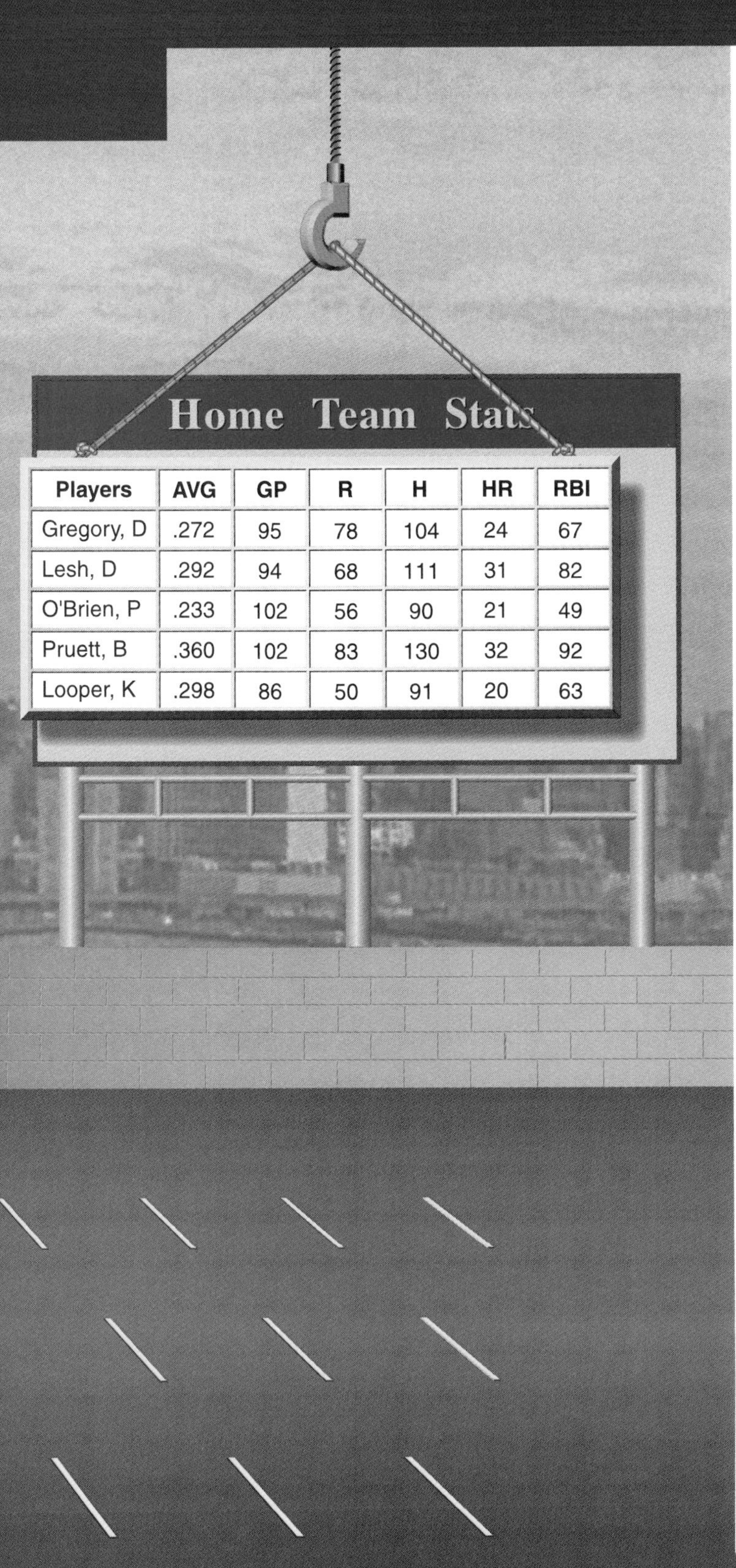

Players	AVG	GP	R	H	HR	RBI
Gregory, D	.272	95	78	104	24	67
Lesh, D	.292	94	68	111	31	82
O'Brien, P	.233	102	56	90	21	49
Pruett, B	.360	102	83	130	32	92
Looper, K	.298	86	50	91	20	63

INSERT A TABLE

You can organize content into columns and rows by inserting tables into your Web page.

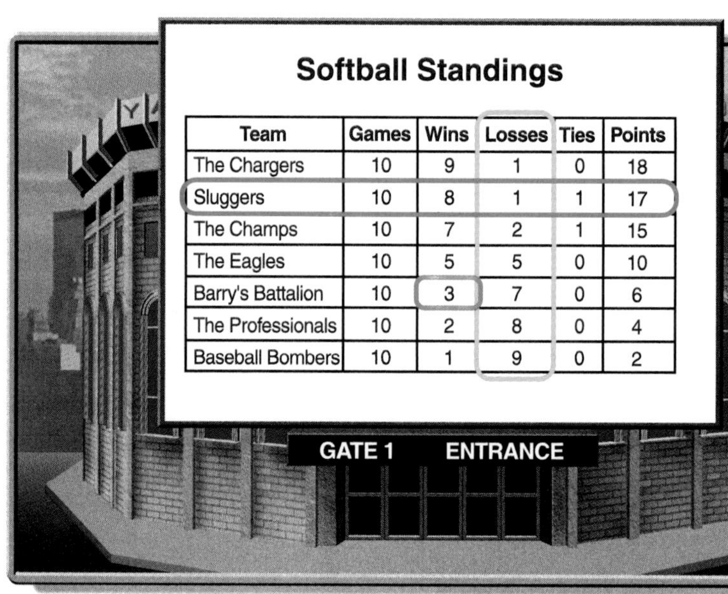
Softball Standings

Team	Games	Wins	Losses	Ties	Points
The Chargers	10	9	1	0	18
Sluggers	10	8	1	1	17
The Champs	10	7	2	1	15
The Eagles	10	5	5	0	10
Barry's Battalion	10	3	7	0	6
The Professionals	10	2	8	0	4
Baseball Bombers	10	1	9	0	2

A table consists of rows, columns and cells.

A row is a horizontal line of boxes.

A column is a vertical line of boxes.

A cell is one box.

INSERT A TABLE

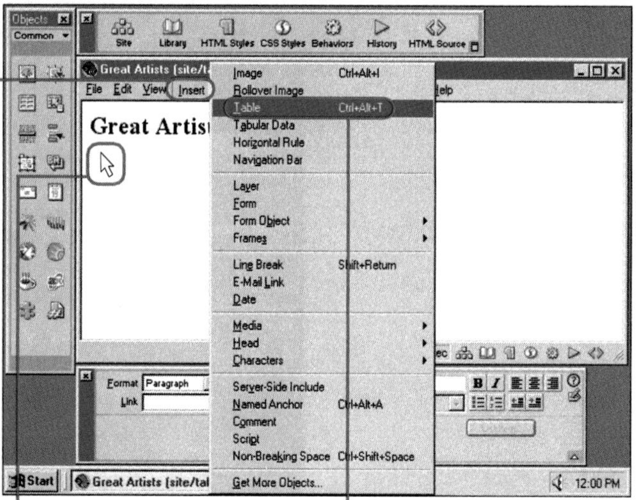

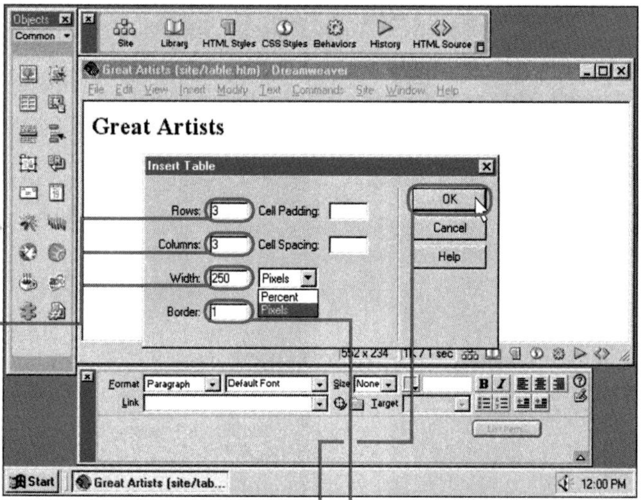

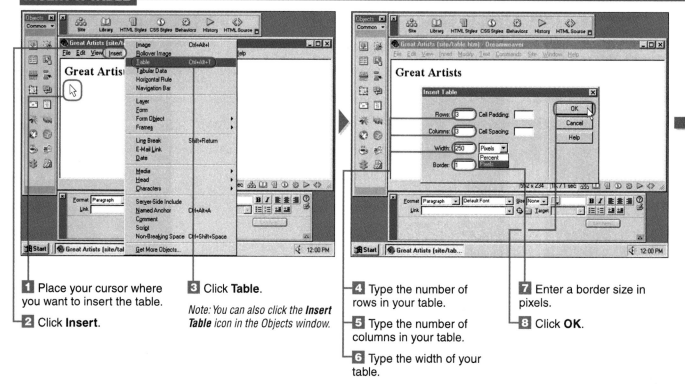

1 Place your cursor where you want to insert the table.

2 Click **Insert**.

3 Click **Table**.

*Note: You can also click the **Insert Table** icon in the Objects window.*

4 Type the number of rows in your table.

5 Type the number of columns in your table.

6 Type the width of your table.

7 Enter a border size in pixels.

8 Click **OK**.

How do I change the appearance of the content inside my table?

You can specify the size, style, and color of text inside a table the same way you format text outside of a table (see Chapter 4). Likewise, you can control the appearance of an image inside a table the same way you control it outside a table (see Chapter 5).

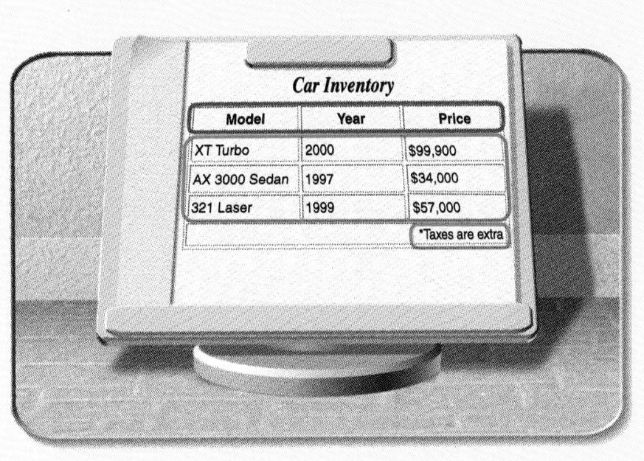

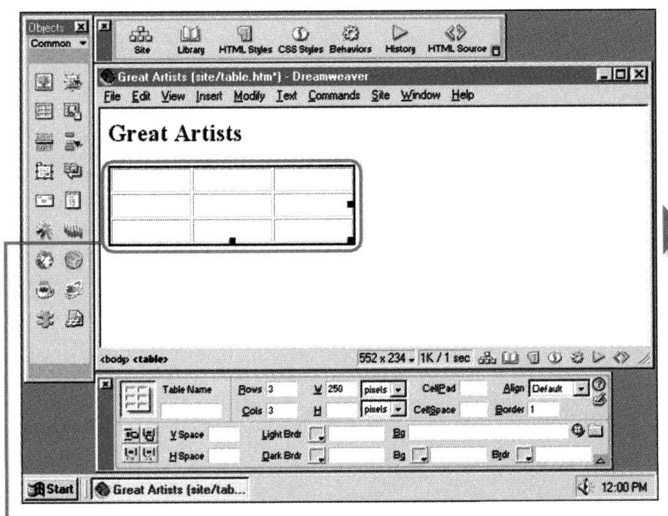

■ Dreamweaver inserts an empty table aligned to the left (the default alignment).

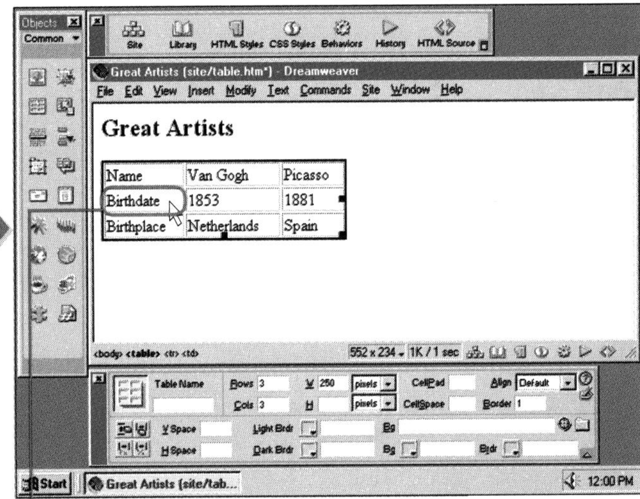

9 Click inside any cell to add text (or other content) into the table.

■ Dreamweaver adjusts the size of the cell to accommodate the content.

CHANGE THE BACKGROUND COLOR OF A TABLE

You can change the background color of a table to make it stand out from the rest of your page. You can also change the background color of individual cells, rows, and columns of a table.

CHANGE THE BACKGROUND COLOR OF A TABLE

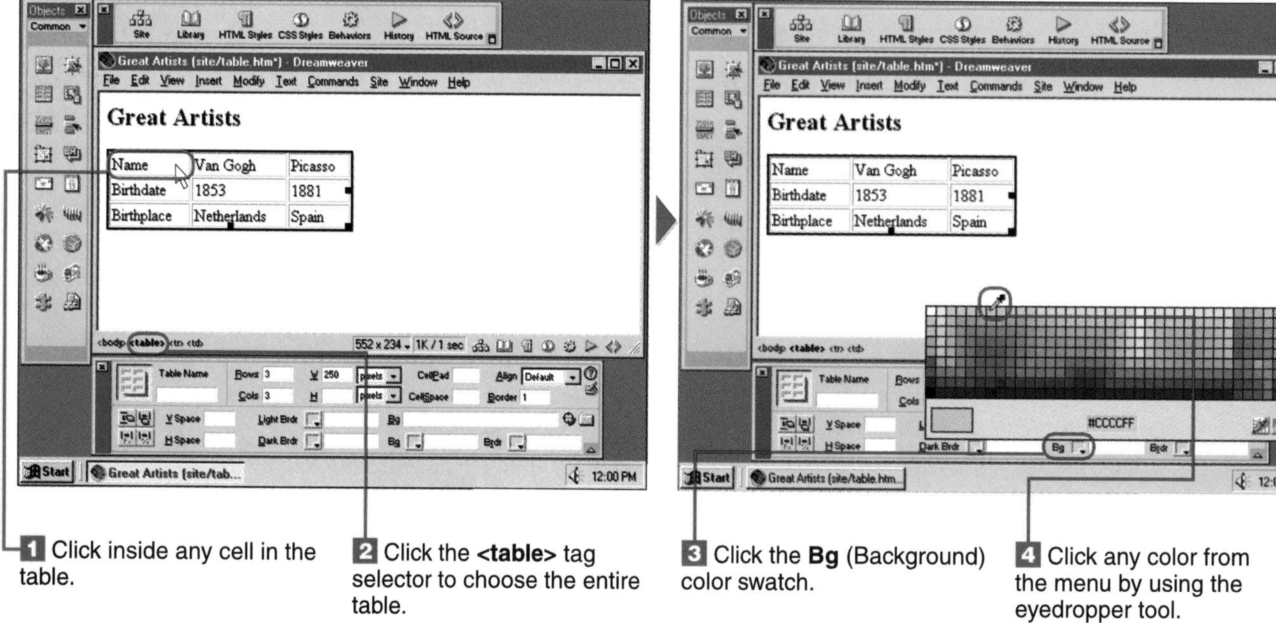

1 Click inside any cell in the table.

2 Click the **<table>** tag selector to choose the entire table.

3 Click the **Bg** (Background) color swatch.

4 Click any color from the menu by using the eyedropper tool.

How do I make the information in my table easier to read?

Varying the colors of alternating columns or rows of your table can make it easier for your viewers to find information. Also, choose contrasting colors for the text and the background when creating tables. Use light backgrounds with dark text and dark backgrounds with light text.

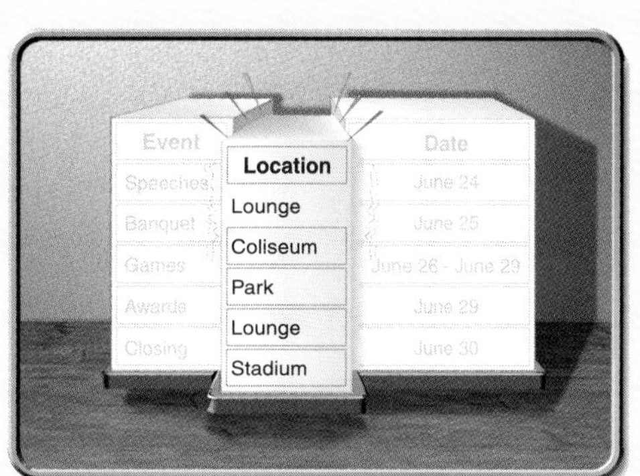

USING THE OBJECT PALETTE

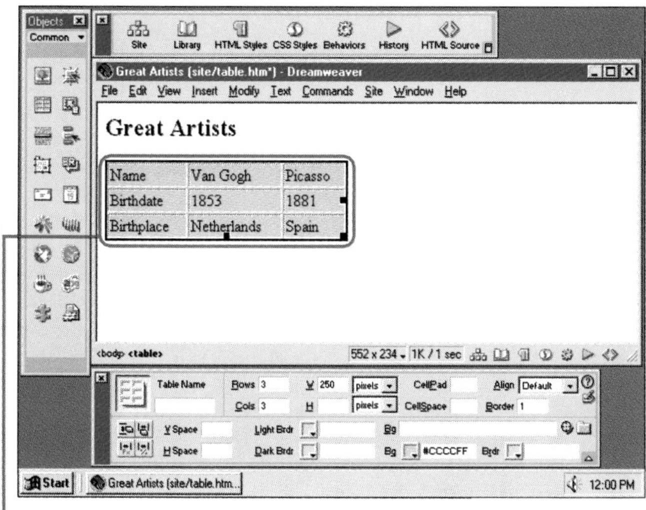

■ The background of the entire table changes to the new color.

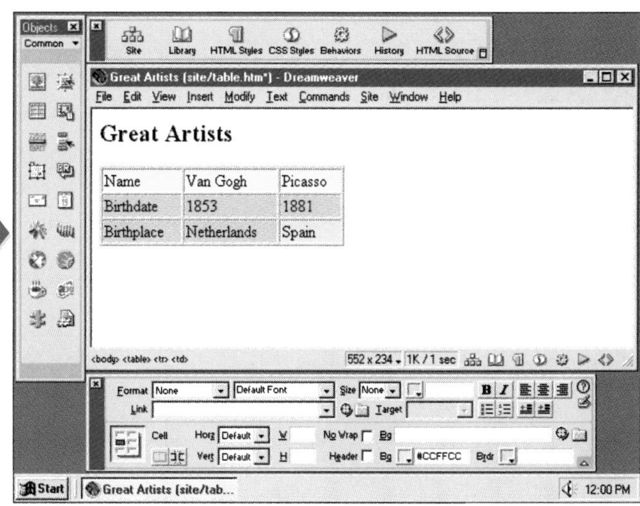

■ To change the background color of individual cells, rows, and columns, select the cells and specify a color using the **Bg** color swatch.

CHANGE THE CELL PADDING IN A TABLE

You can change the cell padding to add space between a table's content and its borders.

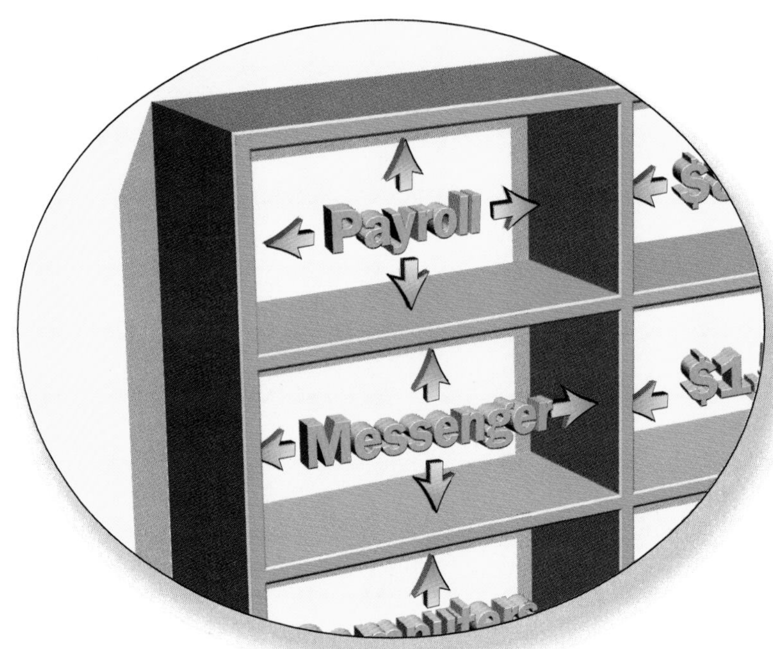

CHANGE THE CELL PADDING IN A TABLE

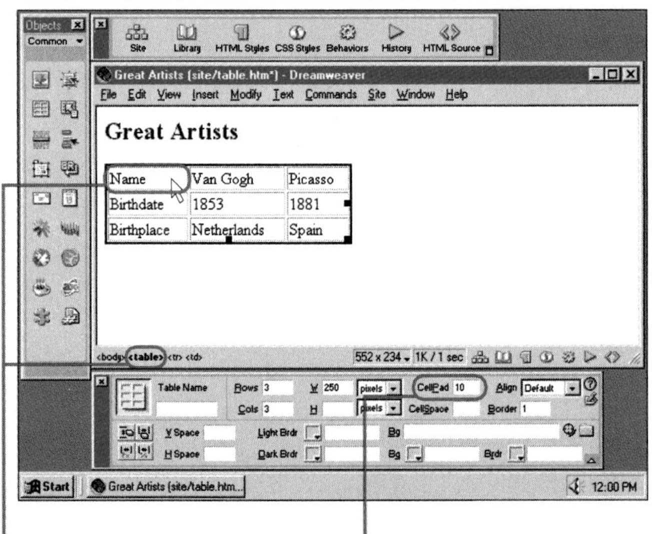

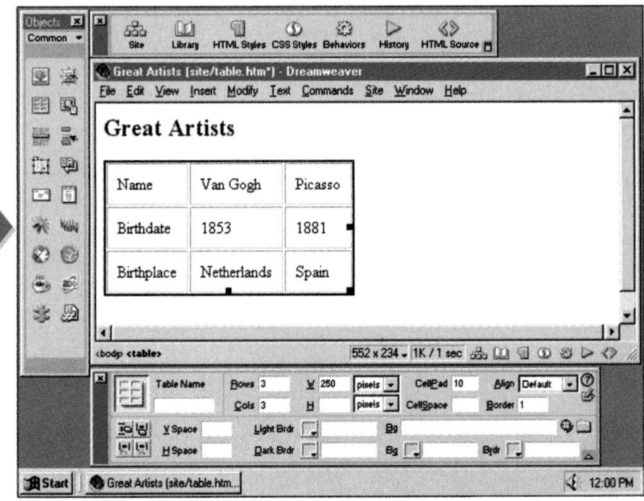

1 Click inside any cell in the table.

2 Click the **<table>** tag selector to select the entire table.

3 Type the amount of padding (in pixels) in the CellPad field.

4 Press **Enter (Return)**.

■ Dreamweaver adjusts the space between the table content and the table borders.

Note: Adjusting the cell padding affects all the cells in a table. There is no way to adjust the padding of individual cells using the CellPad field.

CHANGE THE CELL SPACING IN A TABLE

You can change the cell spacing to adjust the width of your table borders.

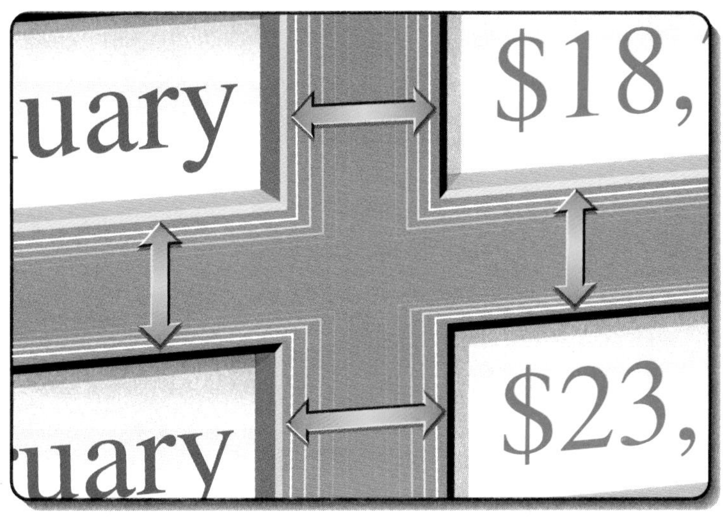

CHANGE THE CELL SPACING IN A TABLE

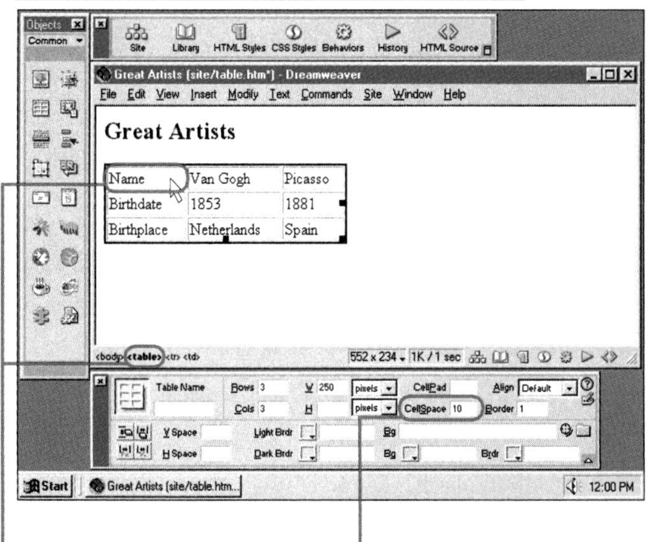

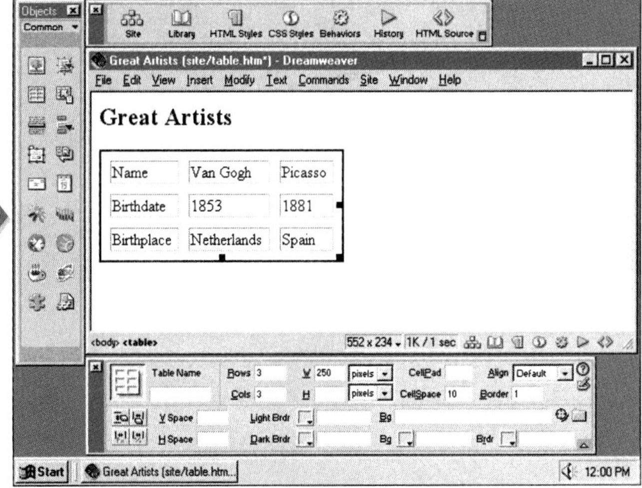

1 Click inside any cell in the table.

2 Click the **<table>** tag selector to select the entire table.

3 Type the amount of spacing (in pixels) in the CellSpace field.

■ Dreamweaver adjusts the width of the table's cell borders.

Note: Adjusting the cell spacing affects all the cell borders in the table. There is no way to adjust the spacing of individual cell borders using the CellSpace field.

CHANGE THE BORDER WIDTH OF A TABLE

You can change the width of the border that surrounds a table.

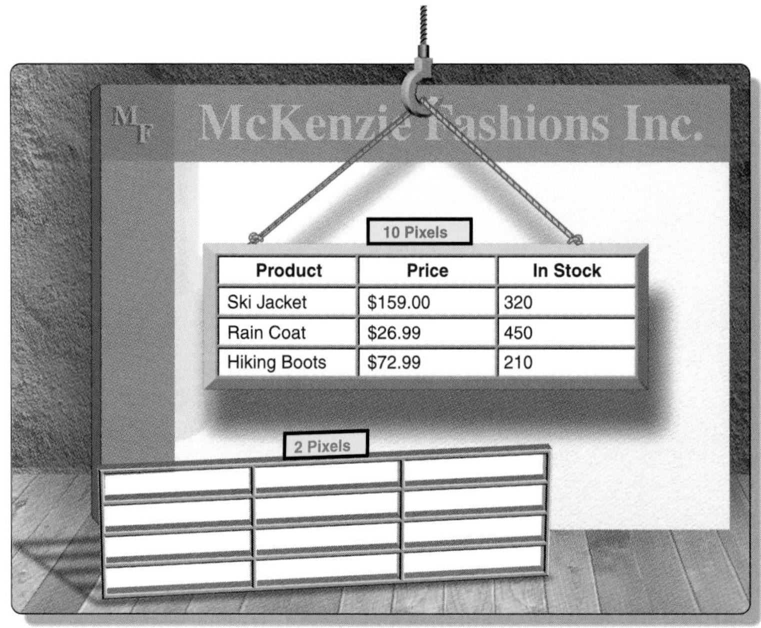

CHANGE THE BORDER WIDTH OF A TABLE

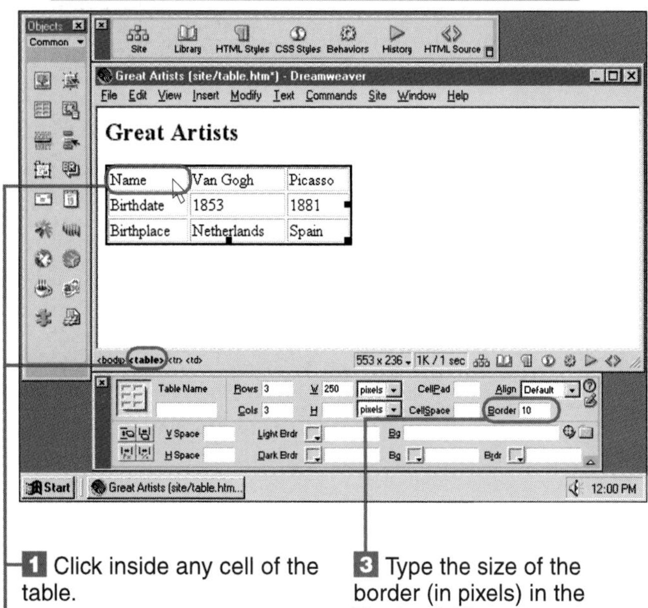

1 Click inside any cell of the table.

2 Click the **<table>** tag selector to select the entire table.

3 Type the size of the border (in pixels) in the Border field.

■ Dreamweaver adjusts the width of the table border.

■ To make your table borders invisible, set the border size to **0**.

Note: The border field does not affect the widths of the borders between cells. To adjust the size of the borders between cells, see "Change the Cell Spacing in a Table."

CHANGE THE BORDER COLOR OF A TABLE

You can change the color of the cell borders of your table.

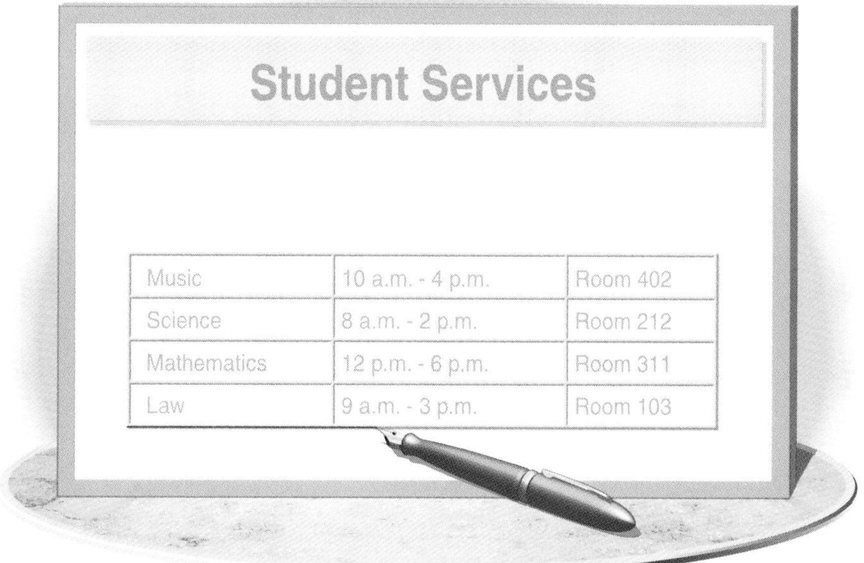

CHANGE THE BORDER COLOR OF A TABLE

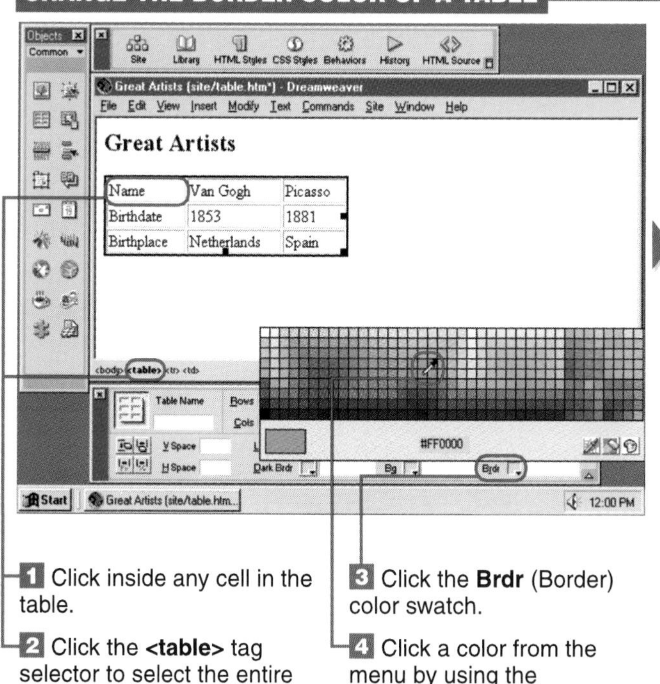

1 Click inside any cell in the table.

2 Click the **<table>** tag selector to select the entire table.

3 Click the **Brdr** (Border) color swatch.

4 Click a color from the menu by using the eyedropper tool.

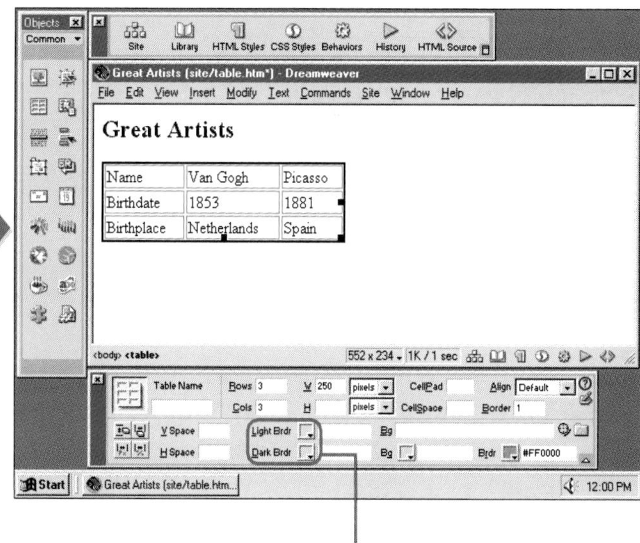

■ The border of the table changes to the new color.

■ You can further fine-tune the look of your table border by using the Light Brdr and Dark Brdr color menus.

INSERT A ROW INTO A TABLE

You can insert a new row into a table.

INSERT A ROW INTO A TABLE

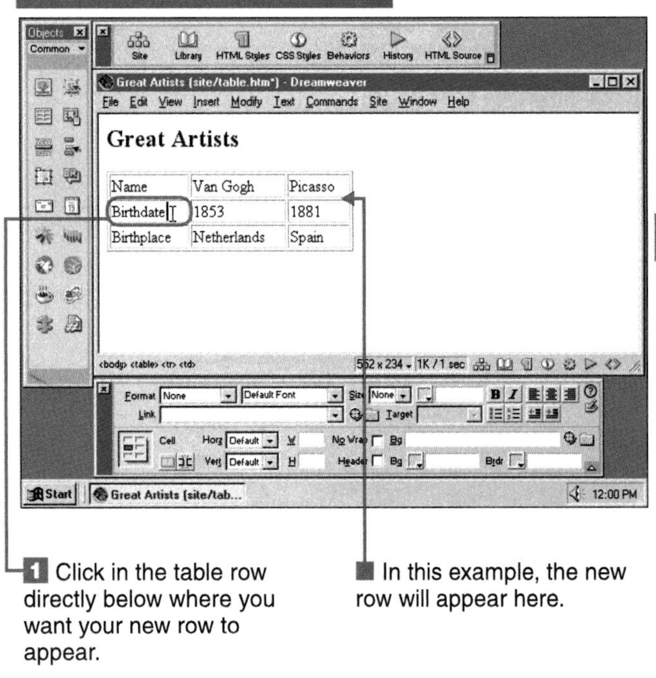

1 Click in the table row directly below where you want your new row to appear.

■ In this example, the new row will appear here.

2 Click **Modify**.

3 Click **Table**.

4 Click **Insert Row**.

*Note: You can use the **Modify⇨Table⇨Insert Rows Or Columns** command to insert multiple rows before or after the selected row.*

How can I add horizontal lines between the rows of my table?

You can add a horizontal line to your table by inserting an empty row, merging the cells to create a single-celled row, then adding a horizontal rule.

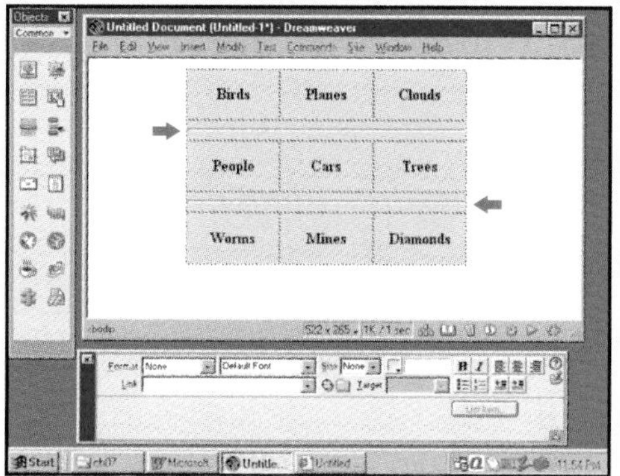

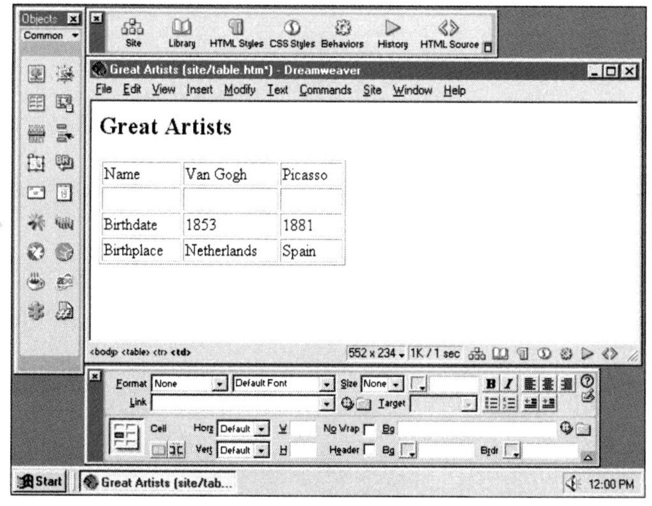

■ Dreamweaver inserts an empty row into the table.

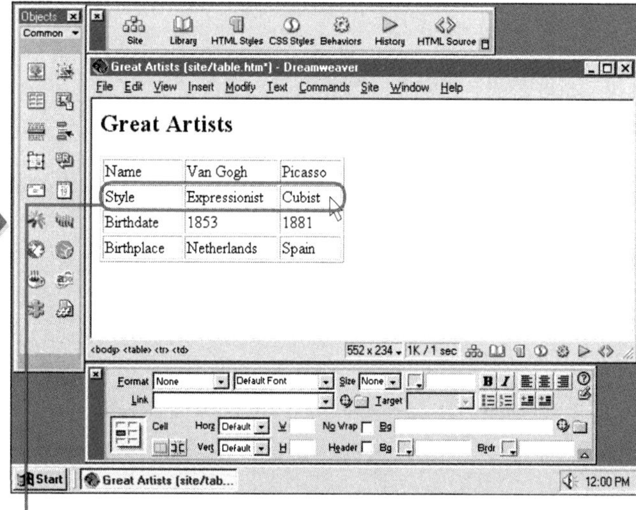

5 Click inside the cells of the new row to add content.

INSERT A COLUMN INTO A TABLE

You can insert a new column into a table.

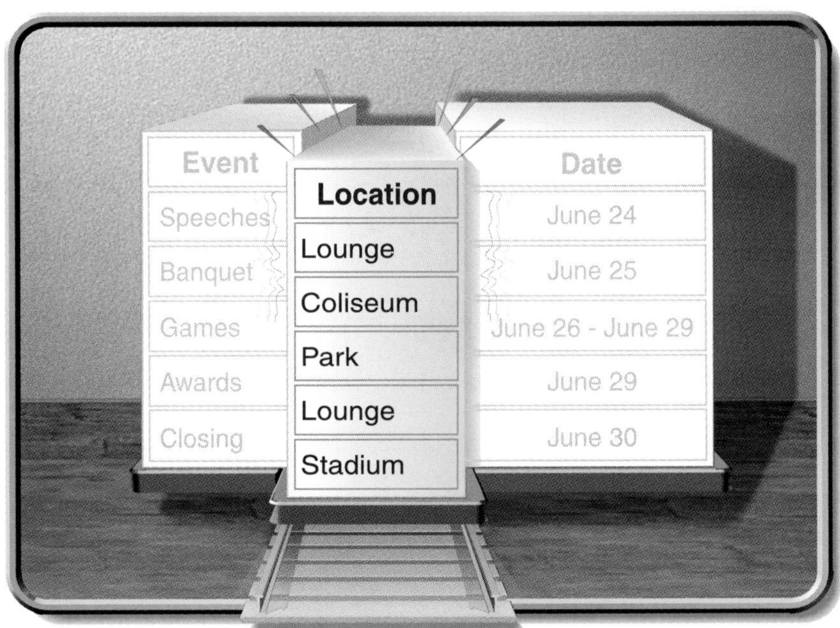

INSERT A COLUMN INTO A TABLE

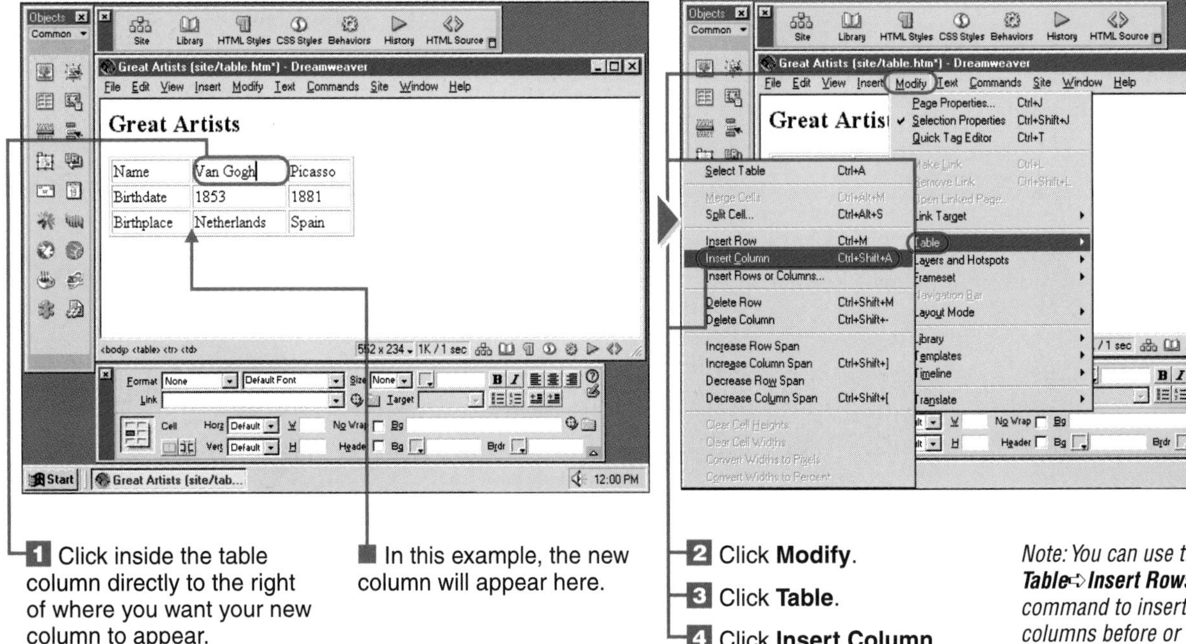

1 Click inside the table column directly to the right of where you want your new column to appear.

■ In this example, the new column will appear here.

2 Click **Modify**.

3 Click **Table**.

4 Click **Insert Column**.

*Note: You can use the **Modify⇨Table⇨Insert Rows Or Columns** command to insert multiple columns before or after the selected column.*

How can I add vertical lines between the columns of my table?

You can add vertical lines to your table by inserting empty columns and merging the cells into a single cell. Specify a background color for those cells to color the lines.

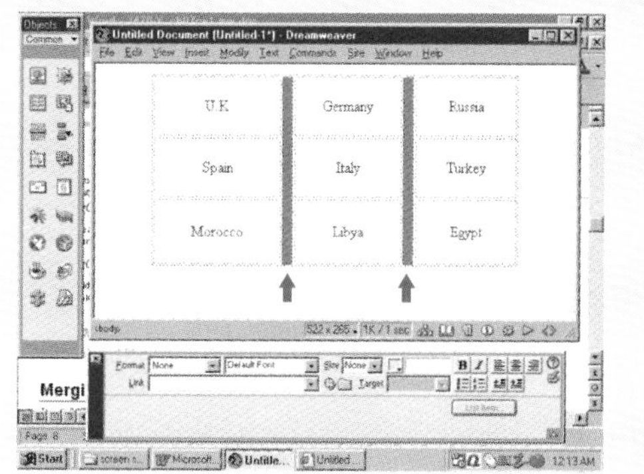

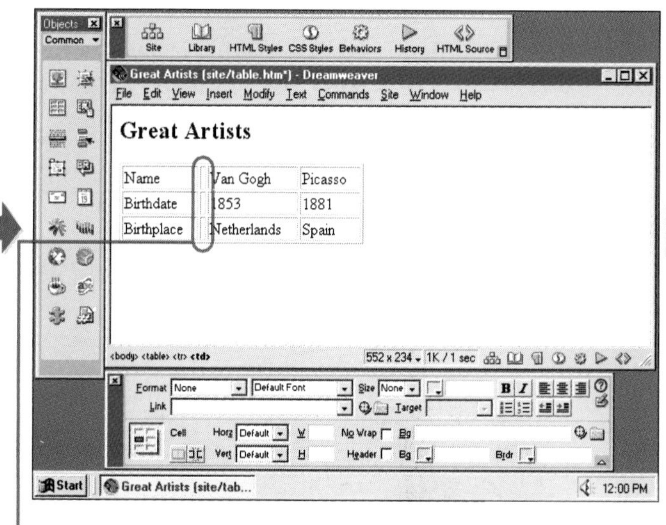

■ Dreamweaver inserts an empty column into the table.

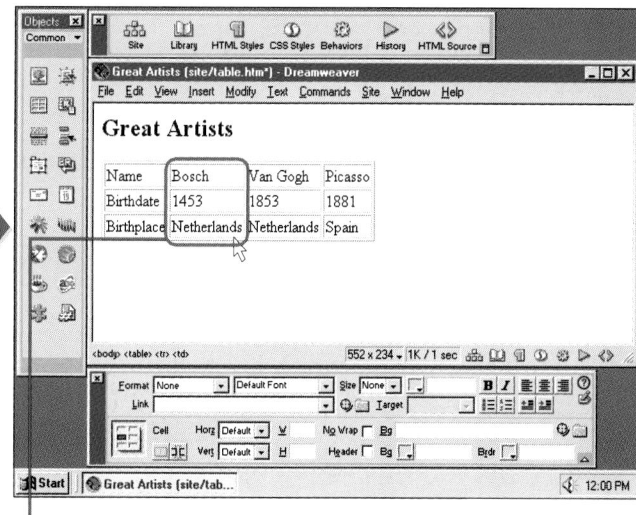

5 Click inside the cells of the new column to add content.

MERGE TABLE CELLS

You can merge table cells so that a single cell spans multiple rows or columns.

Pool A					
Team	Games	Wins	Losses	Ties	Points
The Chargers	10	9	1	0	18
Sluggers	10	8	1	1	17
The Champs	10	7	2	1	15
The Eagles	10	5	5	0	10

MERGE TABLE CELLS

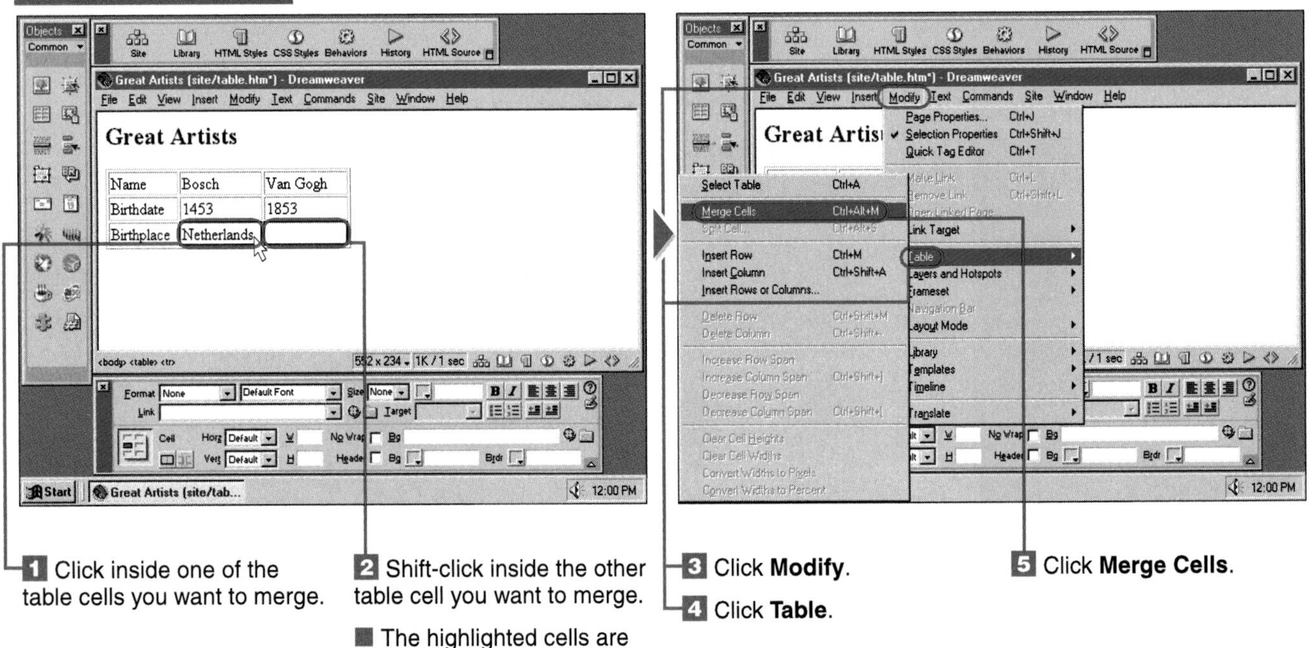

1 Click inside one of the table cells you want to merge.

2 Shift-click inside the other table cell you want to merge.

■ The highlighted cells are selected.

3 Click **Modify**.

4 Click **Table**.

5 Click **Merge Cells**.

Can I merge cells to create any cell shape?

Tables can only contain cells that are rectangular — for instance, you cannot merge multiple cells in a table to create an L-shaped cell. Consequently, Dreamweaver only allows you to Shift-click rectangular combinations of table cells.

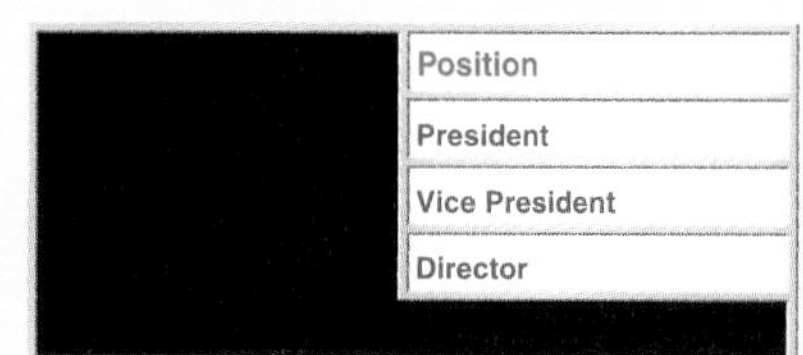

ADD A TITLE TO A WEB PAGE

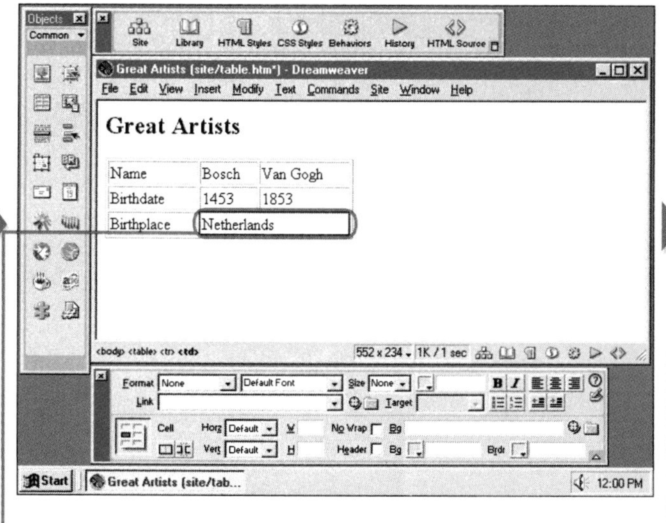

■ Dreamweaver merges the selected cells into a single cell.

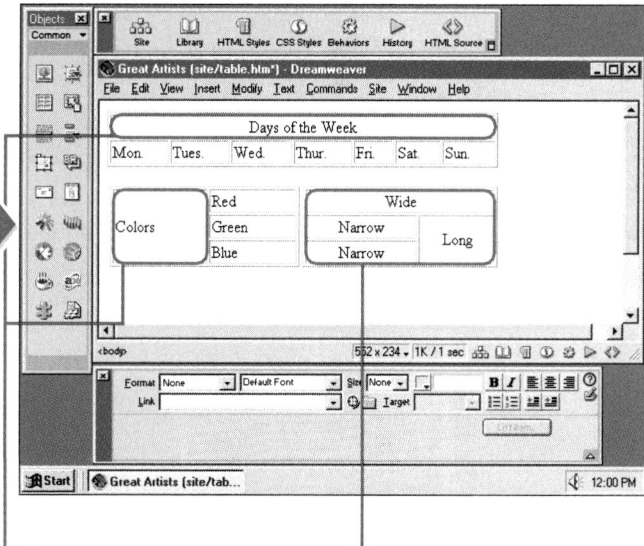

■ You can Shift-click to select multiple cells and merge them to create table cells that span many rows or columns.

■ You can also merge different combinations of cells in the same table.

SPLIT TABLE CELLS

You can split table cells to subdivide parts of your table.

SPLIT TABLE CELLS

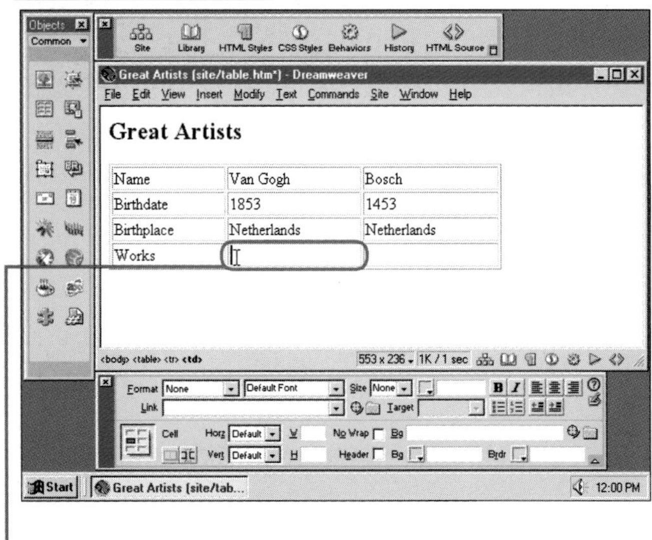

1 Click inside the table cell you want to split.

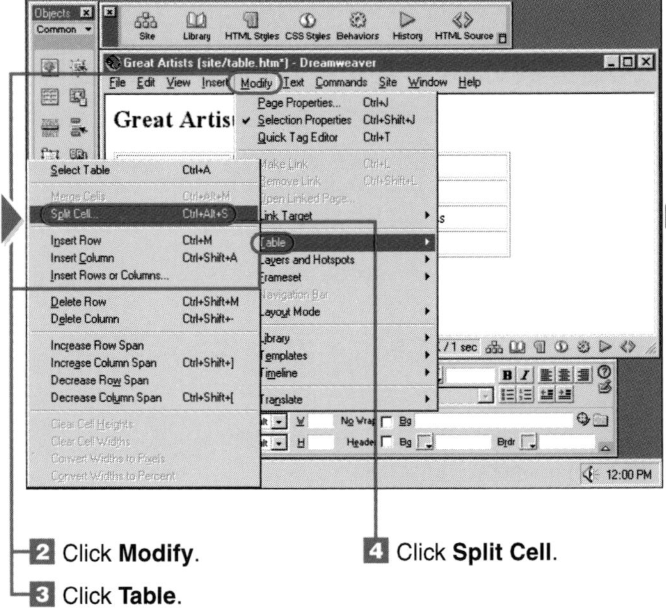

2 Click **Modify**.

3 Click **Table**.

4 Click **Split Cell**.

How do I divide a cell into quadrants?

To divide a single cell into quadrants (two rows and two columns), select the cell and split it into two rows, select the top row and split it into two columns, and then select the bottom row and split it into two columns.

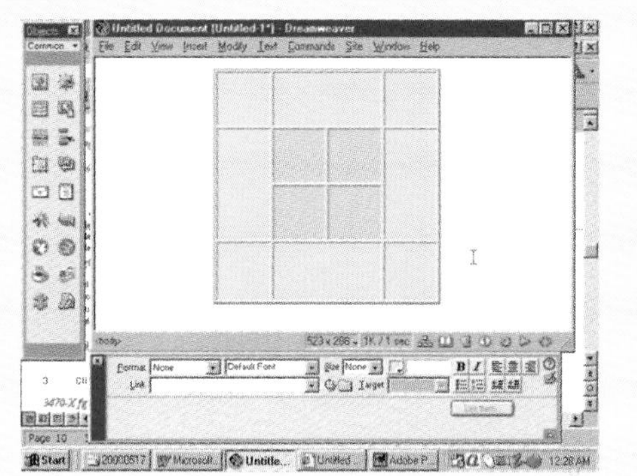

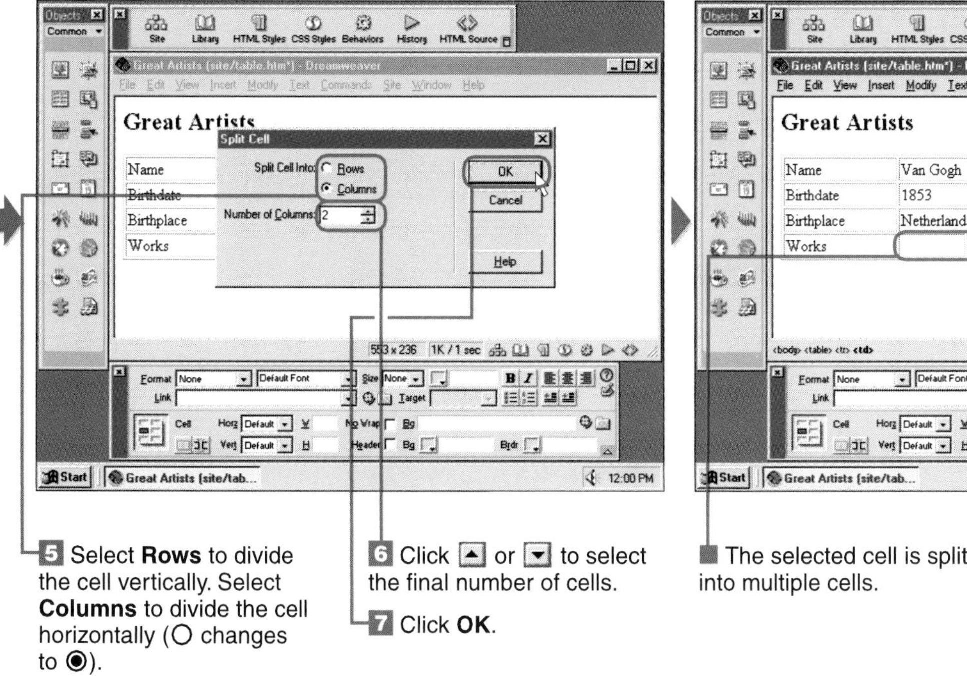

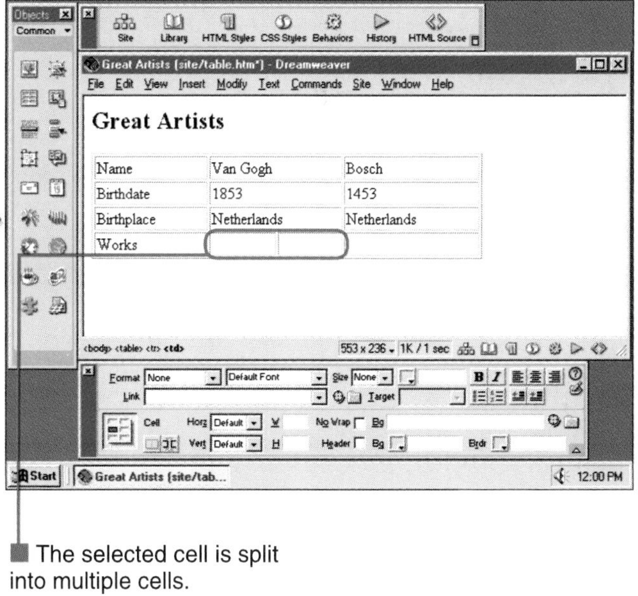

5 Select **Rows** to divide the cell vertically. Select **Columns** to divide the cell horizontally (○ changes to ◉).

6 Click ▲ or ▼ to select the final number of cells.

7 Click **OK**.

■ The selected cell is split into multiple cells.

CHANGE THE WIDTH OF A TABLE

You can change the width of your table.

CHANGE THE WIDTH OF A TABLE

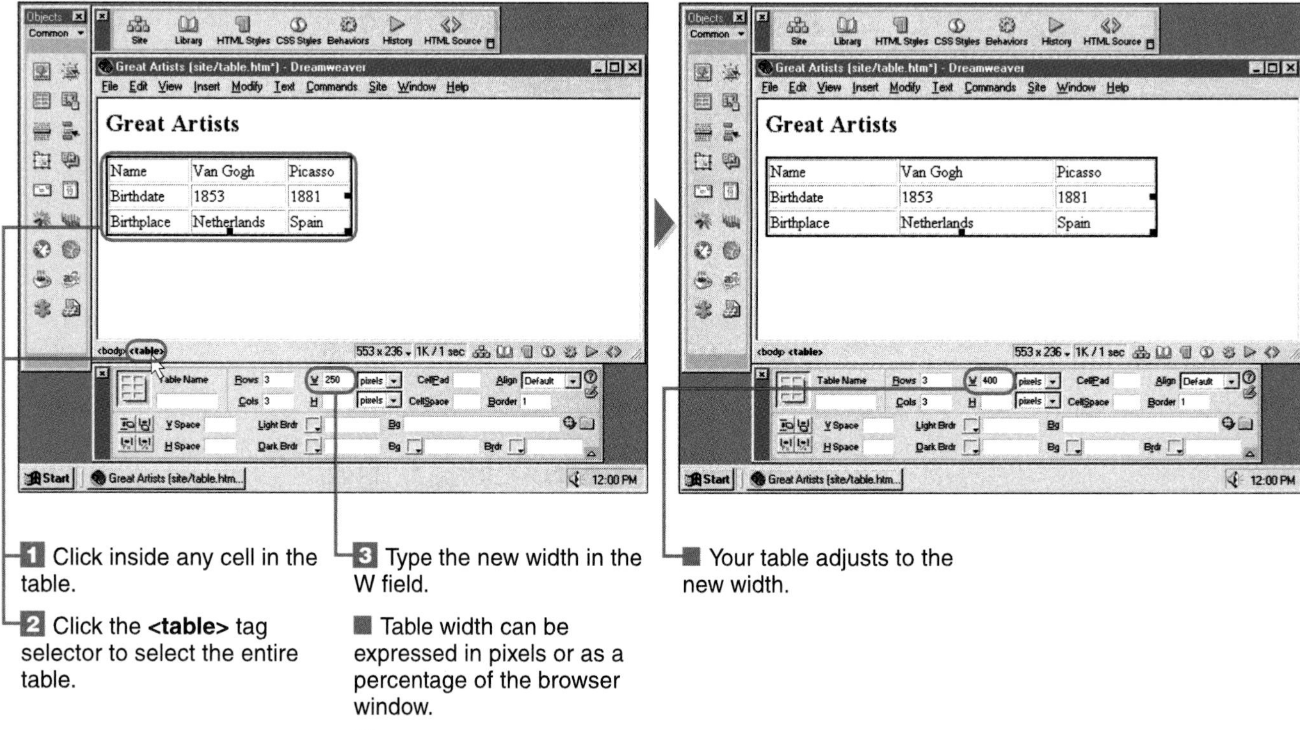

1 Click inside any cell in the table.

2 Click the **<table>** tag selector to select the entire table.

3 Type the new width in the W field.

■ Table width can be expressed in pixels or as a percentage of the browser window.

4 Press **Enter (Return)**.

■ Your table adjusts to the new width.

CHANGE THE WIDTH OF A CELL

You can change the width of individual cells in your table.

CHANGE THE WIDTH OF A CELL

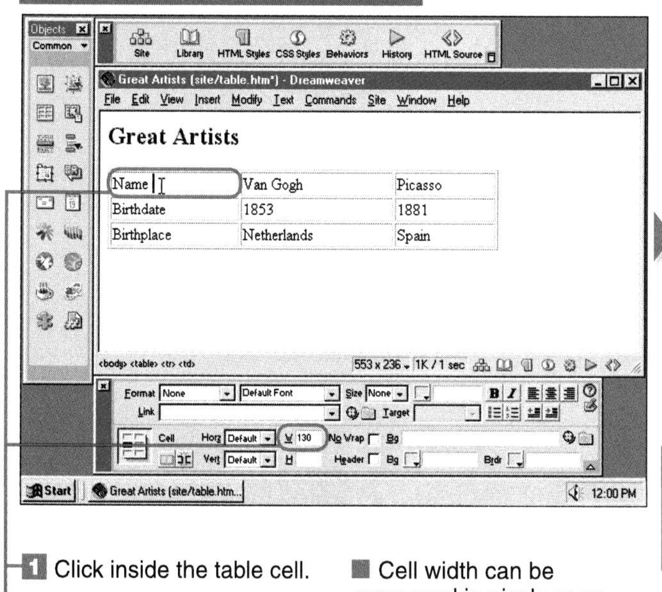

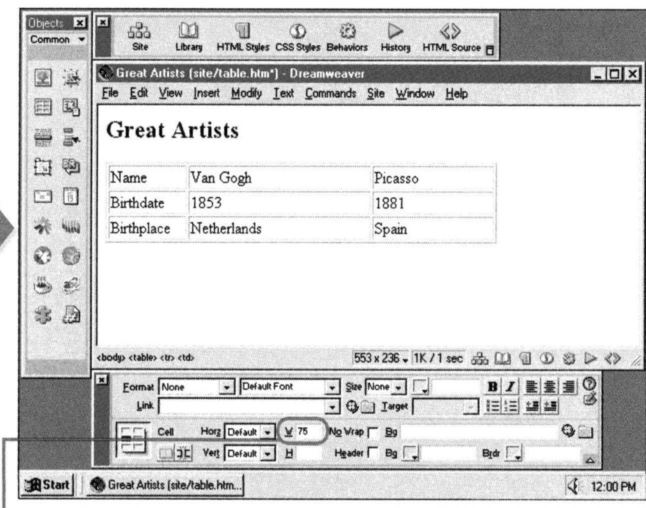

1 Click inside the table cell.

2 Type the new width in the W field.

■ Cell width can be expressed in pixels or as a percentage of the entire table.

3 Press **Enter (Return)**.

■ The table displays the new cell width. Cells above or below the cell are also adjusted.

Note: Dreamweaver will not shrink a cell narrower than the width of the widest item in the cell.

CHANGE THE HEIGHT OF A TABLE

You can change the height of your table.

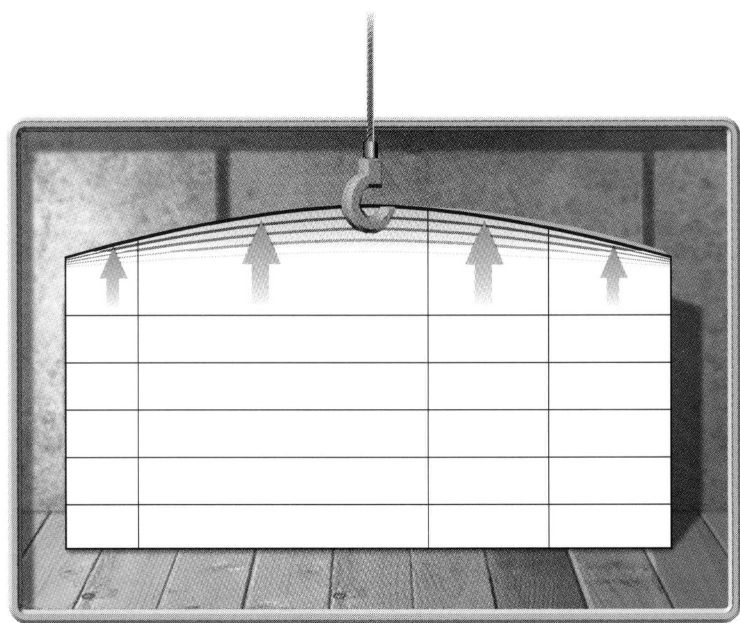

CHANGE THE HEIGHT OF A TABLE

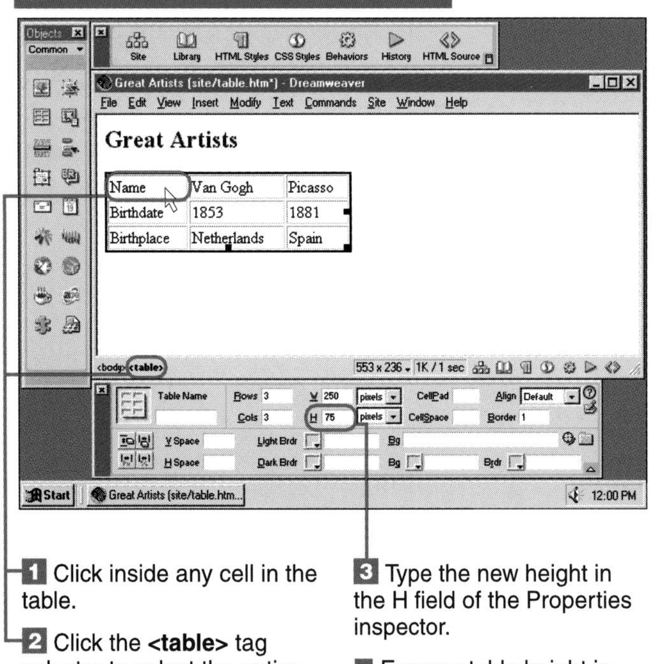

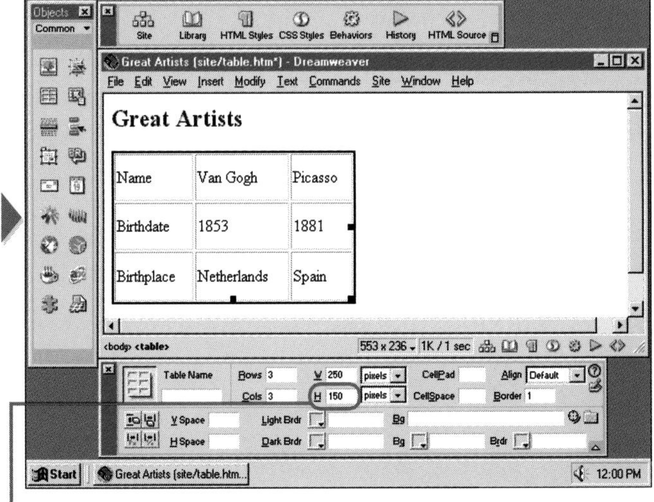

1 Click inside any cell in the table.

2 Click the **<table>** tag selector to select the entire table.

3 Type the new height in the H field of the Properties inspector.

■ Express table height in pixels or as a percentage of the browser window.

4 Press **Enter (Return)**.

■ Your table displays the new height.

CHANGE THE HEIGHT OF A CELL

You can change the height of individual cells in your table.

CHANGE THE HEIGHT OF A CELL

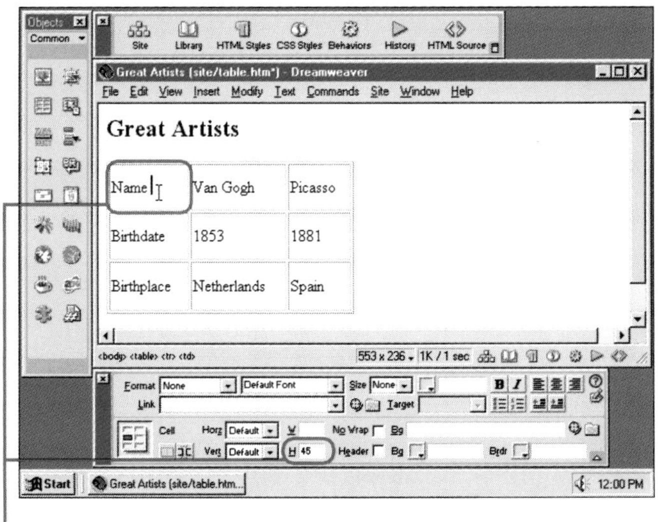

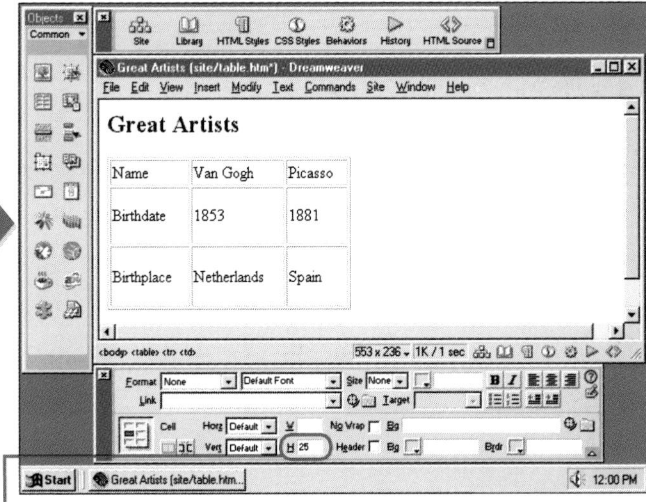

1 Click inside the table cell.

2 Type the new height in the H field.

■ Express the cell height in pixels or as a percentage of the browser window.

3 Press **Enter (Return)**.

■ The new height takes effect. The height of cells to the left or right also adjusts.

Note: Dreamweaver will not shrink a cell shorter than the height of the tallest item in the cell.

CENTER A TABLE

You can center a table on your Web page.

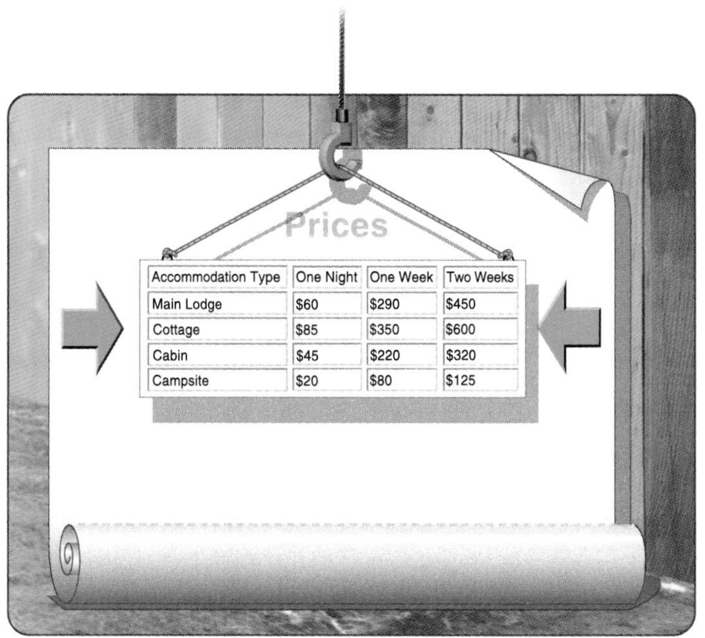

Prices

Accommodation Type	One Night	One Week	Two Weeks
Main Lodge	$60	$290	$450
Cottage	$85	$350	$600
Cabin	$45	$220	$320
Campsite	$20	$80	$125

CENTER A TABLE

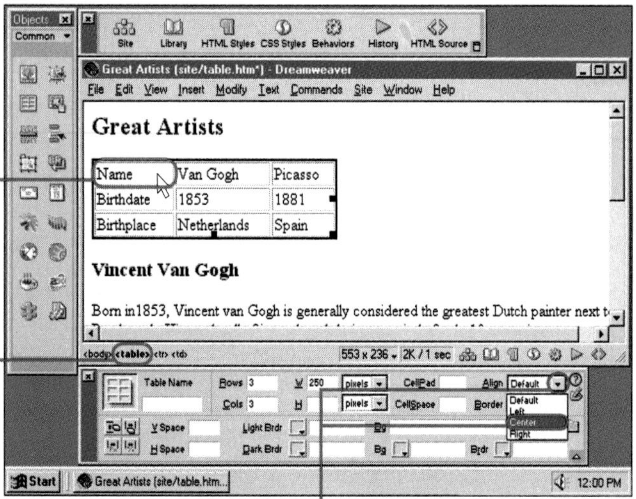

1 Click inside any cell in the table.

2 Click the **<table>** tag selector to select the entire table.

3 Click ▾.

4 Select **Center** in the Align menu.

■ Your table is displayed center-aligned.

WRAP TEXT AROUND A TABLE

You can wrap text around a table by aligning it to the left or right side of your Web page.

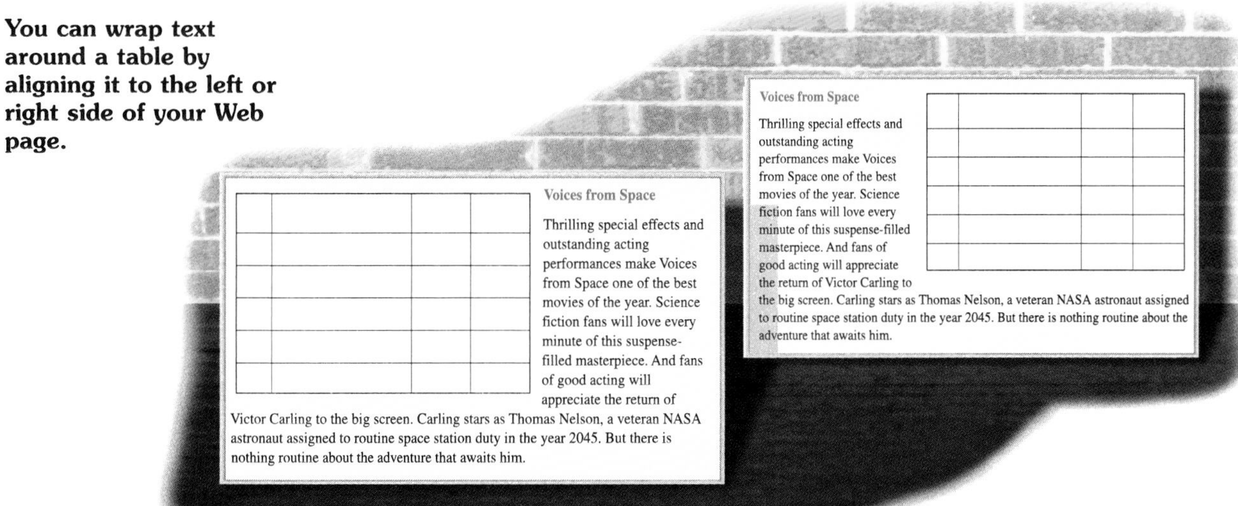

WRAP TEXT AROUND A TABLE

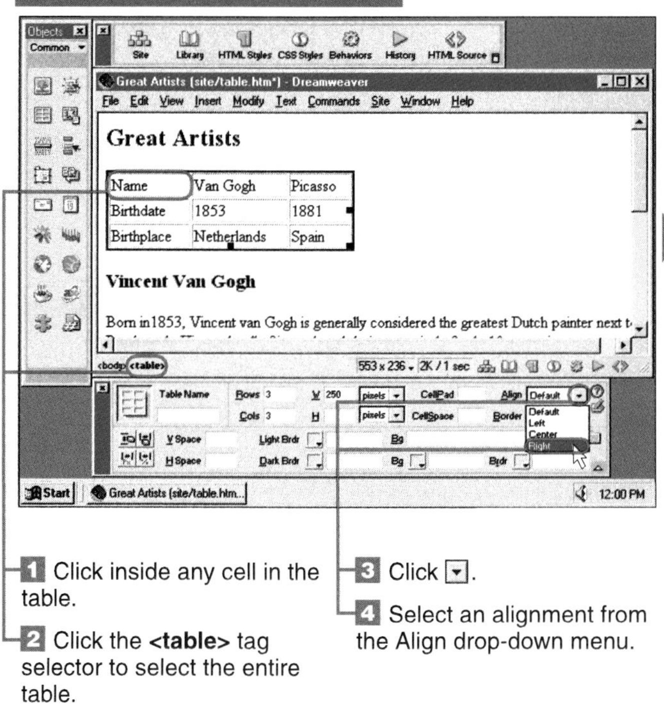

1 Click inside any cell in the table.

2 Click the **<table>** tag selector to select the entire table.

3 Click ▾.

4 Select an alignment from the Align drop-down menu.

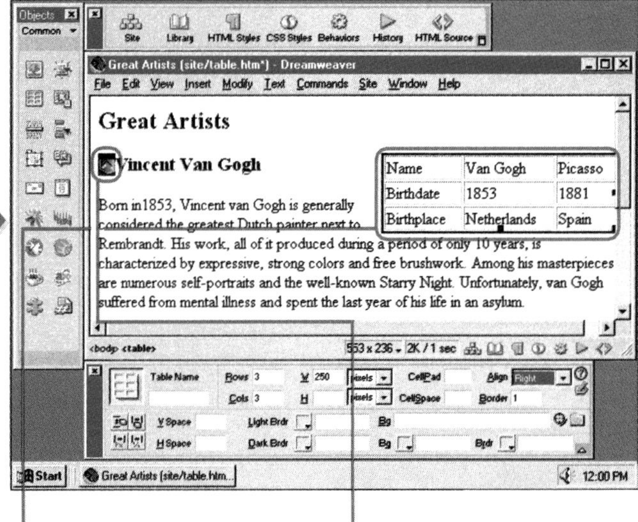

■ The table is displayed with the alignment you have selected. Any text (or other content) that immediately follows the table wraps around it.

■ Dreamweaver inserts an anchor icon to mark where the table was originally inserted. You can click the icon to select the table. This icon does not show up when the page is viewed in Web browsers.

ALIGN TEXT HORIZONTALLY IN A TABLE

You can align text and other content horizontally in your table cells.

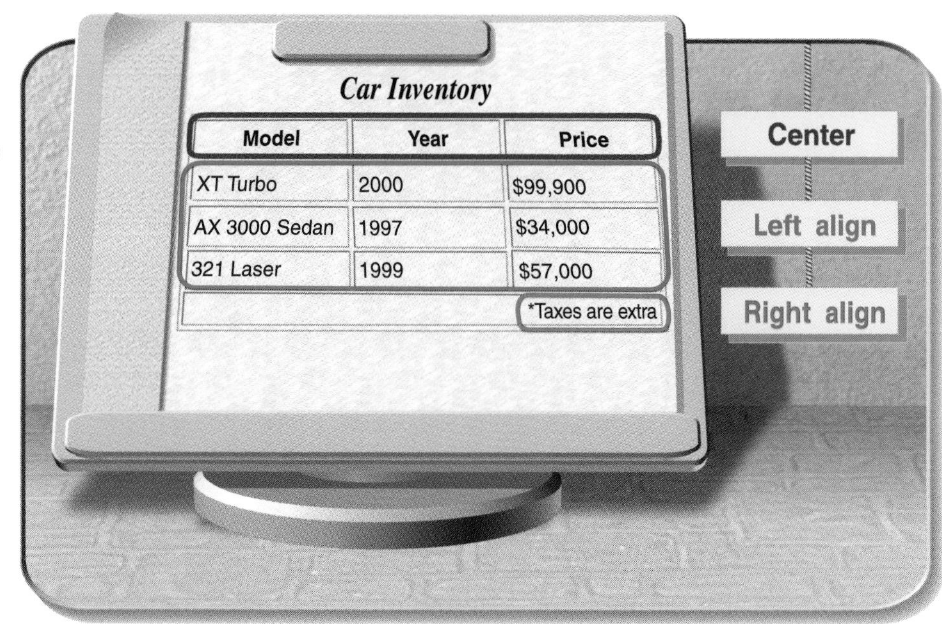

ALIGN TEXT HORIZONTALLY IN A TABLE

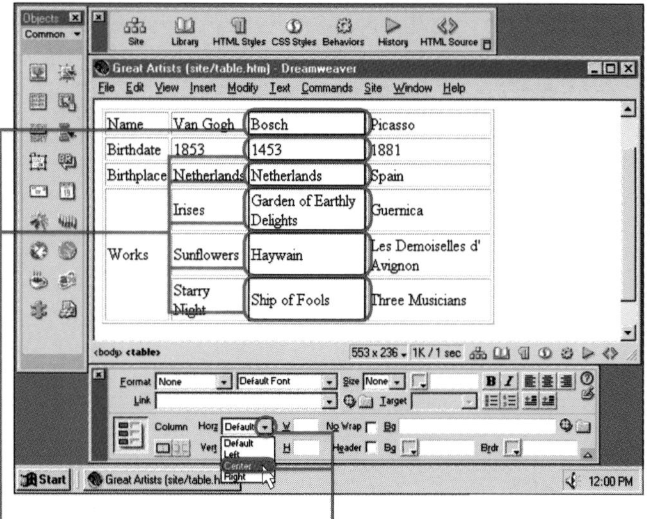

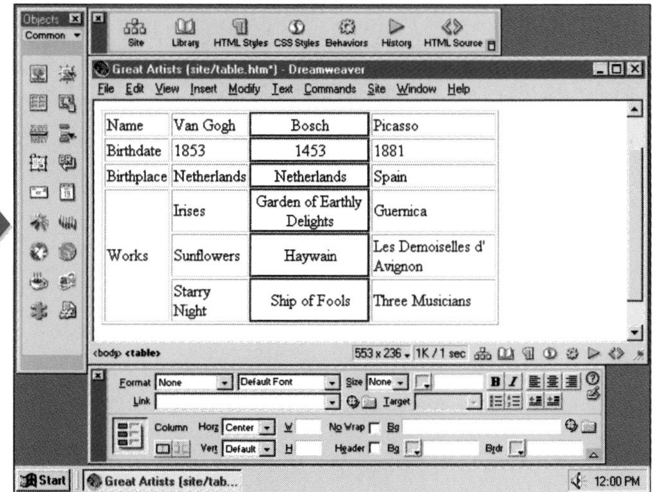

1 Click a cell of the table.

2 To align the content in more than one cell, Shift-click to select the other table cells.

■ The cells appear highlighted.

3 Click ▾.

4 Select an alignment.

■ The text (and other content) in the selected cells is aligned.

Note: The default horizontal alignment for table cells is to the left.

ALIGN TEXT VERTICALLY IN A TABLE

You can align text and other content vertically in your table cells.

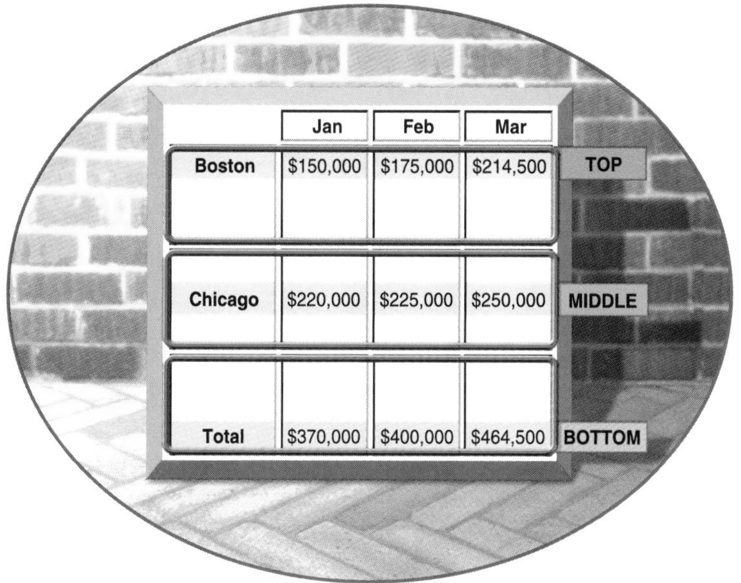

Jan
Feb
Mar
Boston
$150,000
$175,000
$214,500
TOP
Chicago
$220,000
$225,000
$250,000
MIDDLE
Total
$370,000
$400,000
$464,500
BOTTOM

ALIGN TEXT VERTICALLY IN A TABLE

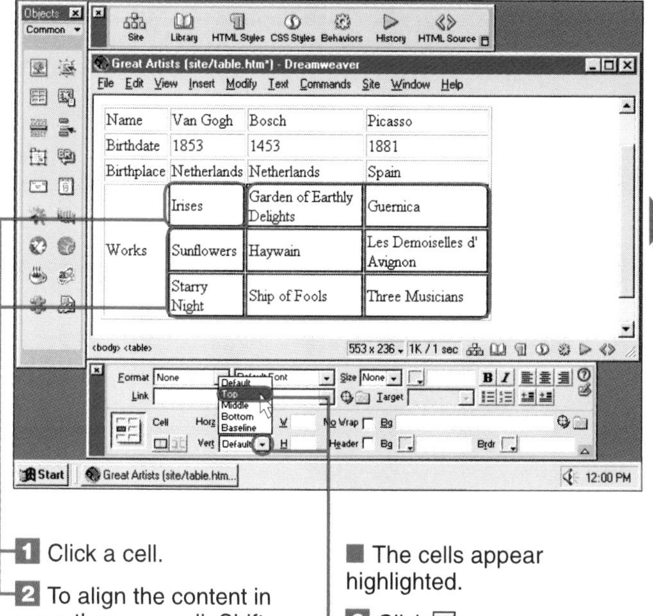

1 Click a cell.

2 To align the content in more than one cell, Shift-click to select the other table cells.

■ The cells appear highlighted.

3 Click ▾.

4 Select an alignment.

■ The text (and other content) in the selected cells is aligned.

Note: The default vertical alignment for table cells is in the middle.

USING A TABLE AS A DESIGN TOOL

To organize your Web page, you can use a table for overall structure. For instance, you can use tables to separate navigational elements on a page from the rest of the its content.

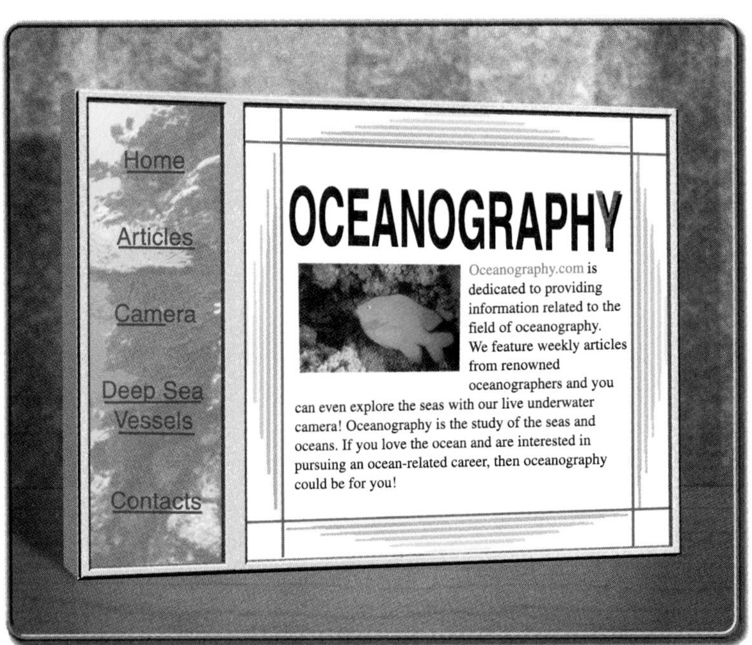

This example uses a one-row, two-column table to separate navigational hyperlinks from site content.

USING A TABLE AS A DESIGN TOOL

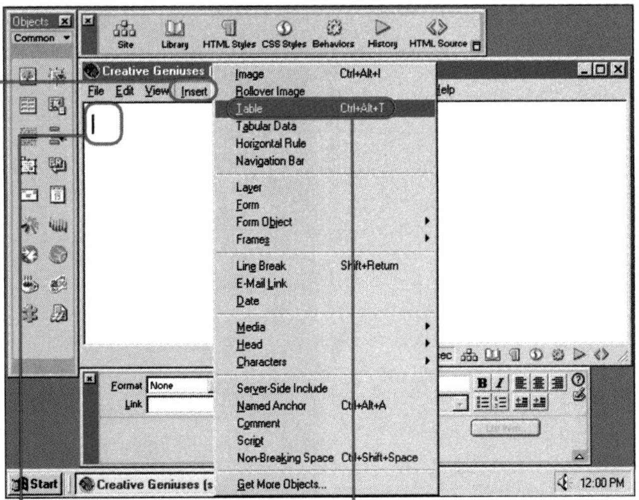

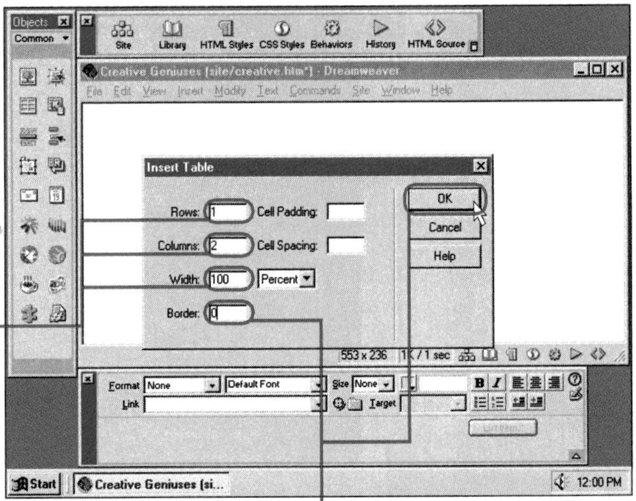

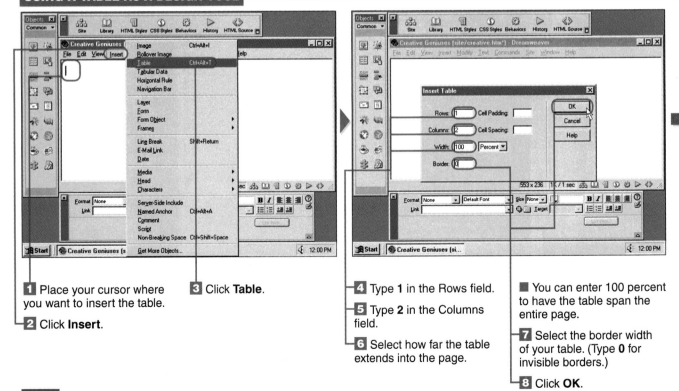

1 Place your cursor where you want to insert the table.

2 Click **Insert**.

3 Click **Table**.

4 Type **1** in the Rows field.

5 Type **2** in the Columns field.

6 Select how far the table extends into the page.

■ You can enter 100 percent to have the table span the entire page.

7 Select the border width of your table. (Type **0** for invisible borders.)

8 Click **OK**.

Can I insert tables inside another table?

Yes, you can insert a table within a table. You can also add smaller tables in those interior tables. Many Web sites use complicated combinations of nested tables to organize their content precisely.

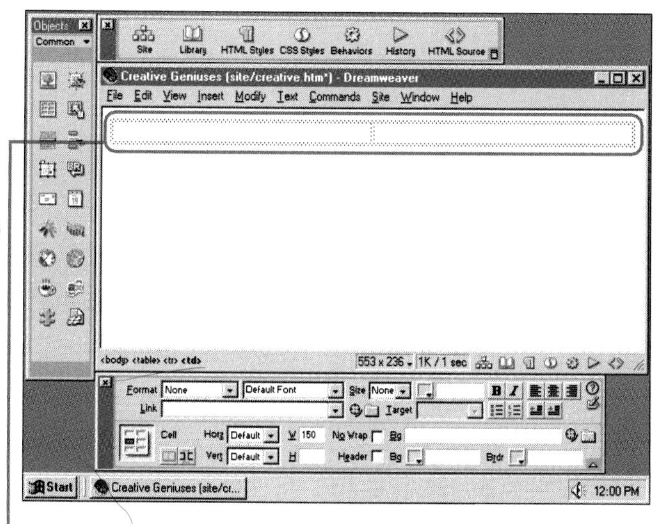

■ Dreamweaver inserts a table matching your specifications. The dashes mean the borders are turned off.

■ Borders do not appear when the page is viewed with a Web browser.

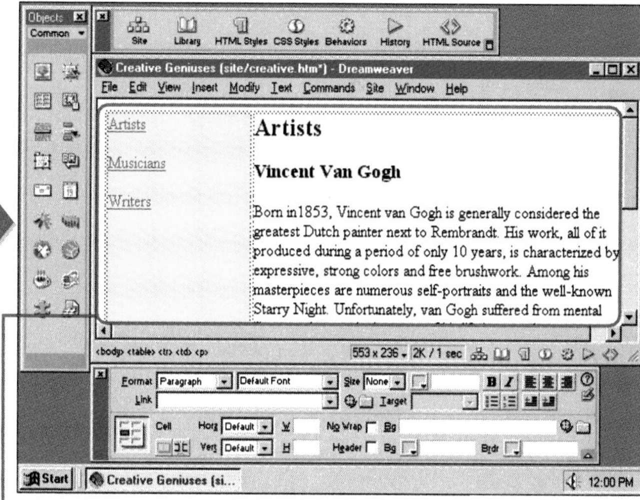

9 Add content to the table columns.

■ In this example, the left column has a background color and contains navigational links set at a width of 150 pixels. The right column contains the main content.

ADD AN IMAGE CAPTION USING A TABLE

You can use a two-cell table to place a caption, above, below, or next to an image.

In this example, the caption is created below the image.

ADD AN IMAGE CAPTION USING A TABLE

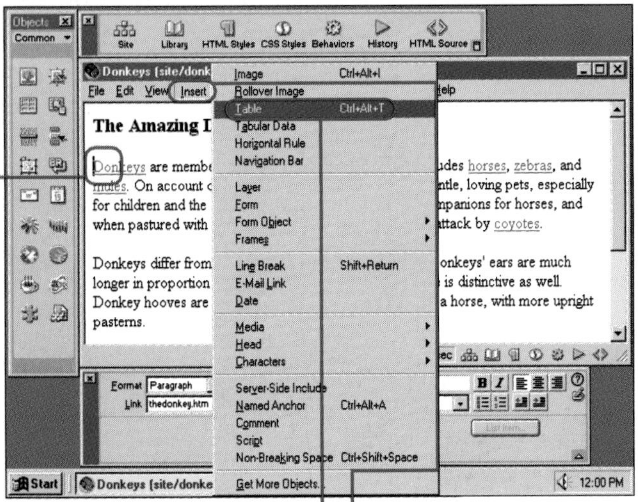

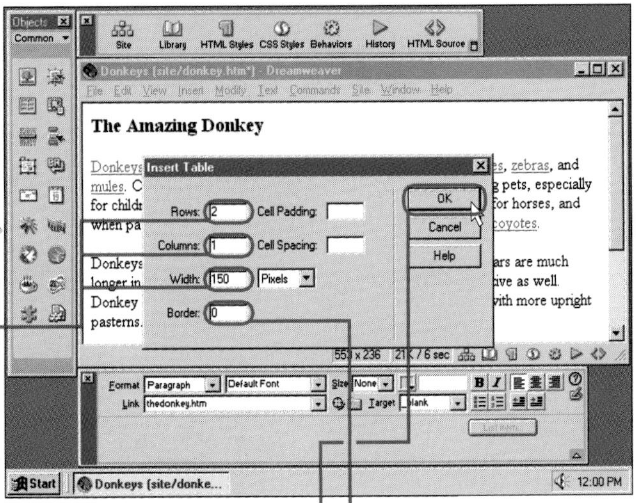

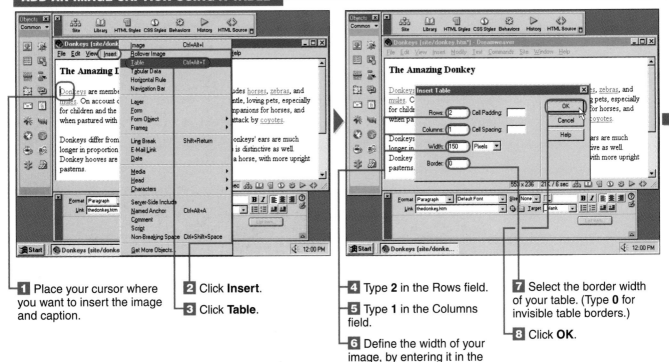

1 Place your cursor where you want to insert the image and caption.

2 Click **Insert**.

3 Click **Table**.

4 Type **2** in the Rows field.

5 Type **1** in the Columns field.

6 Define the width of your image, by entering it in the Width field.

7 Select the border width of your table. (Type **0** for invisible table borders.)

8 Click **OK**.

How can I place captions below several images across a Web page?

Use a two-row table with a column for each image-caption pair.

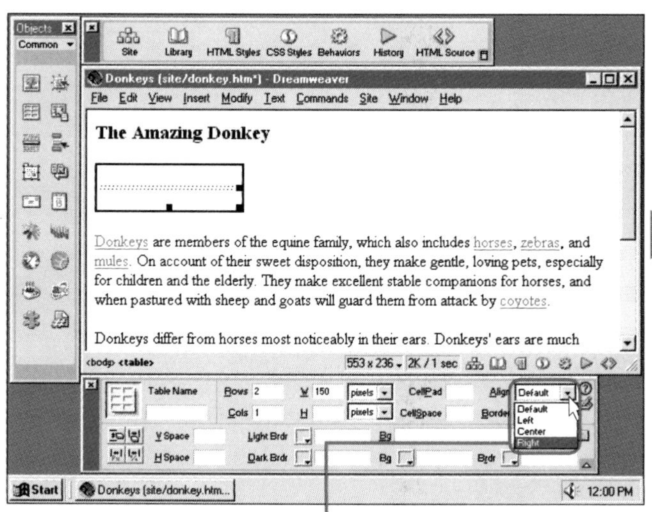

■ Dreamweaver inserts a two-row, one-column table. The dashed border indicates that borders are turned off.

■ Borders do not appear when the page is viewed with a Web browser.

9 To wrap the Web page text around the image and caption, select an alignment.

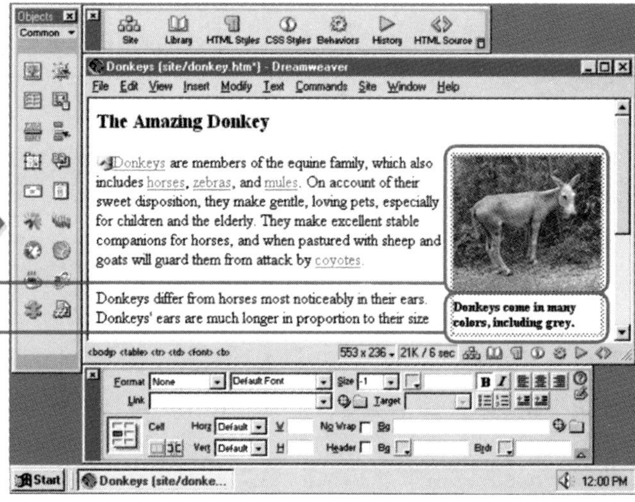

10 Click in the top row of the table and insert the image. (To insert an image, see Chapter 5.)

11 Click in the bottom row of the table and insert the caption text.

Note: You can align a caption to the side of an image by creating a one-row, two-column table.

Form

Creating Forms

Would you like your site visitors to be able to send you feedback and other information? Learn how in this chapter.

INTRODUCTION TO FORMS

You can add forms to your Web site to make it more interactive. Forms enable viewers to enter and submit information to you through your Web pages.

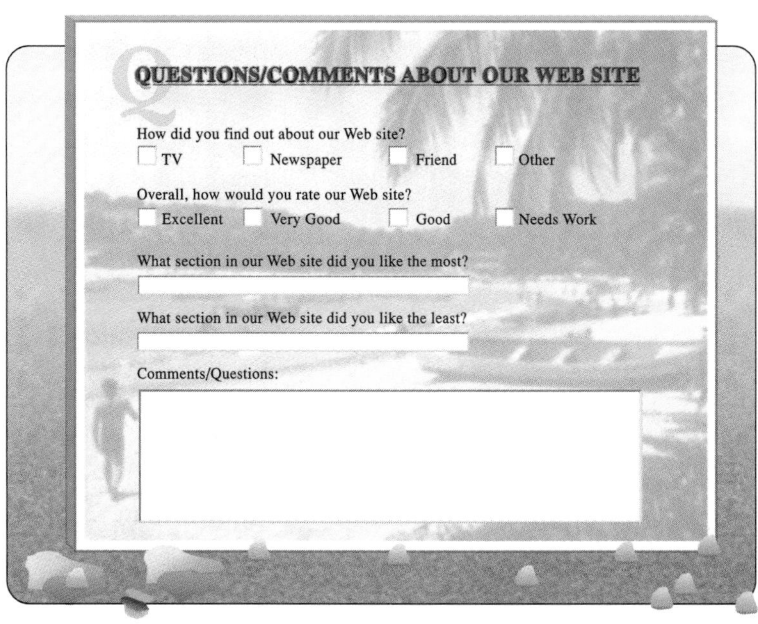

QUESTIONS/COMMENTS ABOUT OUR WEB SITE

How did you find out about our Web site?

☐ TV ☐ Newspaper ☐ Friend ☐ Other

Overall, how would you rate our Web site?

☐ Excellent ☐ Very Good ☐ Good ☐ Needs Work

What section in our Web site did you like the most?

What section in our Web site did you like the least?

Comments/Questions:

Every form works in conjunction with a separate program called a *form handler,* which processes the form information.

CREATING A FORM

You can create a form using text fields, pull-down menus, check boxes, and other interactive elements. You can also assign the Web address of a form handler to process completed forms. Visitors to your Web page fill the form out and send the information to the form handler by clicking a "submit" button.

PROCESSING THE FORM INFORMATION

The *form handler* (also known as a CGI script) processes the form information and does something useful with it, such as forwarding the information to an e-mail address or entering it into a database. You cannot create form handlers with Dreamweaver because creating one requires learning a programming language. However, many ready-made form handlers are available for free on the Web.

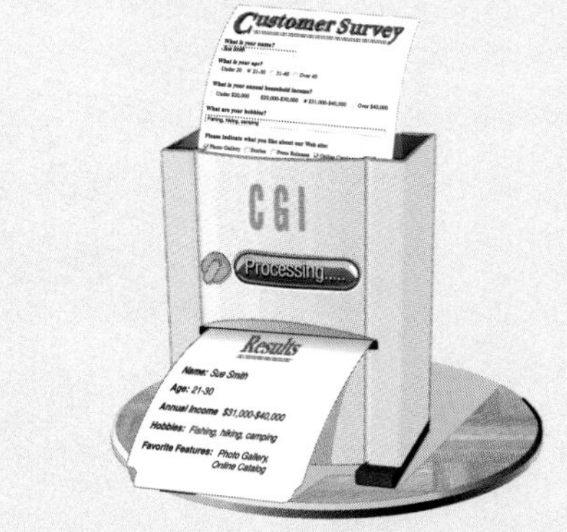

SET UP A FORM

You can set up a form on your Web page by inserting form objects.

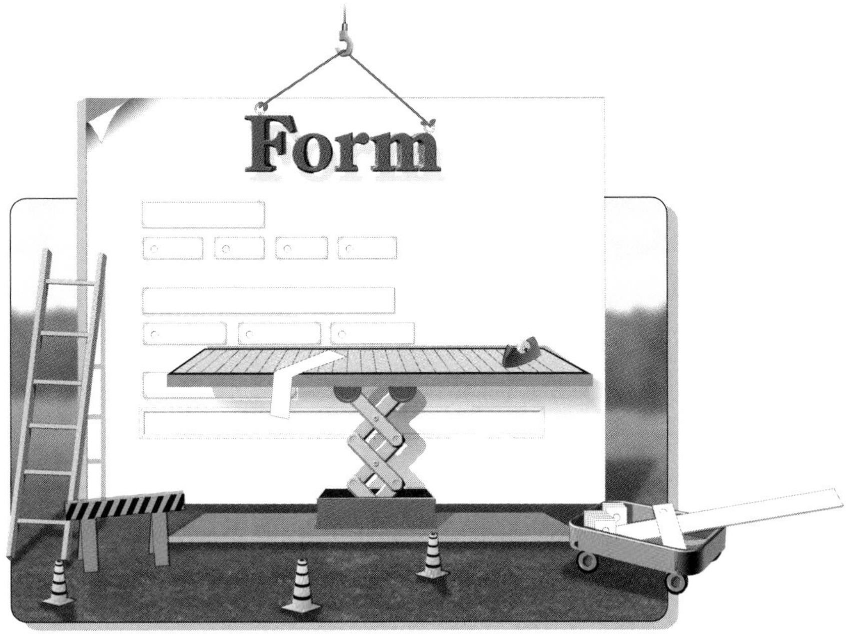

SET UP A FORM

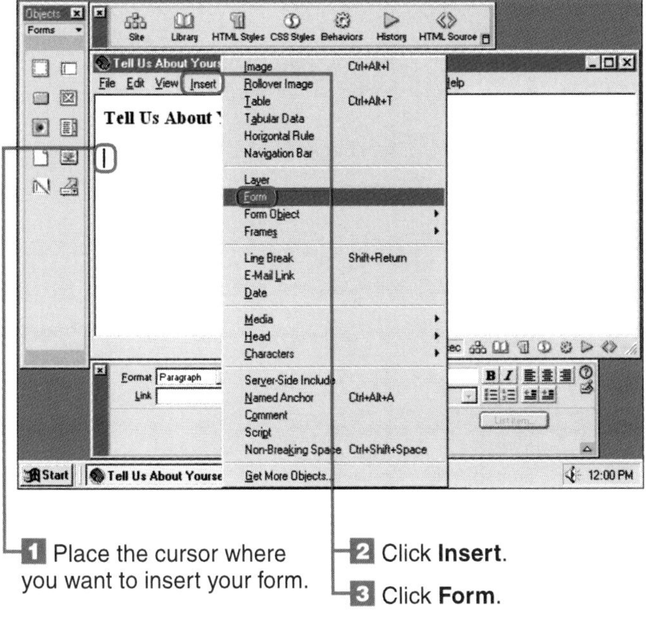

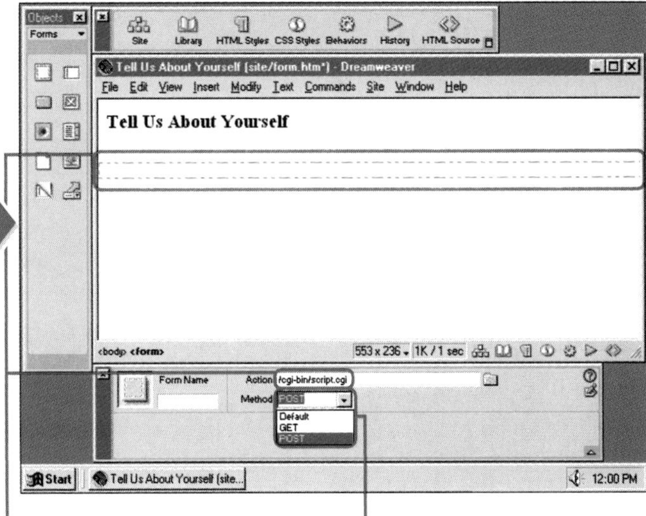

1 Place the cursor where you want to insert your form.

2 Click **Insert**.

3 Click **Form**.

■ Dreamweaver adds a red, dashed box to define where to add a form object.

4 Type the address of the form handler.

5 Click ▾ and select either POST or GET.

6 Add form objects for viewer information.

ADD A TEXT FIELD TO A FORM

You can add a text field that enables viewers to submit text in your form.

ADD A TEXT FIELD TO A FORM

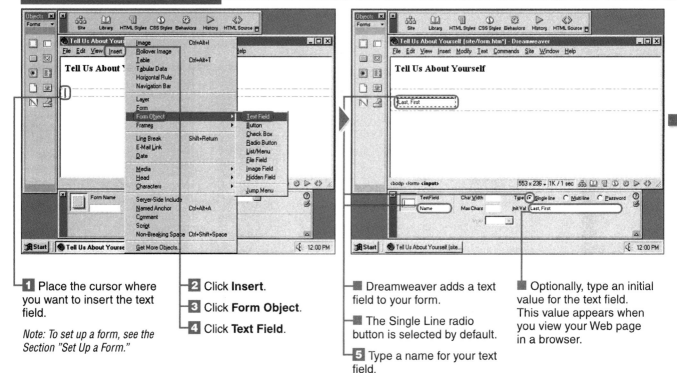

1 Place the cursor where you want to insert the text field.

Note: To set up a form, see the Section "Set Up a Form."

2 Click **Insert**.

3 Click **Form Object**.

4 Click **Text Field**.

■ Dreamweaver adds a text field to your form.

■ The Single Line radio button is selected by default.

5 Type a name for your text field.

■ Optionally, type an initial value for the text field. This value appears when you view your Web page in a browser.

What is sent to the form handler from a text field?

When a user submits a form, the browser sends the text field's name and value (information typed into the field by the user) to the *form handler*. The form handler distinguishes one text field from another by their unique names.

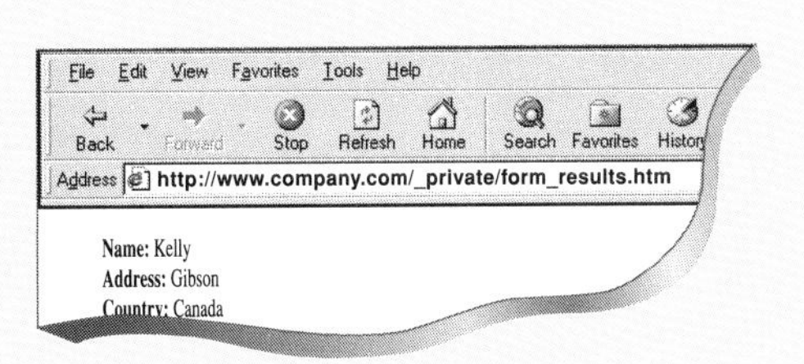

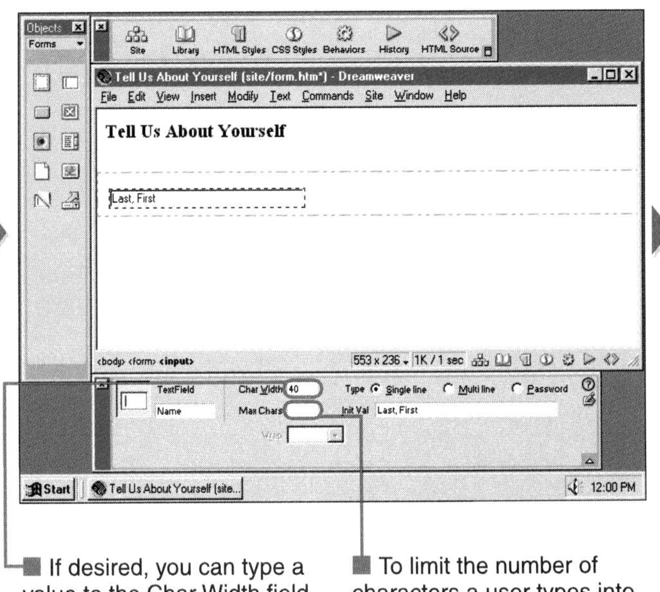

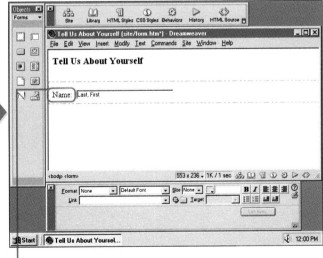

■ If desired, you can type a value to the Char Width field to define the width of the text field.

■ To limit the number of characters a user types into the field, you can type a value to the Max Chars field.

6 Type a label for the text field so that users know what to enter into it.

ADD A MULTI-LINE TEXT FIELD TO A FORM

Multi-line text fields enable viewers to submit large amounts of text with a form.

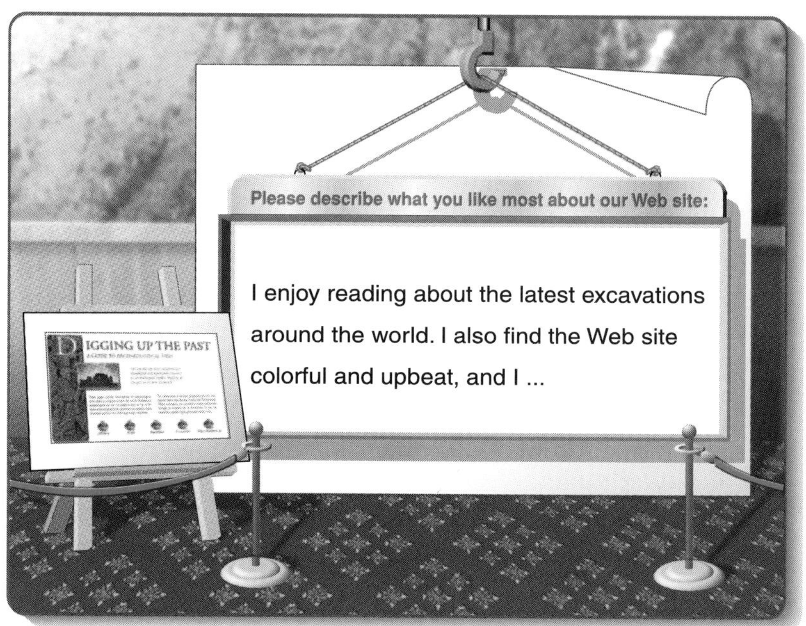

Please describe what you like most about our Web site:
I enjoy reading about the latest excavations around the world. I also find the Web site colorful and upbeat, and I ...
IGGING UP THE PAST

ADD A MULTI-LINE FIELD TO A FORM

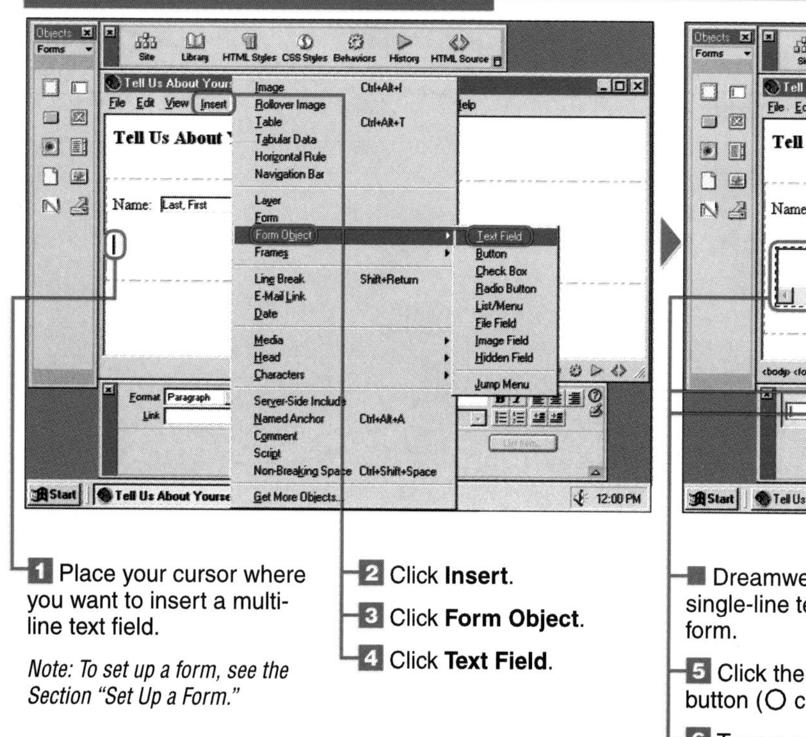

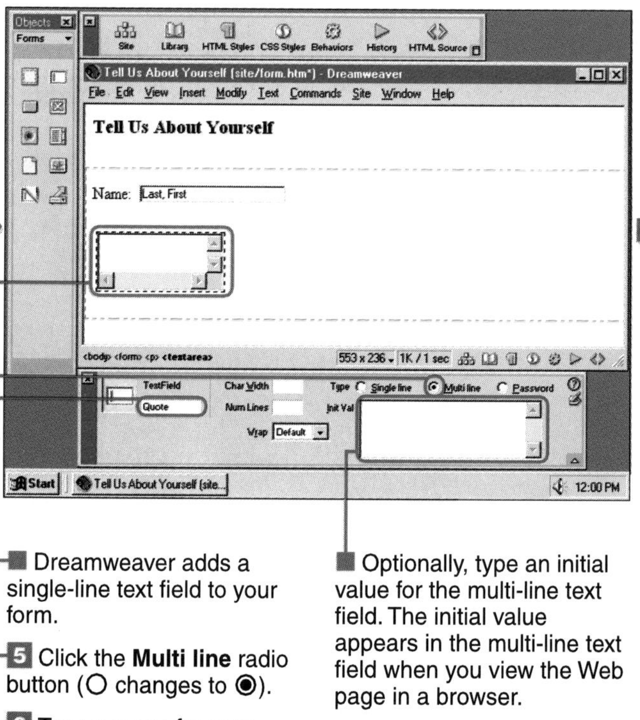

1 Place your cursor where you want to insert a multi-line text field.

Note: To set up a form, see the Section "Set Up a Form."

2 Click **Insert**.

3 Click **Form Object**.

4 Click **Text Field**.

■ Dreamweaver adds a single-line text field to your form.

5 Click the **Multi line** radio button (○ changes to ◉).

6 Type a name for your multi-line text field.

■ Optionally, type an initial value for the multi-line text field. The initial value appears in the multi-line text field when you view the Web page in a browser.

Why is it important to define the `word-wrap` attribute of a multi-line text field?

In some Web browsers, text typed into a multi-line text field does not automatically wrap when it reaches the right edge of the field, which can be annoying for the user. Specifying Virtual or Physical in the Wrap menu ensures that text automatically wraps in a multi-line text field.

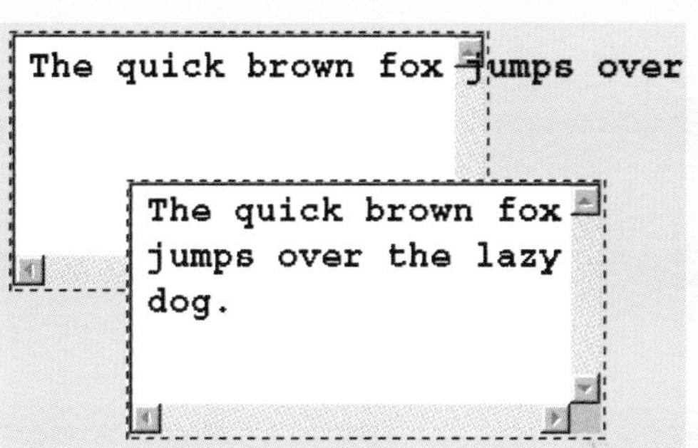

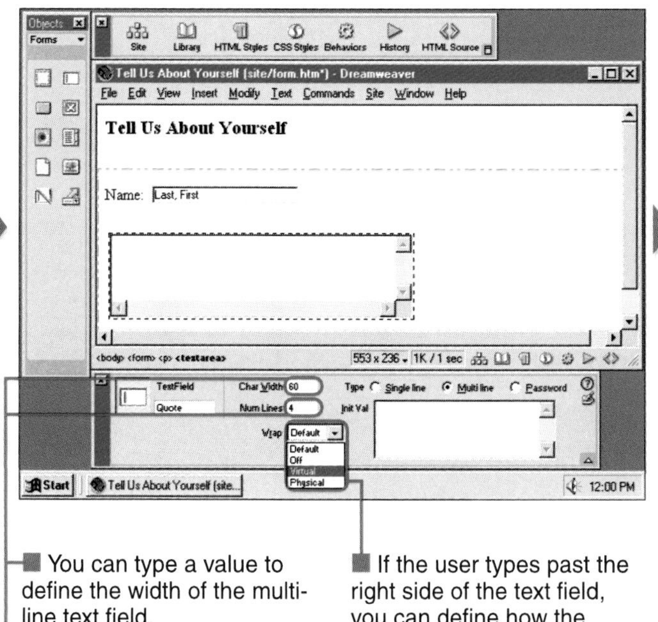

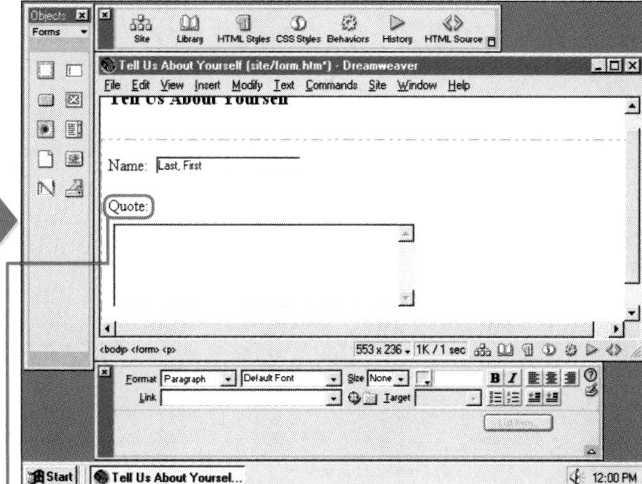

■ You can type a value to define the width of the multi-line text field.

■ You can define the number of lines visible in the multi-line text field.

■ If the user types past the right side of the text field, you can define how the information wraps.

7 Type a label for the multi-line text field so that users can identify what to enter (example: **Quote**).

ADD A PASSWORD FIELD TO A FORM

Dreamweaver allows you to add a password field, which hides information as the user types it into a form. The characters display as asterisks or bullets, depending on the platform.

ADD A PASSWORD FIELD TO A FORM

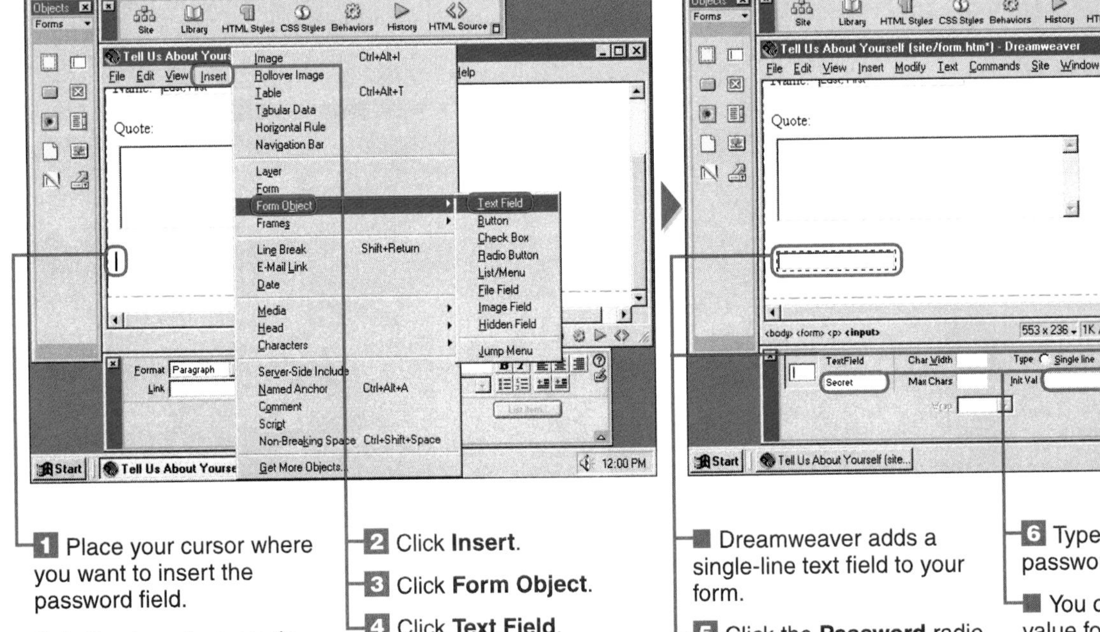

1 Place your cursor where you want to insert the password field.

Note: To set up a form, see the Section "Set Up a Form."

2 Click **Insert**.

3 Click **Form Object**.

4 Click **Text Field**.

■ Dreamweaver adds a single-line text field to your form.

5 Click the **Password** radio button (○ changes to ◉).

6 Type a name in the password field.

■ You can type an initial value for the password field.

Does the password field protect information as it is transmitted over the Internet?

The password field prevents other people from seeing the text a user types into a form. The browser, however, sends the password field information to the form handler as plain text, just like everything else in the form. The the password field does *not* protect your information from someone intercepting it as it travels between the user's computer and the form handler.

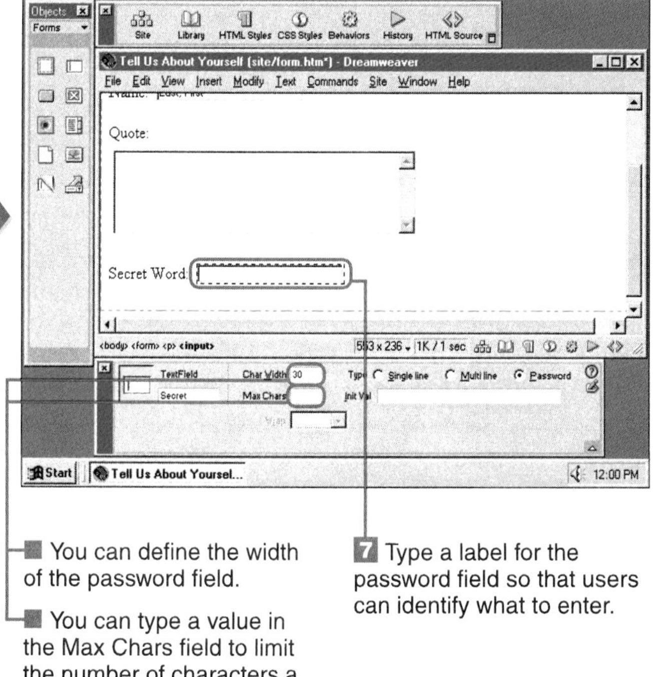

■ You can define the width of the password field.

■ You can type a value in the Max Chars field to limit the number of characters a user enters into the field.

7 Type a label for the password field so that users can identify what to enter.

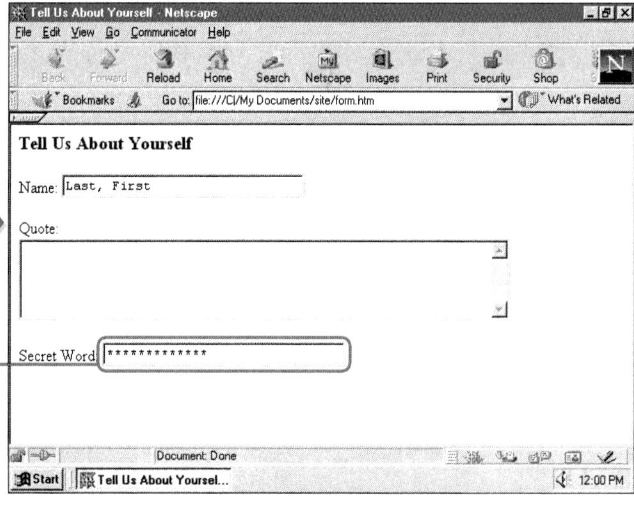

■ When a user types text in the password field, asterisks or bullets will appear in the Web browser (depending on the platform).

ADD CHECK BOXES TO A FORM

Check boxes enable you to select multiple options in a form.

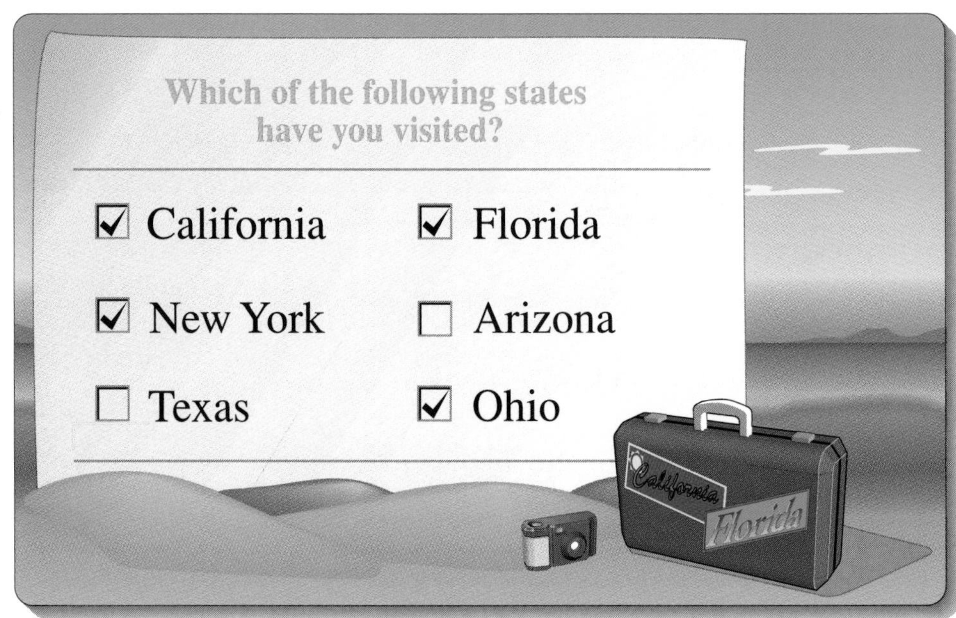

Which of the following states have you visited?
California
Florida
New York
Arizona
Texas
Ohio
California
Florida

ADD CHECK BOXES TO A FORM

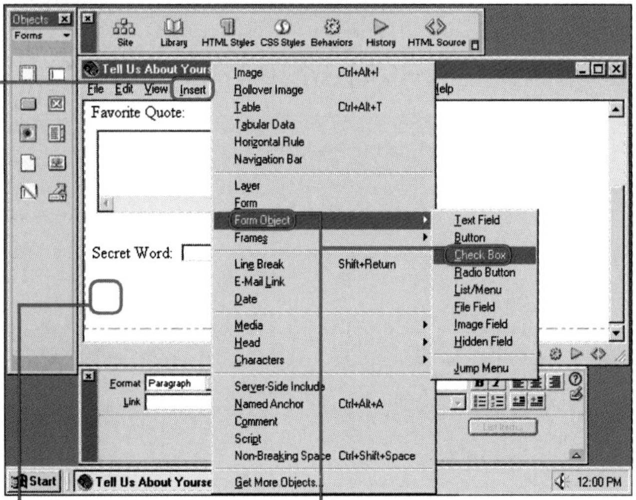

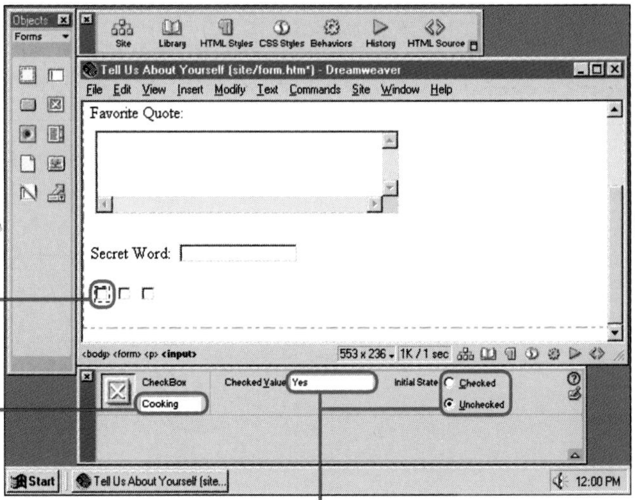

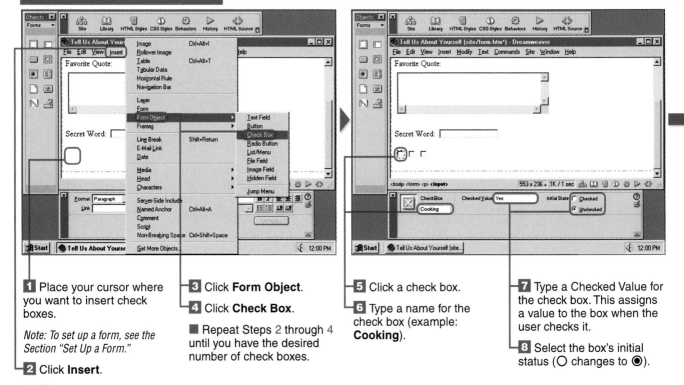

1 Place your cursor where you want to insert check boxes.

Note: To set up a form, see the Section "Set Up a Form."

2 Click **Insert**.

3 Click **Form Object**.

4 Click **Check Box**.

■ Repeat Steps 2 through 4 until you have the desired number of check boxes.

5 Click a check box.

6 Type a name for the check box (example: **Cooking**).

7 Type a Checked Value for the check box. This assigns a value to the box when the user checks it.

8 Select the box's initial status (○ changes to ◉).

What is sent to the form handler from a set of check boxes?

When the user submits a form, the browser sends a name and value for each selected check box to the form handler. It does not send information about check boxes that have not been selected.

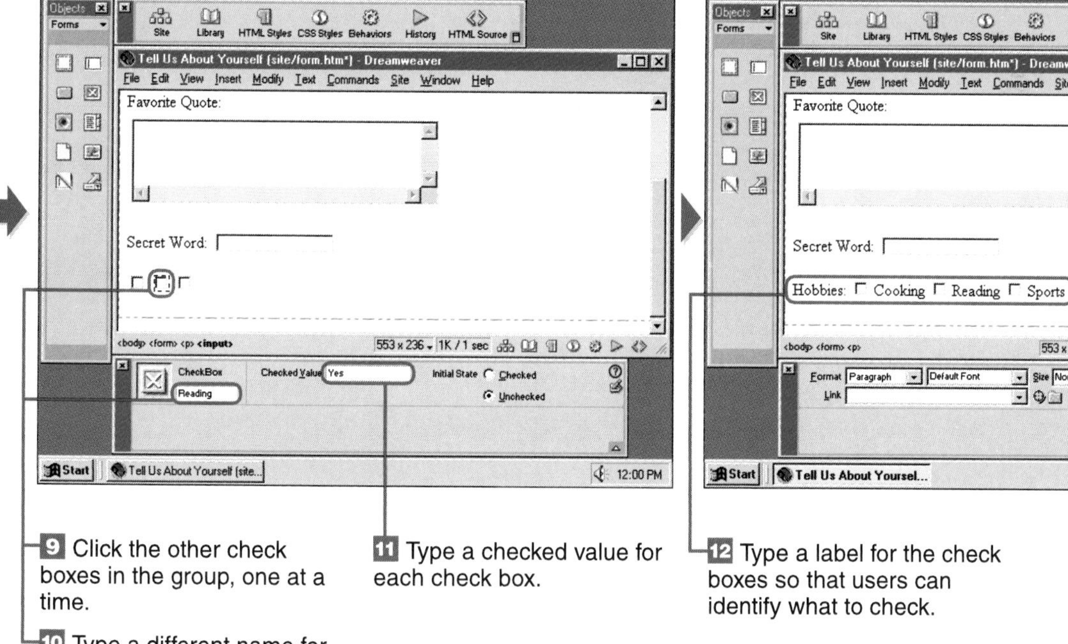

9 Click the other check boxes in the group, one at a time.

10 Type a different name for each check box.

11 Type a checked value for each check box.

12 Type a label for the check boxes so that users can identify what to check.

ADD RADIO BUTTONS TO A FORM

Let your user make one selection (and only one selection) from several options by adding a set of radio buttons to your form.

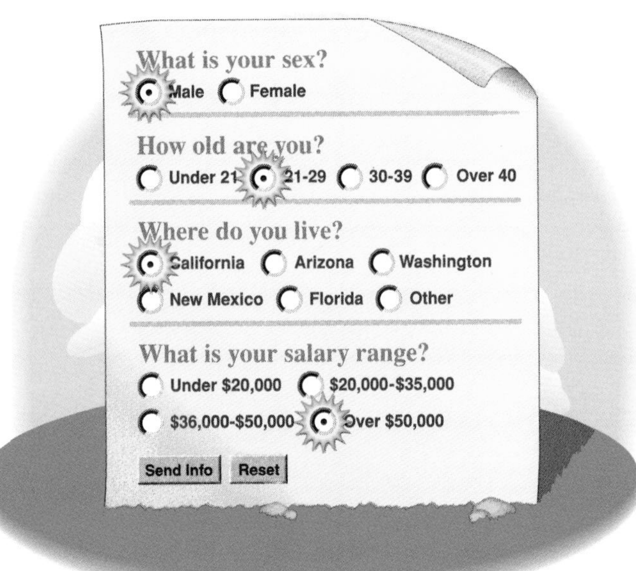

ADD RADIO BUTTONS TO A FORM

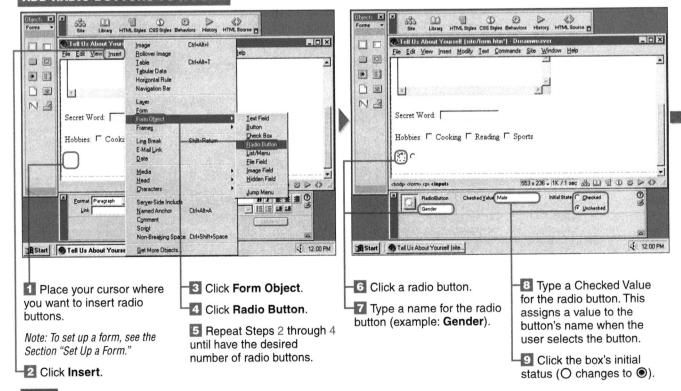

1 Place your cursor where you want to insert radio buttons.

Note: To set up a form, see the Section "Set Up a Form."

2 Click **Insert**.

3 Click **Form Object**.

4 Click **Radio Button**.

5 Repeat Steps 2 through 4 until have the desired number of radio buttons.

6 Click a radio button.

7 Type a name for the radio button (example: **Gender**).

8 Type a Checked Value for the radio button. This assigns a value to the button's name when the user selects the button.

9 Click the box's initial status (○ changes to ◉).

What is sent to the form handler from a set of radio buttons?

When the user submits a form, the browser sends the name assigned to all the buttons in the group and the value of the selected radio button to the form handler. It does not send radio-button information if none have been selected.

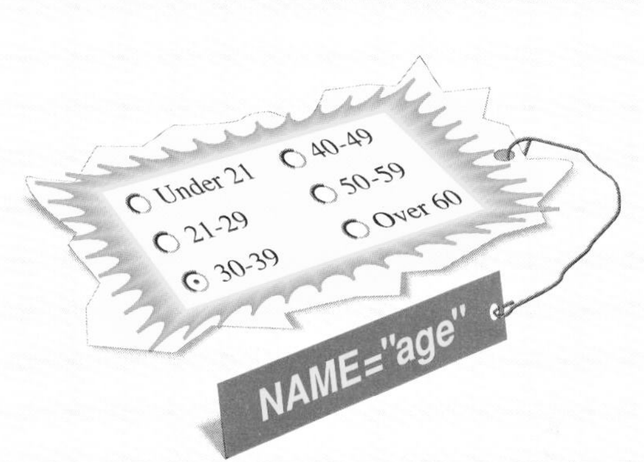

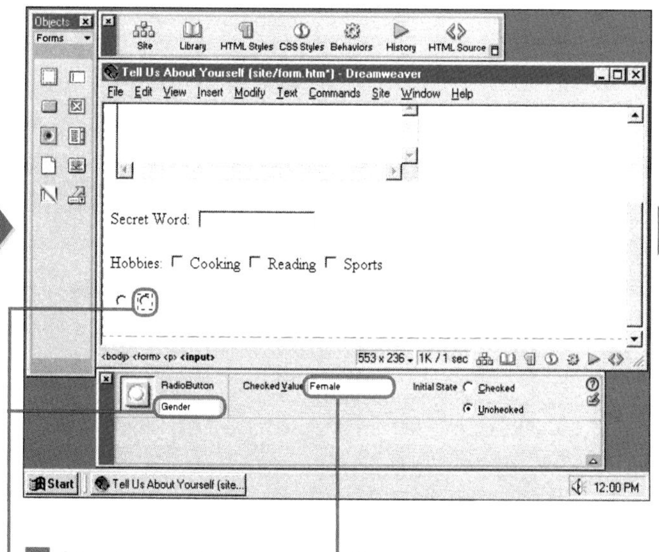

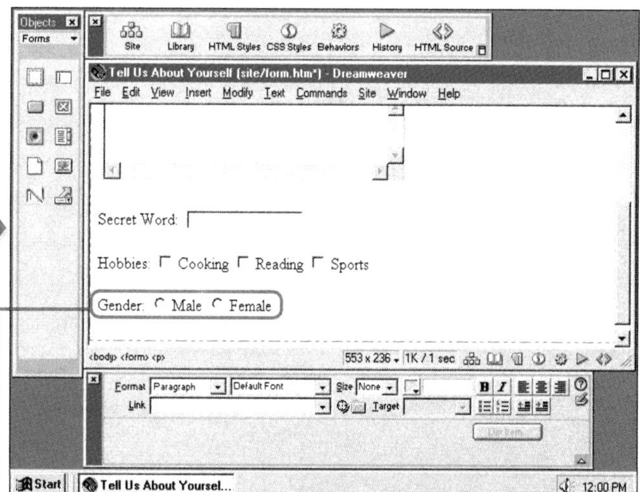

10 Click the next button.

11 Give this radio button the same name as the previous one.

■ Assigning each button the same name with a unique checked value ensures that only one in the set will be "on" at a time.

12 Type a Checked Value for this radio button.

13 Type a label for the radio buttons so that users can identify what to select.

ADD A MENU TO A FORM

A pull-down menu enables you to choose one option from a long list of options.

ADD A MENU TO A FORM

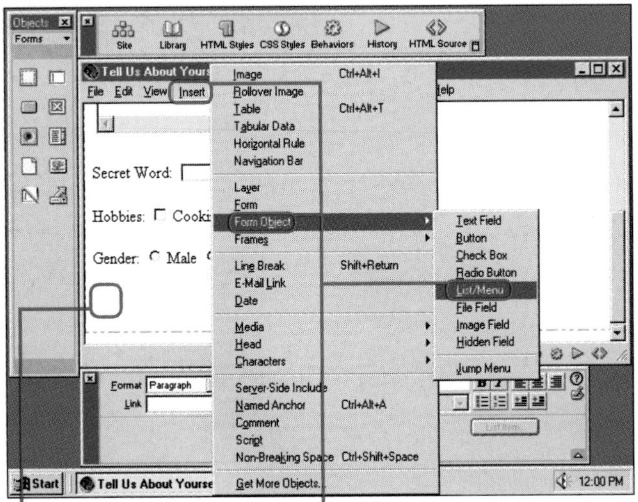

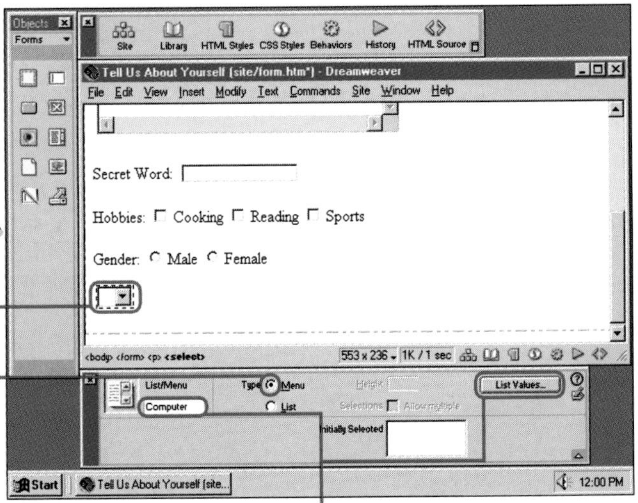

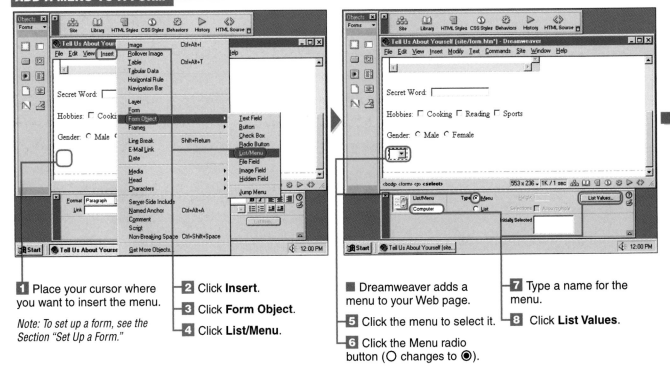

1 Place your cursor where you want to insert the menu.

Note: To set up a form, see the Section "Set Up a Form."

2 Click **Insert**.

3 Click **Form Object**.

4 Click **List/Menu**.

■ Dreamweaver adds a menu to your Web page.

5 Click the menu to select it.

6 Click the Menu radio button (○ changes to ◉).

7 Type a name for the menu.

8 Click **List Values**.

What is the difference between a menu and a list?

Menus and lists serve the same purpose in forms: They enable a user to choose one option from a list of many options. But whereas a menu presents options in a drop-down format, a list presents options in a scrollable window. You can click a radio button in the Property inspector to specify that your form element be a menu or a list.

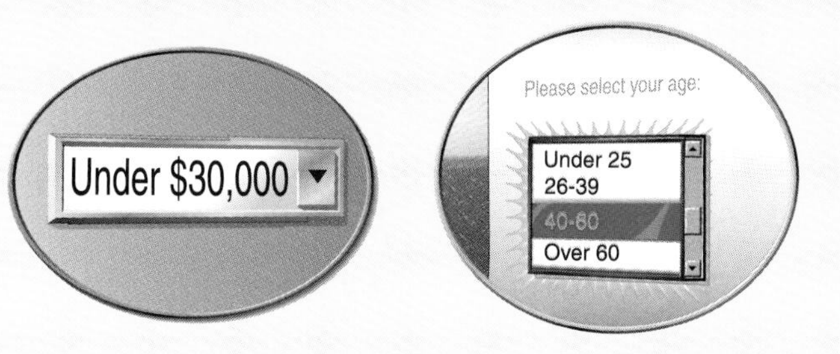

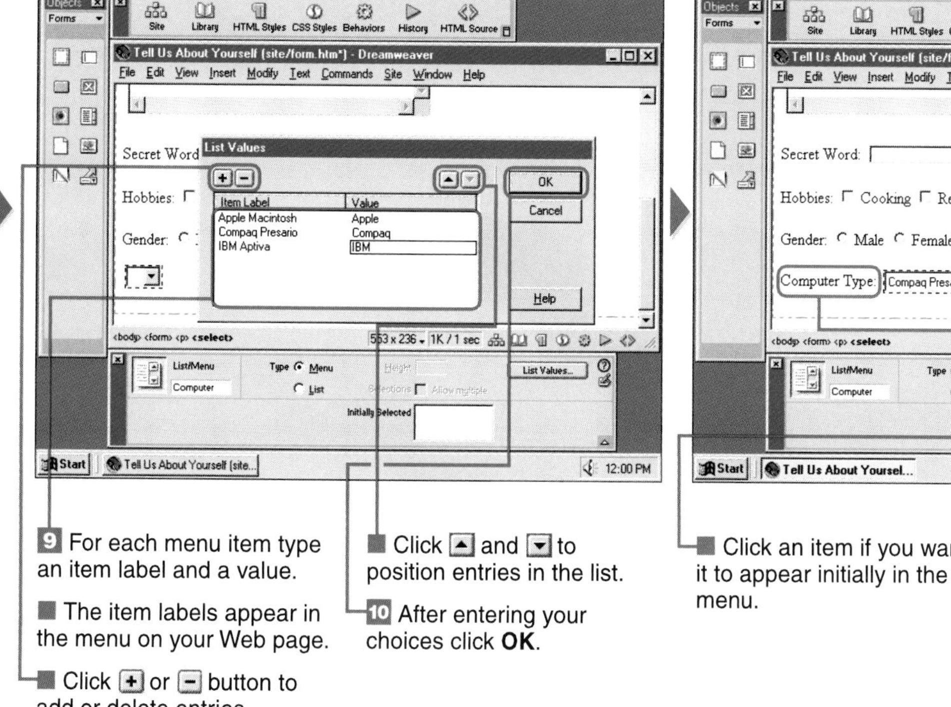

9 For each menu item type an item label and a value.

■ The item labels appear in the menu on your Web page.

■ Click [+] or [−] button to add or delete entries.

■ Click [▲] and [▼] to position entries in the list.

10 After entering your choices click **OK**.

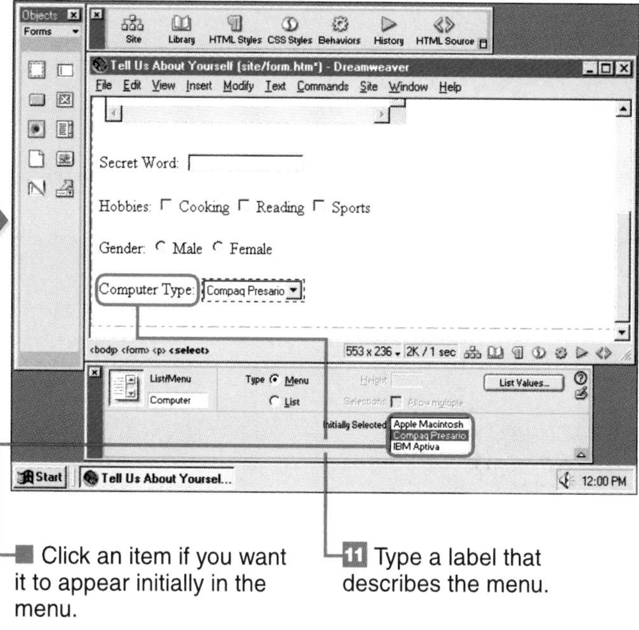

■ Click an item if you want it to appear initially in the menu.

11 Type a label that describes the menu.

ADD A LIST TO A FORM

A list enables you to choose one or more options from a long list of options.

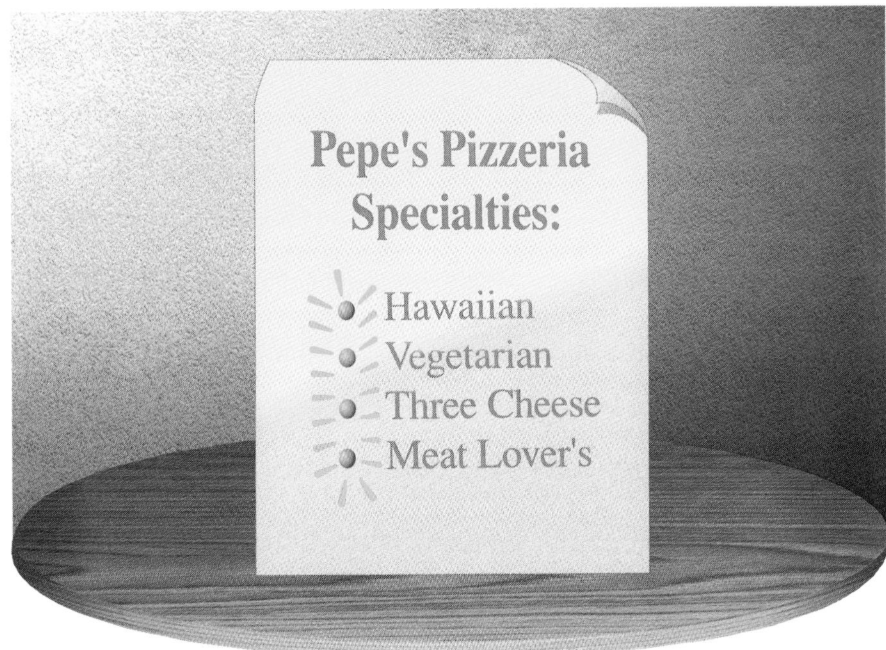

Pepe's Pizzeria
Specialties:
Hawaiian
Vegetarian
Three Cheese
Meat Lover's

ADD A LIST TO A FORM

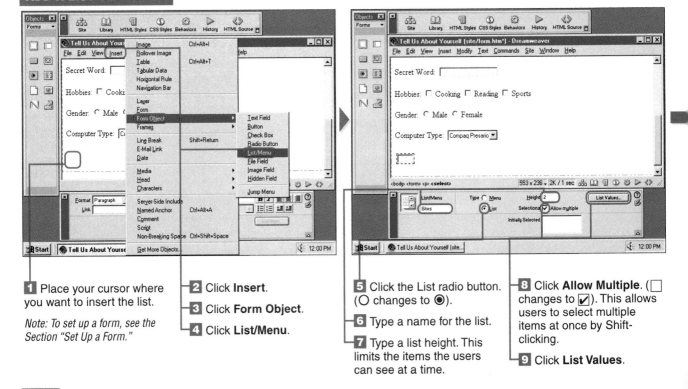

1 Place your cursor where you want to insert the list.

Note: To set up a form, see the Section "Set Up a Form."

2 Click **Insert**.

3 Click **Form Object**.

4 Click **List/Menu**.

5 Click the List radio button. (○ changes to ◉).

6 Type a name for the list.

7 Type a list height. This limits the items the users can see at a time.

8 Click **Allow Multiple**. (☐ changes to ☑). This allows users to select multiple items at once by Shift-clicking.

9 Click **List Values**.

What is sent to the form handler when several items are selected in a list?

When multiple items are selected in a list and the form is submitted, the browser sends the name of the list several times, each time paired with a different value. The form handler makes sense of the multiple instances of the list name.

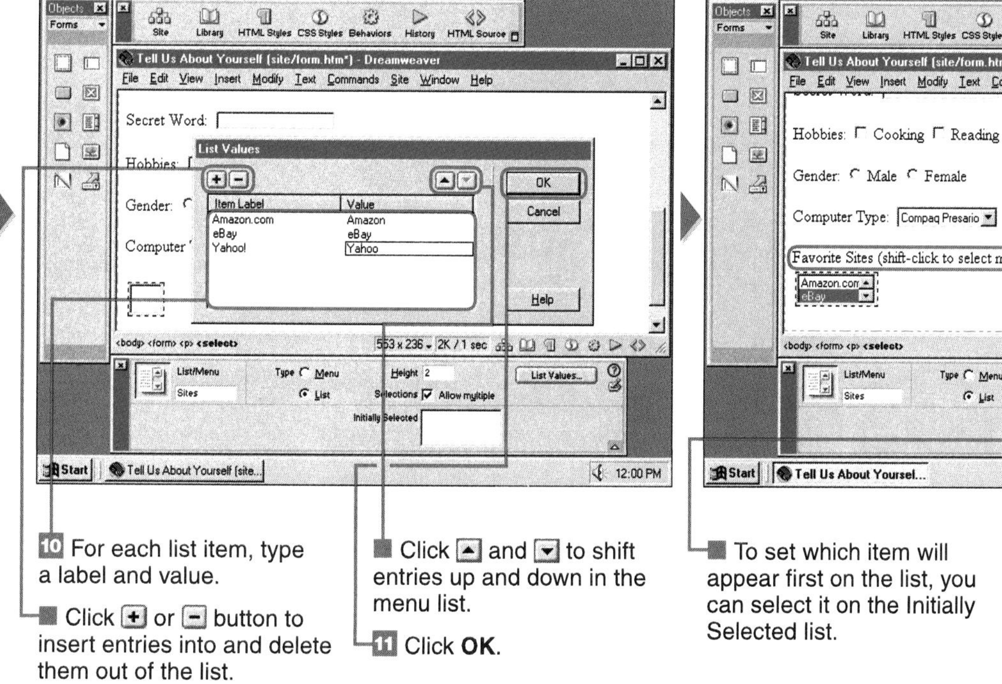

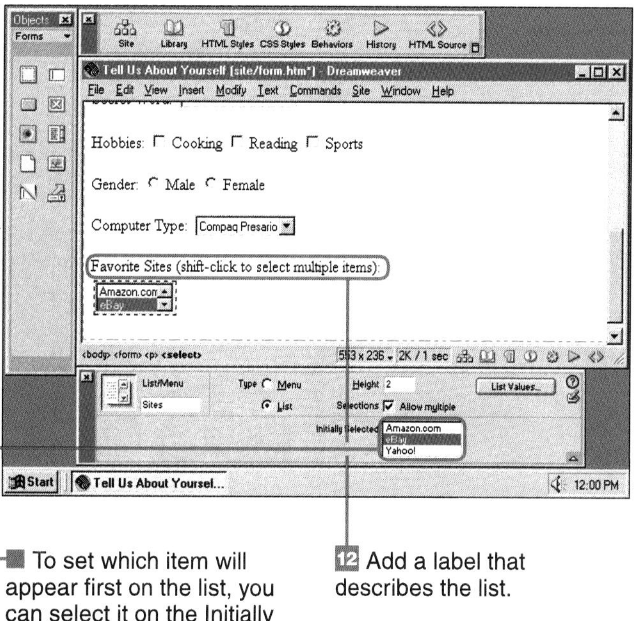

10 For each list item, type a label and value.

■ Click + or − button to insert entries into and delete them out of the list.

■ Click ▲ and ▼ to shift entries up and down in the menu list.

11 Click **OK**.

■ To set which item will appear first on the list, you can select it on the Initially Selected list.

12 Add a label that describes the list.

ADD FILE UPLOADING TO A FORM

Users can select files from their computer and upload them, along with other form information, to the form handler. By clicking a Browse button, a dialog box appears, enabling the user to select a file.

ADD FILE UPLOADING TO A FORM

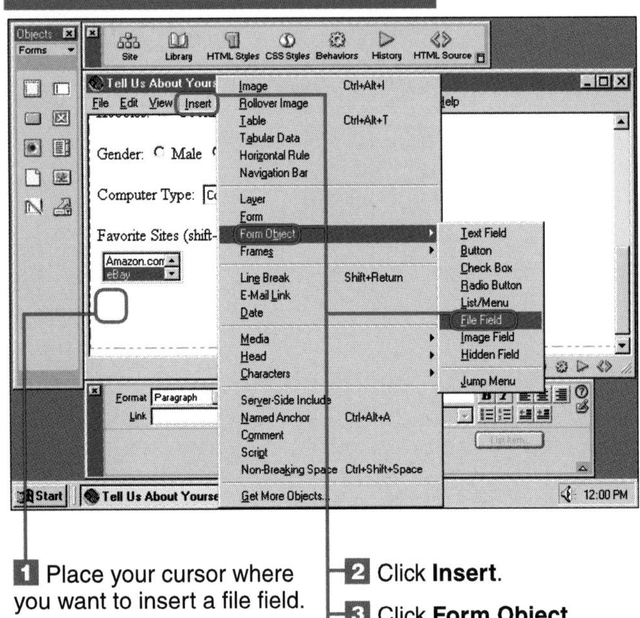

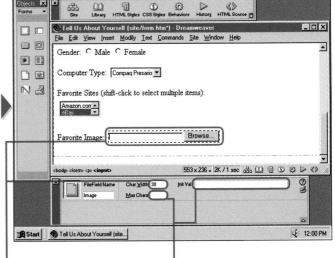

1 Place your cursor where you want to insert a file field.

Note: To set up a form, see the Section "Set Up a Form."

2 Click **Insert**.

3 Click **Form Object**.

4 Click **File Field**.

■ Dreamweaver adds a text field and Browse button to your Web page.

■ You can set the width of the text field where the file path is entered.

■ If you want to limit the number of characters that users may enter, type a value.

■ To have a default file path appear in the text field, type it into the Init Val field.

ADD HIDDEN INFORMATION TO A FORM

You can use hidden form fields to add information to your Web page without the user viewing it.

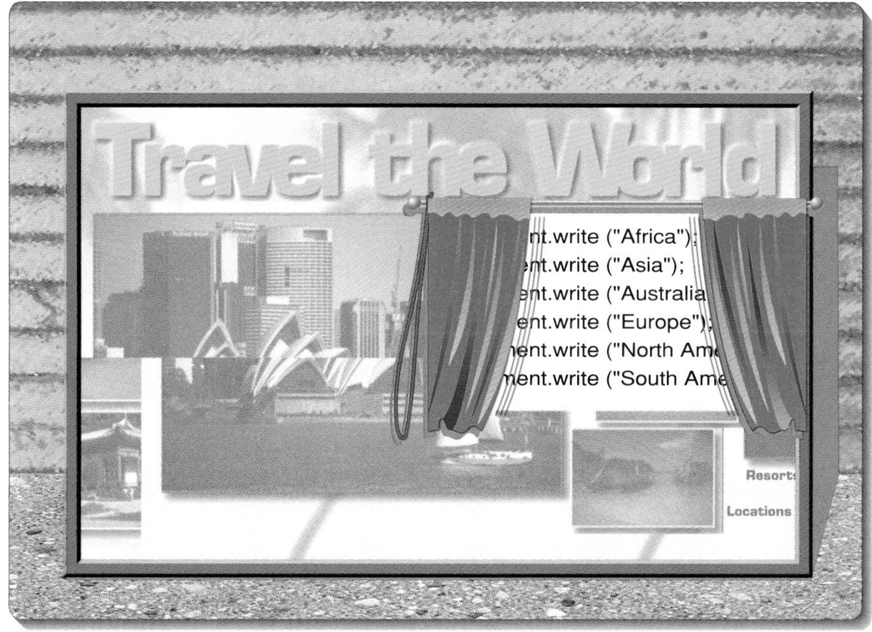

ADD HIDDEN INFORMATION TO A FORM

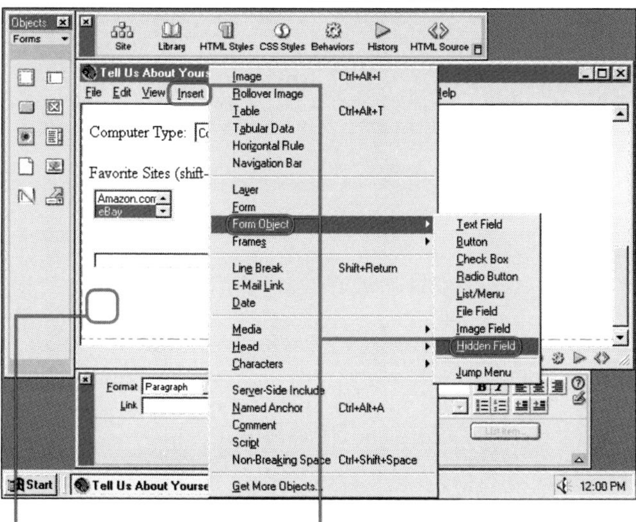

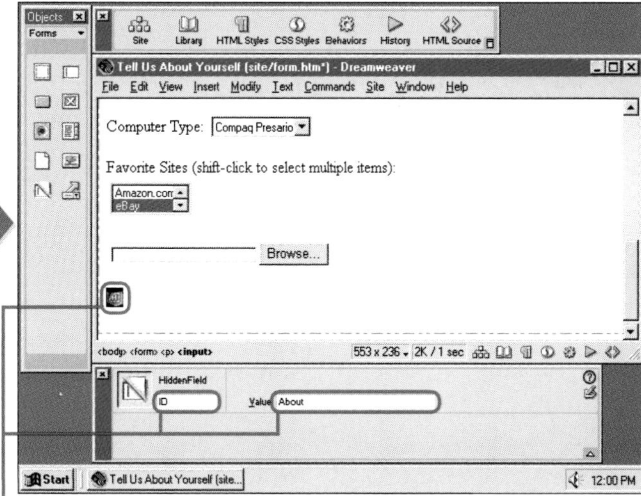

1 Place your cursor where you want to insert the hidden field.

Note: To set up a form, see the Section "Set Up a Form."

2 Click **Insert**.

3 Click **Form Object**.

4 Click **Hidden Field**.

■ The hidden field displays as a hidden field icon in the Document window.

5 Type a name for the hidden field.

6 Type a value to the hidden field.

■ Hidden fields often contain configuration information that the form handler needs to process the form correctly.

ADD A SUBMIT BUTTON TO A FORM

You can add a button that enables users to send the form information to the form handler.

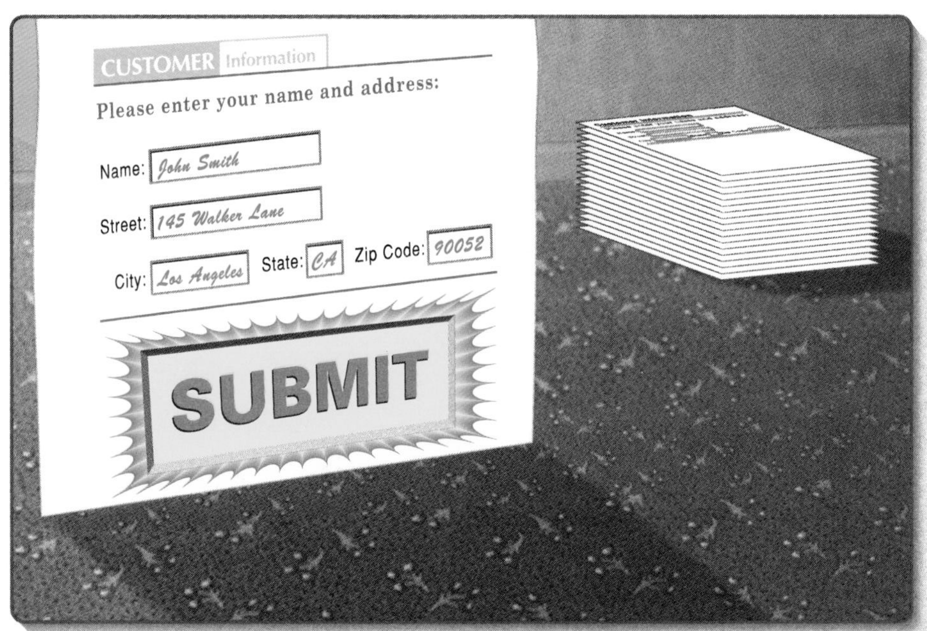

ADD A SUBMIT BUTTON TO A FORM

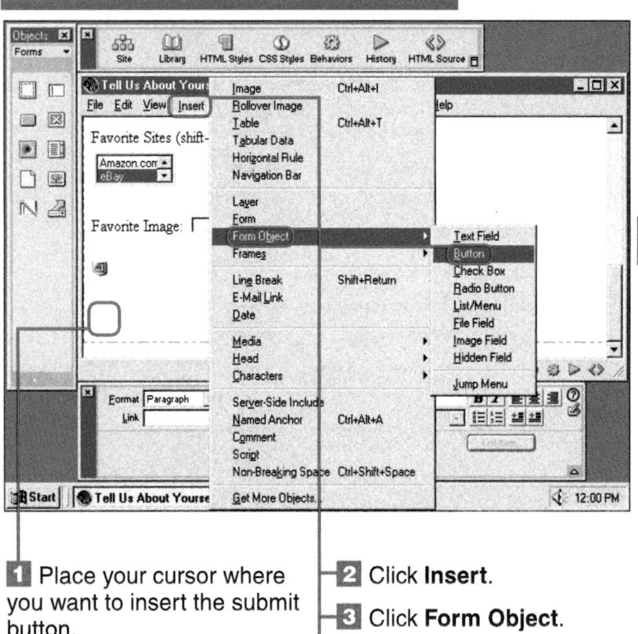

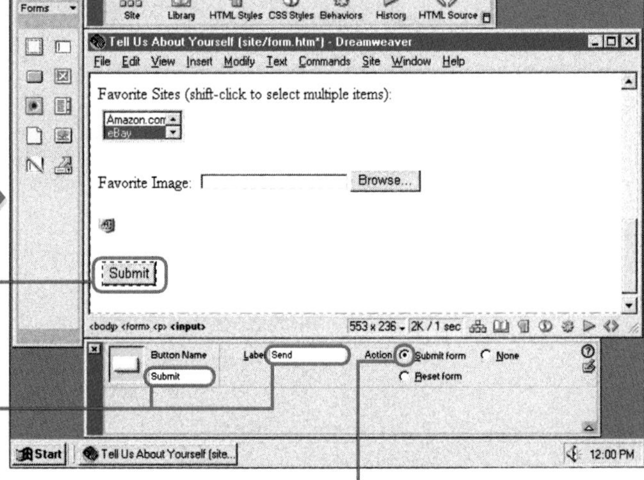

1 Place your cursor where you want to insert the submit button.

Note: To set up a form, see the Section "Set Up a Form."

2 Click **Insert**.

3 Click **Form Object**.

4 Click **Button**.

■ A button appears.

■ You can name the button (example: **Submit**).

5 Type a value in the Label field (example: **Send**).

■ The value appears as text on the button.

6 Select Submit form (○ changes to ◉).

■ When clicked, the submit button sends information to the form handler.

Note: To add the form handler's address to the form, see the Section "Set Up a Form."

ADD A RESET BUTTON TO A FORM

You can add a button to your form that allows users the option of reverting the form to its default values.

ADD A RESET BUTTON TO A FORM

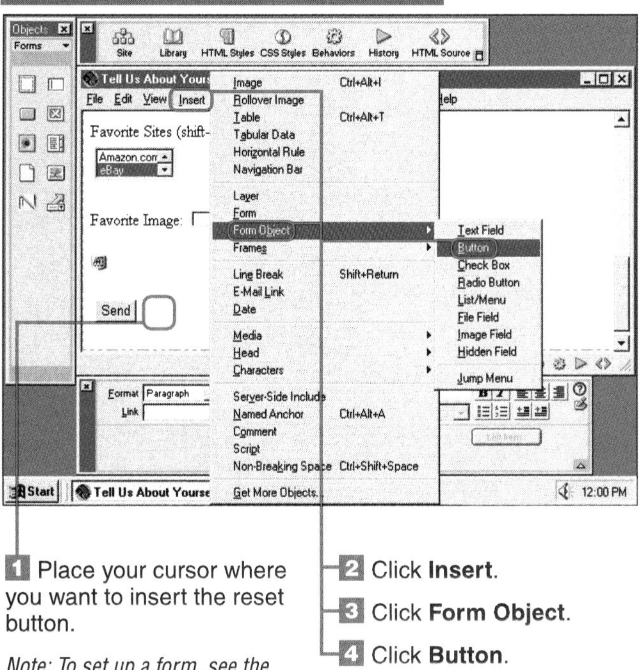

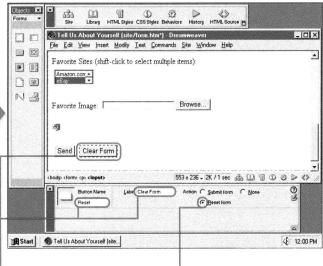

1 Place your cursor where you want to insert the reset button.

Note: To set up a form, see the Section "Set Up a Form."

2 Click **Insert**.

3 Click **Form Object**.

4 Click **Button**.

■ Dreamweaver adds a button to your Web page.

■ You can assign a name to the button (example: **Reset**).

5 Type a value for the Label field (example: **Clear Form**).

6 Select the Reset Form radio button (○ changes to ◉).

■ When the user clicks the Reset button, the browser returns all the objects in the form to their default state.

Reservations
Schedules
Travel Tips
Arrivals
Departures
Sunshine VACATIONS
Plan Your Vacation With Us
At Sunshine Vacations, we make all your vacations memorable ones. Call us today to plan your next trip!
9000

Designing with Frames

Frames can help you organize the information in your Web site. This chapter shows you how to create framed pages.

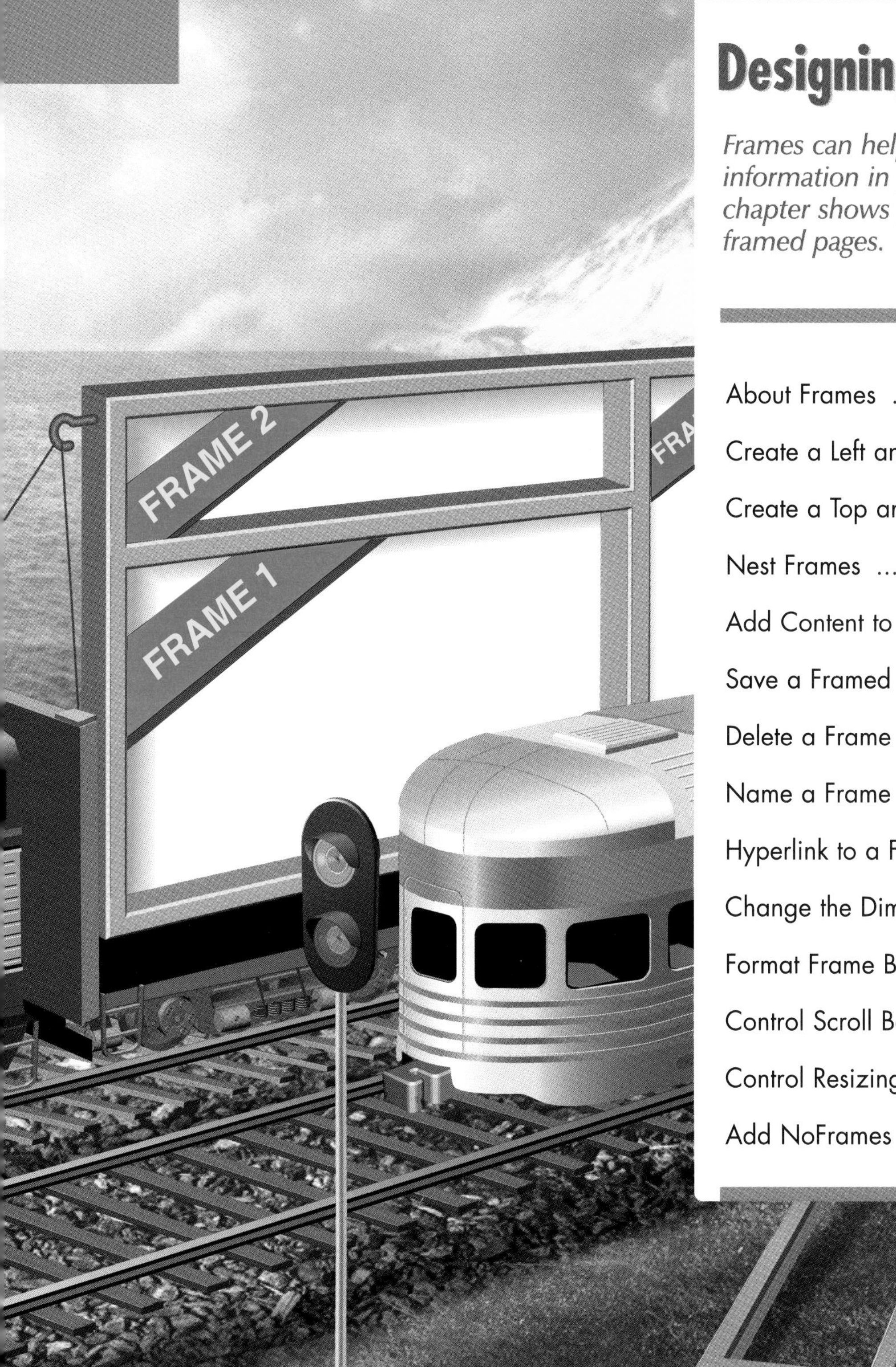

ABOUT FRAMES

In Dreamweaver, you can create frames by dividing a browser window into smaller windows. Each window can display a different Web page.

EAGLE
PUBLISHING

EAGLE PUBLISHING, INC.

Are you looking for a great romance novel? How about science fiction? Or would you prefer a mystery? Whatever you enjoy reading, you're sure to find the perfect book among the new spring releases from Eagle Publishing, Inc. If you would like more information about a book, click on the link corresponding to that book to instantly go to another Web page that presents an in-depth plot summary, an interview with the author and a full-color photo of the book.

Romance

Sophia Love's first novel, Romance in Rome*, was a bestseller, and the highly talented writer now returns with* Passion in Paris*. Love's latest novel features the same intensely romantic writing style that made her first work an international hit.*

Fan favorite Kenny Shaw has worked his magic once again in Symphony of the Heart*, the bittersweet story of a love triangle set in the world of the New York Symphony Orchestra.*

SETTING UP FRAMES

You create a framed Web site by dividing the Document window horizontally or vertically one or more times. You then load a Web page into each frame.

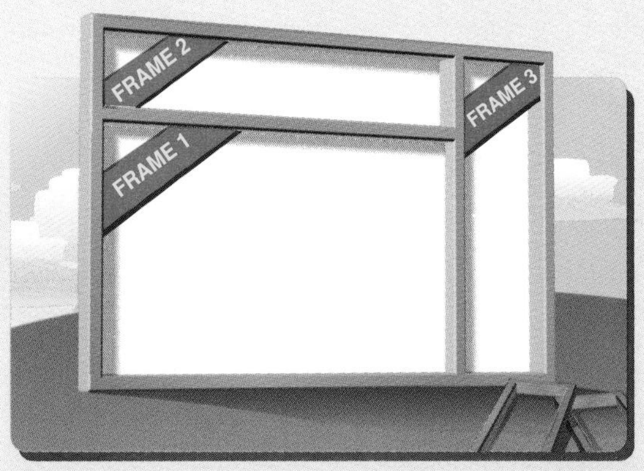

HOW FRAMES WORK

Frames operate independently of one another. As you scroll through the content of a frame, the other frames remain fixed. You can create hyperlinks in one frame that open pages in other frames.

CREATE A LEFT AND RIGHT FRAME

You can split a Document window horizontally to create a frameset with left and right frames.

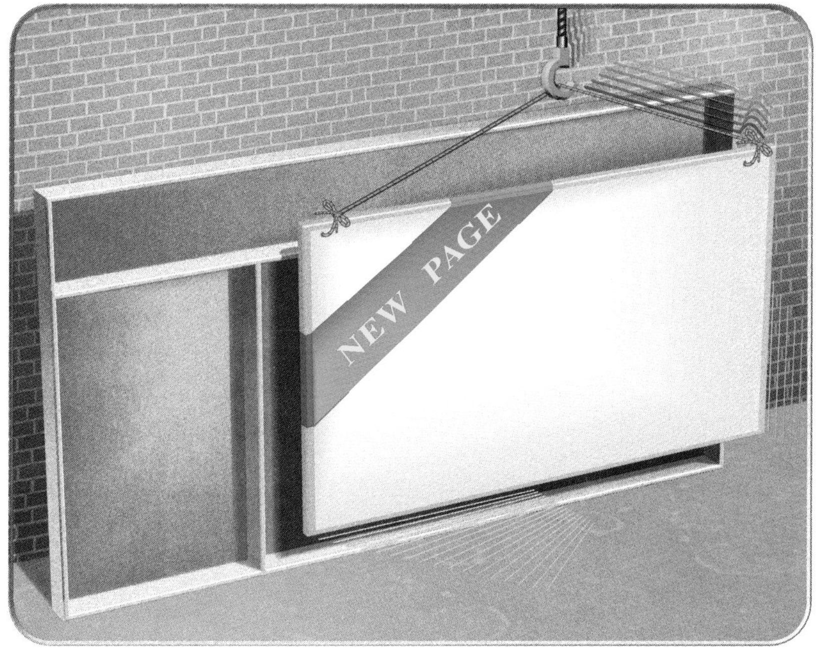

CREATE A LEFT AND RIGHT FRAME

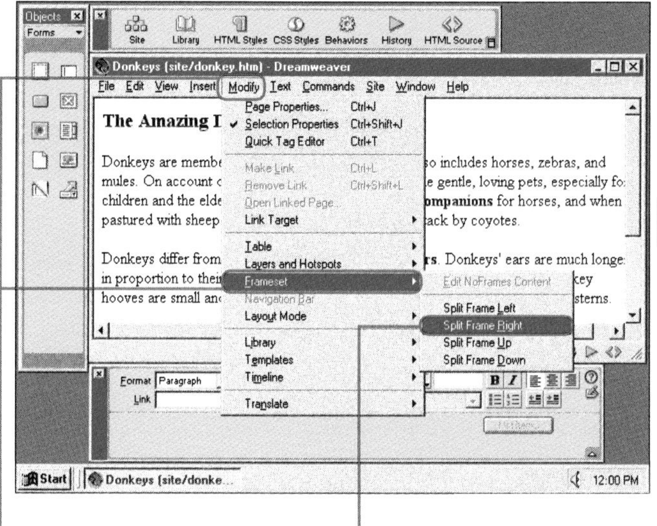

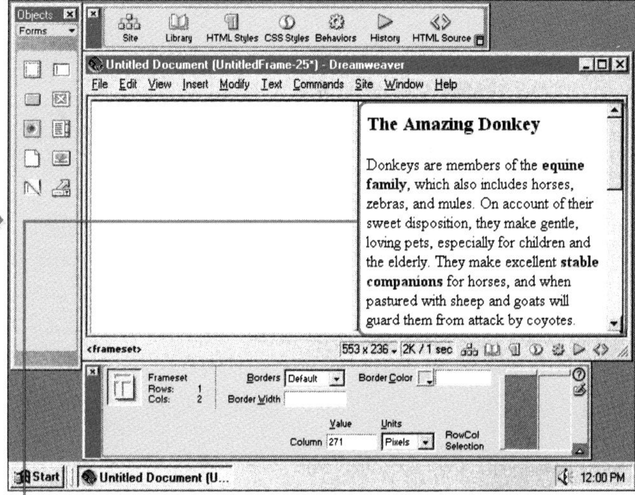

1 Click **Modify**.

2 Click **Frameset**.

3 Click **Split Frame Right** or **Split Frame Left** (example: **Split Frame Right**).

■ The window splits into left and right frames. Information shifts according to your selecton.

Note: To add content to an empty frame, see the section "Add Content to a Frame."

Note: To save your framed page, see the section "Save a Framed Page."

CREATE A TOP AND BOTTOM FRAME

You can split a Document window vertically to create a frameset with a top and bottom frame.

CREATE A TOP AND BOTTOM FRAME

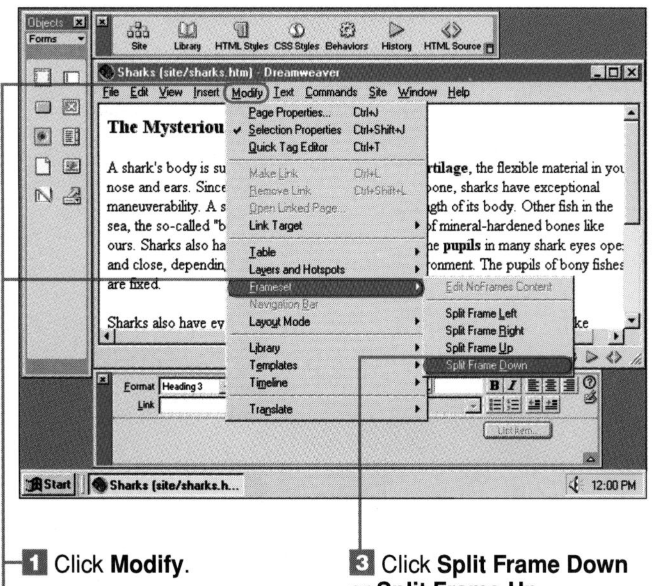

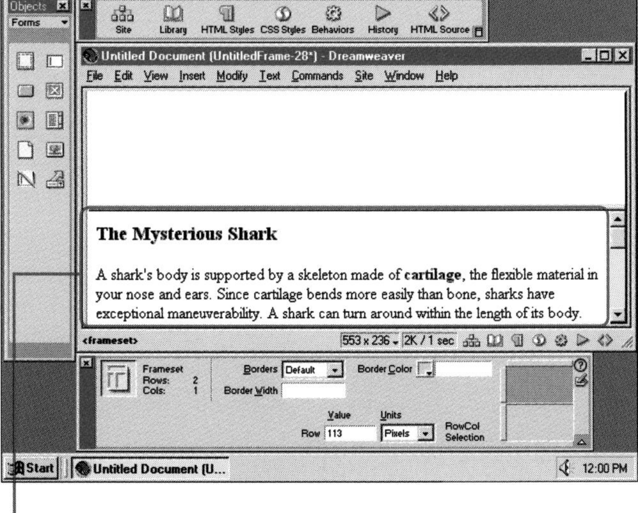

1 Click **Modify**.

2 Click **Frameset**.

3 Click **Split Frame Down** or **Split Frame Up** (example: **Split Frame Up**).

■ The window splits into top and bottom frames. Information shifts according to your selection.

Note: To add content in an empty frame, see the section "Add Content to a Frame."

Note: To save your framed page, see the section "Save a Framed Page."

With Dreamweaver you can subdivide an existing frame to create a nested frameset, which gives you more frames in which to organize your information.

NEST FRAMES

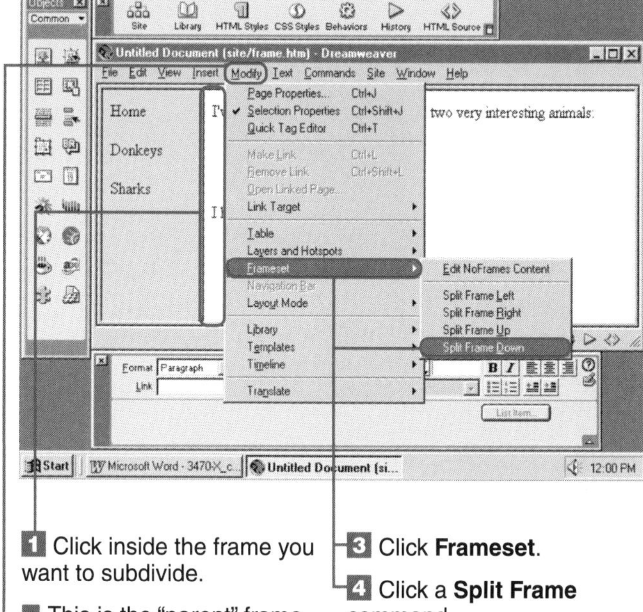

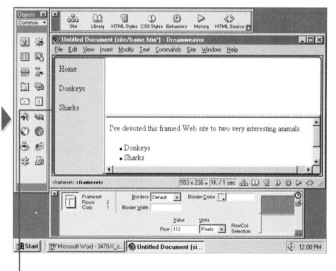

1 Click inside the frame you want to subdivide.

■ This is the "parent" frame.

2 Click **Modify**.

3 Click **Frameset**.

4 Click a **Split Frame** command.

■ Dreamweaver splits the selected frame into two frames. You now have a frameset inside a frameset.

Note: To add content to the empty frame see the section "Add Content to a Frame."

■ You can continue to split frames into more frames.

ADD CONTENT TO A FRAME

You can add content to a frame by opening an existing HTML document in the frame. You can also add content by typing text or inserting elements into a frame just as you would an unframed page.

ADD CONTENT TO A FRAME

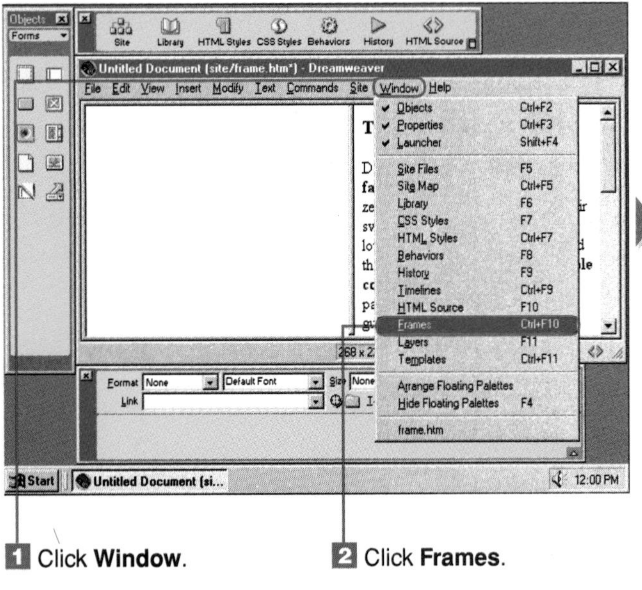

1 Click **Window**.

2 Click **Frames**.

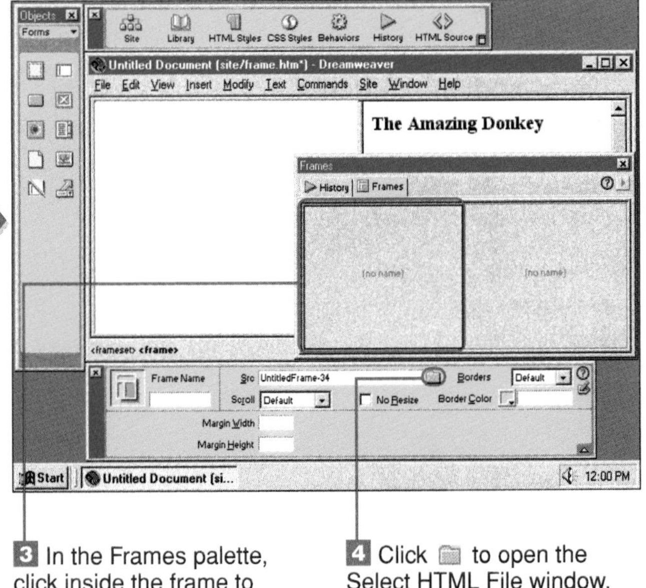

3 In the Frames palette, click inside the frame to which you want to add content.

4 Click [folder icon] to open the Select HTML File window.

■ The Select HTML file window opens.

Can I load a page from a different Web site into one of my frames?

Yes. To load an external Web page into a frame, enter the page's address in the URL field of the Select HTML File window (see Step 5 in this section). Because Dreamweaver cannot display external files, the external page does not appear in the Document window; it appears when you open the document online in a Web browser.

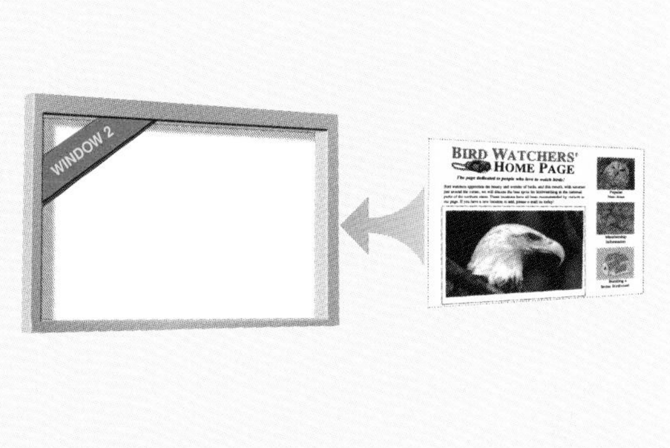

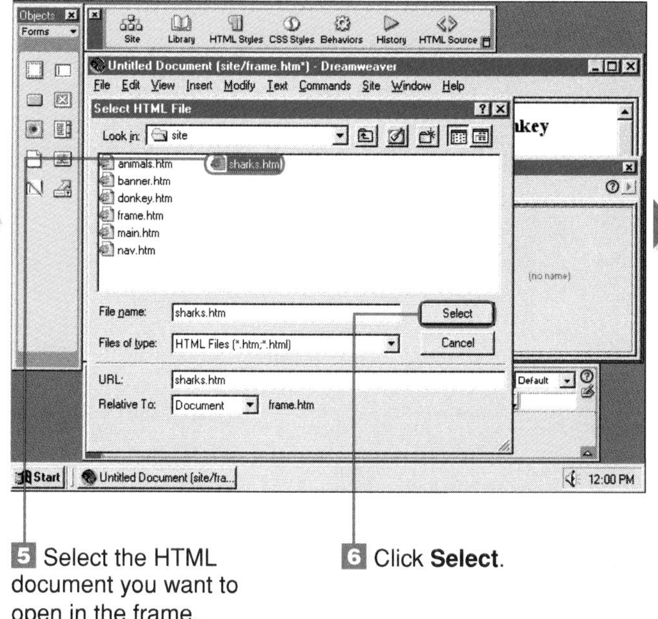

5 Select the HTML document you want to open in the frame.

6 Click **Select**.

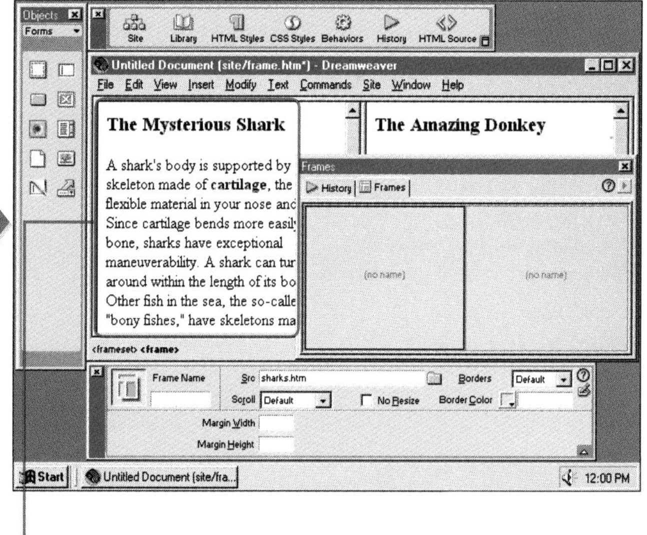

■ Dreamweaver displays the document in the frame.

SAVE A FRAMED PAGE

Saving your framed Web page requires you to save all documents in the individual frames as well as the page's frameset.

SAVE INDIVIDUAL FRAMES

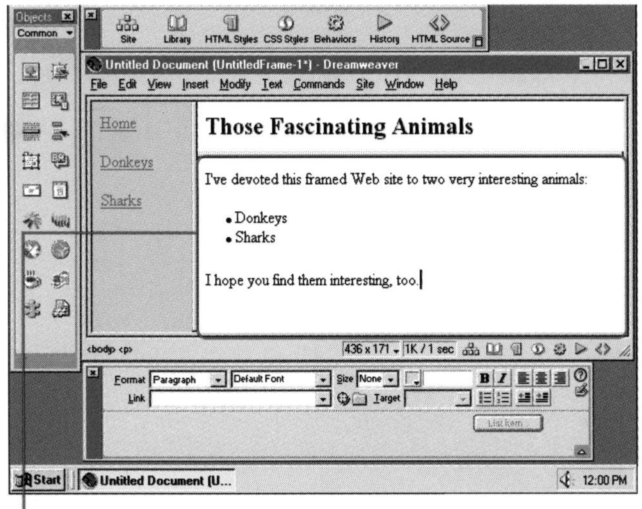

1 To save an HTML file in a frame, click inside one of the frames of the Web page.

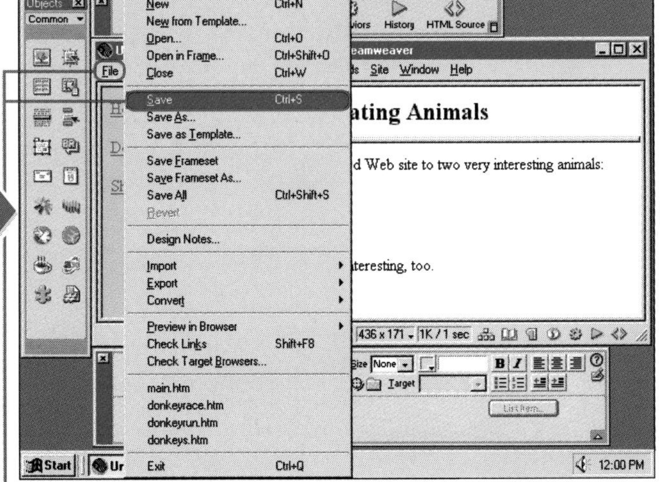

2 Click **File**.

3 Click **Save**.

Note: If the Save button is grayed out, you do not need to save the frame.

TEACH YOURSELF TY

Is there a shortcut for saving all the documents in my framed page?

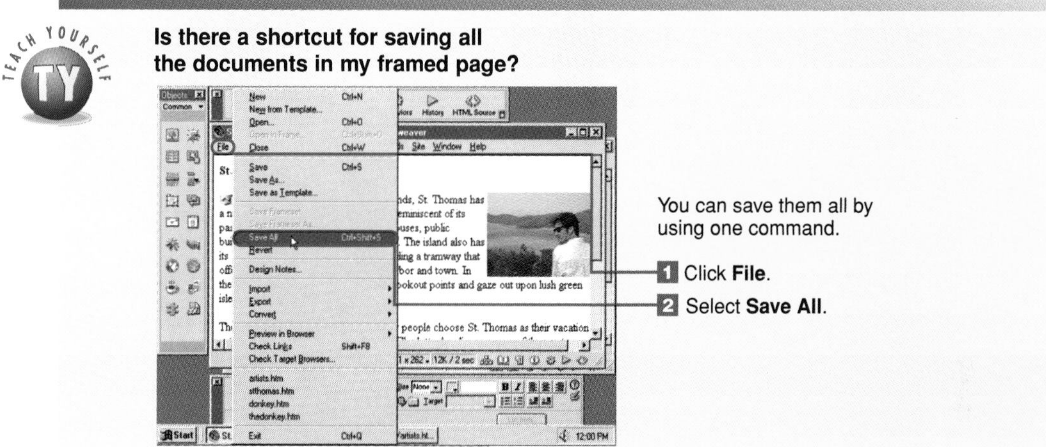

You can save them all by using one command.

1 Click **File**.

2 Select **Save All**.

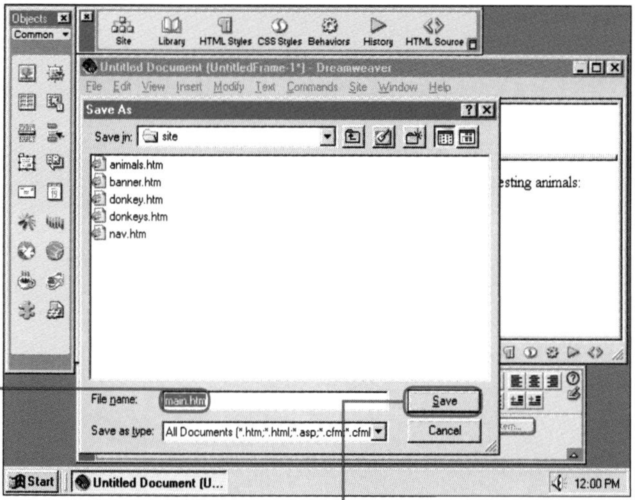

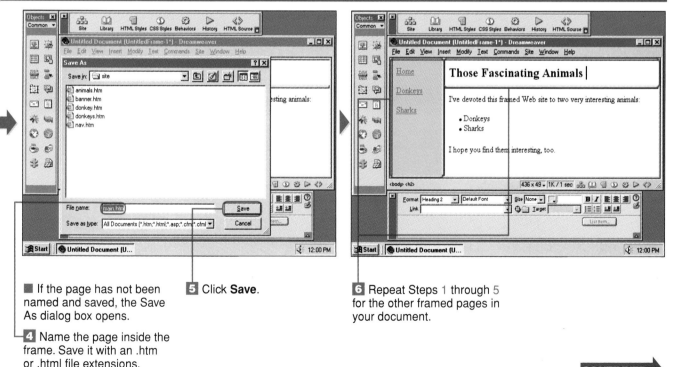

■ If the page has not been named and saved, the Save As dialog box opens.

4 Name the page inside the frame. Save it with an .htm or .html file extensions.

5 Click **Save**.

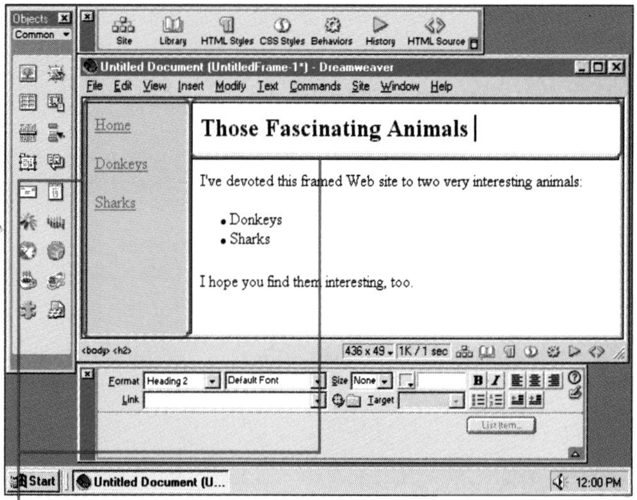

6 Repeat Steps 1 through 5 for the other framed pages in your document.

CONTINUED

To finish saving your framed page, you must save the frameset. The frameset is a separate HTML document that defines the dimensions, organization, and other characteristics of the framed page. It must be saved separately.

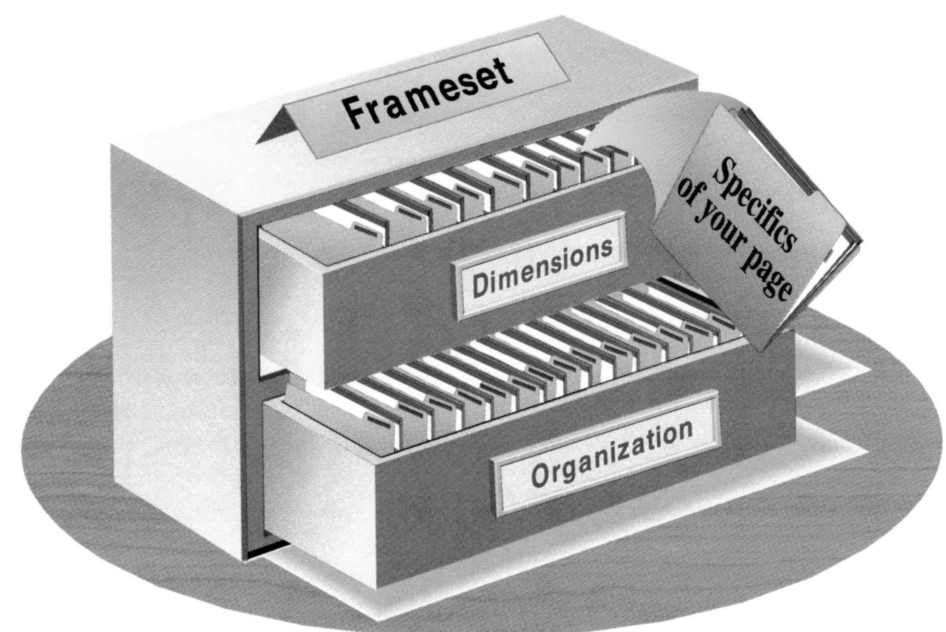

SAVE THE FRAMESET

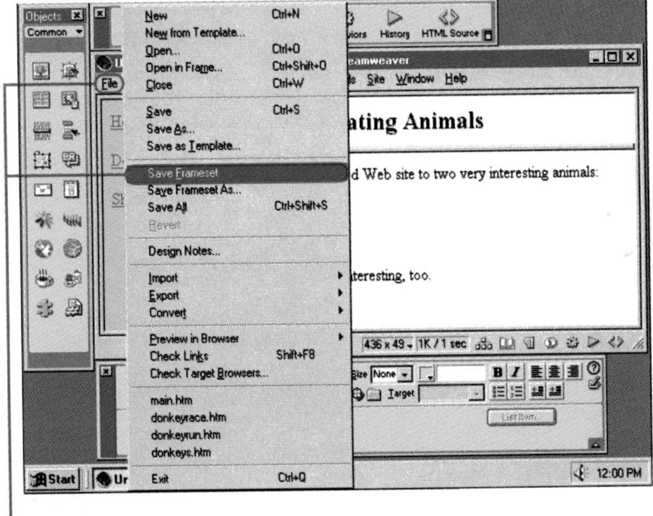

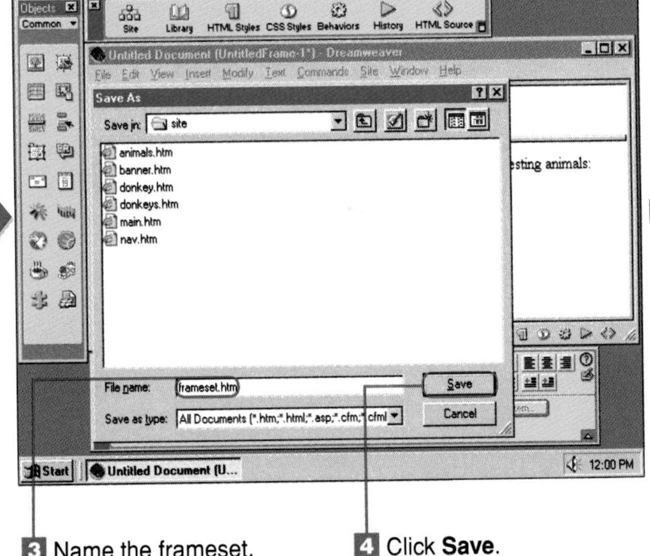

1 Click **File**.

2 Click **Save Frameset**.

■ If the frameset has not been named and saved, a Save As dialog box opens.

3 Name the frameset.

Note: Because framesets are HTML documents, they require .htm or .html file extensions.

4 Click **Save**.

Can pages saved as part of a frameset be viewed on their own outside the frameset?

Yes. The pages inside frames are HTML documents and can be viewed separately just like any other HTML document.

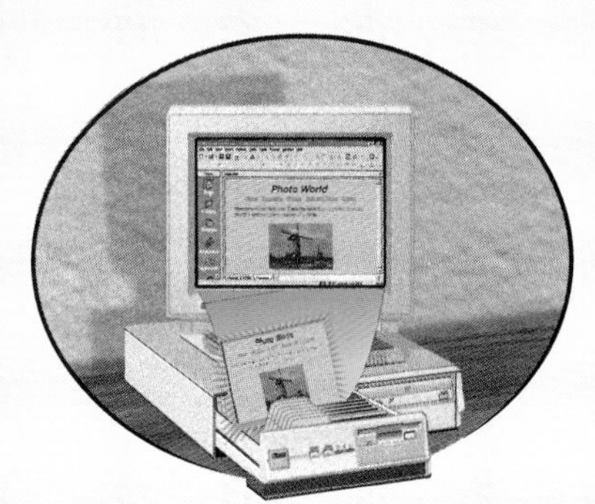

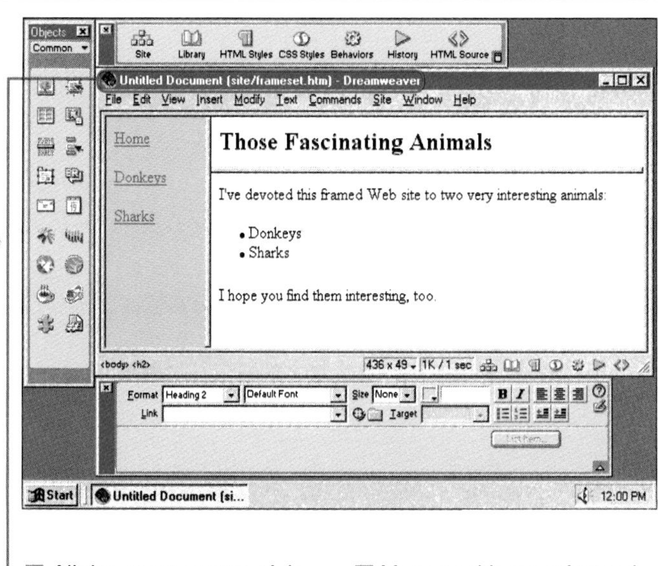

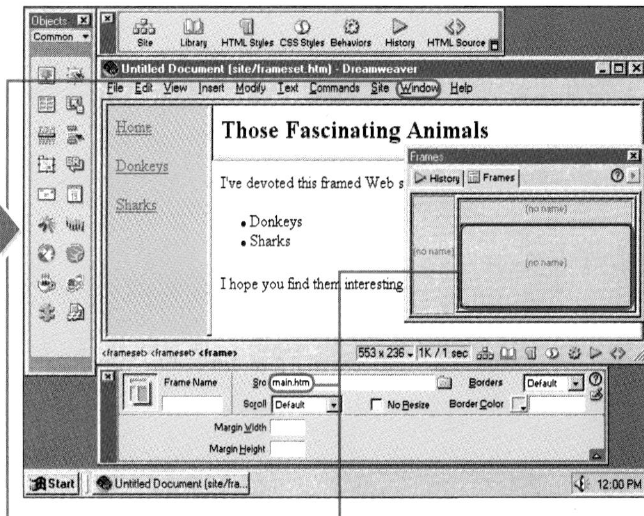

■ All the components of the framed Web page are now saved.

■ The frameset name appears in the Document window bar.

■ You can title your framed Web page the same way you title a non-framed Web page.

Note: See Chapter 2 to title your framed web page.

■ You can view the saved filenames of the pages in each frame with the Frames inspector.

5 Select **Window** and select **Frames**.

■ The Frame palette appears.

6 Click inside a frame.

■ The filename appears in the Src field.

DELETE A FRAME

You can delete a frame by clicking and dragging to minimize it.

DELETE A FRAME

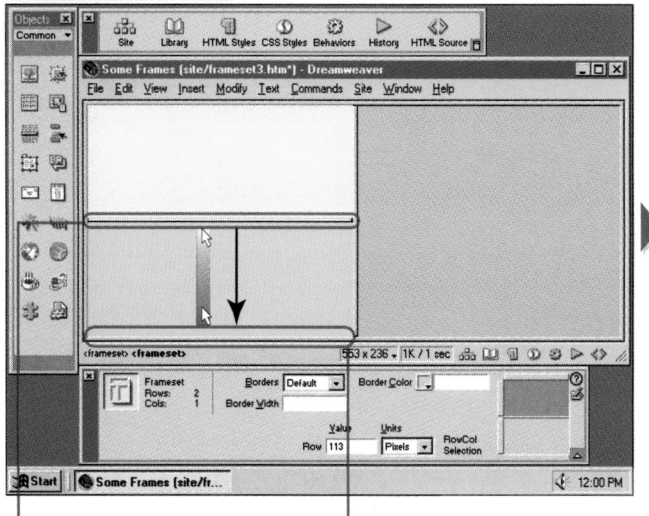

1 Click and drag the border of the frame you want to delete.

2 Drag the border to the edge of the window.

■ The frame is deleted.

NAME A FRAME

Dreamweaver enables you to name a frame so that it can be referenced by a hyperlink. This allows hyperlinks to open up new Web pages in a different frame.

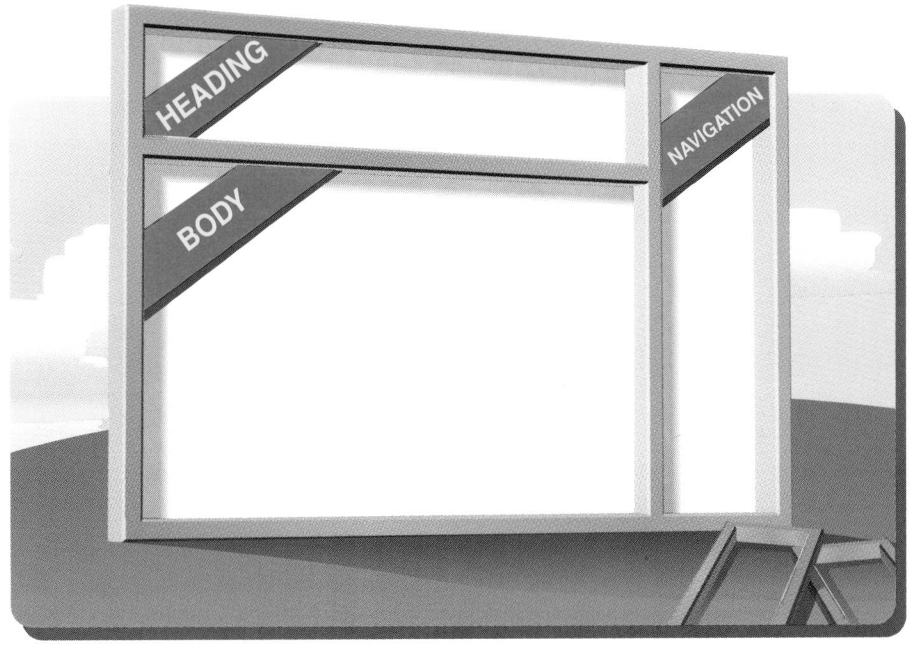

NAME A FRAME

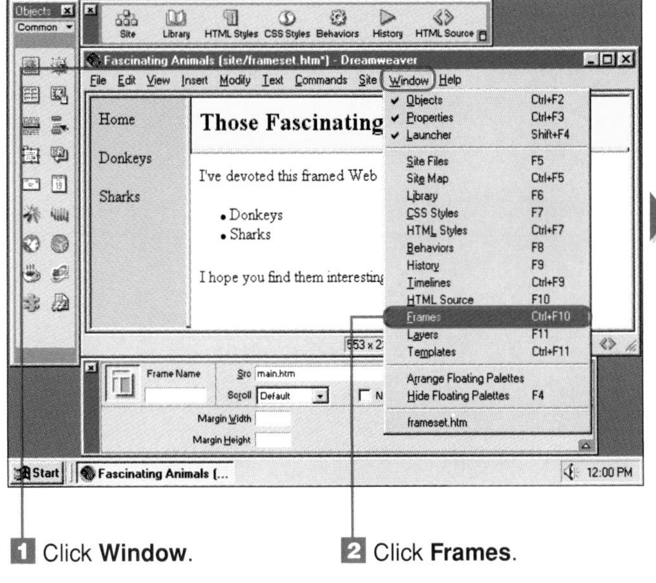

1 Click **Window**.

2 Click **Frames**.

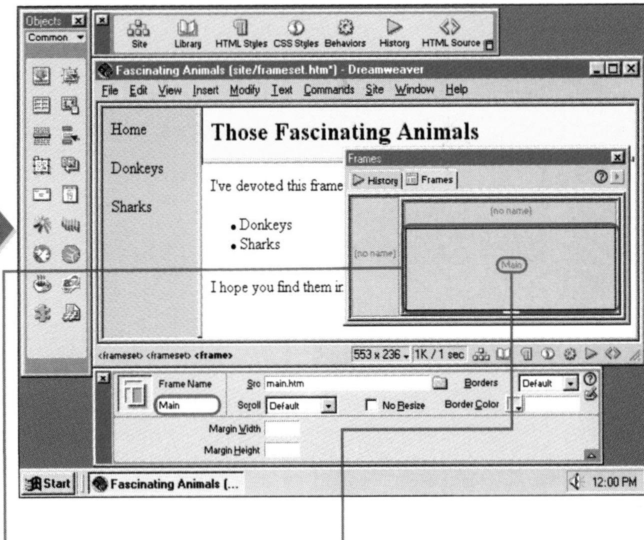

3 Click inside the frame you want to name.

4 Type a name for the frame.

5 Press **Enter** (**Return**).

■ The name of the frame appears in the Frames window.

HYPERLINK TO A FRAME

You can create a hyperlink that opens a page in a different frame.

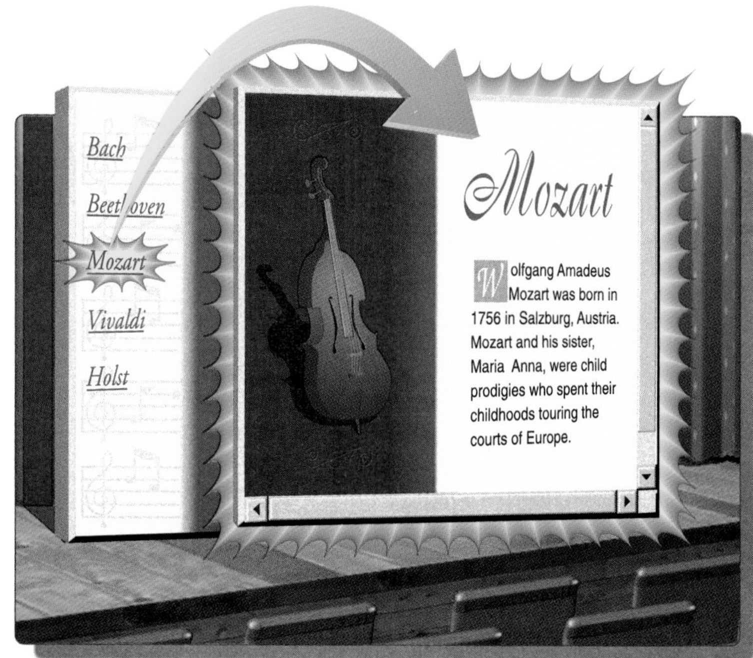

HYPERLINK TO A FRAME

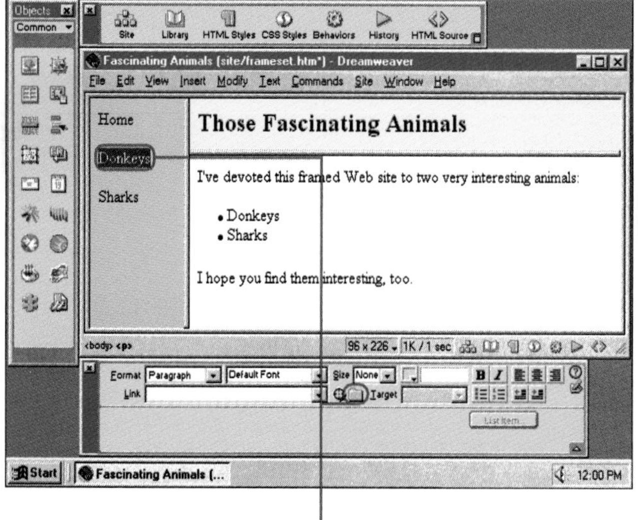

Note: For the hyperlink to work correctly, you must name the target frame. To name a frame, see the Section "Name a Frame."

1 Select the text to be hyperlinked.

2 Click ▢.

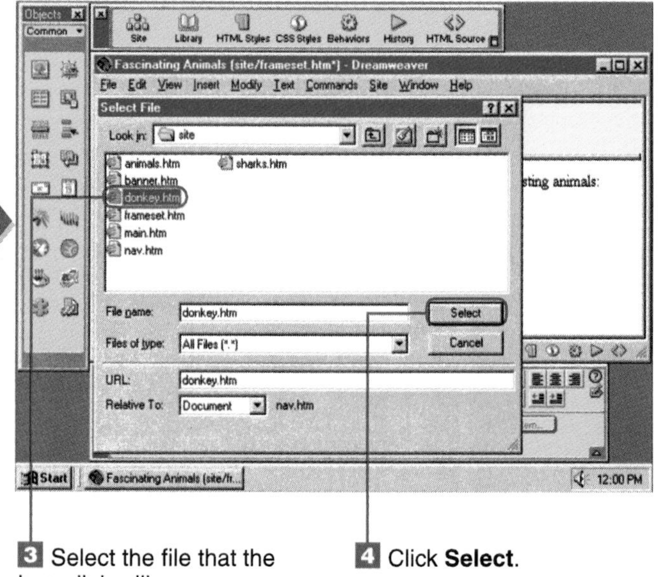

3 Select the file that the hyperlink will open.

4 Click **Select**.

What do some of the special items in the Target Menu do?

-**blank** causes a link to open in a new browser window.

-**top** causes a link to open on top of the current page, replacing any existing framesets.

-**parent** causes the link to open in the parent frame (the frame enclosing the hyperlink frame in a nested frameset).

-**self** causes the link to open in the same frame as the link (the default behavior of a hyperlink).

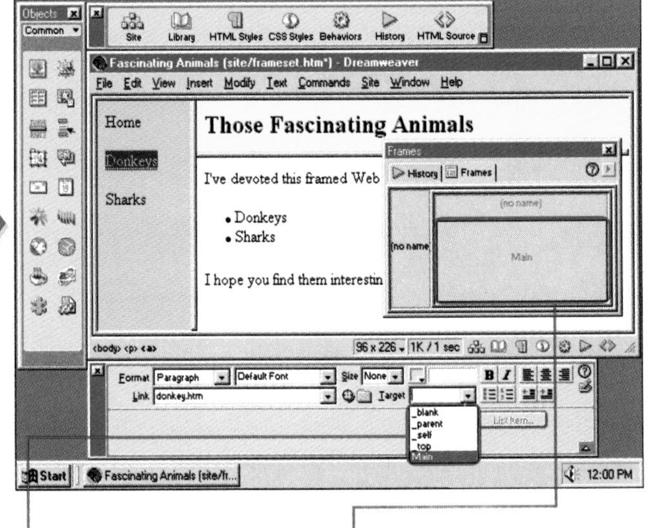

5 Select the name of the frame where the target file will open. If you have named the frame, it appears in the menu.

■ You can also view the frame names in the Frames window (to open it, select **Window⇨Frames**).

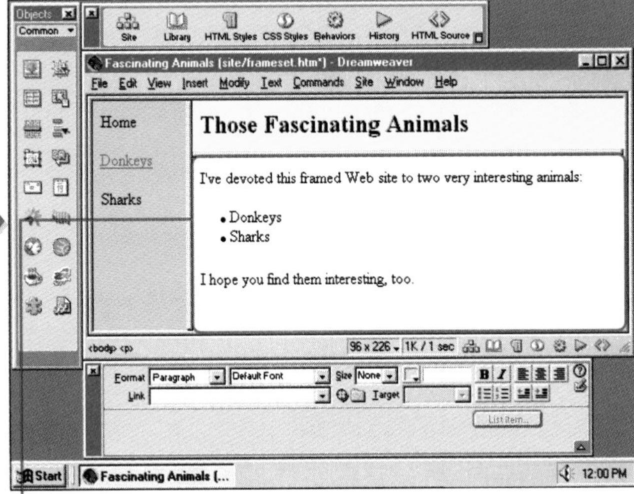

■ When you open the framed page in a Web browser and click the hyperlink, the destination page opens inside the targeted frame.

CHANGE THE DIMENSIONS OF A FRAME

By changing the dimensions of a frame you can display its information more effectively.

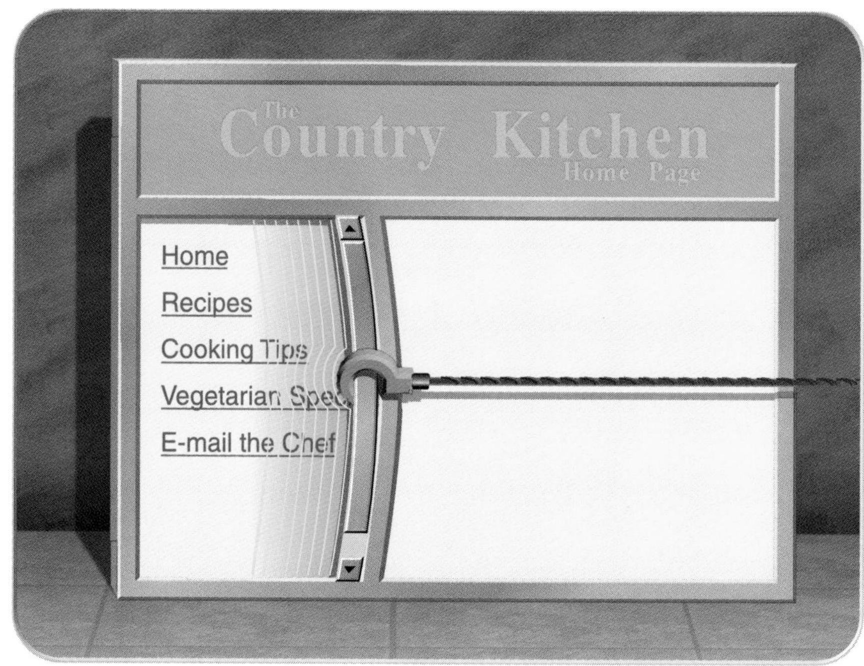

CHANGE THE DIMENSIONS OF A FRAME

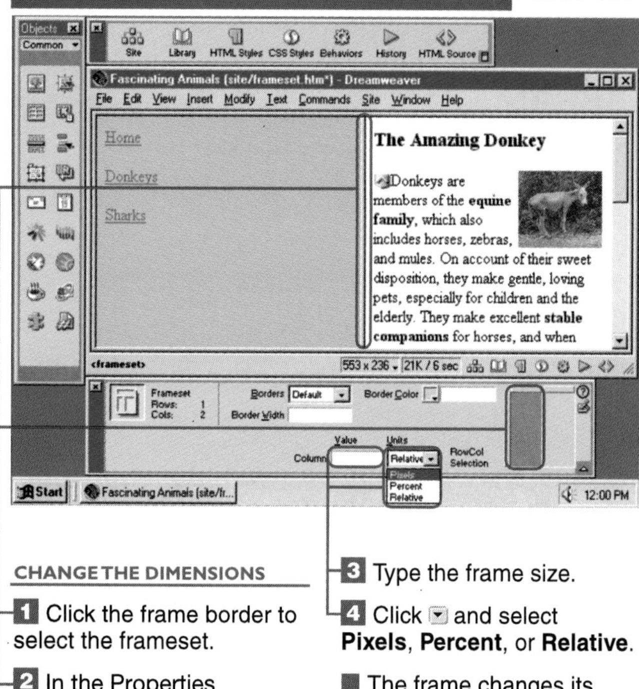

CHANGE THE DIMENSIONS

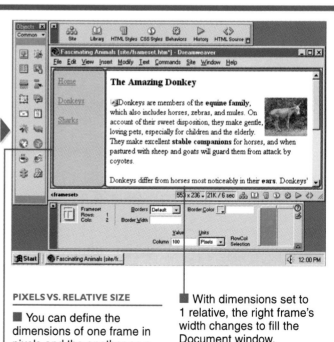

1. Click the frame border to select the frameset.
2. In the Properties Inspector, click the frame whose dimensions you want to change.
3. Type the frame size.
4. Click ▾ and select **Pixels**, **Percent**, or **Relative**.

■ The frame changes its dimensions.

PIXELS VS. RELATIVE SIZE

■ You can define the dimensions of one frame in pixels and the another as a relative size.

■ In this example, the left frame's width is 100 pixels. Its width remains static.

■ With dimensions set to 1 relative, the right frame's width changes to fill the Document window.

Is there a quick way to change the dimensions of a frameset?

You can click and drag a frame border to quickly adjust the dimensions of a frameset. The values in the Properties inspector change accordingly.

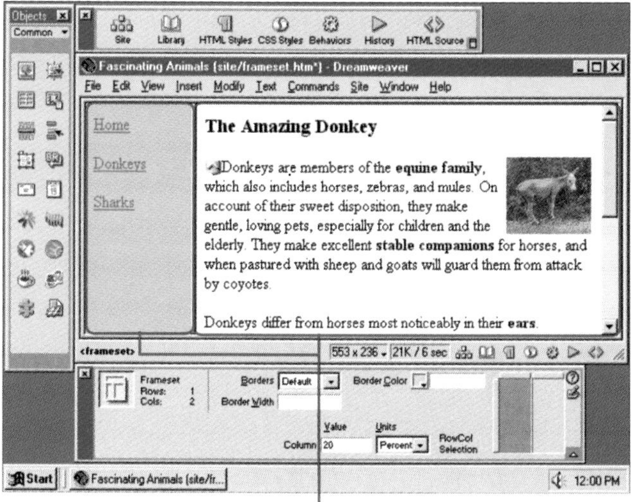

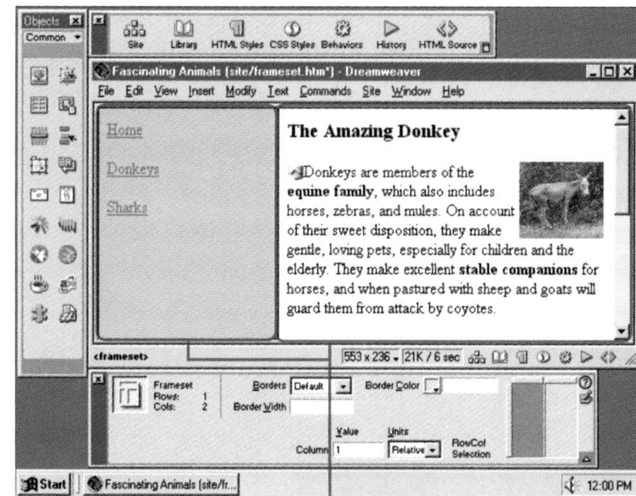

CHANGE THE PERCENTAGE

■ You can allocate the window area proportionally by defining frame dimensions as percentages.

■ In this example, the left frame's width is 20 percent and takes up one-fifth of the window.

■ The frame's width is 80 percent and it takes up four-fifths of the window.

CHANGE THE RELATIVE SIZE

■ Relative sizes for frames are similar to percentage sizes. They enable you to allocate the window area proportionally.

■ In this example, the left frame's relative width is set to 1.

■ Set to 2 relative, the right frame's width takes up twice as much space as the other frame.

FORMAT FRAME BORDERS

To create an eye-catching Web pages, Dreamweaver enables you to change the appearance, size, and color of frame borders.

FORMAT FRAME BORDERS

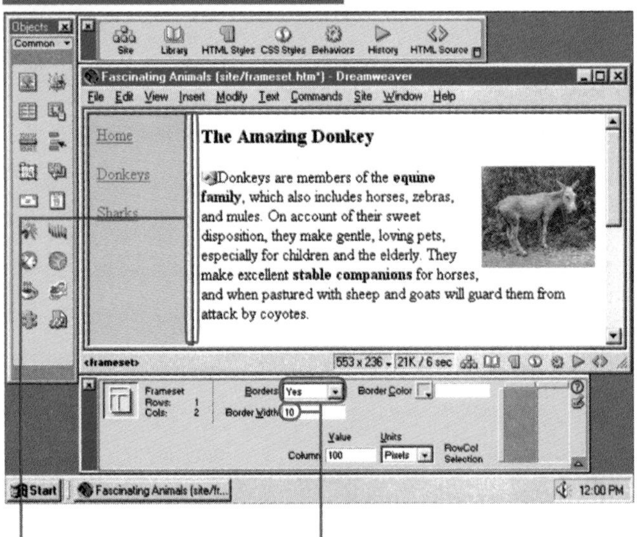

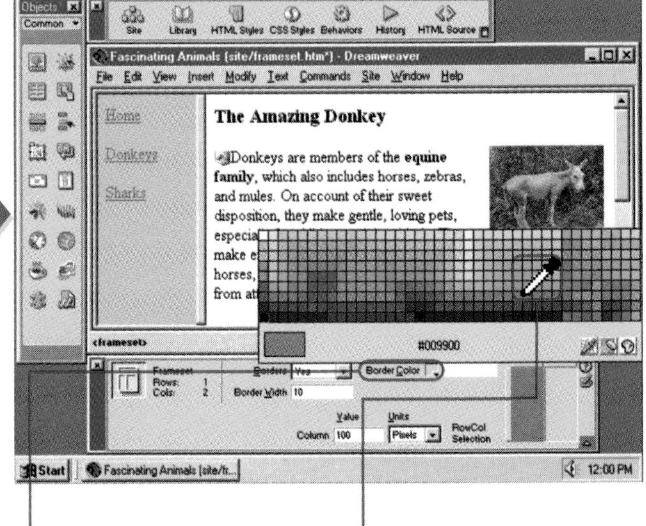

1 Click the frame border to select the frameset.

■ The Properties inspector displays the frameset's information.

2 Click ▼ and select **Yes**, **No**, or **Default** in the Borders menu. This controls whether or not borders appear (most browsers display borders as the default).

3 Type a size in pixels for the frame borders.

4 Click the **Border Color** swatch to open the color menu.

5 Select a color by using the eyedropper tool.

Why would I want to make a frame border invisible?

You may not want the visitors to your site to realize you have used frames. You can do this by turning off frame borders and making the background color identical for all the framed pages.

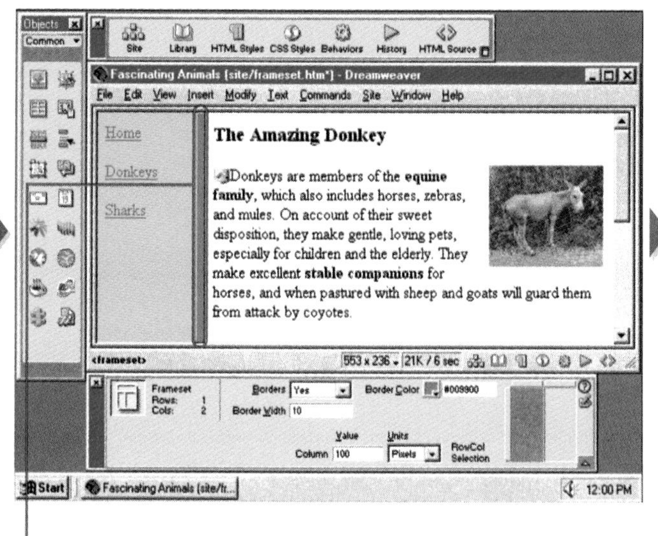

■ In this example, the frameset has a green, 10-pixel-wide border.

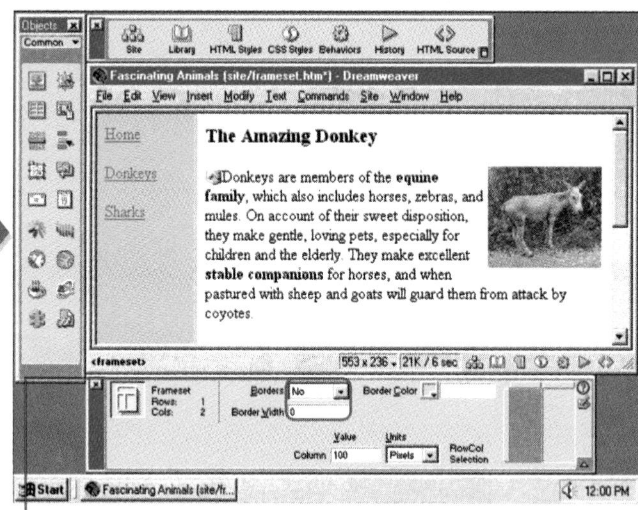

■ To eliminate frame borders, select **No** in the Borders menu and **0** in the Border Width menu. The border is invisible when viewed in a Web browser.

CONTROL SCROLL BARS IN FRAMES

Dreamweaver enables you to control whether or not scroll bars appear in a frame. Scroll bars let users view information that extends outside the borders of your frames.

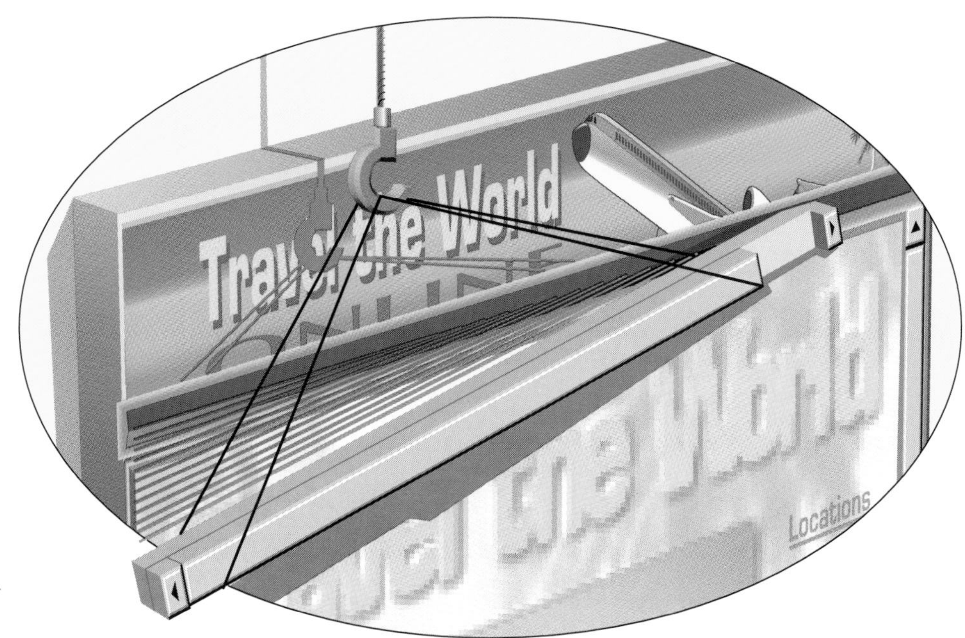

CONTROL SCROLL BARS IN FRAMES

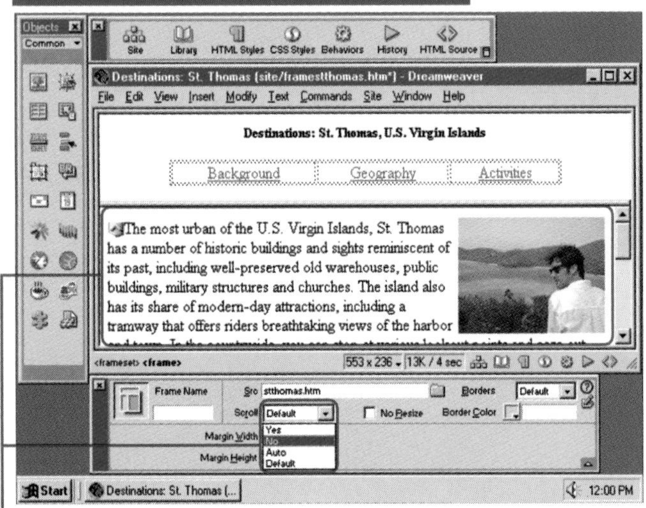

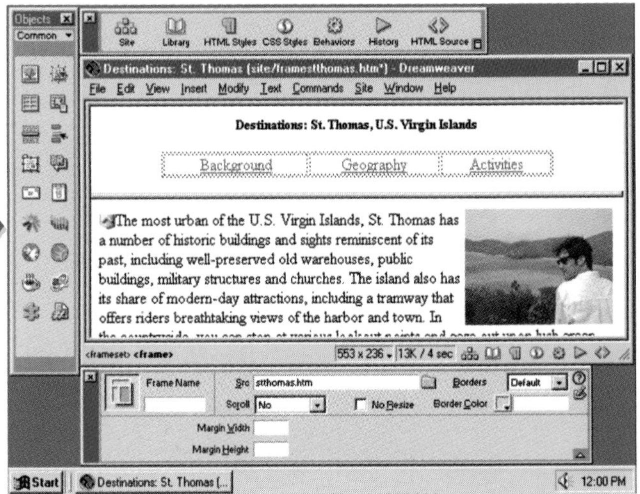

1 Alt-click (Option-click) a frame.

2 Click ▾ and select a value from the Scroll menu.

■ If you select **Auto**, scroll bars appear in the frame when content extends outside the frame. For most browsers, **Default** has the same effect as **Auto**.

■ In this example, scroll bars are turned off in the bottom frame.

Note: Turning scroll bars off may prevent users with low-resolution monitors from accessing all the content on your page.

CONTROL RESIZING OF FRAMES

You can prevent users from resizing your frames. This is useful when you do not want the layout of your frames to ever change. The default behavior for most browsers enables the user to resize frames by clicking and dragging the frame borders.

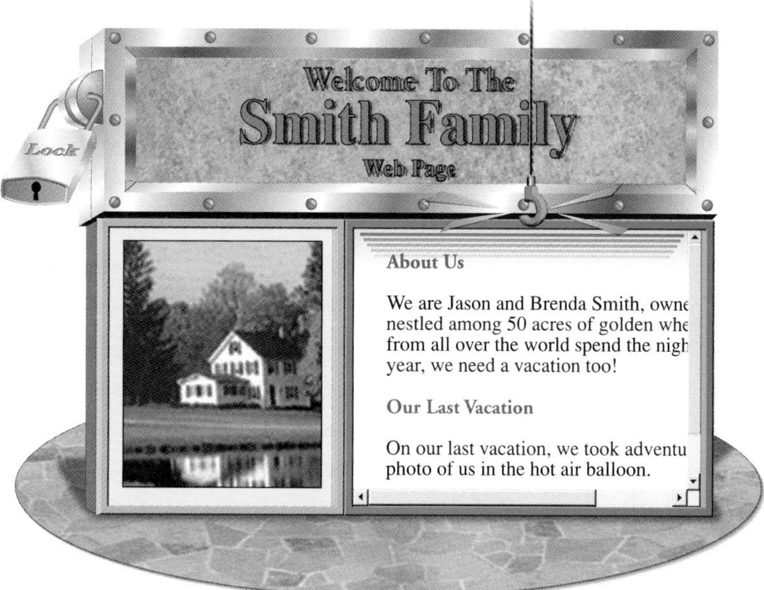

CONTROL RESIZING OF FRAMES

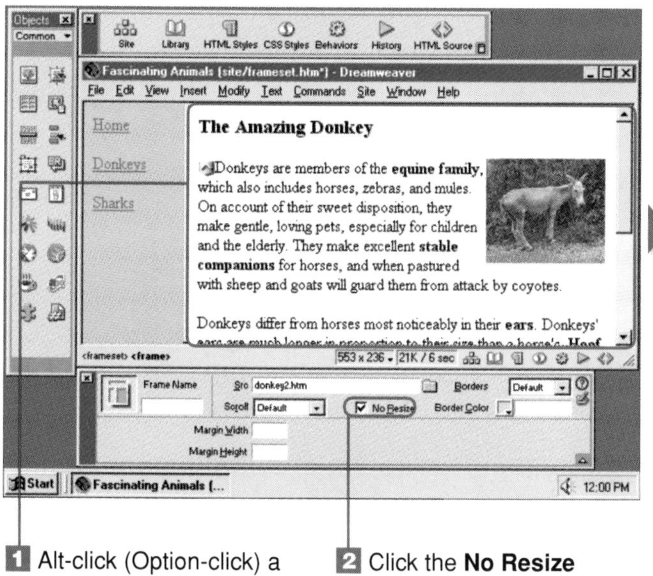

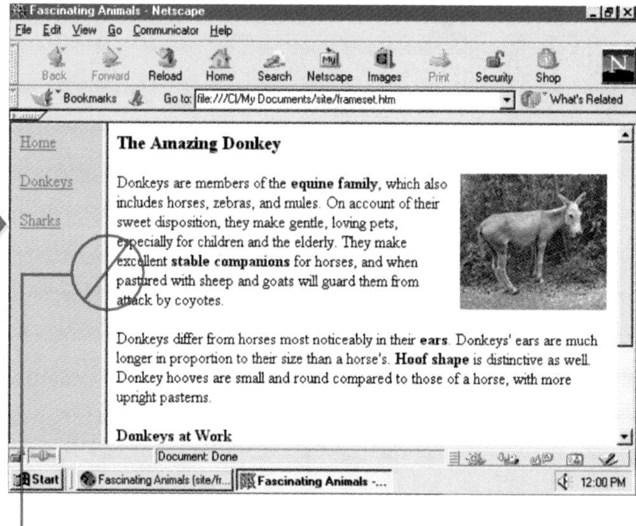

1 Alt-click (Option-click) a frame.

2 Click the **No Resize** check box to prevent resizing of that frame (☐ changes to ☑).

■ Users cannot click and drag the frame border to resize the frameset.

Note: Preventing resizing can keep users from closing a frame. Users might also miss important content.

ADD NOFRAMES CONTENT

Because not every user has a browser that displays frames, you can provide content that displays when these frame-challenged users view your Web site.

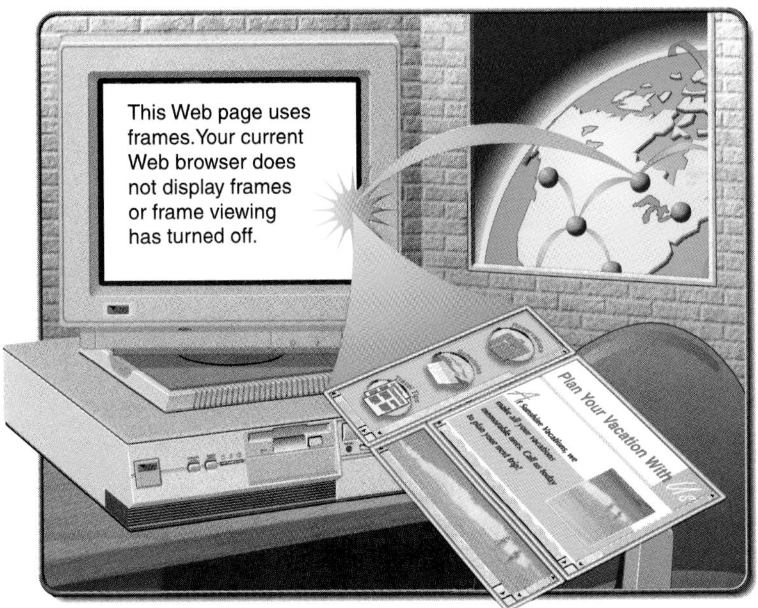
This Web page uses frames. Your current Web browser does not display frames or frame viewing has turned off.
Plan Your Vacation With Us

ADD NOFRAMES CONTENT

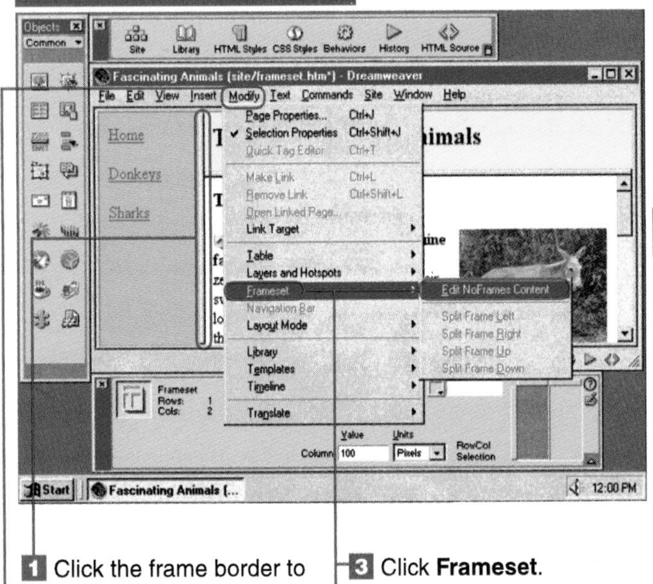

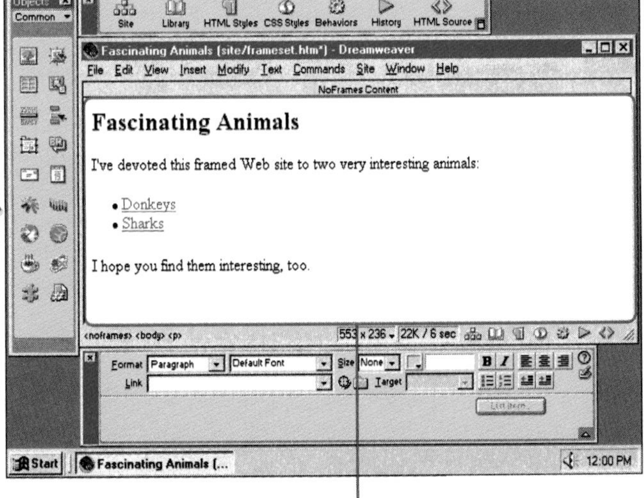

1 Click the frame border to select the frameset.

Note: You must select the outermost frameset if your Document window has nested framesets.

2 Click **Modify**.

3 Click **Frameset**.

4 Click **Edit NoFrames Content**.

■ Dreamweaver displays a NoFrames Content page.

5 Add the content you want to display.

What kinds of users are unable to view frames?

Users with nongraphical browsers are usually unable to view frames, as are users with older versions of graphical browsers.

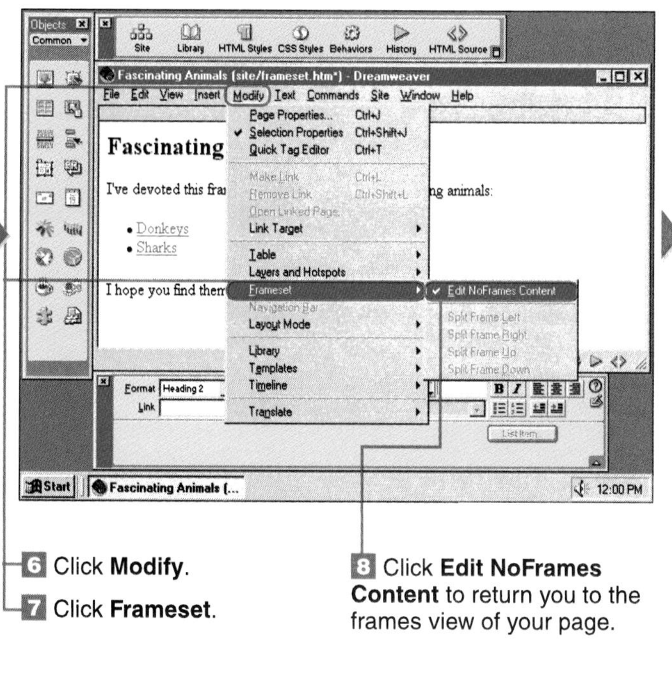

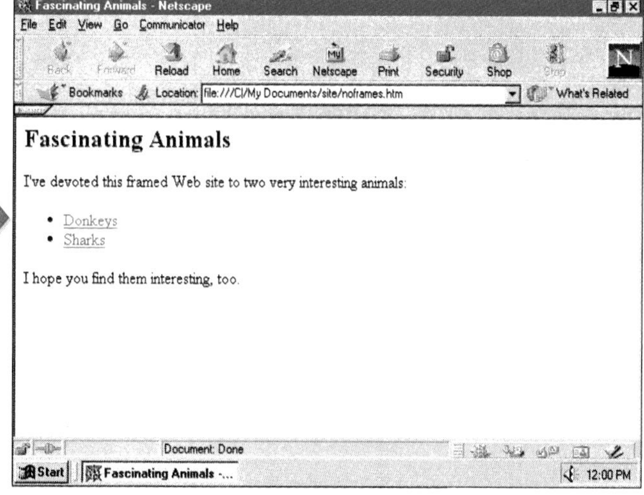

6 Click **Modify**.

7 Click **Frameset**.

8 Click **Edit NoFrames Content** to return you to the frames view of your page.

■ A browser that is not capable of displaying frames will display the NoFrames content when it opens the framed page.

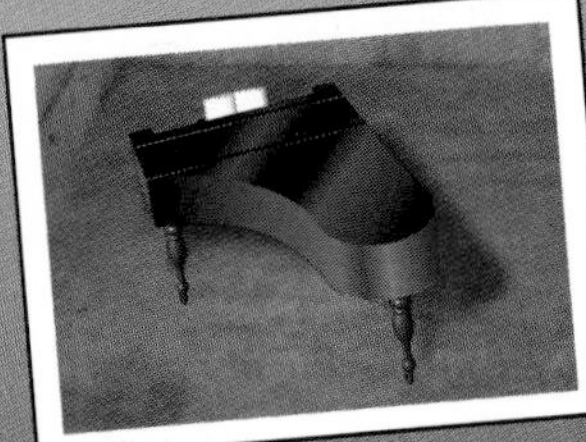

Composers From The Past

Bach

Johann Sebastian Bach was born into a family of musicians in 1685 in Eisenach, Germany. Bach's works include church organ and choral music, music for chamber orchestras and over 200 cantatas. Although he was more respected as an organist during his lifetime, Bach's compositions influenced many later composers including Beethoven and Mozart.

Beethoven

Ludwig van Beethoven was born in Bonn, Germany in 1770. He spent most of his life in Vienna, where he earned a living giving concerts, teaching piano and selling his compositions. One of the most fascinating aspects of Beethoven's life was his triumph over deafness, which struck him during adulthood. In fact, he composed some of his most powerful works after losing his hearing.

Using Libraries and Templates

Would you like to save time by storing frequently used Web-page elements and layouts? This chapter shows you how.

ABOUT LIBRARY ITEMS AND TEMPLATES

Library items and templates let you avoid repetitive work by storing copies of frequently used page elements and layouts.

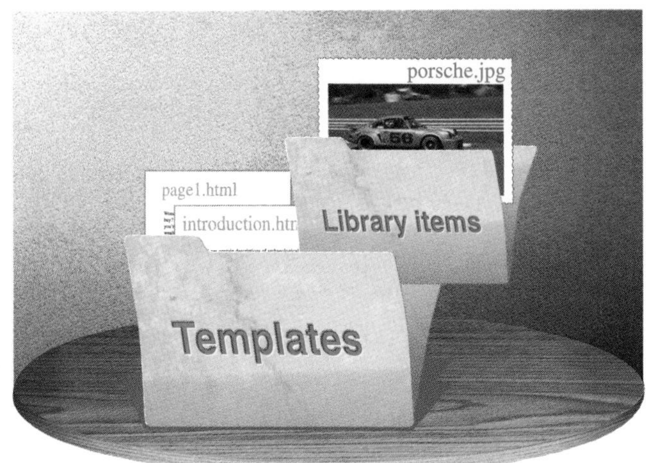

LIBRARY ITEMS

You can define parts of your Web pages that you want to repeat in your site as *library items,* so you do not have to create them from scratch over and over. After you make changes to a library item, Dreamweaver automatically updates all the instances of the item across your Web site.

TEMPLATES

You can define commonly used Web-page layouts as *templates* to save time as you build your pages. After you make changes to a template, Dreamweaver automatically updates all of the site's pages that are based on that template.

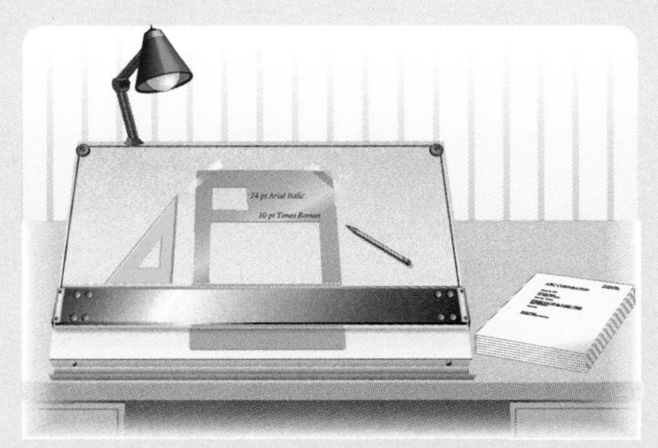

VIEW LIBRARY AND TEMPLATES PALETTES

You can view the library items and templates you have created for your site by using the Library and Templates palettes.

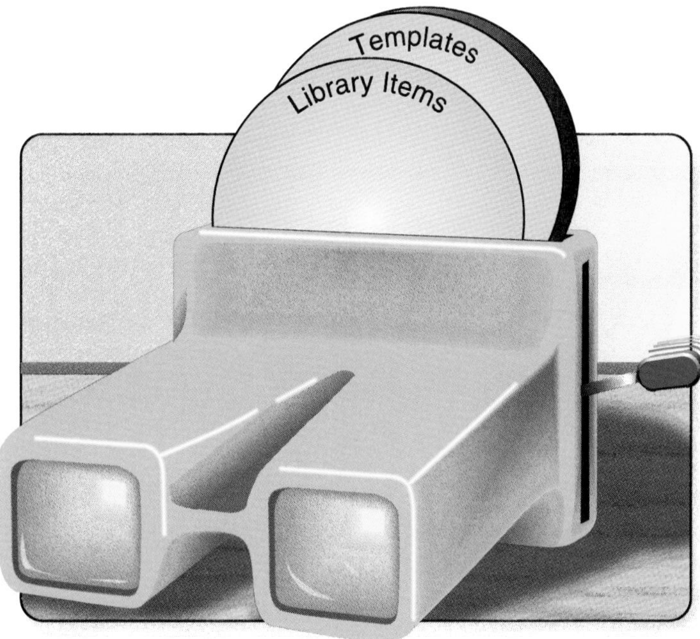

VIEW LIBRARY AND TEMPLATES PALETTES

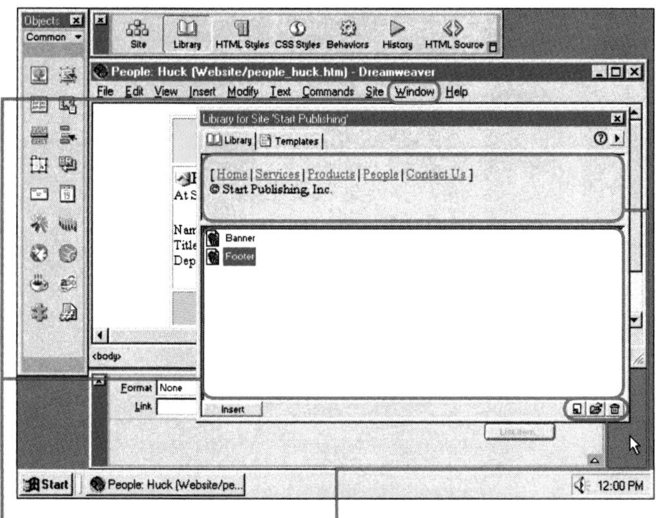

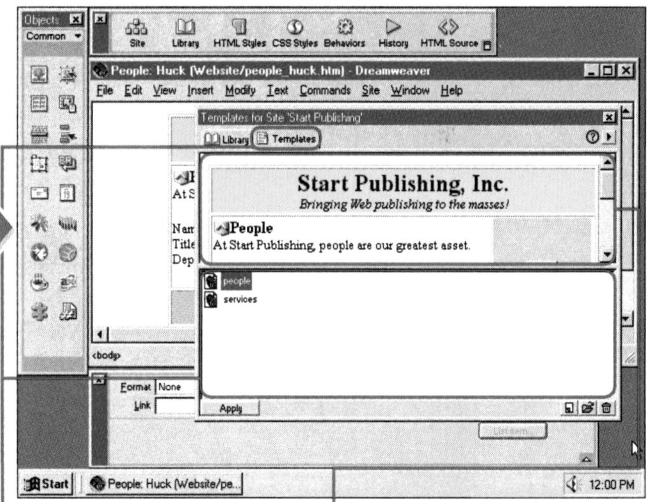

1 Click **Window** and then **Library** to open the Library palette.

■ The bottom window displays a list of the library items for your site.

■ The top window displays the library item selected in the list below.

■ You can create, open, or delete items by clicking the shortcut buttons, , and , respectively.

2 Click the **Templates** tab to access the Templates palette (or you can click **Window⇨Templates**).

■ The bottom window displays a list of the templates for your site.

■ The top window displays the template selected in the list below.

CREATE A LIBRARY ITEM

You can define a frequently used element on your Web page as a library item to avoid having to re-create it on other pages.

CREATE A LIBRARY ITEM

1 Drag your cursor to select the part of your Web page that you want to define as a library item.

Note: To create library items for your Web pages, the pages must be associated with a site. To create a site in Dreamweaver, see Chapter 2.

2 Select **Modify**.

3 Select **Library**.

4 Select **Add Object To Library**.

What page elements should I consider defining as library items?

Anything that appears multiple times in a Web site is a good candidate for a library item. This can include headers, footers, navigational menus, contact information, and disclaimers.

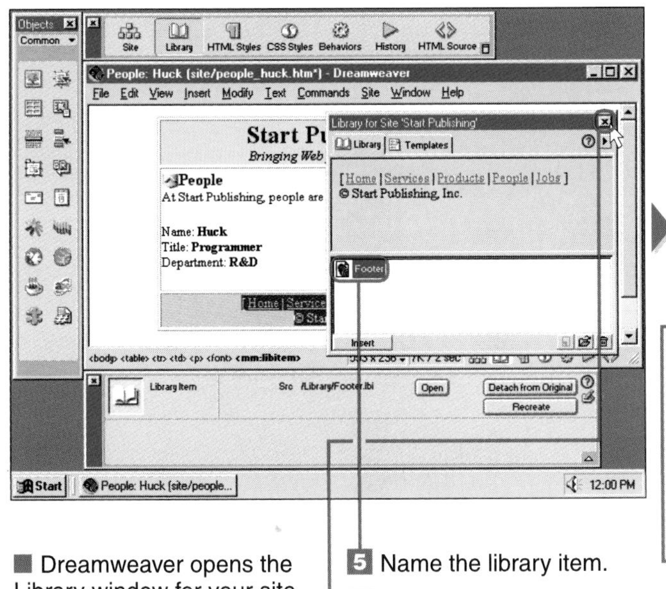

■ Dreamweaver opens the Library window for your site and creates a new, untitled library item.

5 Name the library item.

6 Press **Enter (Return)**.

7 Click ☒ to close the Library window.

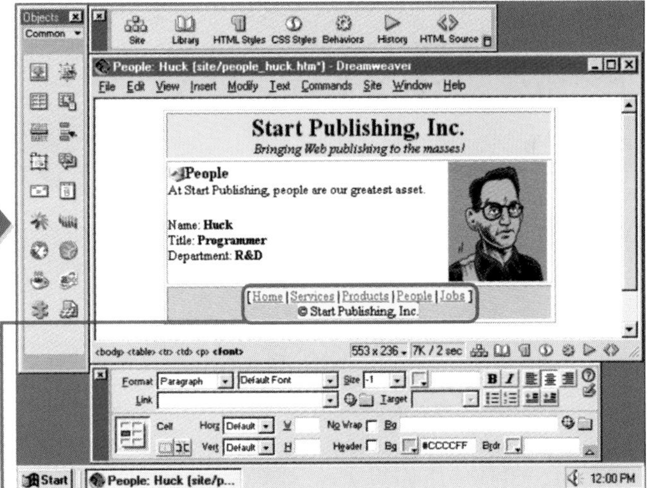

■ The new library item is highlighted in yellow and appears only in Dreamweaver.

■ You can change the highlight color by clicking **Edit⇨Preferences⇨ Highlighting**.

Note: Defining an element as a library item prevents you from editing it in the Document window. (To edit library items, see the section "Edit a Library Item and Update the Site").

Inserting items from the library into your Web pages can save you hours of repetitive work. All the pages in a site have access to the same library items.

INSERT A LIBRARY ITEM

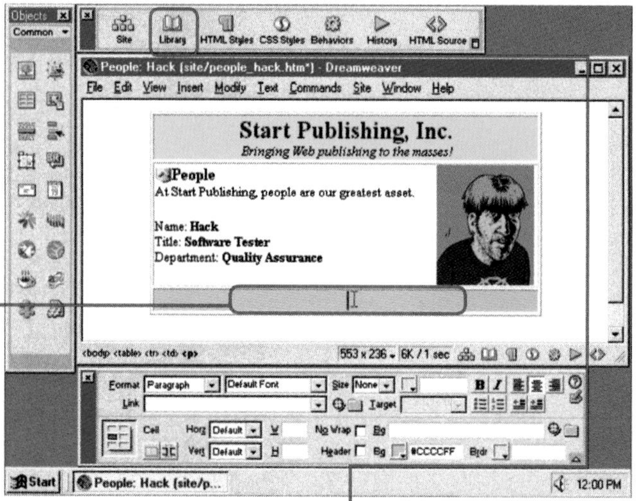

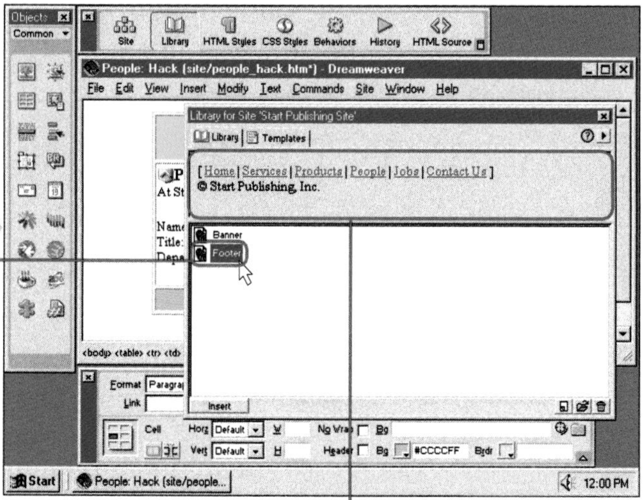

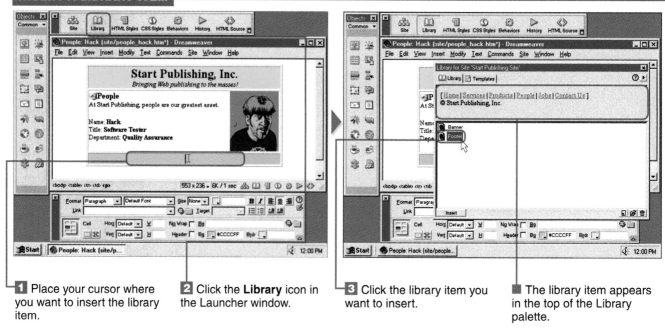

1 Place your cursor where you want to insert the library item.

2 Click the **Library** icon in the Launcher window.

3 Click the library item you want to insert.

■ The library item appears in the top of the Library palette.

Can I insert more than one copy of a library item on a Web page?

Yes. This can come in handy when you have stylistic elements, such as custom horizontal rules or list bullets, that appear repeatedly on a page.

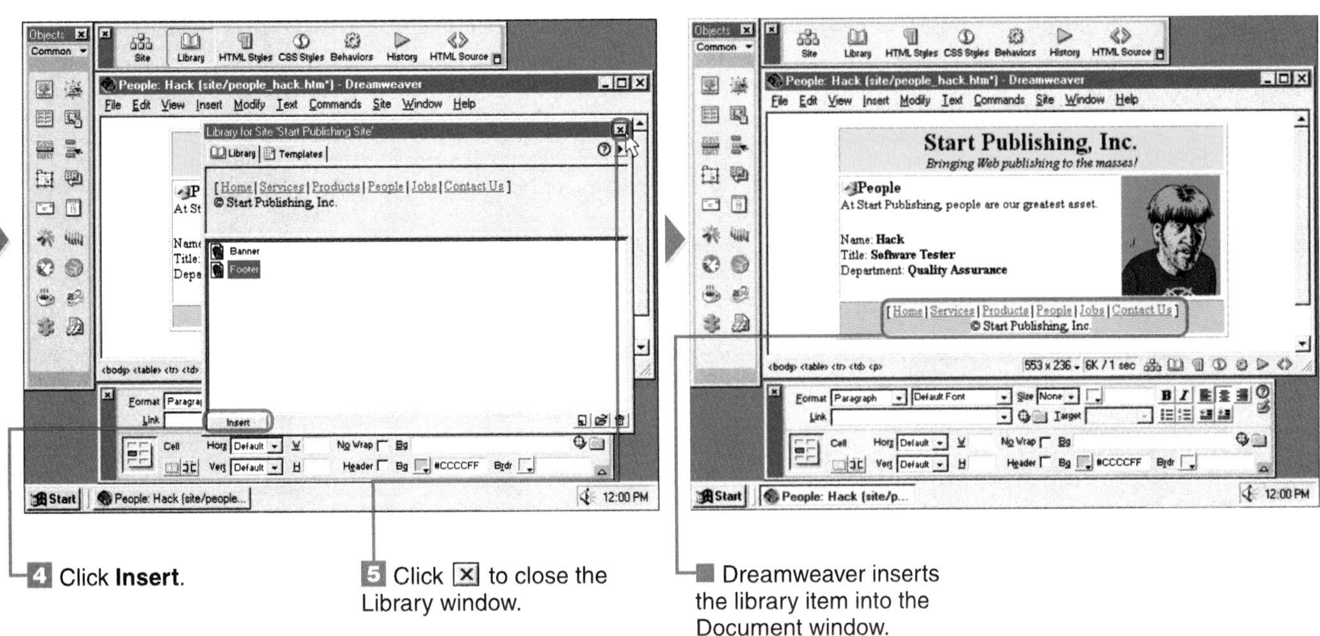

4 Click **Insert**.

5 Click ☒ to close the Library window.

■ Dreamweaver inserts the library item into the Document window.

EDIT A LIBRARY ITEM AND UPDATE THE SITE

You can edit a library item and then automatically update all the pages in your site that use that item.

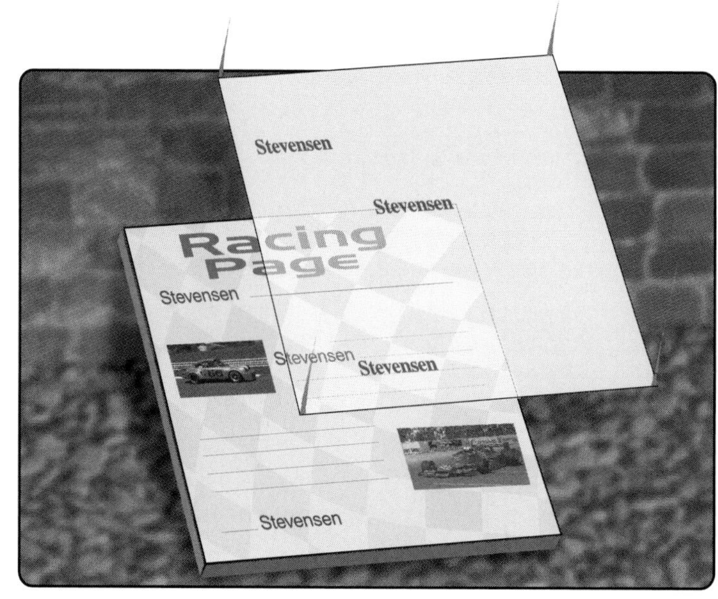

To detach a specific instance of a library item from the library so you can edit it, see the section "Detach Content from the Library."

EDIT A LIBRARY ITEM AND UPDATE THE SITE

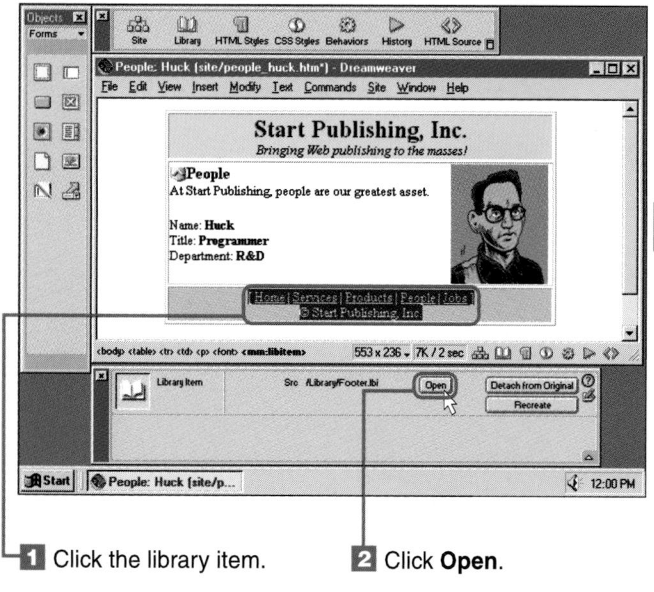

1 Click the library item.

2 Click **Open**.

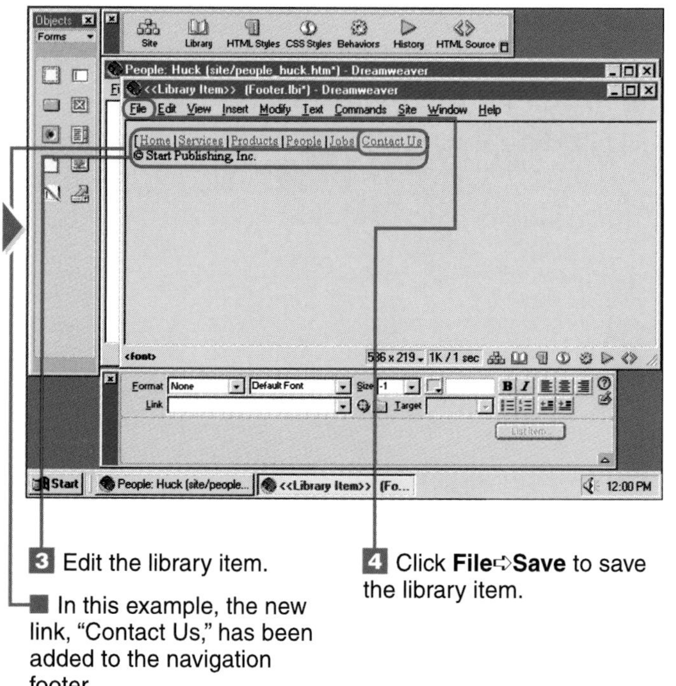

3 Edit the library item.

■ In this example, the new link, "Contact Us," has been added to the navigation footer.

4 Click **File**⇨**Save** to save the library item.

What will my pages look like after I have edited a library item and updated my site?

All the pages in your site that contain the library item will be replaced with the edited version. By using the library feature, you can make a change to a single library item and have hundreds of Web pages (or more) updated automatically.

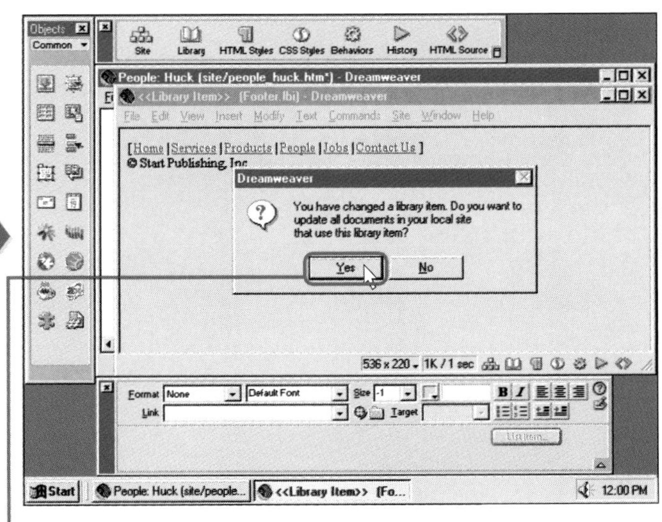

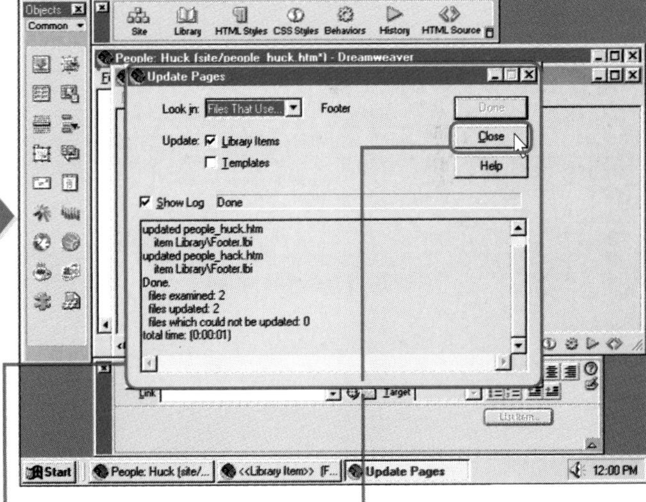

■ An alert box appears asking if you want to update all the instances of the library item in the site.

5 Click **Yes**.

Note: If you have updated the library item previously, a slightly different box appears. The box lists the files that feature the library item and asks you if you want to update the site.

■ A dialog box appears showing the progress of the updates.

6 After Dreamweaver is finished updating the site, click **Close**.

DETACH CONTENT FROM THE LIBRARY

To edit the content of a library item on a specific Web page (and nowhere else), you can detach it from the library.

DETACH CONTENT FROM THE LIBRARY

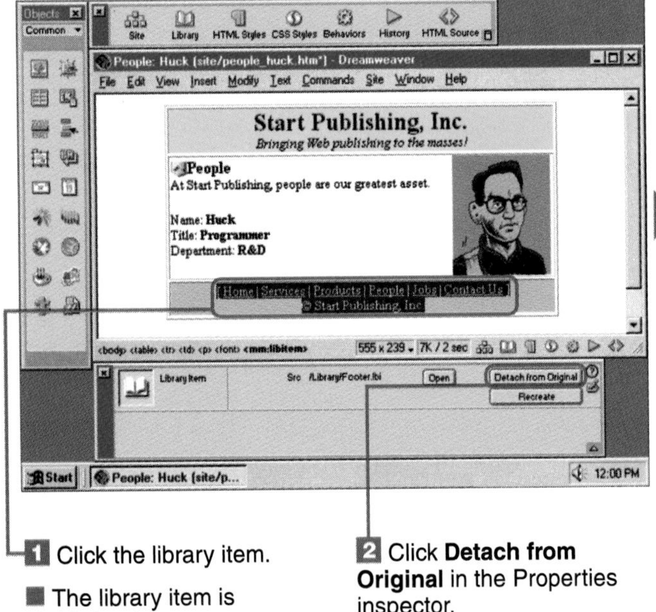

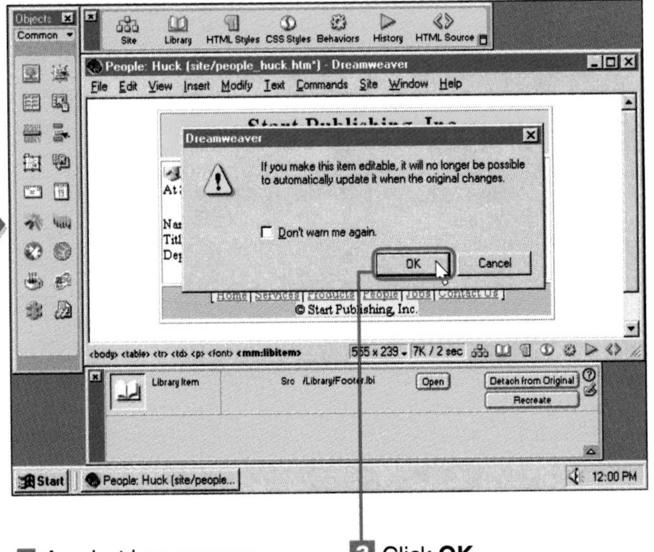

1 Click the library item.

■ The library item is highlighted.

2 Click **Detach from Original** in the Properties inspector.

■ An alert box appears asking if you want to make the item editable.

3 Click **OK**.

Why would I want to detach content from the library?

The ability to detach content from the library lets you use library items as templates. For instance, if you know that you need numerous captioned images in your Web site, you can create a library item that has a two-cell table with a generic image and caption. To place an image and caption, you insert the library item and then detach the item from the library to make it editable.

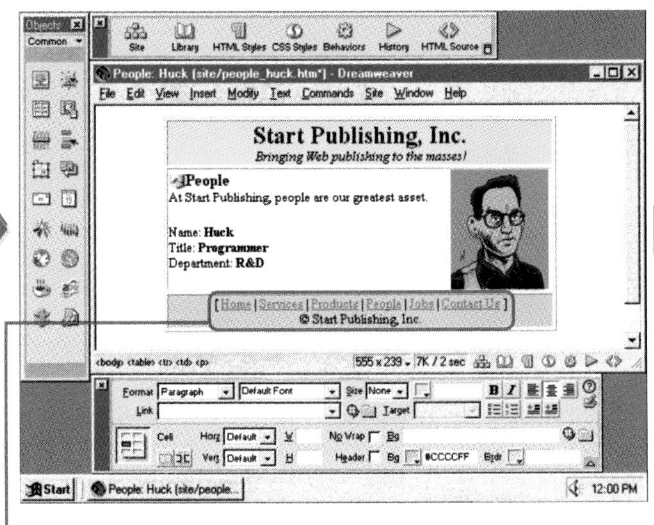

■ The text is no longer a library item, and no longer has the distinctive highlighting.

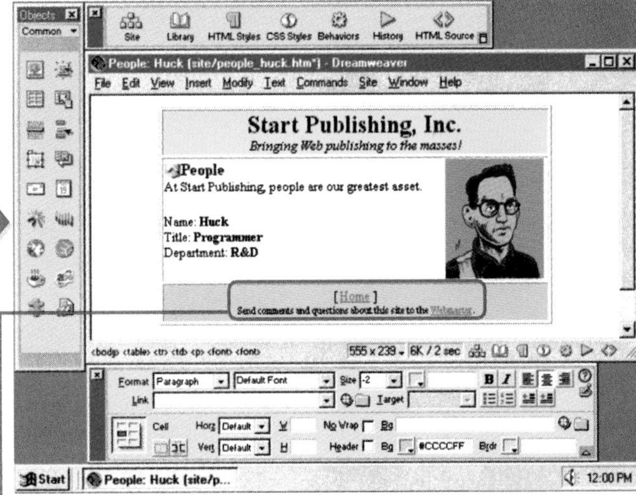

■ In this example, the footer was detached from the library. It is now editable.

You can define a Web page layout as a template to save time when building your site's pages.

CREATE A TEMPLATE

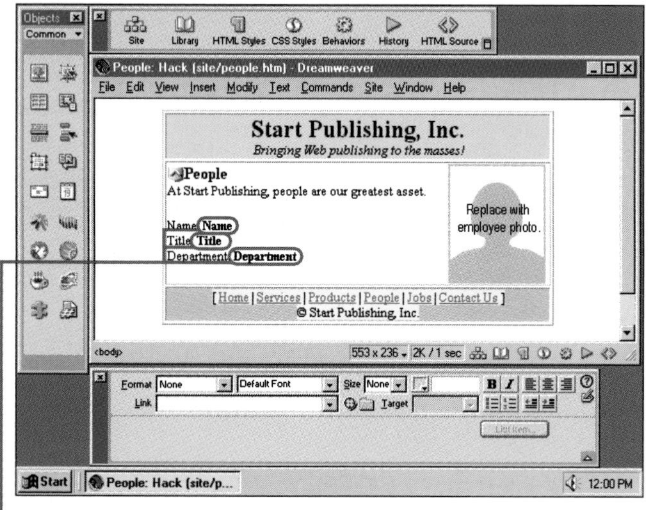

1 Create the Web page that will serve as a template (to create a Web page, see Chapter 2).

■ You can add placeholders where information will be changing from page to page.

Note: To create a template for your Web pages, your pages must be associated with a site (see Chapter 2 for how to create a local site).

■ In this example, the yellow highlighted library item will be included in the template.

2 Click **File**.

3 Click **Save As Template**.

What are the different types of content in a template?

A template usually contains two types of content: editable and noneditable. When you create a new Web page based on a template, you can only change the parts of the page that are defined as editable. To change noneditable regions, you must edit the template.

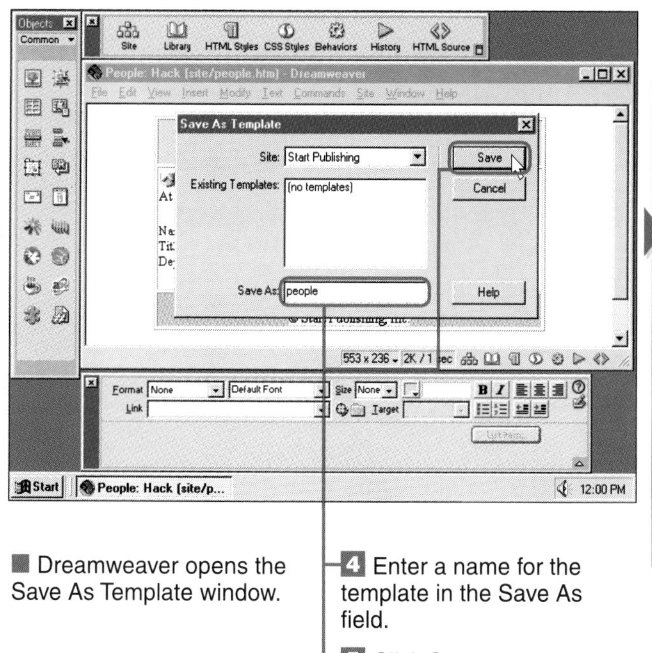

■ Dreamweaver opens the Save As Template window.

4 Enter a name for the template in the Save As field.

5 Click **Save**.

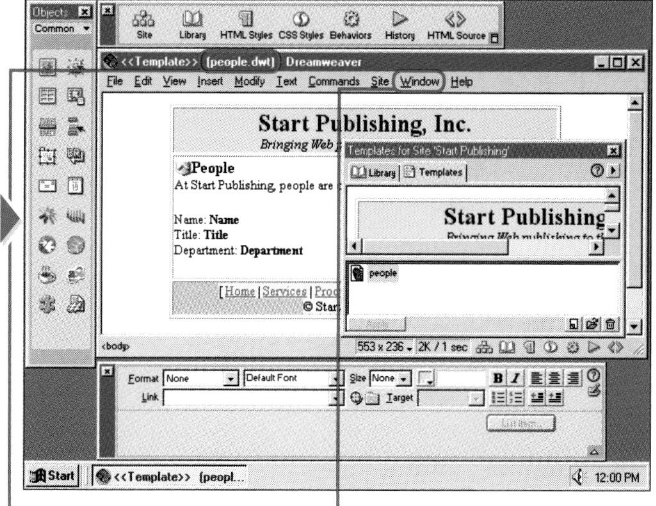

■ Dreamweaver saves the Web page as a template, gives it a .dwt extension, and stores it in a Templates folder in your site folder.

■ To make the template functional, define your placeholder text as editable regions.

Note: See the Section "Set a Template's Editable Regions".

■ Click **Window⇨Templates** to view the template.

SET A TEMPLATE'S EDITABLE REGIONS

You can define regions of a template as editable. This capability lets you specify which areas of your site's pages will change from page to page. When you create a new Web page by using a template, you can change only the parts of the new page that are defined as editable.

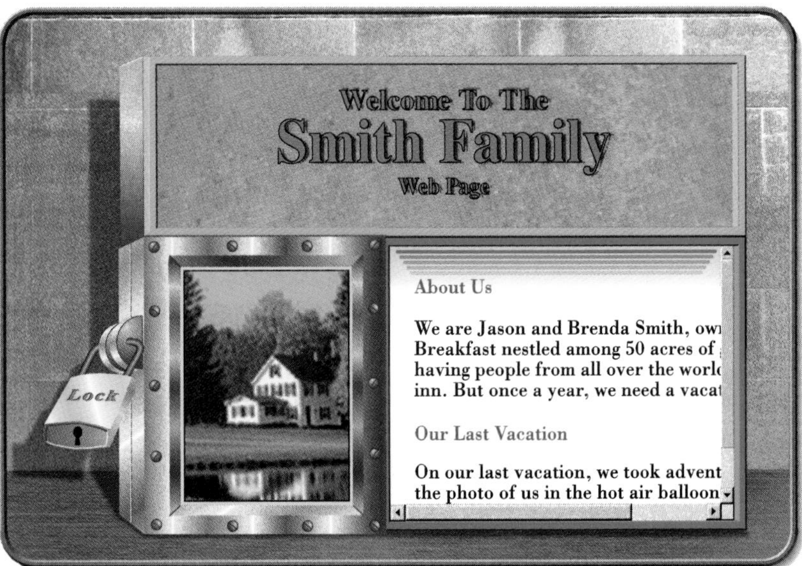

SET A TEMPLATE'S EDITABLE REGIONS

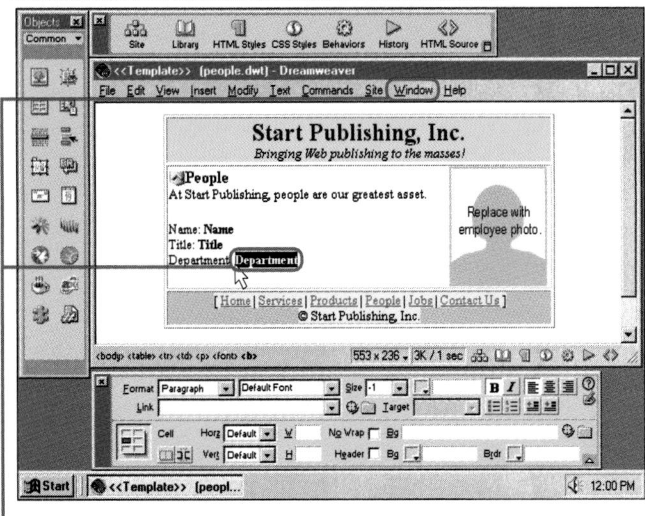

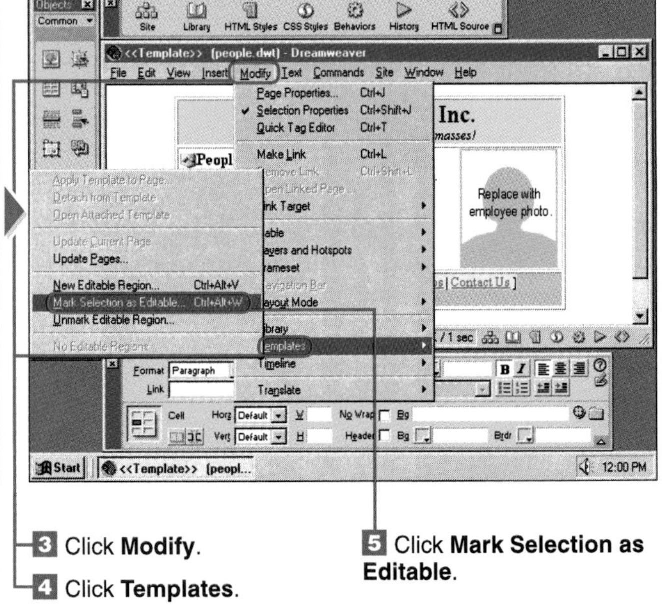

1 Open the template by clicking **Window⇨Templates** and double-clicking the template's name in the window.

2 Drag to select the text you want to define as editable.

■ You can also click and drag to select images, tables, forms, and other template elements that you want to define as editable.

3 Click **Modify**.

4 Click **Templates**.

5 Click **Mark Selection as Editable**.

What parts of a Web-page template should be defined as editable?

Any part that needs to change from page to page. Generally, variable areas in the page body are defined as editable while site navigation and copyright information are defined as noneditable.

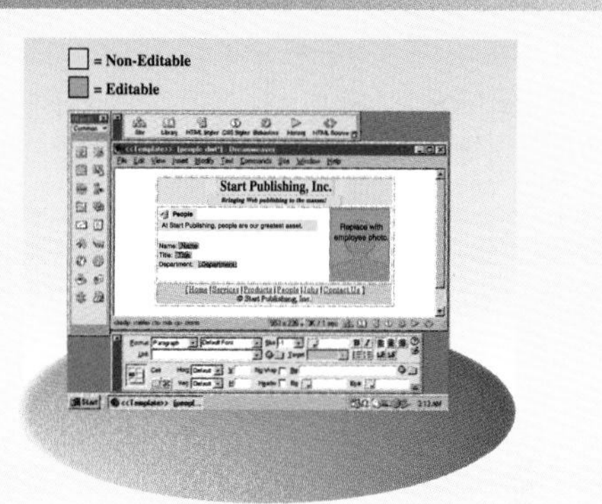

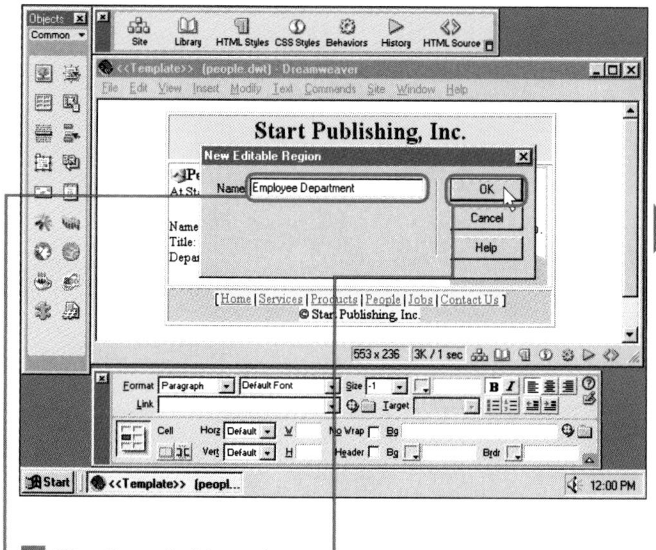

6 Give the editable region a name that distinguishes it from other editable regions on the page.

Note: You cannot use the characters &, ", ', <, or > in the name.

7 Click **OK**.

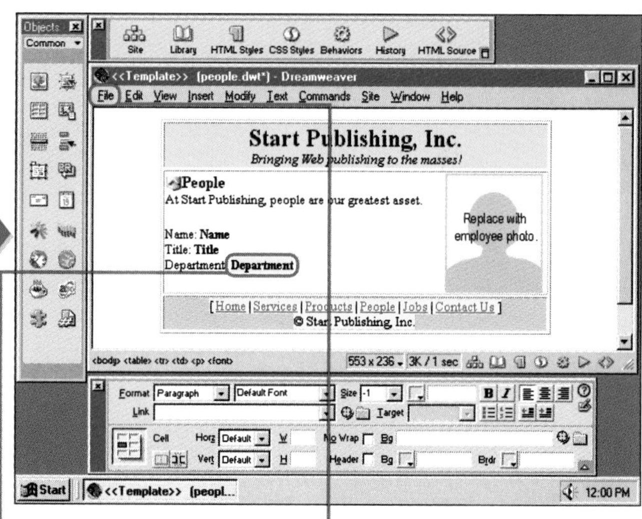

■ The editable text is highlighted in light blue on your Web page.

Note: You can change the highlight color for editable text by selecting Edit ⇨ Preferences and selecting Highlighting from the list.

8 Repeat Steps 1 through 6 for all the regions on the page that you want to be editable in the template.

9 Click **File⇨Save** to save the template.

CREATE A PAGE USING A TEMPLATE

You can create a Web page based on a template instead of creating the page from scratch.

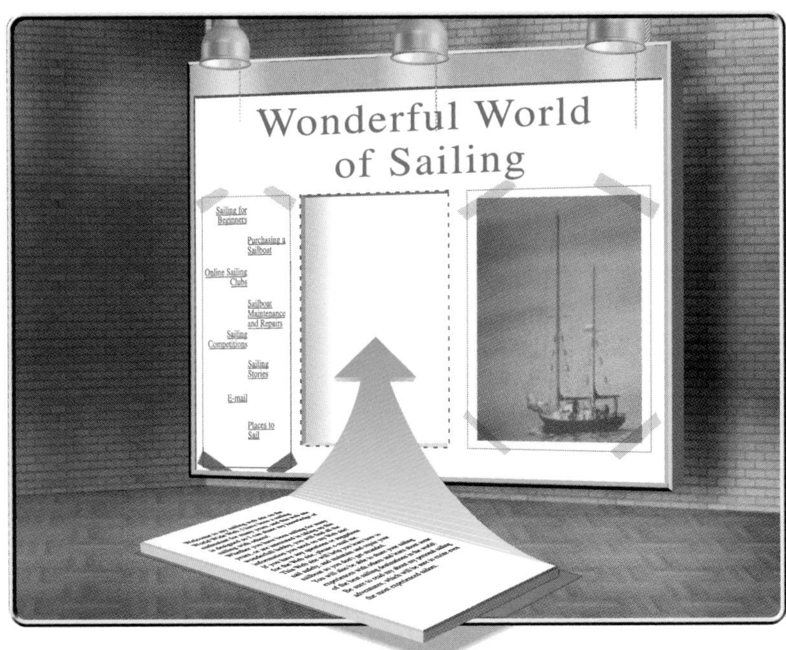

CREATE A PAGE USING A TEMPLATE

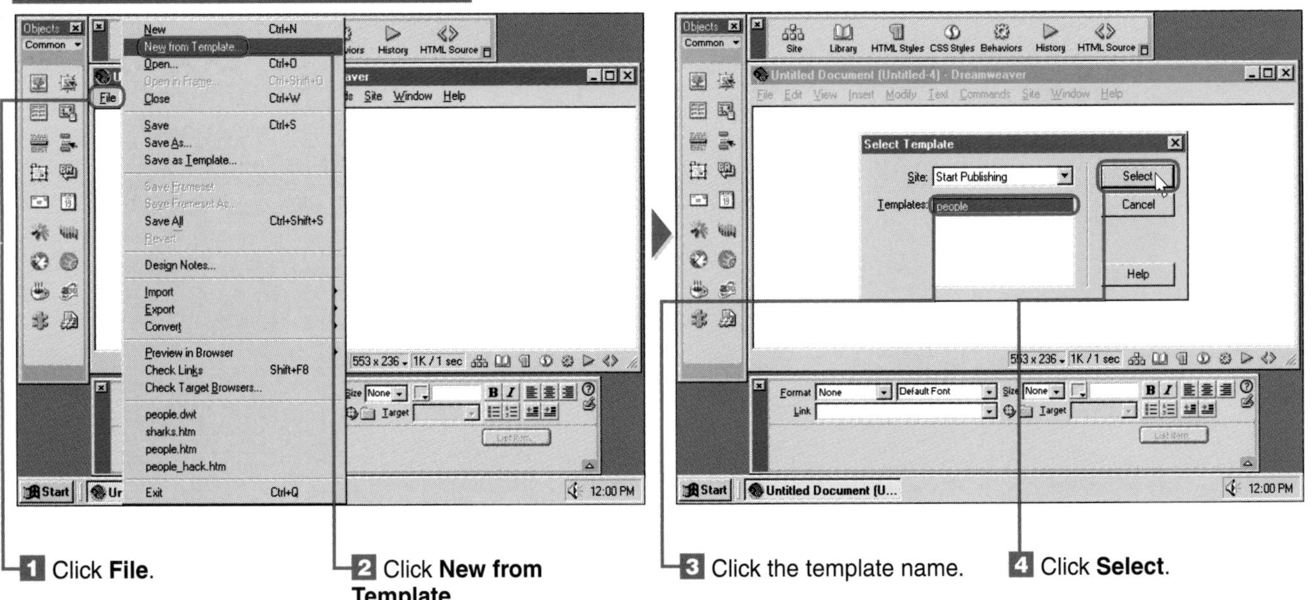

1 Click **File**.

2 Click **New from Template**.

3 Click the template name.

4 Click **Select**.

How can I change the noneditable regions of a Web page that was created using a template?

To change the noneditable regions, you have to detach the page from the template. To detach a page, click **Modify⇨Templates⇨Detach From Template**.

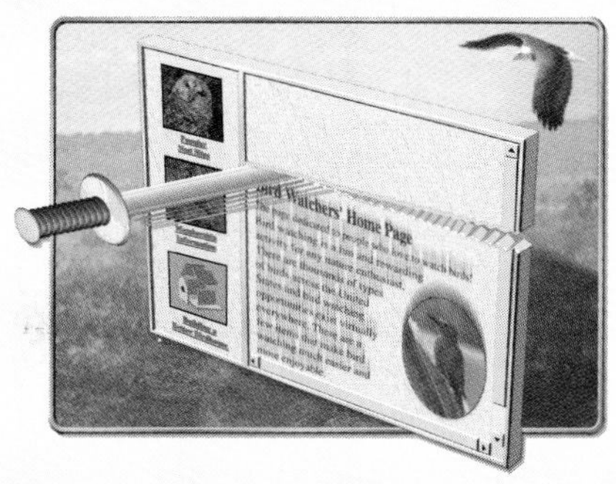

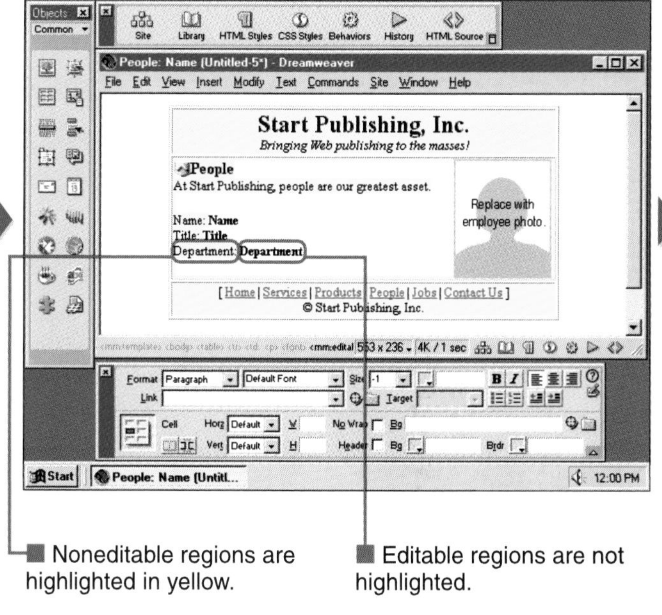

■ Noneditable regions are highlighted in yellow.

■ Editable regions are not highlighted.

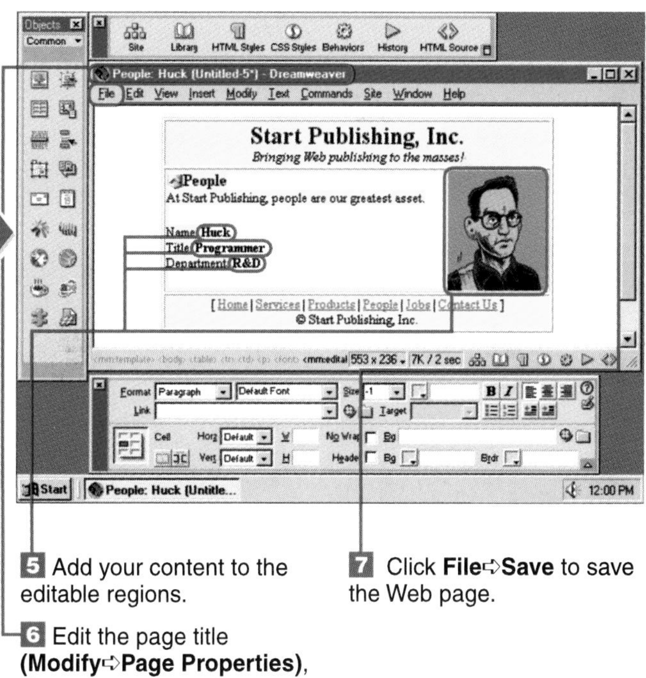

5 Add your content to the editable regions.

6 Edit the page title **(Modify⇨Page Properties)**, if necessary.

7 Click **File⇨Save** to save the Web page.

EDIT A TEMPLATE AND UPDATE THE SITE

You can edit a template and automatically update all the pages that use that template.

EDIT A TEMPLATE AND UPDATE THE SITE

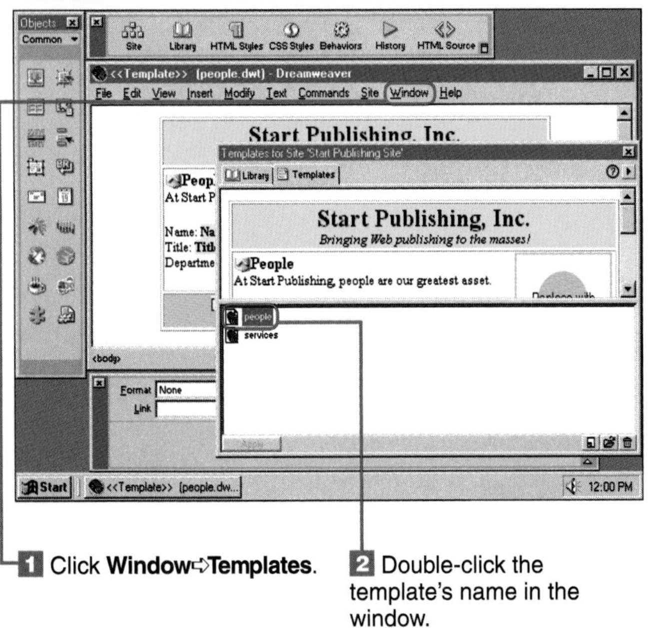

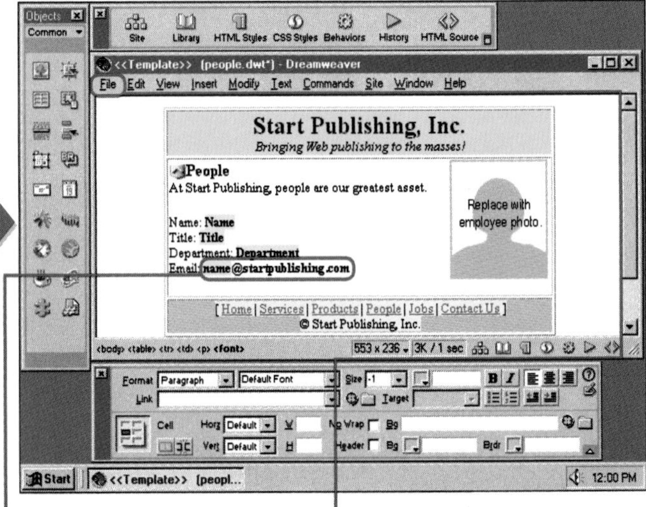

1 Click **Window⇨Templates**.

2 Double-click the template's name in the window.

3 Make your edits to the template. This can include adding or deleting editable and noneditable content. To define content as editable, see the Section "Set a Template's Editable Regions."

■ In this example, an e-mail entry has been added to the template. The "E-mail:" label is noneditable, while the e-mail address is editable.

4 Save the page by clicking **File⇨Save**.

Where are template files stored?

Dreamweaver stores template files in a Templates folder inside the site folder. You can open template files directly by clicking **File⇨Open** and going to the Templates folder. Be sure to have the Files of type menu in the Open dialog box set to Template files.

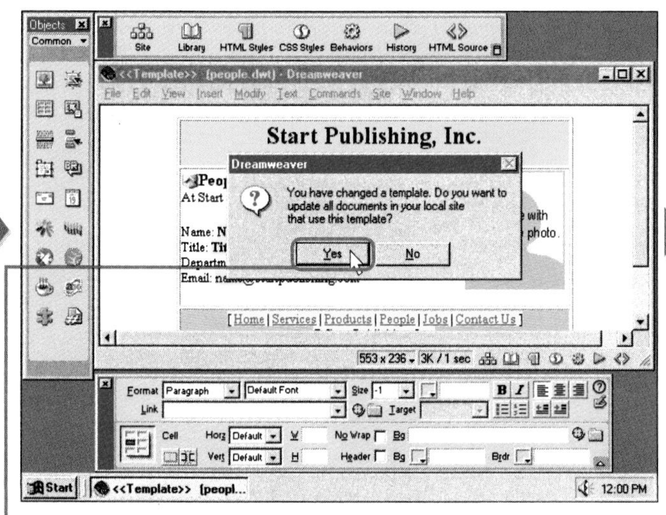

■ An alert box appears asking if you want to update all the pages that are based on the template.

5 Click **Yes**.

Note: If you've previously updated the library item, a slightly different box appears. The box lists the files that are based on the template and asks you if you want to update the site.

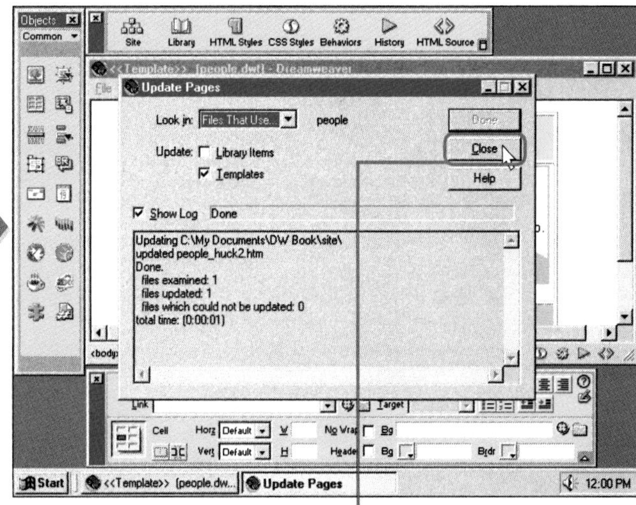

■ A dialog box appears showing the progress of the updates.

6 After Dreamweaver is finished updating the site, click **Close**.

Here at Sunshine Vacations,
we are commited to making
your vacation or business trip
a memorable one! We provide
the best rates available for
flights, accommodations and
rental cars and important advice
about what to see and do at your
destination city.
Kick back, relax and enjoy the
peace of mind that comes with
knowing Sunshine Vacations is
available 24 hours a day should
you need our assistance.

STYLE SHEET

BANNER

IMAGE

PARAGRAPH

CHAPTER 11

Implementing Style Sheets

Would you like to add complex formatting to your text and other Web page elements? This chapter shows you how by using style sheets.

INTRODUCTION TO STYLE SHEETS

You can apply many different types of formatting to your Web pages with style sheets (also known as *Cascading Style Sheets*, or CSS).

FORMAT TEXT

A standard separate from HTML, style sheets let you format fonts; adjust character, paragraph, and margin spacing; customize the look of hyperlinks; tailor the colors on your page; and more.

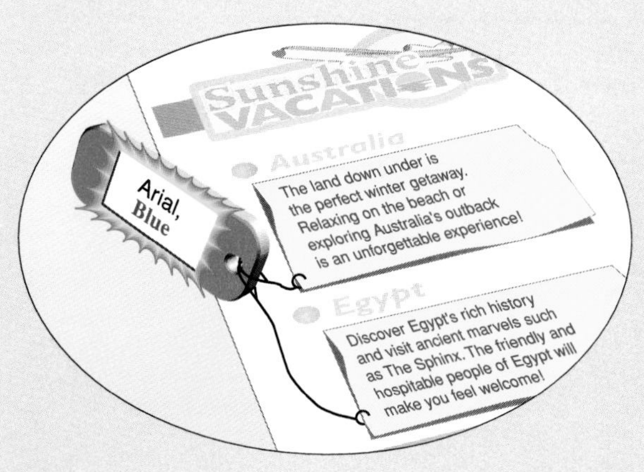

POSITION WEB PAGE ELEMENTS

You can use style sheets to position images, text, and other elements precisely on your Web page, something that is not possible with HTML. Dreamweaver's layer feature offers a user-friendly way to apply style sheets' positioning capabilities.

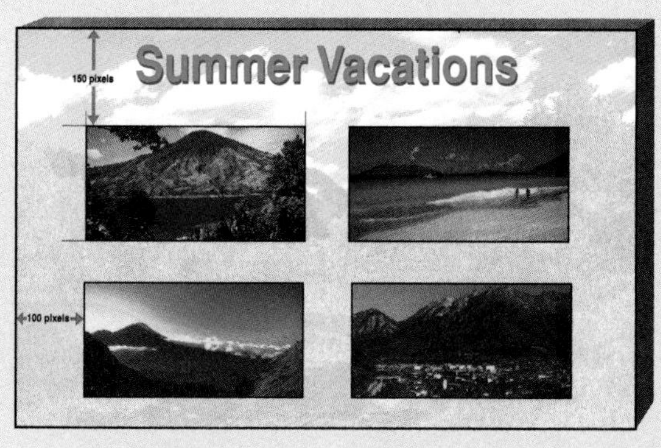

USE STYLE SHEETS INSTEAD OF HTML

Many of the HTML-based formatting features discussed in Chapter 4 can be performed using style sheets. Style sheets can also be used to apply more elaborate formatting to your pages than is possible with regular HTML.

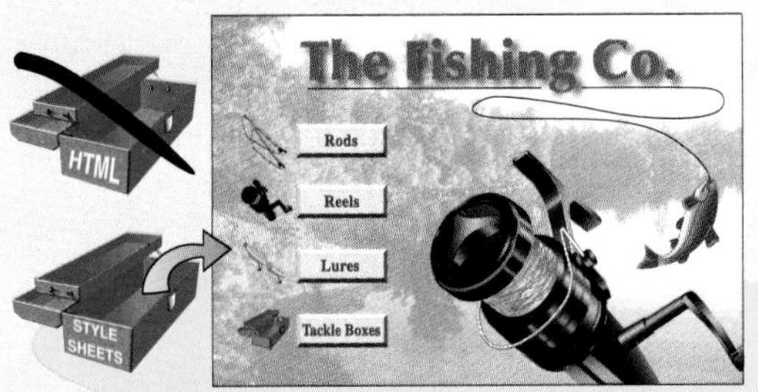

EMBEDDED STYLE SHEETS

A style sheet that is saved inside a particular Web page is called an *embedded style sheet.* Embedded style sheet rules apply only to the page in which they are embedded.

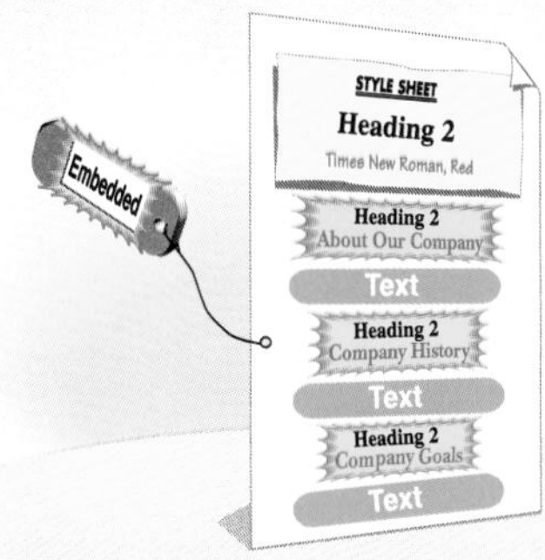

EXTERNAL STYLE SHEETS

You can save style sheets as separate files; these external style sheets exist independently of your HTML pages. Different Web pages can access a common set of style rules by linking to the same external style sheet.

STYLE SHEETS AND BROWSERS

Style sheets are a relatively new feature on the Web. They are supported by Microsoft Internet Explorer Version 3 and greater and Netscape Navigator Version 4 and greater (the more recent browser versions support more style sheet features). Unfortunately, the two major browsers implement style sheets in slightly different ways, so it is important to test pages using style sheets on both browsers before they go live.

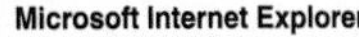

Netscape Communicator

CUSTOMIZE AN HTML TAG

You can use style sheets to customize an HTML tag.

CUSTOMIZE AN HTML TAG

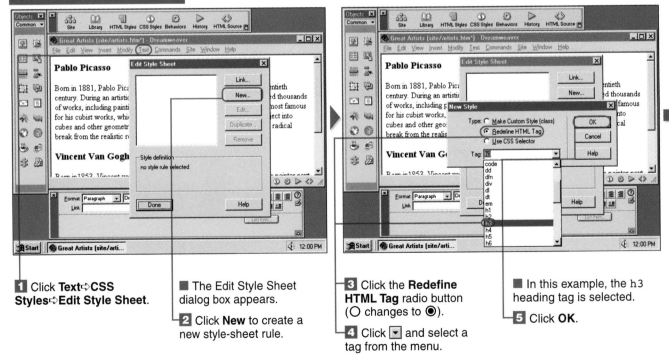

1 Click **Text⇨CSS Styles⇨Edit Style Sheet**.

■ The Edit Style Sheet dialog box appears.

2 Click **New** to create a new style-sheet rule.

3 Click the **Redefine HTML Tag** radio button (○ changes to ◉).

4 Click ▼ and select a tag from the menu.

■ In this example, the `h3` heading tag is selected.

5 Click **OK**.

What is the advantage of redefining an HTML tag?

Redefining an HTML tag using style sheets can help you work faster. For instance, to make h4 subtitles that are red, italicized, and underlined without using style sheets, you must perform four steps for each: define each subtitle as h4, color it red, italicize it, and underline it. With style sheets, you can simply redefine h4 as red, italicized, and underlined, and then create each subtitle in one step — by defining the text as h4.

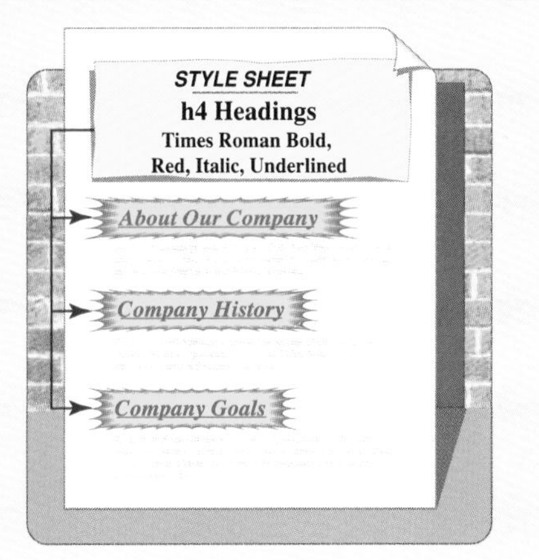

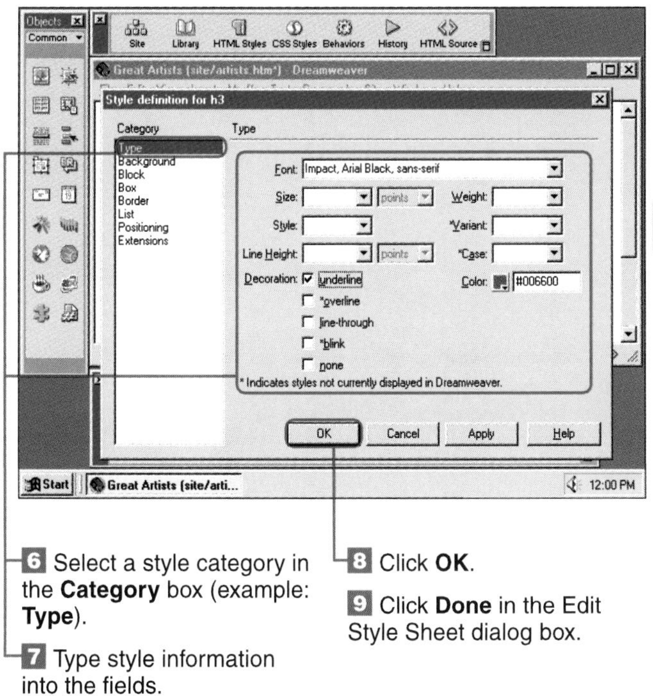

6 Select a style category in the **Category** box (example: **Type**).

7 Type style information into the fields.

8 Click **OK**.

9 Click **Done** in the Edit Style Sheet dialog box.

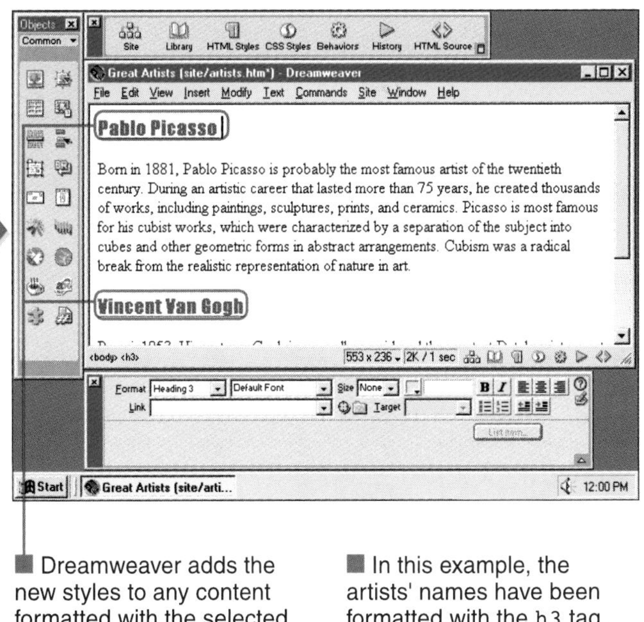

■ Dreamweaver adds the new styles to any content formatted with the selected tag in the page.

■ In this example, the artists' names have been formatted with the h3 tag.

CREATE A CLASS

You can define specific style attributes as a style-sheet class. You can then apply that class to elements on your Web page.

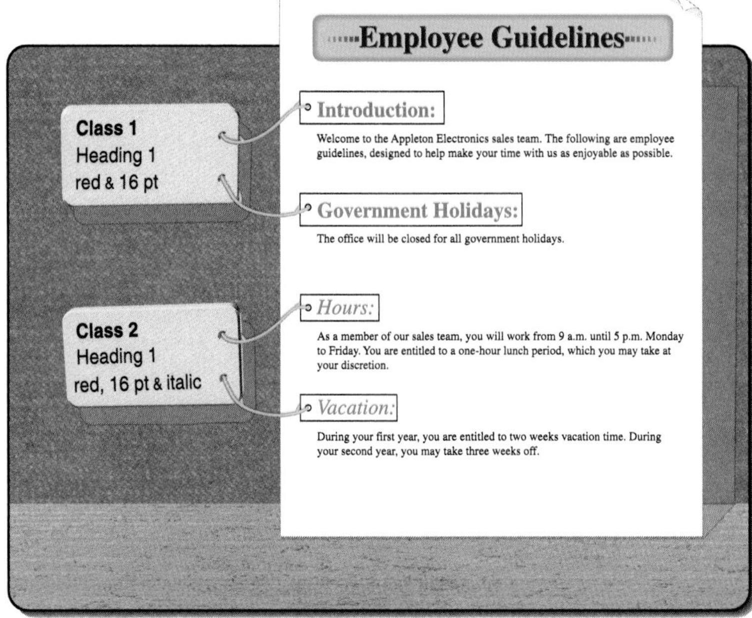

Employee Guidelines
Class 1
Heading 1
red & 16 pt
Class 2
Heading 1
red, 16 pt & italic
Introduction:
Welcome to the Appleton Electronics sales team. The following are employee guidelines, designed to help make your time with us as enjoyable as possible.
Government Holidays:
The office will be closed for all government holidays.
Hours:
As a member of our sales team, you will work from 9 a.m. until 5 p.m. Monday to Friday. You are entitled to a one-hour lunch period, which you may take at your discretion.
Vacation:
During your first year, you are entitled to two weeks vacation time. During your second year, you may take three weeks off.

CREATE A CLASS

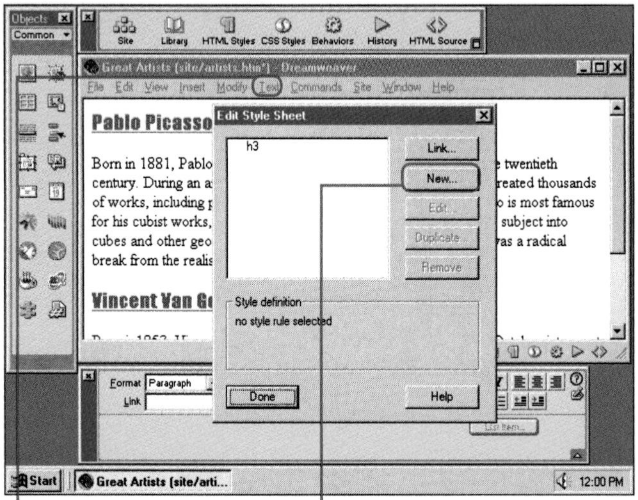

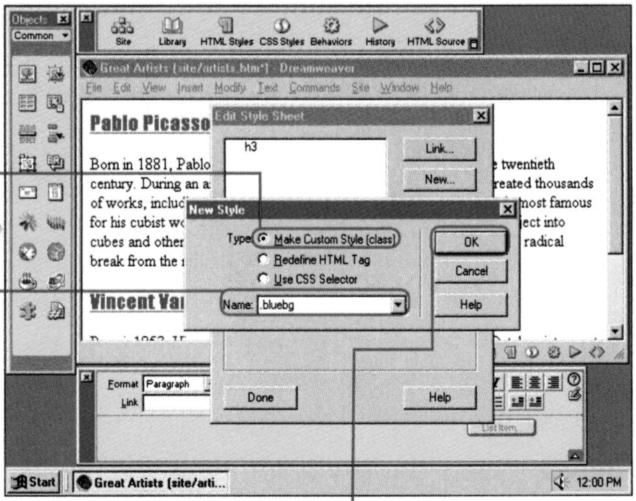

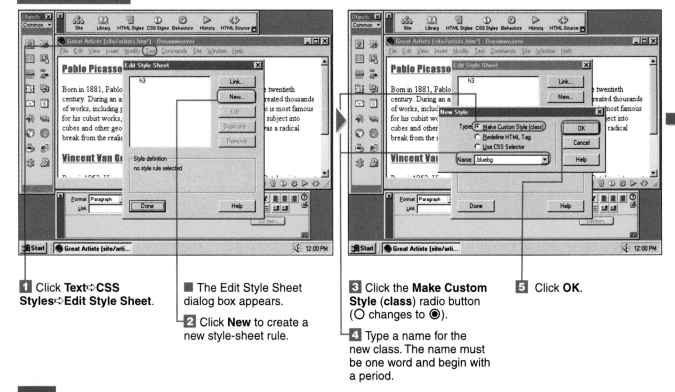

1 Click **Text⇨CSS Styles⇨Edit Style Sheet**.

■ The Edit Style Sheet dialog box appears.

2 Click **New** to create a new style-sheet rule.

3 Click the **Make Custom Style (class)** radio button (○ changes to ◉).

4 Type a name for the new class. The name must be one word and begin with a period.

5 Click **OK**.

What is the difference between customizing an HTML tag and creating a class?

Customizing an HTML tag applies a custom style to a specific tag. The new style affects every instance of that tag on your Web page. If you customize your paragraph tags as green using style sheets, every paragraph in your page will be green. Classes let you define custom styles that are independent of specific HTML tags. For a class to work, you have to apply it to an element on your page. A class that turns text green can be applied to a paragraph, an h3 heading, or another text-based tag.

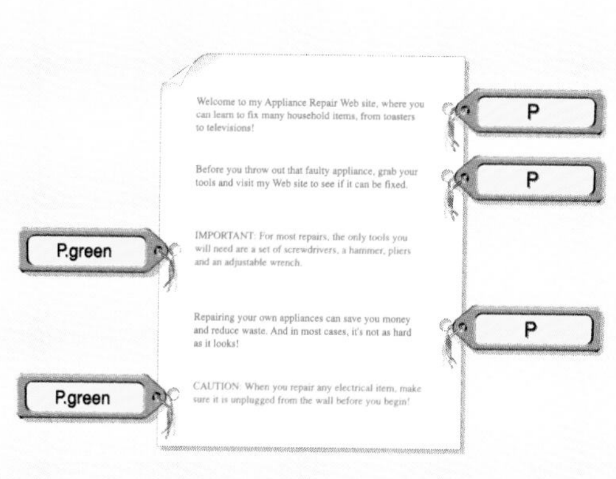

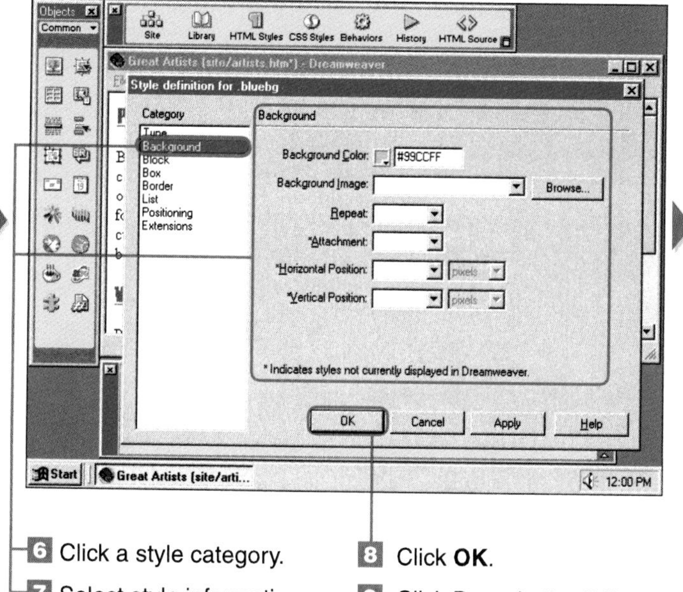

6 Click a style category.

7 Select style information using the menus.

■ In this example, a light-blue background style has been selected (example: **Background**).

8 Click **OK**.

9 Click **Done** in the Edit Style Sheet dialog box.

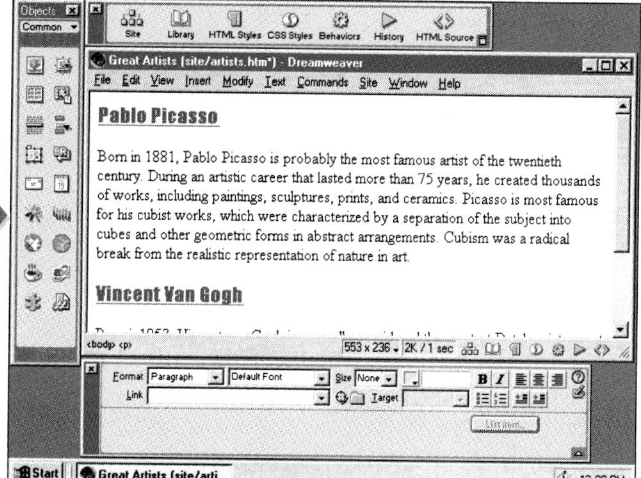

■ The new class has no effect until you apply it to something in your Web page.

Note: See the Section "Apply a Class."

APPLY A CLASS

You can apply a style-sheet class to content on your Web page. To create a class, see the Section "Create a Class."

APPLY A CLASS

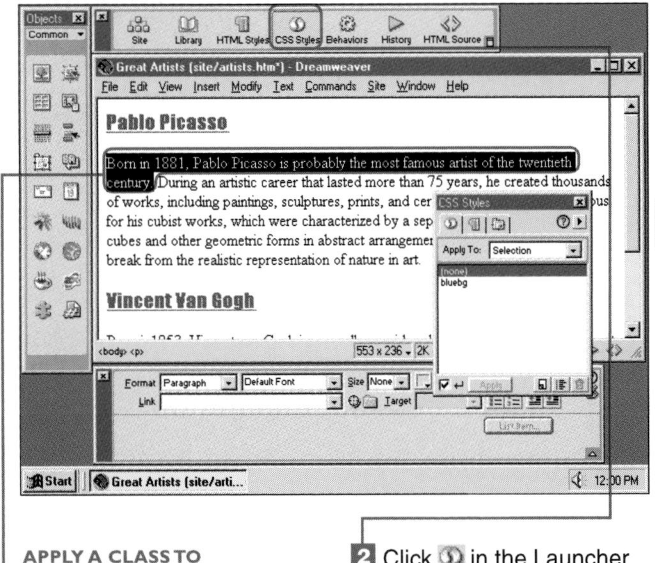

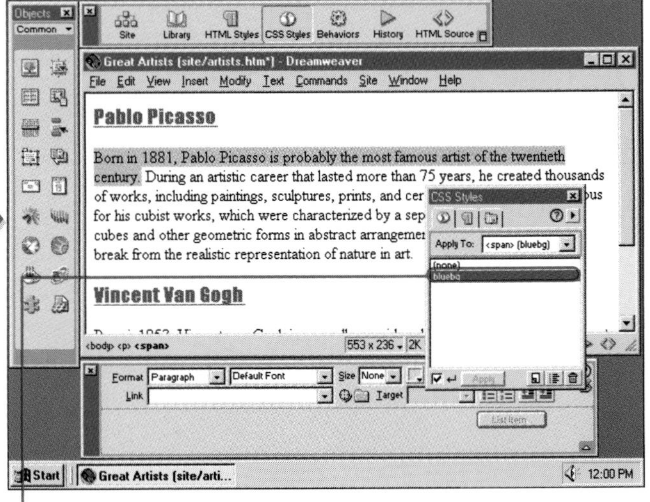

APPLY A CLASS TO SELECTED TEXT

1 Drag your cursor over the text to which you want to apply the class.

2 Click in the Launcher.

■ The CSS Styles palette displays all the classes available for the page.

3 Click a class in the CSS Styles palette.

■ Dreamweaver applies the style-sheet class to the selected content on the page.

Do different Web browsers interpret style sheets differently?

Yes. There are differences between the way the current versions of Microsoft Internet Explorer and Netscape Navigator interpret some style-sheet attributes. Paragraph borders, for instance, may look one way when a page is viewed in Navigator but slightly different when viewed in Explorer. For this reason, it is important to test pages that use style sheets in different browsers.

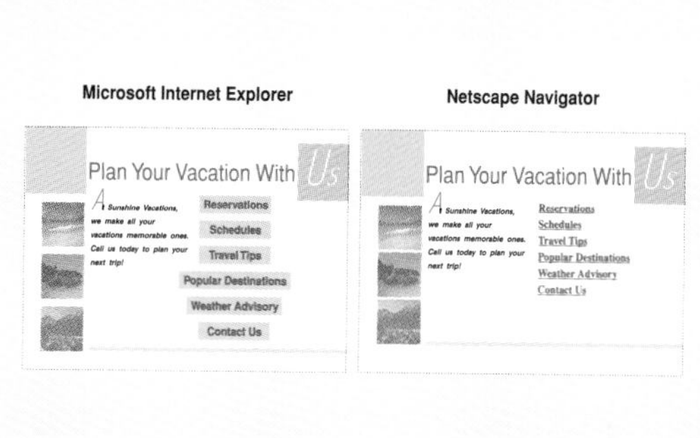

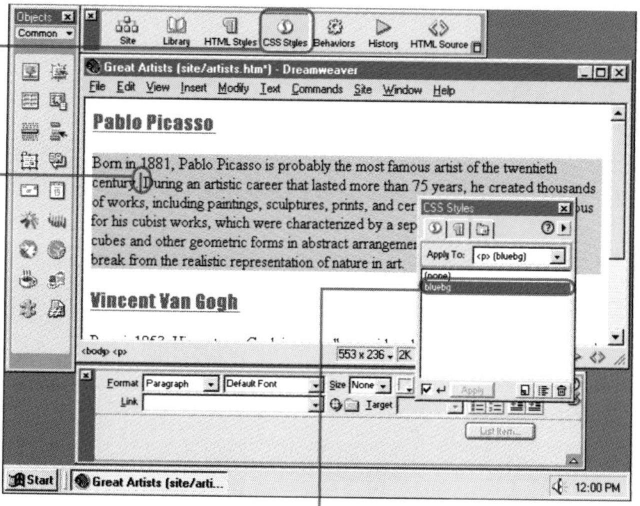

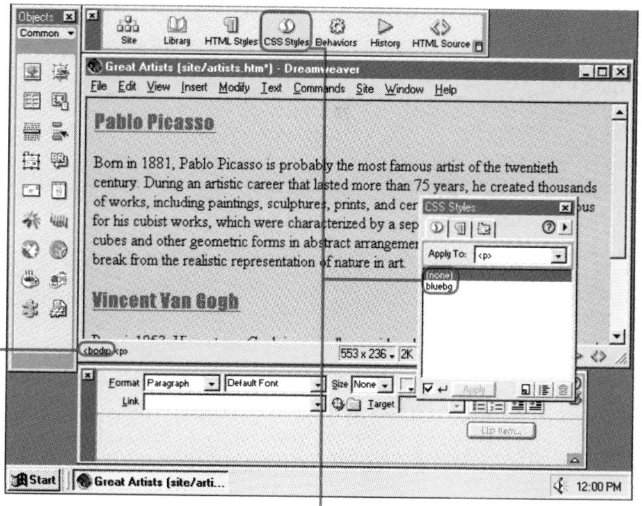

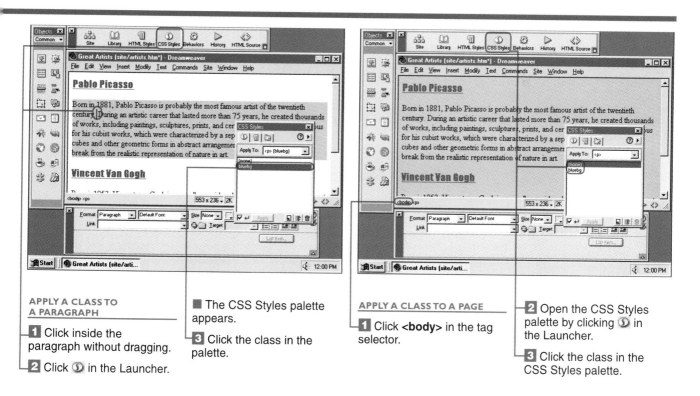

APPLY A CLASS TO A PARAGRAPH

1 Click inside the paragraph without dragging.

2 Click in the Launcher.

■ The CSS Styles palette appears.

3 Click the class in the palette.

APPLY A CLASS TO A PAGE

1 Click **<body>** in the tag selector.

2 Open the CSS Styles palette by clicking in the Launcher.

3 Click the class in the CSS Styles palette.

EDIT A STYLE-SHEET CLASS

You can edit the style definitions of a class. To create a style-sheet class, see the Section "Create a Class."

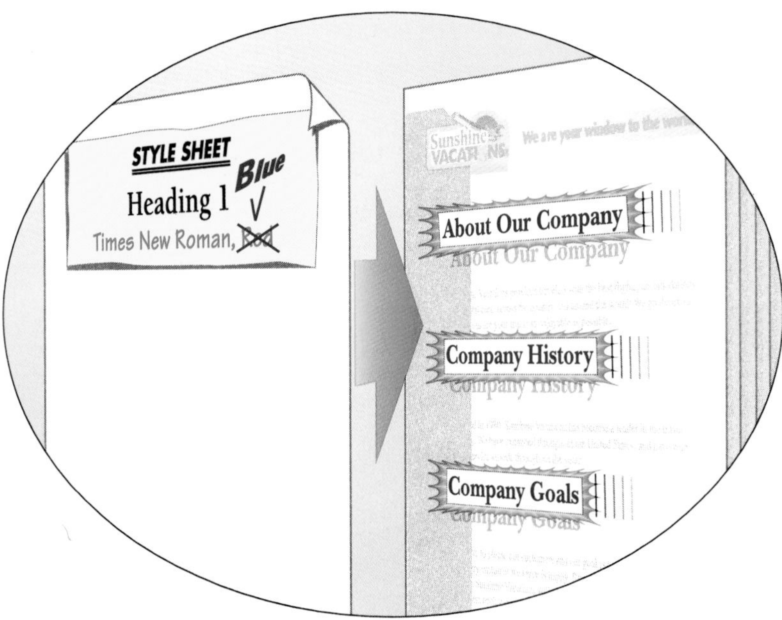

EDIT A STYLE-SHEET CLASS

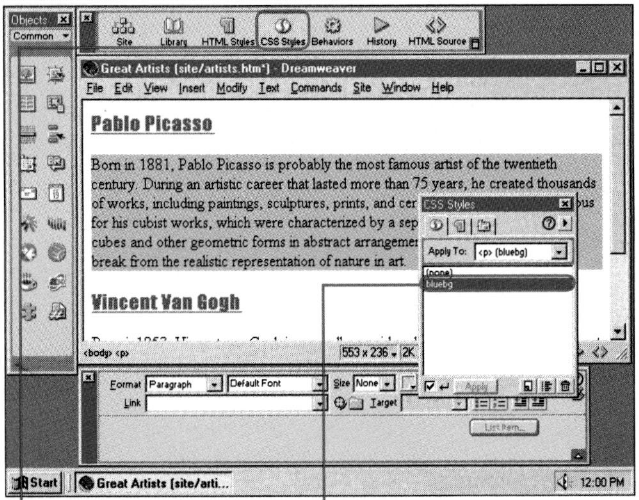

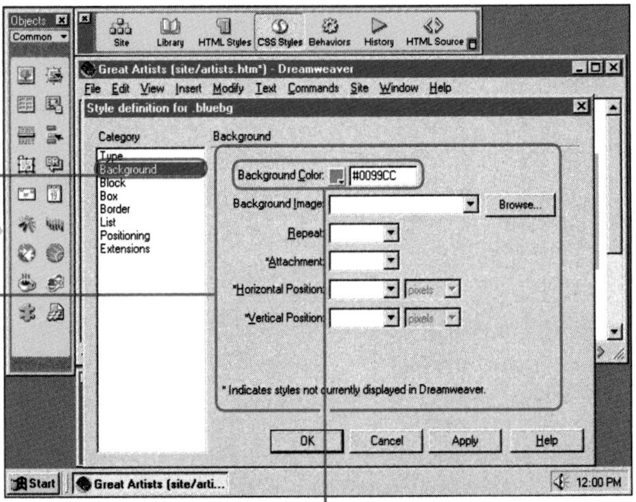

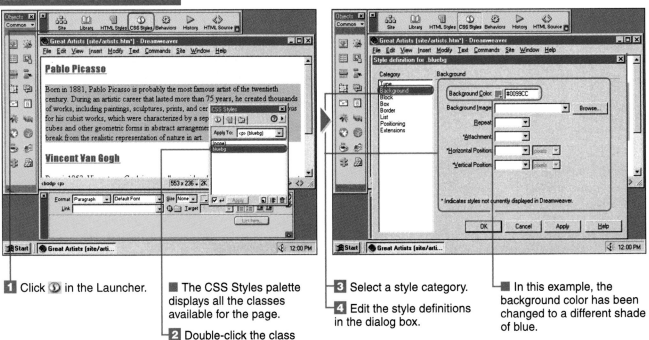

1 Click in the Launcher.

■ The CSS Styles palette displays all the classes available for the page.

2 Double-click the class you want to edit.

3 Select a style category.

4 Edit the style definitions in the dialog box.

■ In this example, the background color has been changed to a different shade of blue.

When I edit a style class, what happens to the instances where the rule was applied?

Changes you make to a class take effect automatically in the pages that use that style rule. This is the case for classes defined in embedded style sheets and in external style sheets. The fact that you can affect many different parts of a Web page — or many different Web pages — by changing a class makes style sheets powerful tools for maintaining Web content.

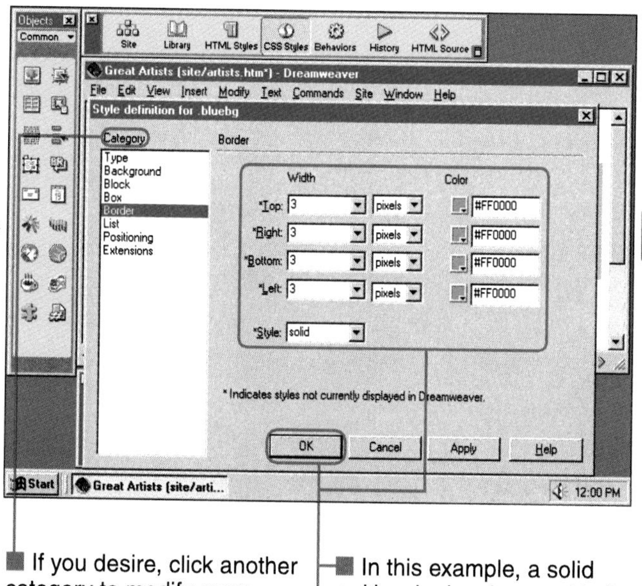

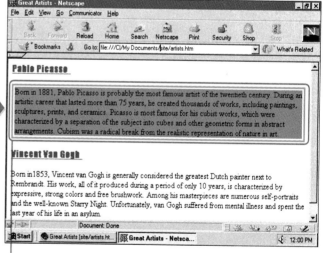

■ If you desire, click another category to modify more style definitions.

■ In this example, a solid red border has been added to the class.

5 Click **OK**.

■ In a Web browser, the paragraph displays the new changes.

Note: Dreamweaver cannot display some style definitions — for instance, border styles. Sometimes you must open the page in a Web browser to see the full effect of your edits.

USING CSS SELECTORS TO MODIFY LINKS

Style-sheet selectors can be used to customize the hyperlinks on your page.

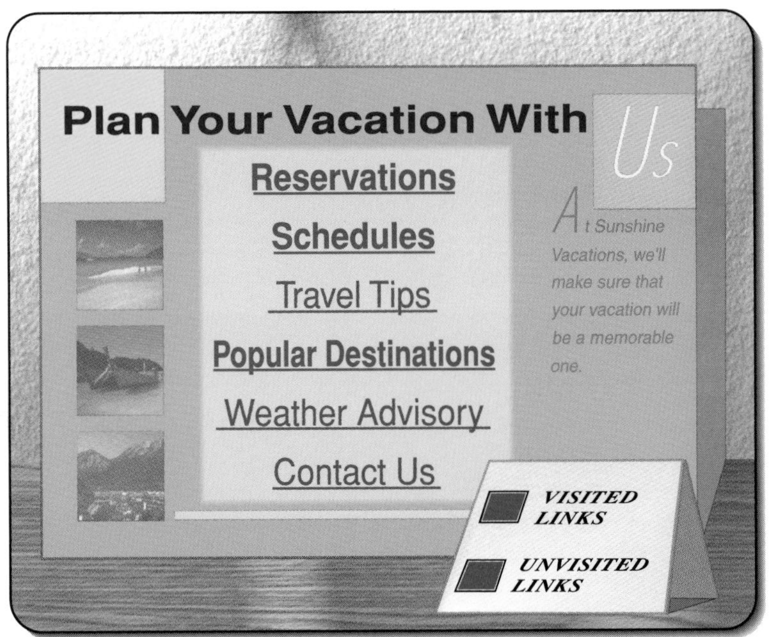

USING CSS SELECTORS TO MODIFY LINKS

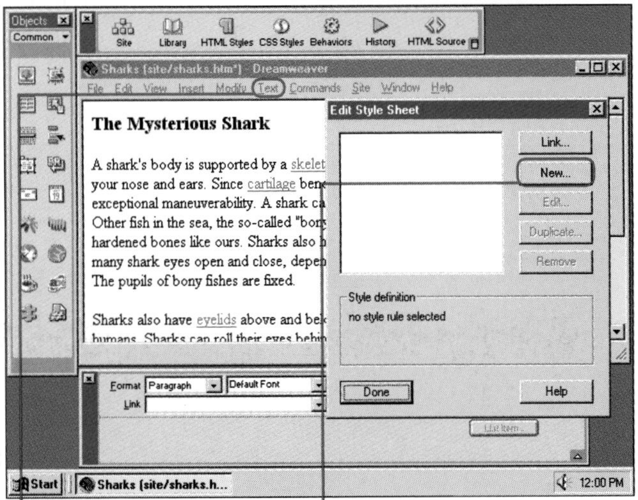

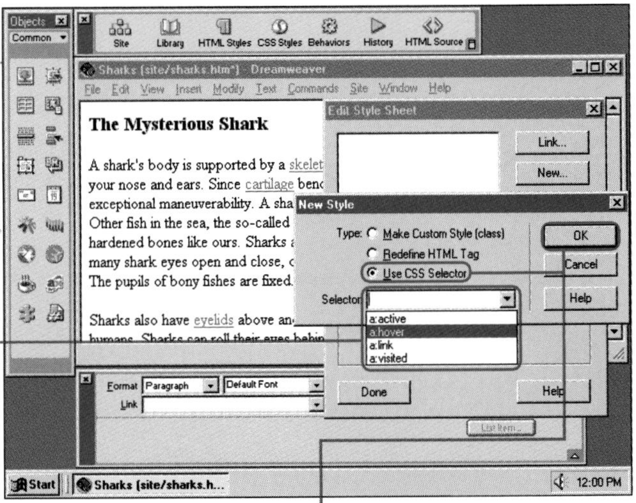

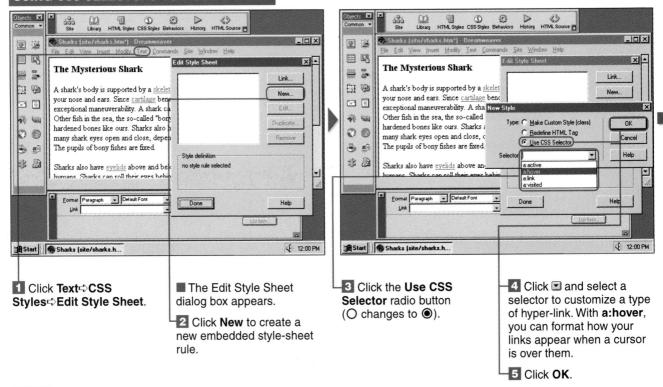

1 Click **Text⇨CSS Styles⇨Edit Style Sheet**.

■ The Edit Style Sheet dialog box appears.

2 Click **New** to create a new embedded style-sheet rule.

3 Click the **Use CSS Selector** radio button (○ changes to ◉).

4 Click ▾ and select a selector to customize a type of hyper-link. With **a:hover**, you can format how your links appear when a cursor is over them.

5 Click **OK**.

How do I eliminate the underlining on my hyperlinks?

You can remove the underlining that is normally applied to hyperlinks by modifying CSS selectors. Select the "none" decoration in the style definition window (as shown in the example in this section) for the four different selectors. If you want underlining to appear only when the user places the cursor over a link, modify all the selectors except **a:hover**.

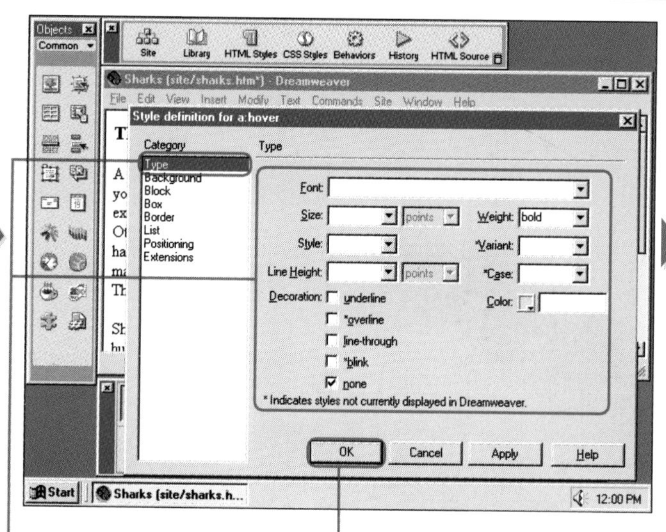

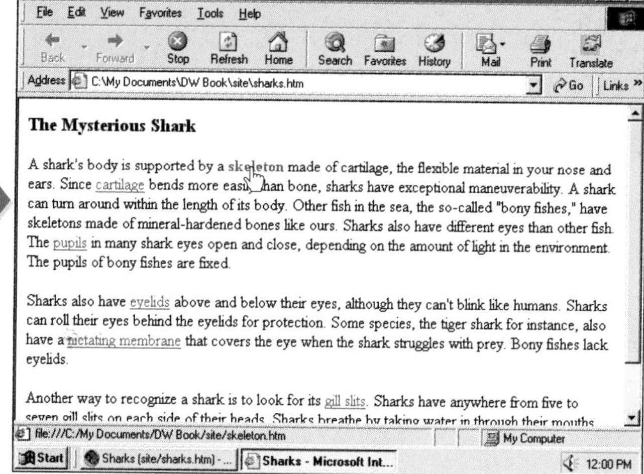

6 Select a style category in the Category box. This example uses **type**, which enables you to modify the text style of your links.

7 Select style information using the menus.

■ This example uses **none** for text decoration and **bold** for weight.

8 Click **OK**.

9 Click **Done** in the Edit Style Sheet dialog box.

■ When the page is opened in the Web browser and the cursor is placed over a link, the style of the link changes.

■ In this example, the underlining disappears and the text becomes bold.

CREATE AN EXTERNAL STYLE SHEET

You can save style-sheet rules in a separate file. In this manner, you can easily apply the same styles to multiple Web pages.

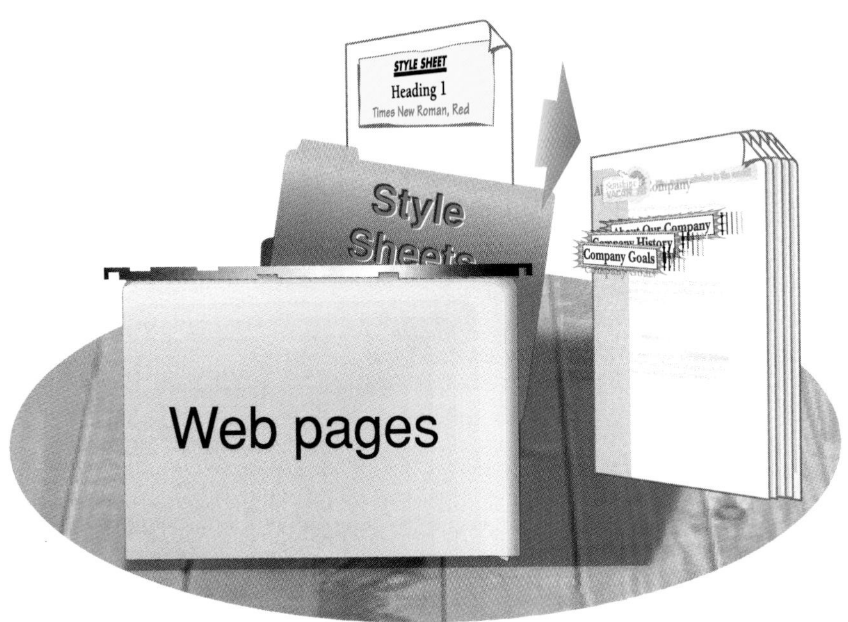

CREATE AN EXTERNAL STYLE SHEET

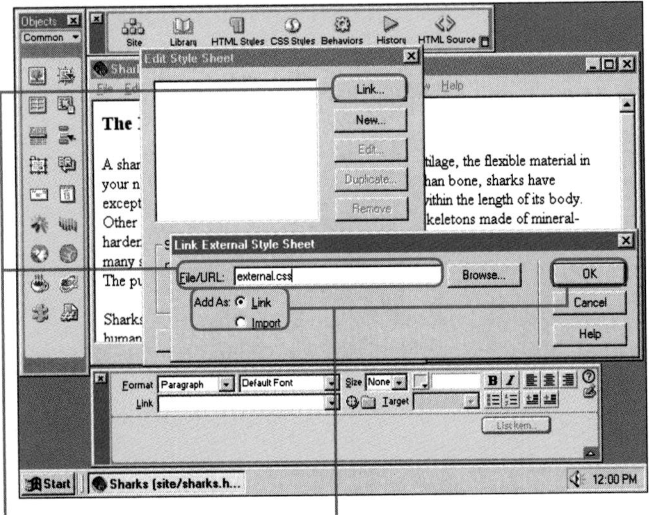

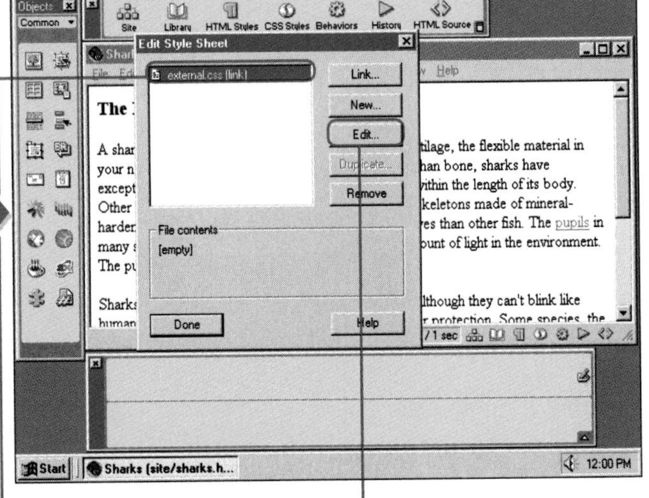

1 Click **Text ⇨CSS Styles⇨Edit Style Sheet.**

2 Click **Link**.

■ The Link External Style Sheet box appears.

3 Type the filename.

Note: The Filename must end in .css for your external style sheet.

4 Select **Link** or **Import** to determine how the external style sheet is associated with your page (○ changes to ◉).

5 Click **OK**.

■ The new external style sheet appears in the list.

6 To add style definitions to your external style sheet, select the style sheet's name in the list.

7 Click **Edit**.

What are the advantages of external style sheets?

External style sheets are helpful when maintaining large Web sites. By creating an external style sheet to which many developers can link, you can keep a consistent look and feel across a site.

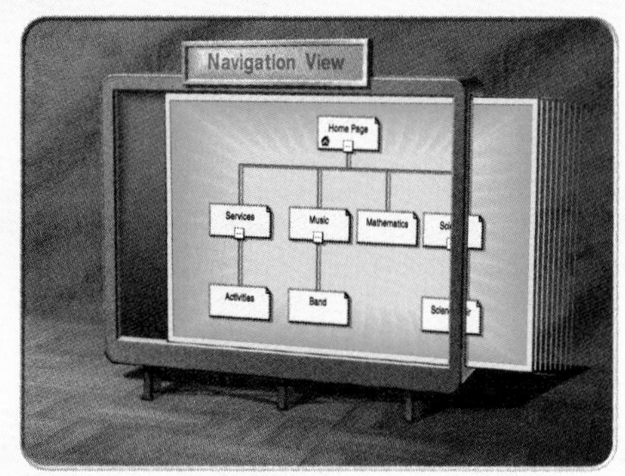

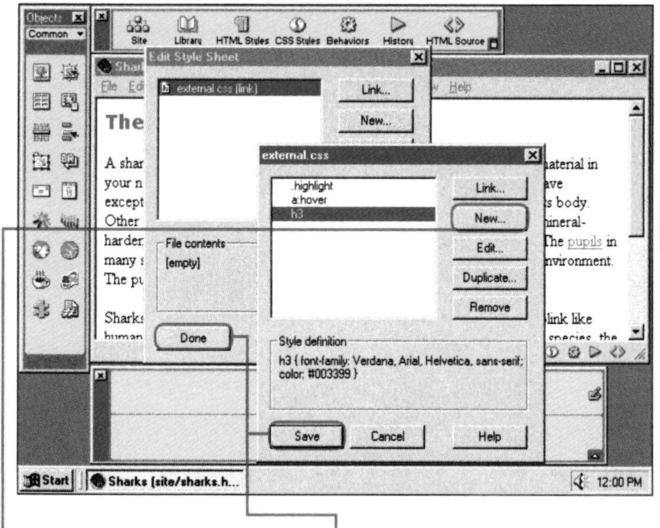

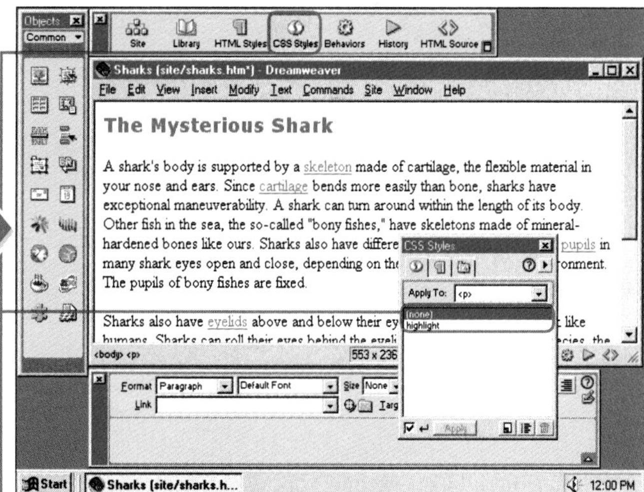

■ A separate dialog box opens for the external style sheet.

7 Click **New** to create each new style-sheet rule.

■ In this example, a tag was customized, a selector was used, and a class was defined on an external style.

8 Click **Save**.

9 Click **Done** in the Edit Style Sheet dialog box.

■ The rules from the new style sheet are automatically applied to the current document.

10 Click the CSS Styles button.

■ Any classes you created in the external style sheet are available in the CSS Styles palette.

*Note: The link to the style sheet can be removed by clicking **Text ⇨ CSS ⇨ Styles ⇨ Edit Style Sheet**, highlighting the style-sheet name, and clicking **Remove**.*

APPLY AN EXTERNAL STYLE SHEET

External style sheets let you define a set of style definitions once, and applies them to many pages—even pages on different Web sites. To create an external style sheet, see the Section "Create an External Style Sheet."

APPLY AN EXTERNAL STYLE SHEET

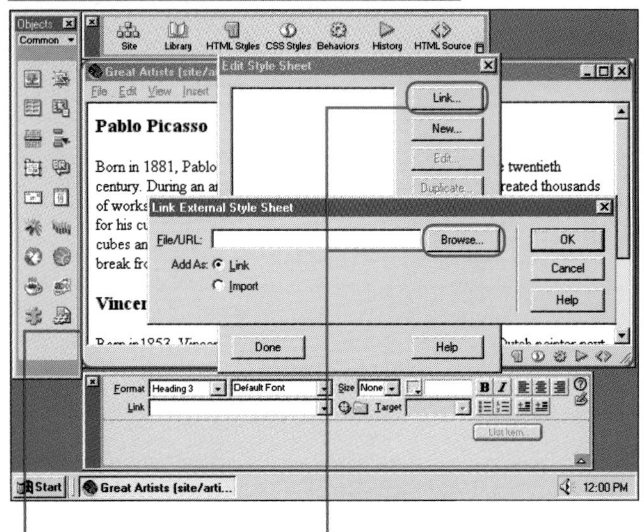

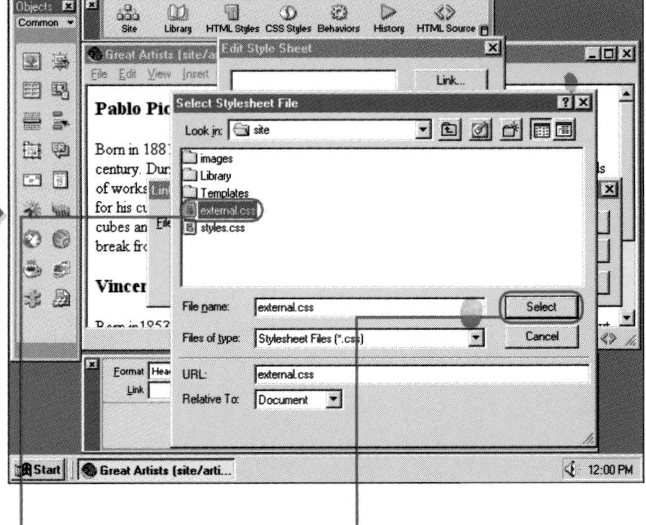

1 Open the page to which you want to apply the external style sheet.

2 Click **Text⇨CSS Styles⇨Edit Style Sheet**.

■ The Edit Style Sheet dialog box appears.

3 Click **Link** (○ changes to ◉).

4 Click **Browse**.

■ If the style sheet is on an external Web server, you can enter its Web address in the URL field.

5 Select the style-sheet file you want to attach to your Web page (example: **external.css**).

6 Click **Select**.

Can I make a style sheet publically available on the Web?

You can make a style sheet freely available to others by saving it as an external style sheet and uploading it to a Web server, just like you would a Web page. Others can link to it using the Web address (URL) of the style sheet.

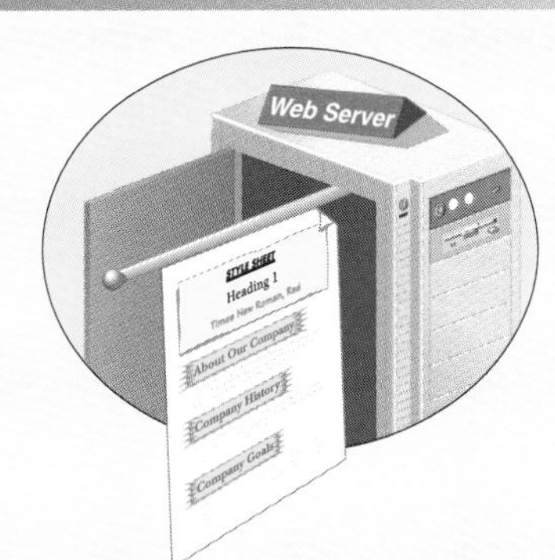

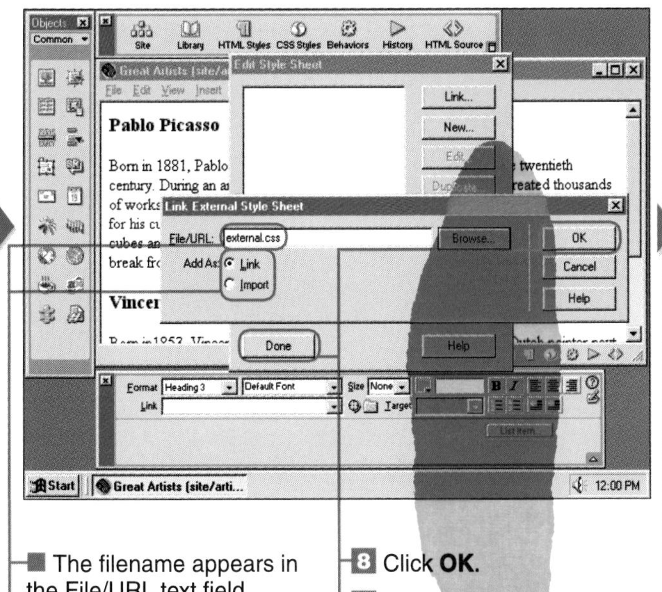

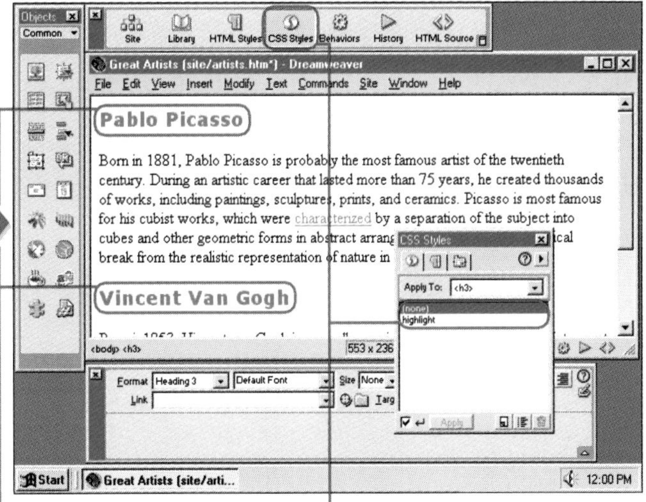

■ The filename appears in the File/URL text field.

7 Select the **Link** or **Import** radio button (○ changes to ◉) to determine how the external style sheet is associated with your page.

8 Click **OK.**

9 Click **Done** in the Edit Style Sheet dialog box.

■ Dreamweaver applies the external style to the page.

■ In this example, the external style sheet has redefined the h3 tag (with a Verdana font face and blue color).

10 Click the CSS Styles icon in the Launcher.

■ Classes defined in the external style sheet appear in the CSS Styles palette.

Note: To apply a class, see the Section "Apply a Class".

Elements can be precisely positioned on your Web page by using style sheets. You can also position elements using layers (see the section "Create a Layer").

POSITION PAGE ELEMENTS

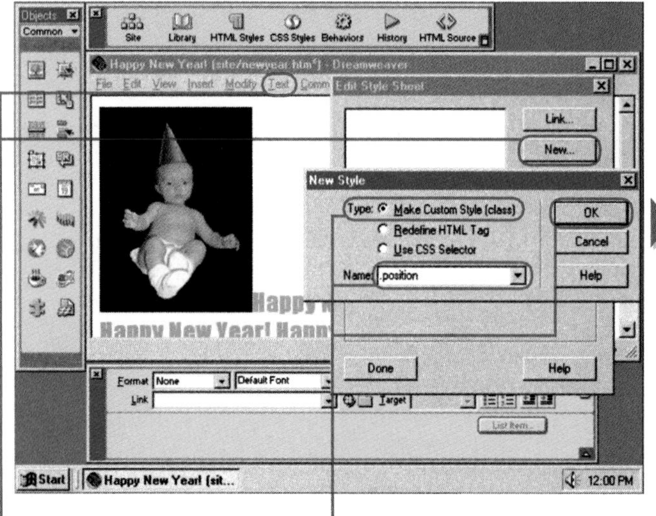

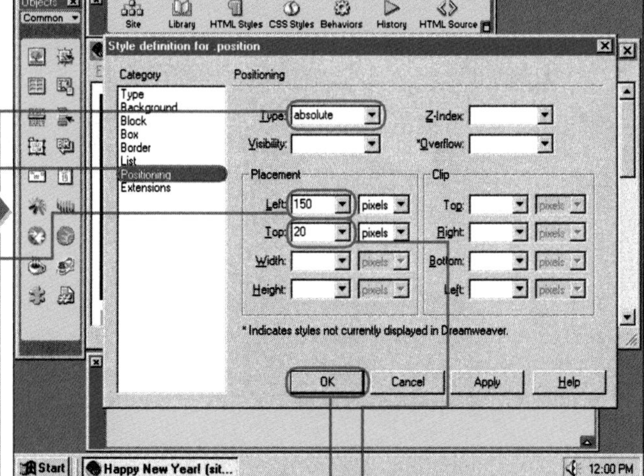

1 Click **Text⇨CSS Styles⇨Edit Style Sheet**.

■ The Edit Style Sheet dialog box appears.

2 Click **New** to open the New Style dialog box.

3 Click the **Make Custom Style** (**Class**) radio button (○ changes to ◉).

4 Type a name for the new class. The name must be one word and begin with a period.

5 Click **OK**.

6 Click **Positioning**.

7 Click ▼ and select **absolute** as the type.

8 Type a value in the Left text field. This will be the element's offset from the left side of the window.

9 Type a value in the Top text field. This will be the element's offset from the top of the window.

10 Click **OK**.

11 Click **Done** in the Edit Styles dialog box.

Why would I want to use style sheets to position elements on my page?

Positioning with style sheets allows you to arrange elements of your Web page much more precisely (to the pixel) than is possible with HTML. Positioning also allows you to place elements in your Web page on top of one another.

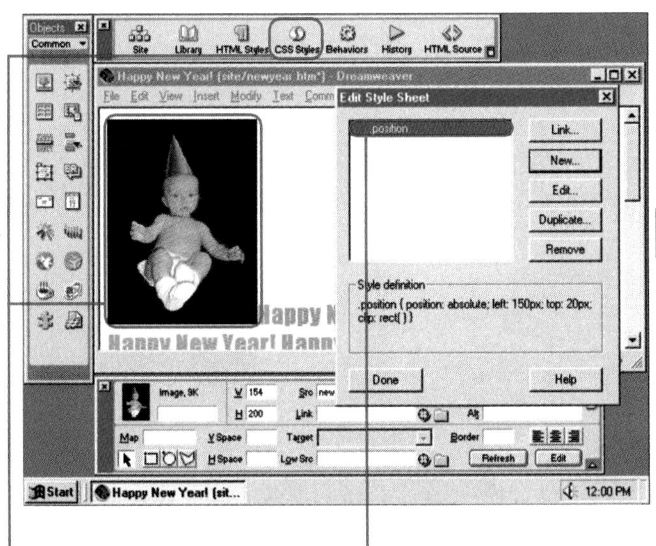

12 Click the element you want to position.

13 Click the (CSS Styles icon) in the Launcher.

■ The Edit Style Sheet dialog box appears.

14 Select the name of the class you just created in the list.

■ The element you selected is removed from the flow of the page and positioned according to your specifications.

Note: Although this example used an image, you can position text, tables, and other page elements.

CREATE A LAYER

Layers give you the option of overlapping elements on your page while positioning them precisely. Your layers can contain text, images, and other page elements.

CREATE A LAYER

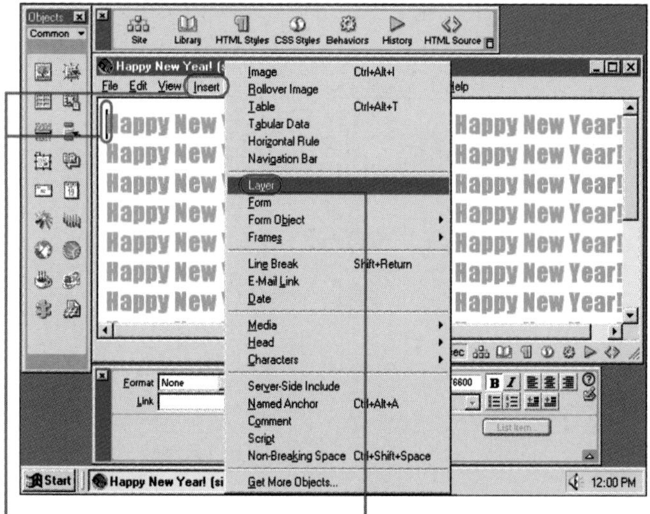

1 Place your cursor where you want to insert a layer.

2 Click **Insert**.

3 Click **Layer**.

Note: You can also insert a layer by clicking the layer icon in the Object window, then clicking and dragging it in the document window.

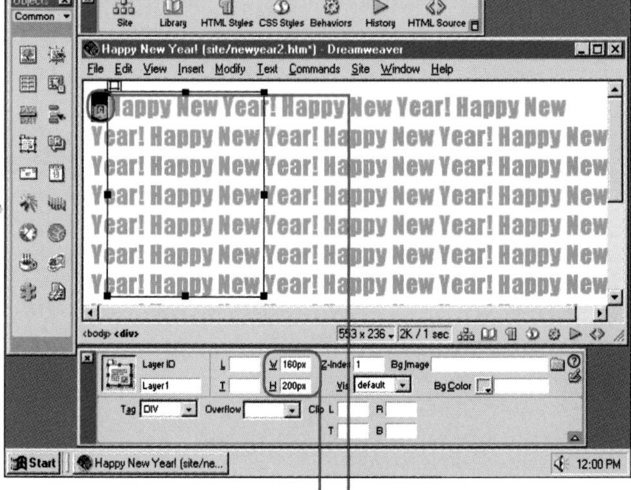

■ Dreamweaver inserts a layer. The layer floats above any existing content.

4 Click [icon] to select your layer.

5 Type the width of the layer in the W field and the height of the layer in the H field.

How can I change the properties of the default layer that is initially inserted when I create a layer?

You can change the properties of the default layer by clicking **Edit⇨Preferences,** and then **Layers** in the menu. This enables you to change the default layer's visibility, dimensions, color, and other properties.

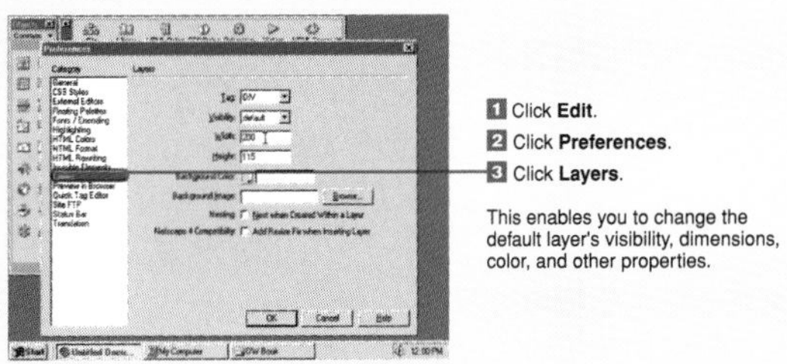

1 Click **Edit**.

2 Click **Preferences**.

3 Click **Layers**.

This enables you to change the default layer's visibility, dimensions, color, and other properties.

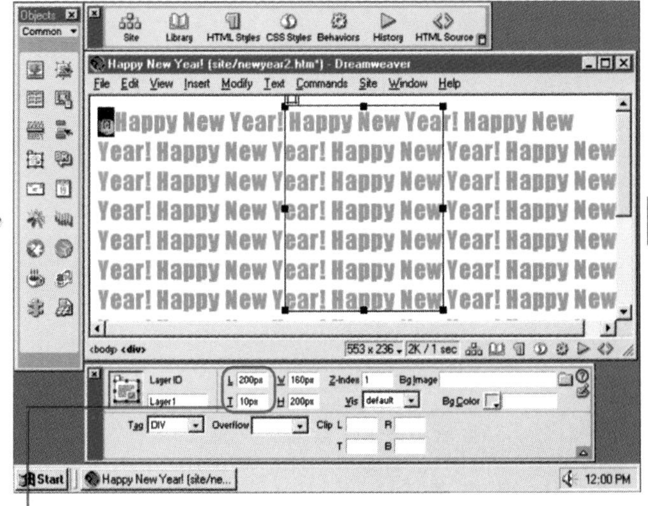

6 To position your layer, type its distance from the left side of the window in the L field and its distance from the top of the window in the T field.

7 Label the values by typing **px** for pixels, **in** for inches, or **cm** for centimeters.

8 To add content to a layer, click inside it.

■ In the example, an image was added. You can also add text, tables, and other page elements to layers.

You can change the dimensions and positioning of a layer.

RESIZE A LAYER

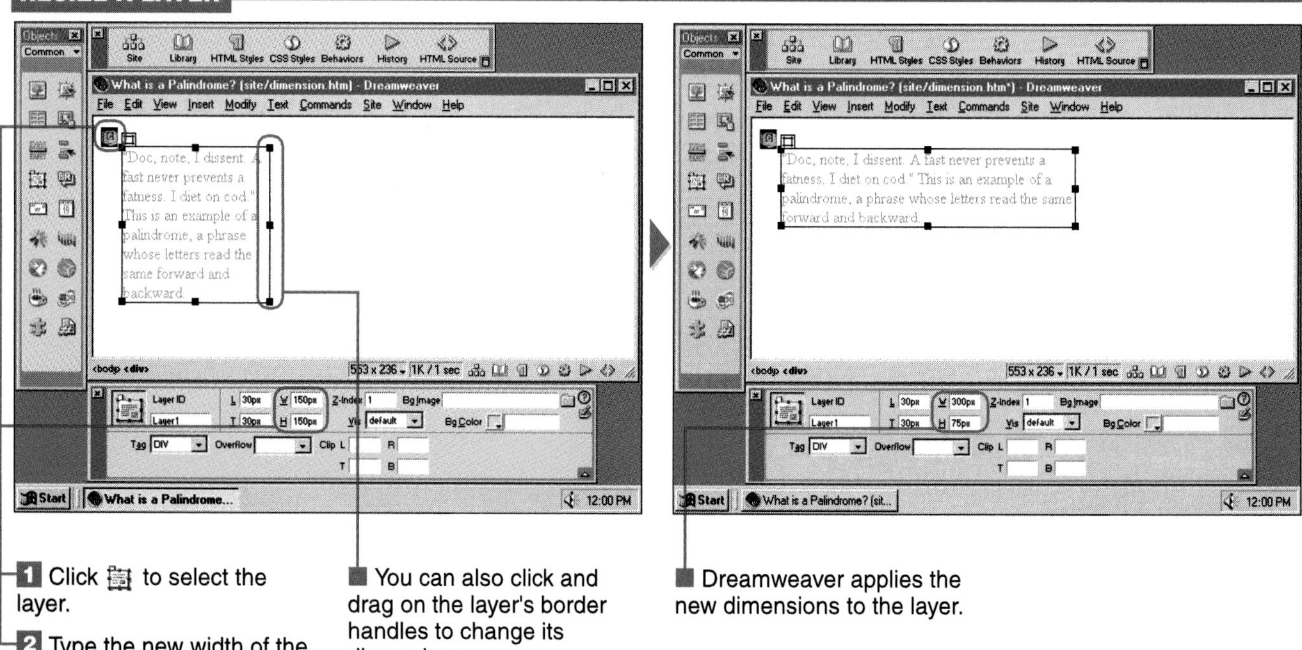

1 Click [icon] to select the layer.

2 Type the new width of the layer in the W field and the new height of the layer in the H field.

■ You can also click and drag on the layer's border handles to change its dimensions.

■ Dreamweaver applies the new dimensions to the layer.

How will moving a layer affect other layers on my page?

Layers are positioned relative to the upper left corner of the page, not relative to one another. So moving one layer will not affect the positioning of other layers. This allows layers to be stacked on top of one another.

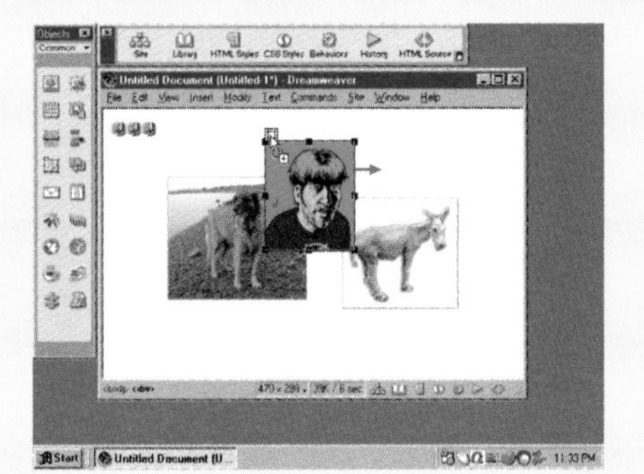

REPOSITION A LAYER

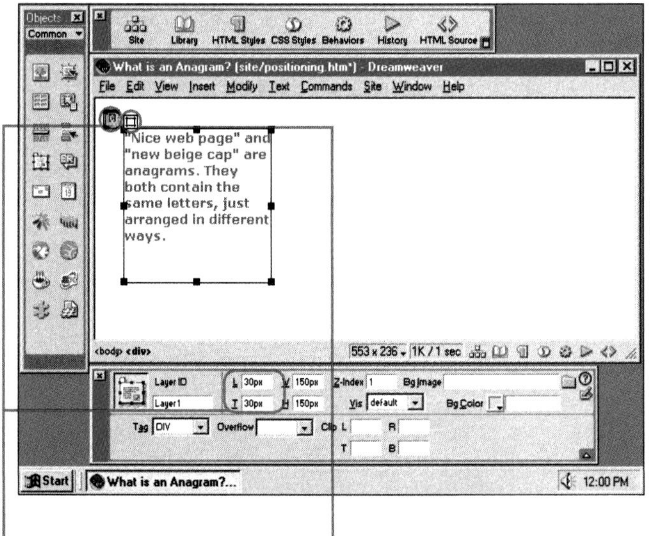

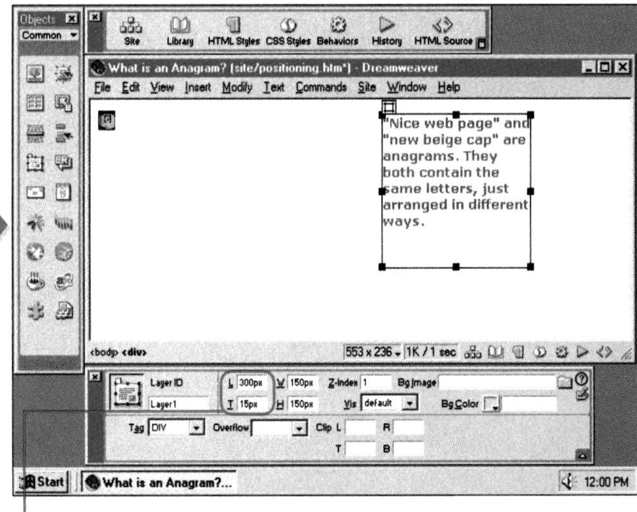

1 Click ▣ to select the layer.

2 Type the new distance from the left side of the window in the L field and the new distance distance from the top of the window in the T field.

3 Label the values by typing **px** for pixels, **in** for inches, or **cm** for centimeters.

■ You can also click and drag ▣ to change a layer's position.

■ Dreamweaver applies the new positioning to the layer.

CONTROL OVERLAP IN A LAYER

You can control whether content that overlaps the borders of a layer is displayed.

CONTROL OVERLAP IN A LAYER

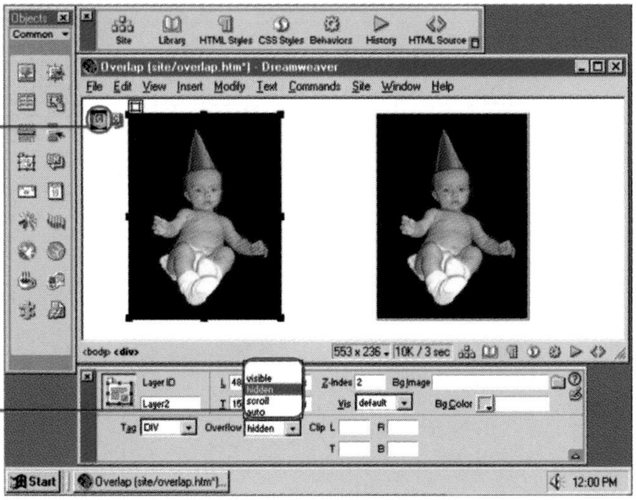

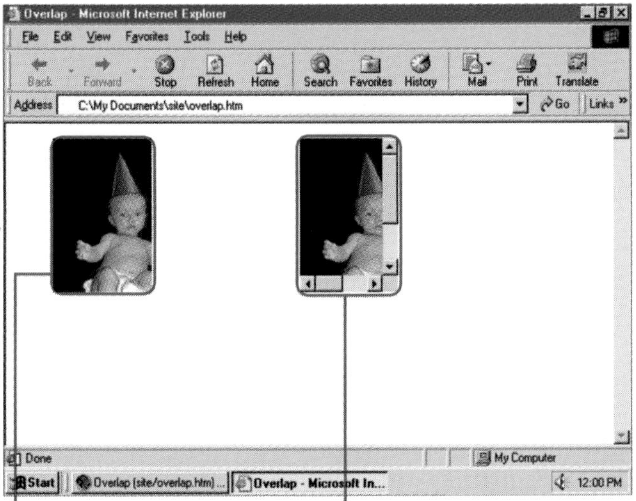

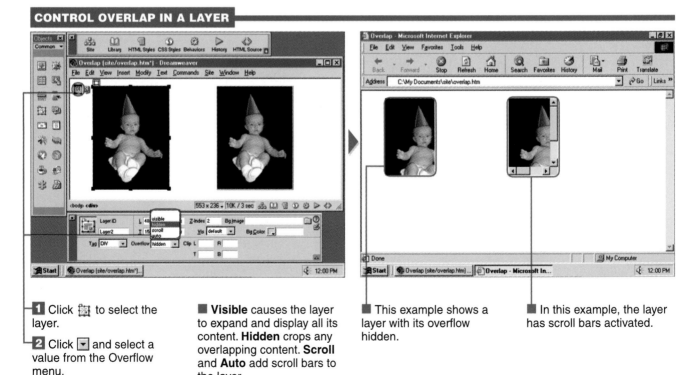

1 Click to select the layer.

2 Click and select a value from the Overflow menu.

■ **Visible** causes the layer to expand and display all its content. **Hidden** crops any overlapping content. **Scroll** and **Auto** add scroll bars to the layer.

■ This example shows a layer with its overflow hidden.

■ In this example, the layer has scroll bars activated.

HIDE A LAYER

You can hide a layer to display information behind it.

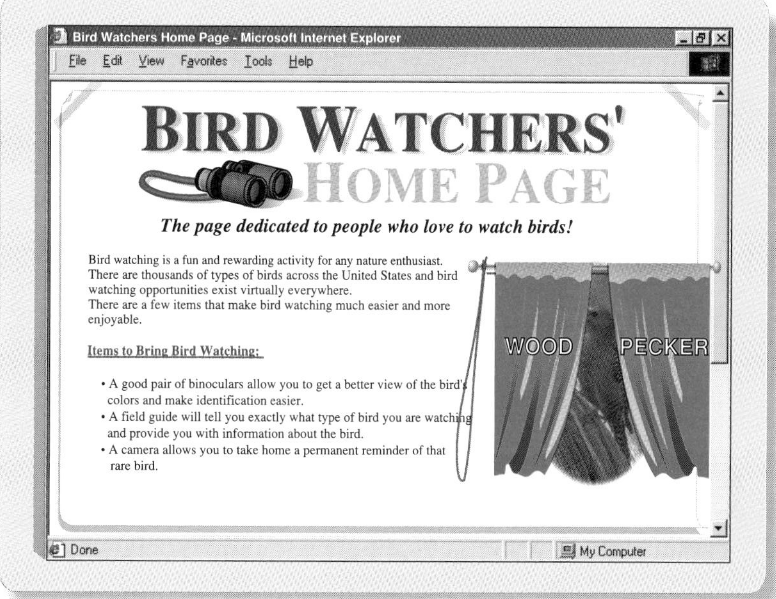

HIDE A LAYER

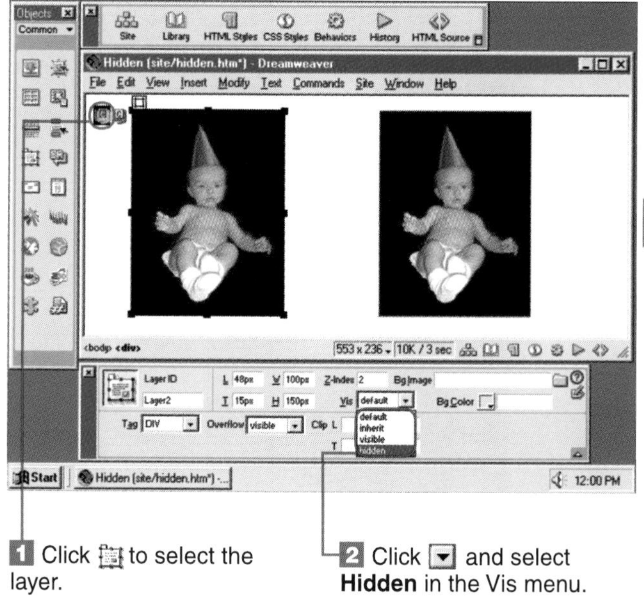

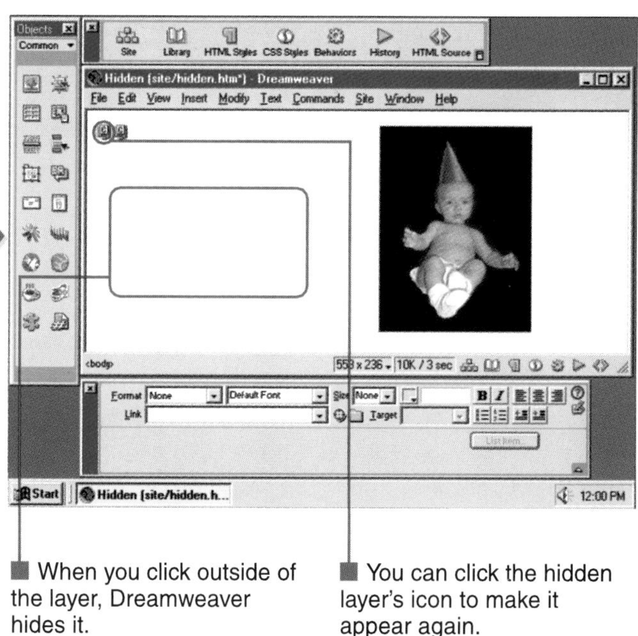

1 Click ▦ to select the layer.

2 Click ▾ and select **Hidden** in the Vis menu.

■ When you click outside of the layer, Dreamweaver hides it.

■ You can click the hidden layer's icon to make it appear again.

ADD BACKGROUND COLOR TO A LAYER

You can add background color to a layer to make it contrast with the rest of the Web page.

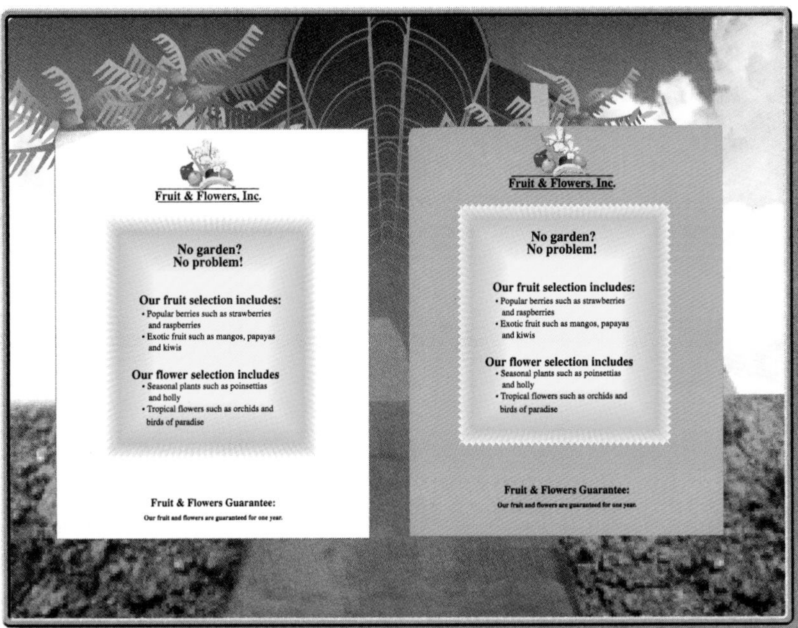

ADD BACKGROUND COLOR TO A LAYER

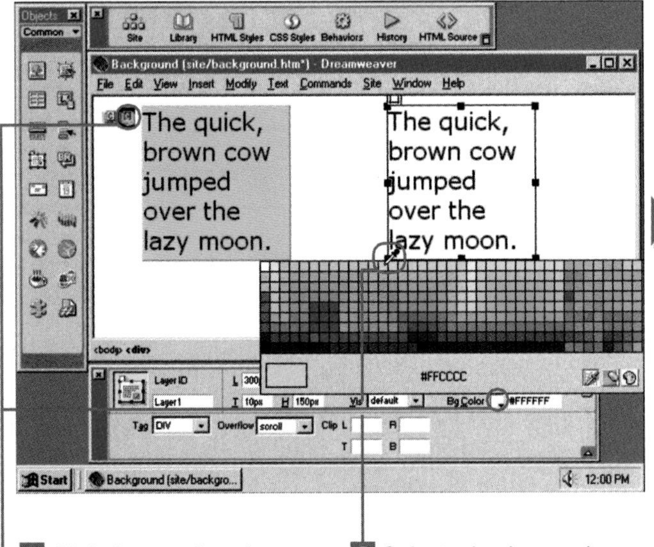

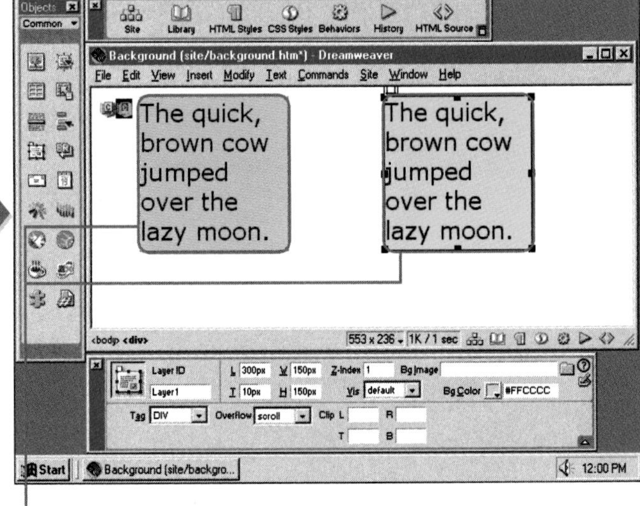

1 Click [icon] to select the layer.

2 Click **BgColor** to open the color menu.

3 Select a background color using the eyedropper.

■ You can click [icon] to select a background image for the layer.

■ In this example, the layers have different background colors.

CHANGE THE STACKING ORDER OF LAYERS

The Layers palette lets you easily rearrange the stacking order of layers on a page. The stacking order determines which layers are visible when they overlap.

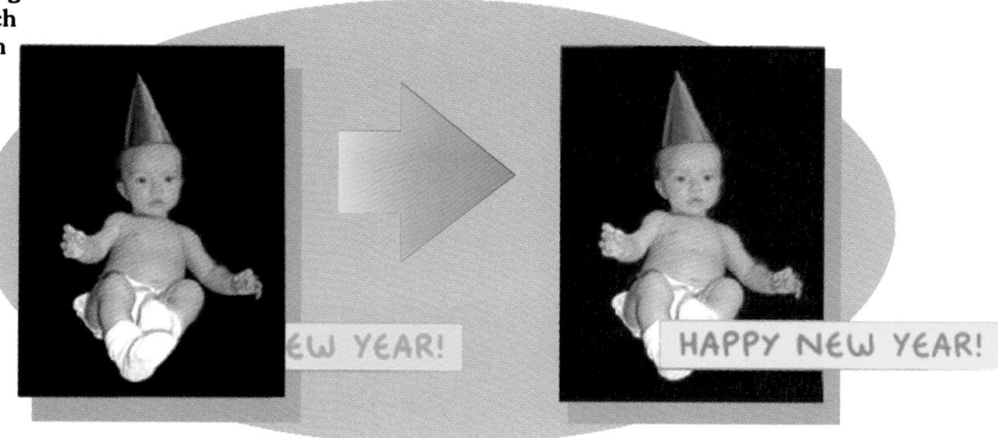

CHANGE THE STACKING ORDER OF LAYERS

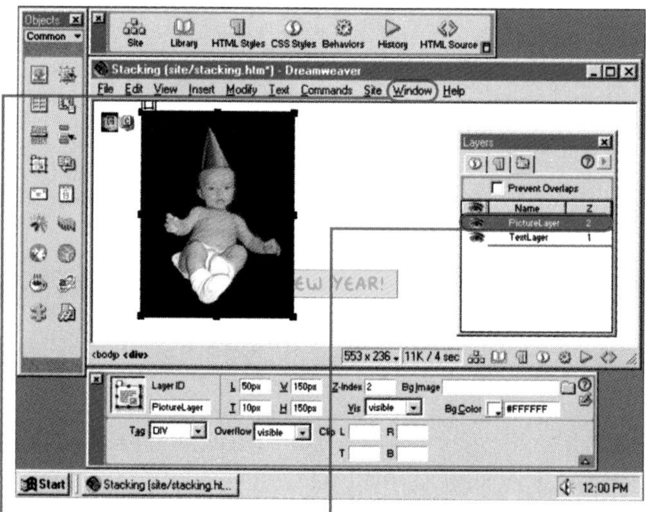

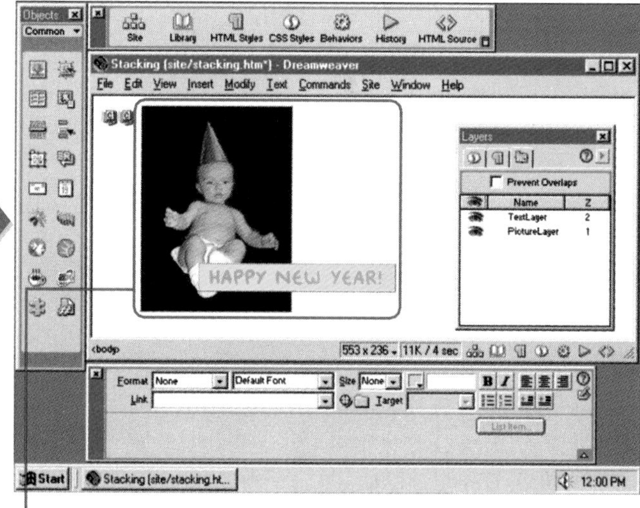

■ In this example, the baby layer is over the banner layer.

1 Click **Window⇨Layers**.

■ The page's layers appear in the Layers palette.

2 Click and drag a layer name to change the stacking order. Drag the layer name up to move it higher in the stack; drag it down to send it down.

■ Dreamweaver changes the stacking order of the layers.

The Fishing Co.
CUSTOMER INFORMATION
NAME: J. Anderson
ADDRESS:
CITY:
ZIP CODE: 47777-8844
VALIDATED

VALIDATED

CHAPTER 12

Implementing Behavior

Dreamweaver's behaviors let you include interactive features in your site. This chapter shows you how to add behaviors to your pages.

ABOUT BEHAVIORS

Your can add interactive features to your Web pages with Dreamweaver's *behaviors*. Behaviors let you create image rollovers, validate forms, check browser versions, and more.

WHAT IS A BEHAVIOR?

A *behavior* is a cause-and-effect feature that you set up in your Web page. You specify a user event (such as a mouse click) and the resulting action (such as a pop-up window appearing) that should take place when that event occurs.

DREAMWEAVER CREATES BEHAVIORS WITH JAVASCRIPT

Dreamweaver builds behaviors with *JavaScript,* a popular programming language for adding dynamic features to Web sites. You apply behaviors to specific objects on your Web page using dialog boxes, then Dreamweaver writes the JavaScript code behind the scenes to create the behaviors.

BEHAVIORS AND BROWSERS

Dreamweaver's standard behaviors all work in Version 4.0 or later of Netscape Navigator and Microsoft Internet Explorer. Some of the behaviors will also work in earlier browsers.

WHAT IS AN IMAGE ROLLOVER?

An *image rollover* behavior replaces an image on your page in response a user action, such as a cursor passing over it or a mouse clicking it.

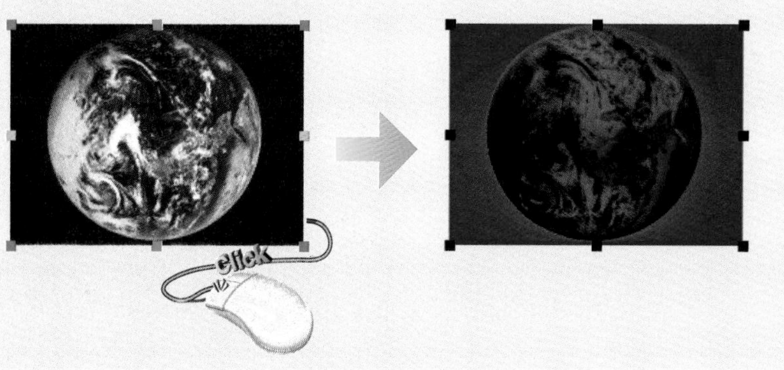

WHAT IS FORM VALIDATION?

You can make sure users do not enter erroneous information on your forms by using a behavior to validate your entry fields. You can cause an alert to appear if invalid data is submitted.

WHY CHECK BROWSER VERSIONS?

It can be difficult to design a page that works equally well in all browsers, especially if you use advanced features such as style sheets. You can use a behavior to check the type of browser a person is using and send them to a page built specifically for that browser.

Version 1

Version 2

CREATE A BEHAVIOR

Defining a behavior requires you to select three things: the element on your Web page to be associated with the behavior, the action you want performed, and the event that triggers the action.

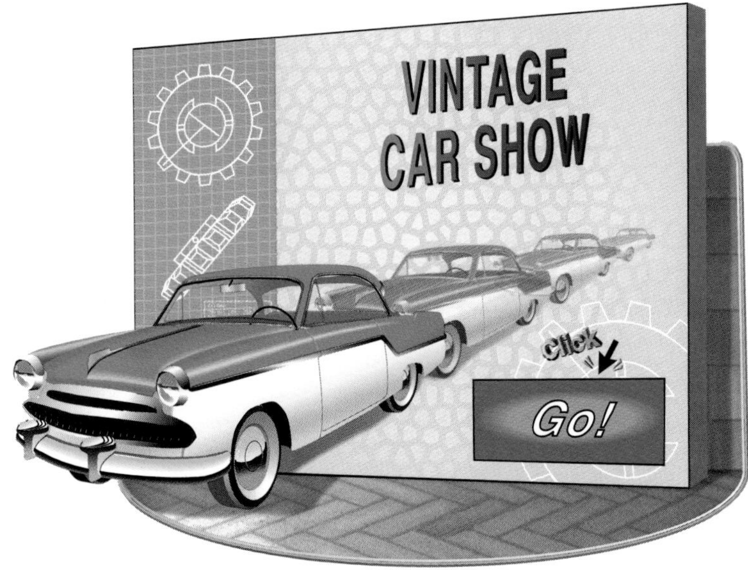

CREATE A BEHAVIOR

1 Select the object on your Web page that you want associated with a behavior.

2 Click to open the Behaviors inspector.

3 Click and select a browser compatibility.

■ Dreamweaver limits the available behaviors to those that work in that browser. (The greater the browser version, the more behaviors it supports.)

4 Click to display the actions.

■ The actions available depend on the object selected and the browser compatibility.

5 Select an action.

How does JavaScript create behaviors?

JavaScript is a programming language that can be written into the text of your HTML document. Many of its uses involve changing elements of a page in response to user activities such as mouse clicks. In short, JavaScript enhances HTML, making Web pages more dynamic.

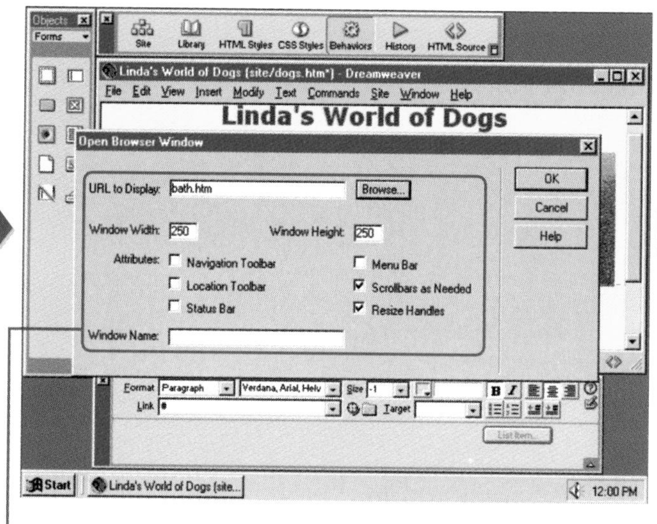

■ Dreamweaver displays a dialog box specific to that action.

6 Define your action in the dialog box.

7 Click **OK**.

■ To define specific actions, see the rest of the sections in this chapter.

8 Click ▼ to display the events.

■ The events available depend on the object selected, the action you selected, and browser compatibility.

9 Select an event.

■ The browser compatibility, action, and event for the behavior are displayed in the Behaviors window.

■ You can delete an action by selecting it in the window and clicking –.

CREATE AN IMAGE ROLLOVER

Dreamweaver's behaviors can replace an image when the cursor rolls over it. Rollover effects are often used to enhance navigation graphics.

CREATE AN IMAGE ROLLOVER

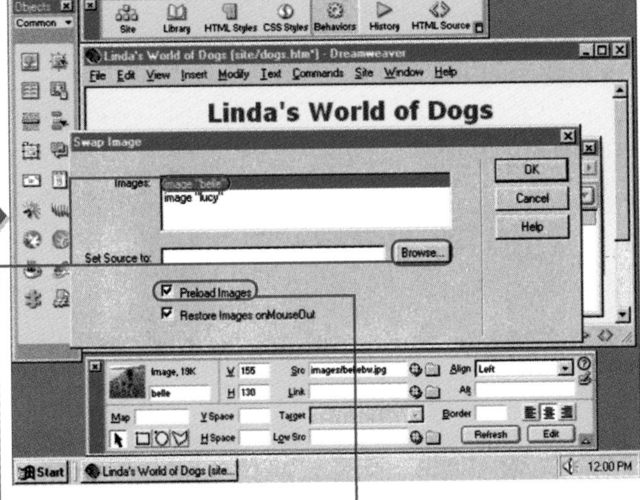

1 Select the image to be replaced.

■ In this example, a color image of a dog replaces a black-and-white one.

2 Name the image.

3 Click ⚙ to open the Behaviors inspector.

4 Click ▾ and select **4.0 and Later Browsers**.

5 Click + and select **Swap Image**.

■ The list displays all the named images on the page.

6 Select the image to be replaced.

7 Click **Browse** to select a replacement image.

■ To load the replacement image as the Web page loads, check **Preload Images** (☐ changes to ☑).

How do I create a rollover navigation button?

First you create "on" and "off" versions of the button in an image editor (such as Adobe Photoshop or Macromedia Fireworks). Then you add the "off" image to your page and apply the image-swap behavior to it (see below). Some common ways to create the "on" version of a rollover button are to reverse its colors, add a border, or shift the art slightly so it looks like the graphic has been pressed down.

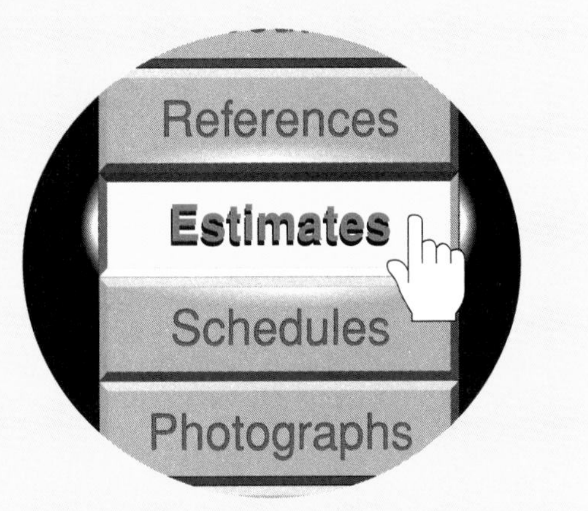

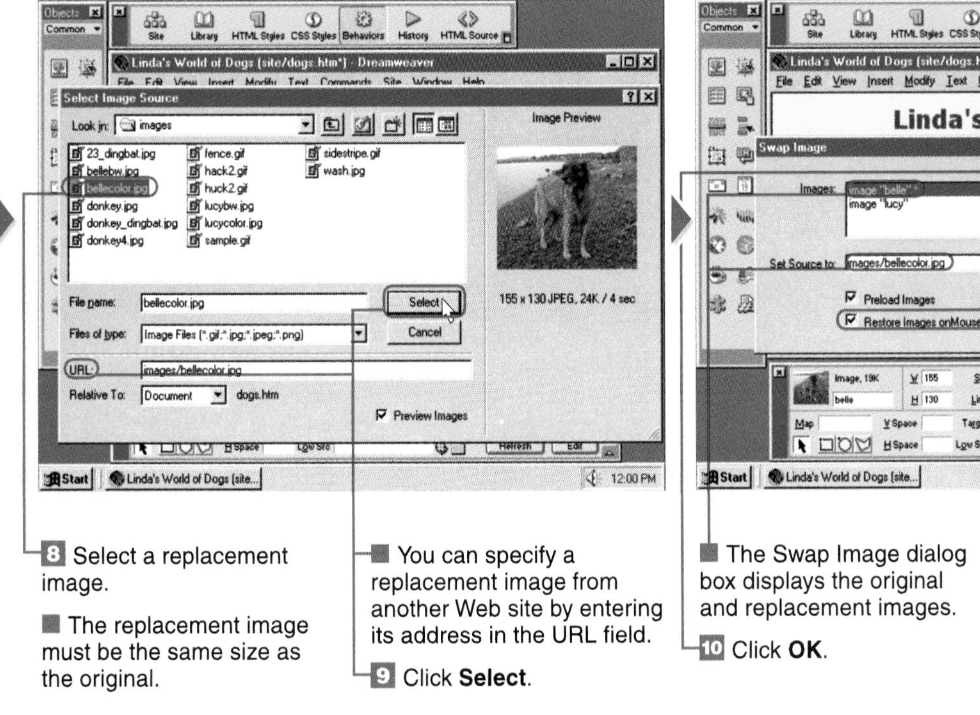

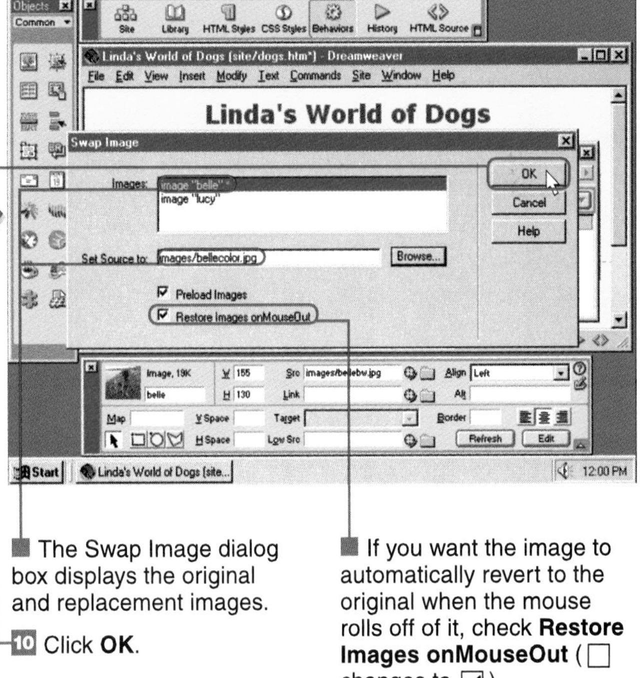

8 Select a replacement image.

■ The replacement image must be the same size as the original.

■ You can specify a replacement image from another Web site by entering its address in the URL field.

9 Click **Select**.

■ The Swap Image dialog box displays the original and replacement images.

10 Click **OK**.

■ If you want the image to automatically revert to the original when the mouse rolls off of it, check **Restore Images onMouseOut** (☐ changes to ☑).

CONTINUED

CREATE AN IMAGE ROLLOVER (CONTINUED)

Creating an image rollover involves defining an existing image on the page, a replacement image, and the user action to trigger the rollover. You can test the final result in a browser.

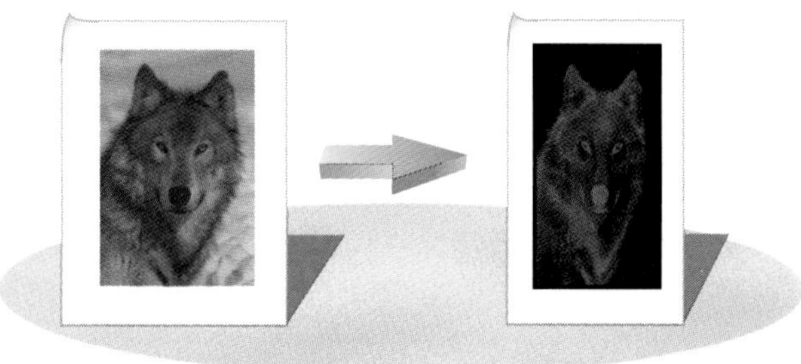

CREATE AN IMAGE ROLLOVER (CONTINUED)

■ The Behavior window lists the events and actions for the image selected in Step 1.

■ In this example, Dreamweaver created two event/action pairs because **Restore Images** was checked.

■ By default, Swap Image is triggered by an onMouseOver event (the cursor rolling over the image).

■ To change the event that triggers the rollover, you can click ▾ and select a new event.

Can I create a rollover effect where the image that is replaced is different from the image that is rolled over?

Yes. You do this by choosing an image in the Swap Image window (Step 6 in this section) that is different than the image selected in the document window (Step 1 in this section).

CHECK AN IMAGE ROLLOVER

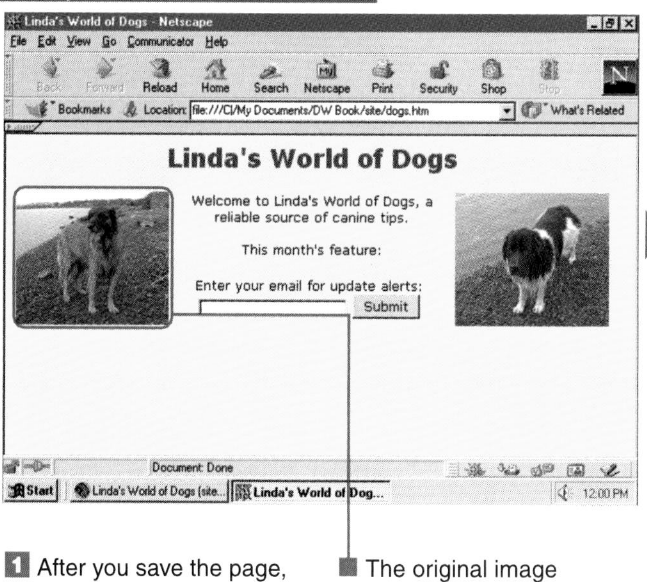

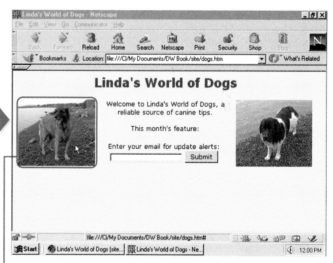

1 After you save the page, open it in a Web browser.

■ The original image appears when the page loads.

2 Roll the cursor over the image to ensure that the original image changes to the new image.

■ When you roll off of the image, it reverts to the original one.

CREATE A STATUS BAR MESSAGE

You can make a message appear in the browser's status bar in response to a user's action.

CREATE A STATUS BAR MESSAGE

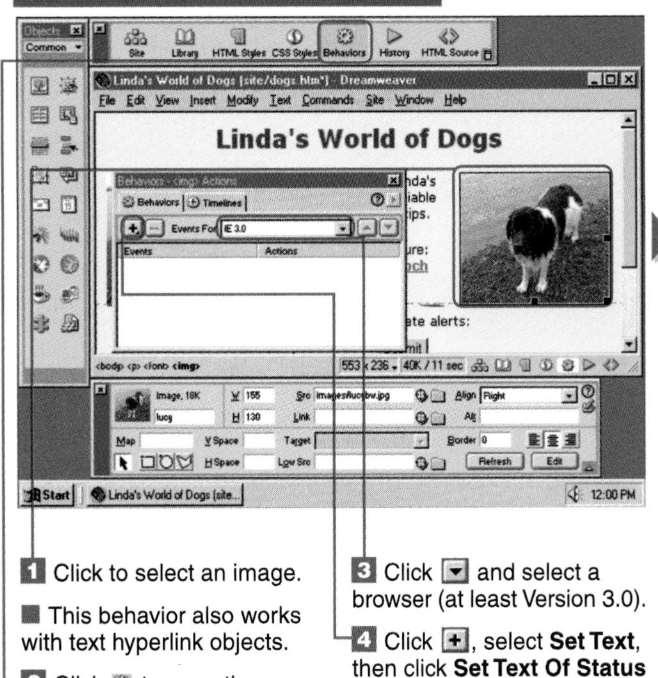

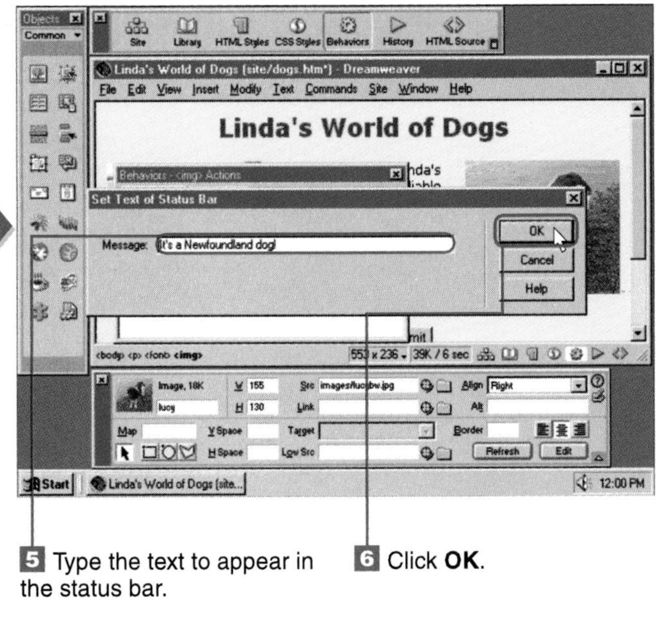

1 Click to select an image.

■ This behavior also works with text hyperlink objects.

2 Click ⚙ to open the Behaviors inspector.

3 Click ▼ and select a browser (at least Version 3.0).

4 Click **+**, select **Set Text**, then click **Set Text Of Status Bar**.

5 Type the text to appear in the status bar.

6 Click **OK**.

How do I make the status message go away?

You can hide the status message by assigning a second behavior to your object. For instance, if you assigned a behavior that makes an `onMouseOver` event trigger a status message (as I do below), you can create a second behavior that makes an `onMouseOff` event erase the message. (Just make the `onMouseOff` event trigger a blank message in the status bar.)

■ The default event for status-bar messages is `onMouseOver` (rolling the mouse over the object triggers the message).

■ You can click ▾ to select a different event.

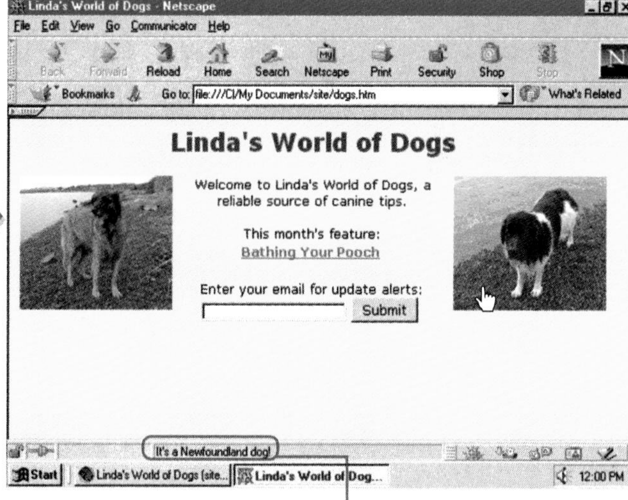

7 Save the Web page. (See Chapter 2.)

■ When you open the Web page in a Web browser, and roll the cursor over the image, the message appears in the status bar.

VALIDATE A FORM

You can double-check a user's form entries to make sure valid data is submitted.

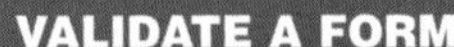

VALIDATE A FORM

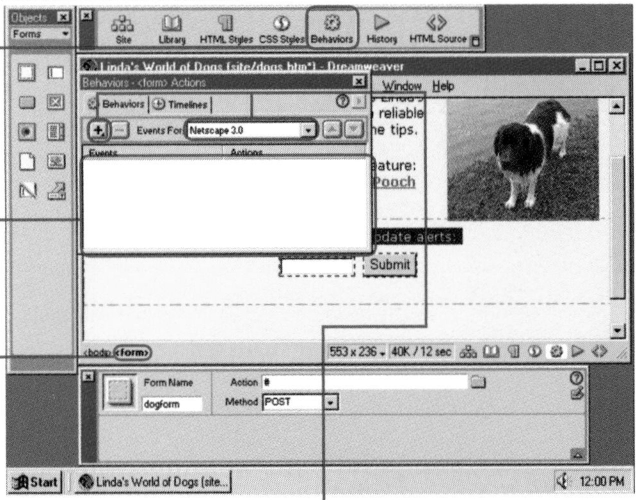

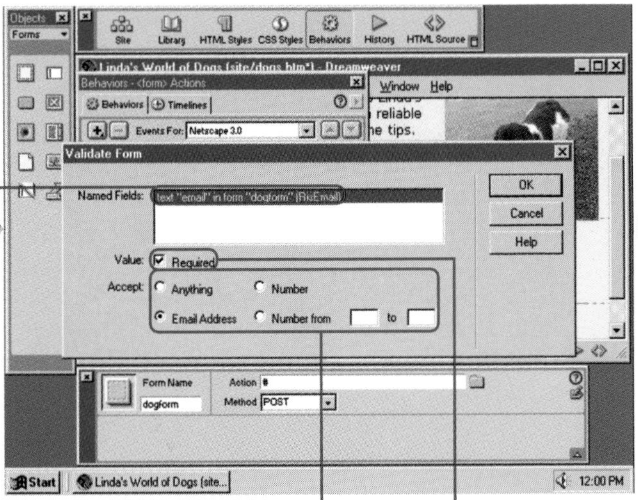

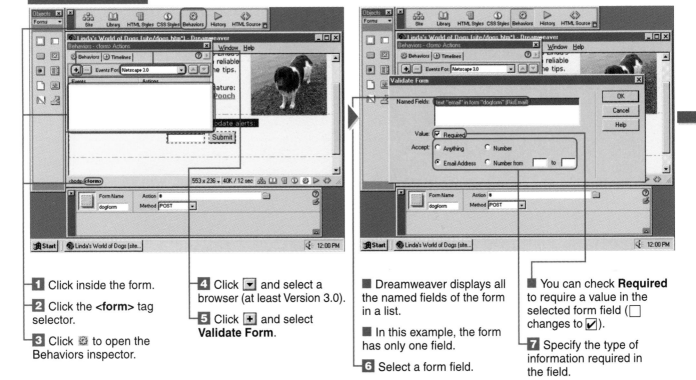

1 Click inside the form.

2 Click the **<form>** tag selector.

3 Click to open the Behaviors inspector.

4 Click and select a browser (at least Version 3.0).

5 Click and select **Validate Form**.

■ Dreamweaver displays all the named fields of the form in a list.

■ In this example, the form has only one field.

6 Select a form field.

■ You can check **Required** to require a value in the selected form field (☐ changes to ☑).

7 Specify the type of information required in the field.

Are behaviors the only way to validate a form?

No. Behaviors use JavaScript to validate the form on the client side (the browser checks to see if the values are okay before it sends anything to the form handler). Forms can also be validated on the server side. This involves programming the form handler to check the form values and return any error messages to the browser (which are things Dreamweaver cannot do).

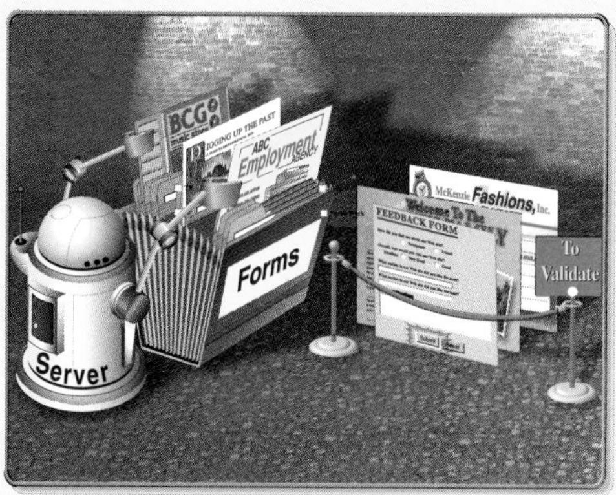

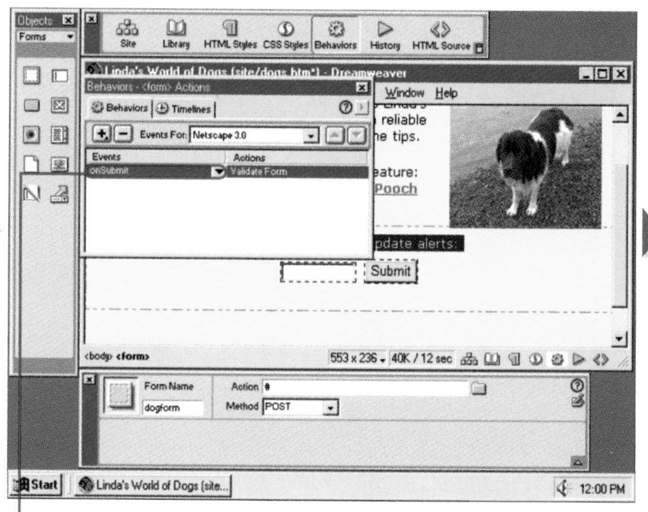

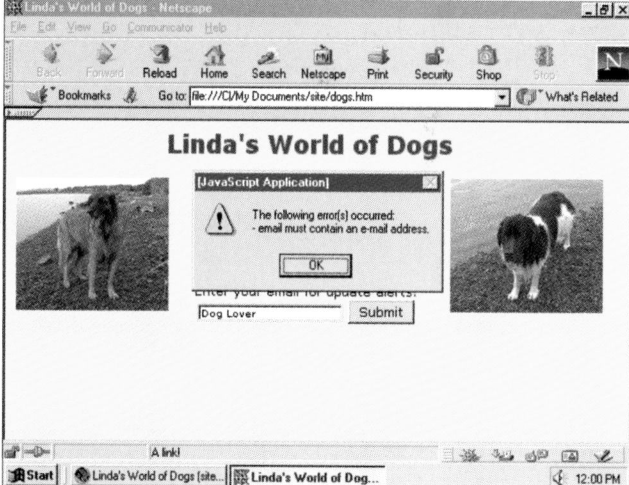

■ The default event for form validation is `onSubmit`. When the user clicks the submit button, the behavior validates the form.

■ You can click ▾ to select a different event.

8 Save the Web page.

■ You can open the page in a Web browser to test the form. If you submit the form with invalid content, the browser generates a pop-up alert.

■ In this example, an alert appears because an invalid e-mail address was entered.

CREATE A POP-UP MESSAGE

You can create a pop-up message that appears in response to a user's action.

CREATE A POP-UP MESSAGE

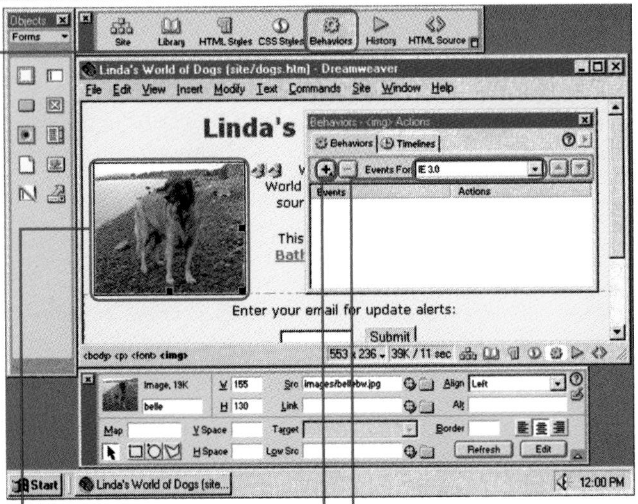

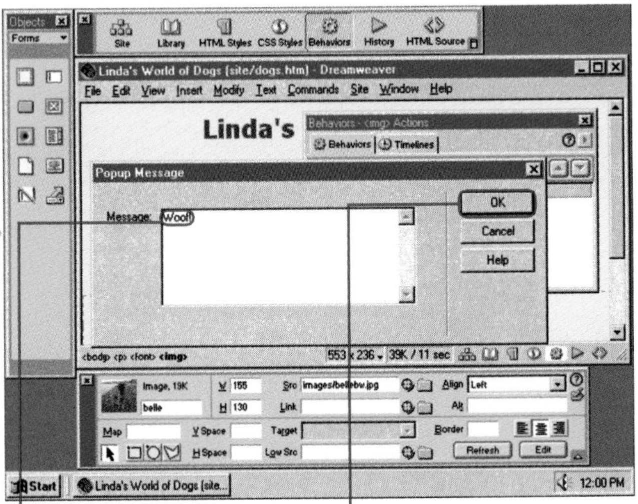

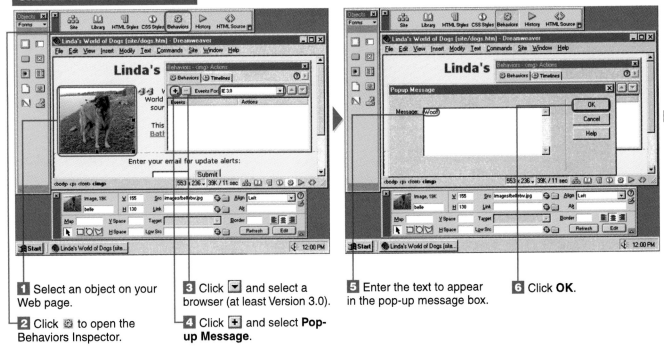

1. Select an object on your Web page.
2. Click ⚙ to open the Behaviors Inspector.
3. Click ▾ and select a browser (at least Version 3.0).
4. Click + and select **Pop-up Message**.
5. Enter the text to appear in the pop-up message box.
6. Click **OK**.

Can I modify the button, size, and other attributes of a pop-up message box?

Only the message text can be modified. This makes the pop-up message feature somewhat limited.

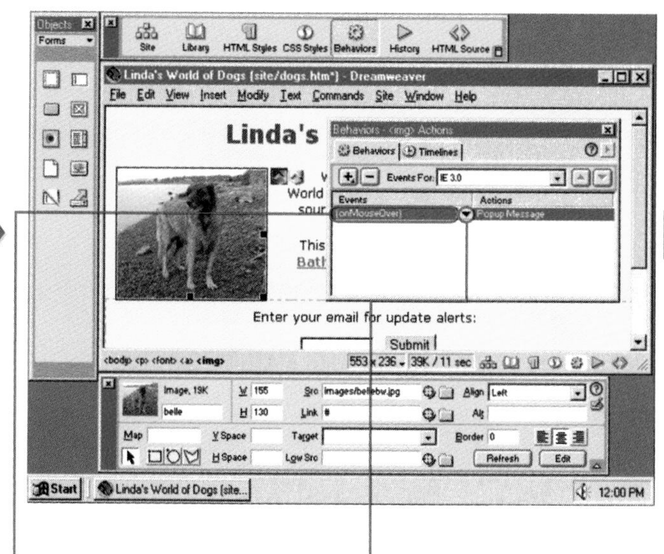

■ The default event for pop-up messages using Internet Explorer 3.0 browser compatibility is `onMouseOver` (rolling the cursor over the object triggers the pop-up message).

■ You can click ▾ to select a different event.

7 Save the Web page. (See Chapter 2.)

■ When you open the page in a Web browser and roll the cursor over the image, the pop-up message appears.

OPEN A CUSTOMIZED WINDOW

You can open hyperlinked information in a new, customized browser window.

OPEN A CUSTOMIZED WINDOW

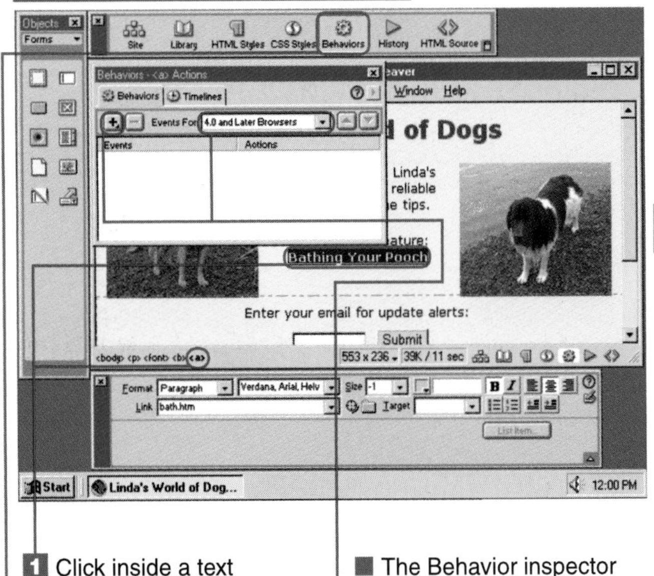

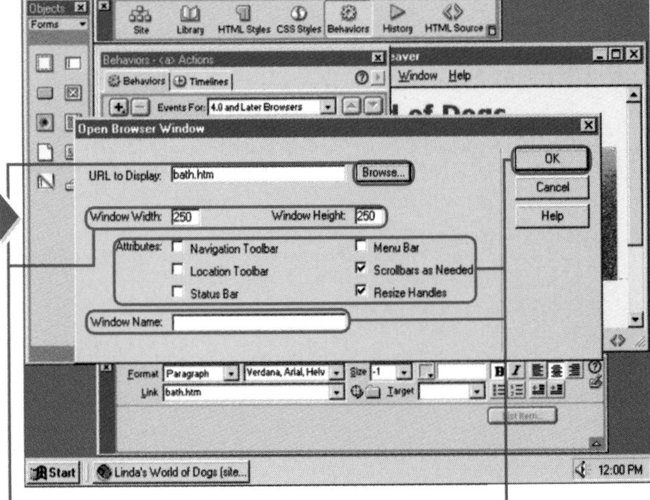

1 Click inside a text hyperlink and click the **<a>** tag selector to select it. This behavior also works with image hyperlinks.

2 Click ⚙.

■ The Behavior inspector opens.

3 Click ▼ and select a browser (at least Version 3.0).

4 Click + and select **Open Browser Window**.

5 Click **Browse** and select a file to open in the new window (or enter the file's URL in the field).

6 Type the new window's width and height in pixels.

7 Click the toolbars or window attributes you want the new window to have (☐ changes to ☑).

8 Name the window if you plan to target it with other hyperlinks.

9 Click **OK**.

Why would you want to keep toolbars out of a new browser window?

To keep the new window compact. This enables the user to see more of the old browser window beneath it (see this section).

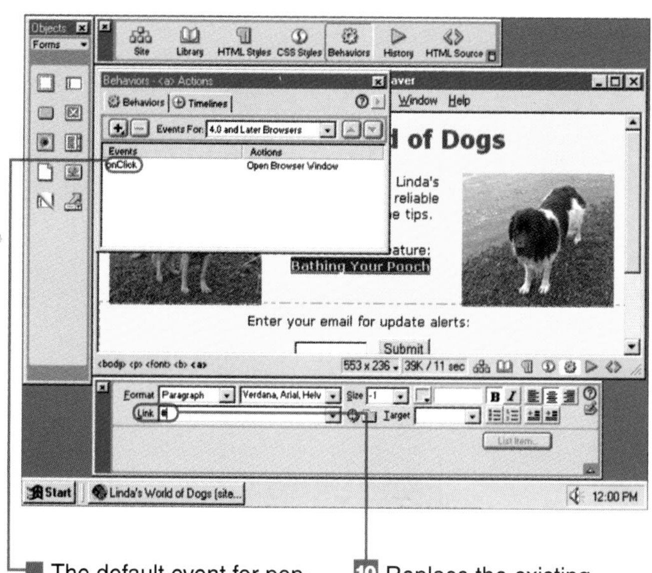

■ The default event for pop-up messages using 4.0 browser compatibility is `onClick` (clicking the element opens the window).

10 Replace the existing hyperlink destination with a pound sign (#) to prevent pages from opening in the old window when you click the object.

11 Save the Web page. (See Chapter 2.)

■ When you open it in a Web browser and click the hyperlink, the new browser window appears.

■ In this example, the page specified in Step 5 loads into the window.

CHECK A USER'S BROWSER

Dreamweaver's behaviors allow you to check the brand and version of a user's browser. You can then send users to a page tailored to their browser.

CHECK A USER'S BROWSER

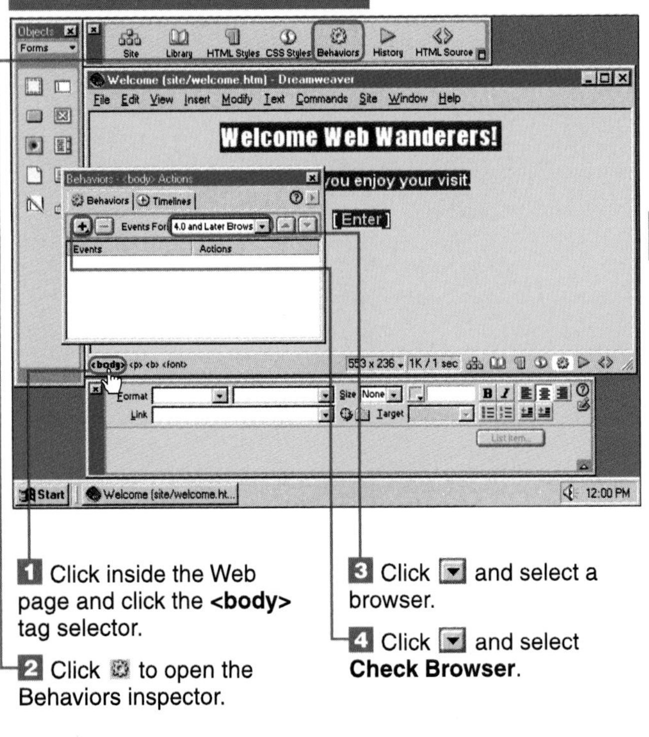

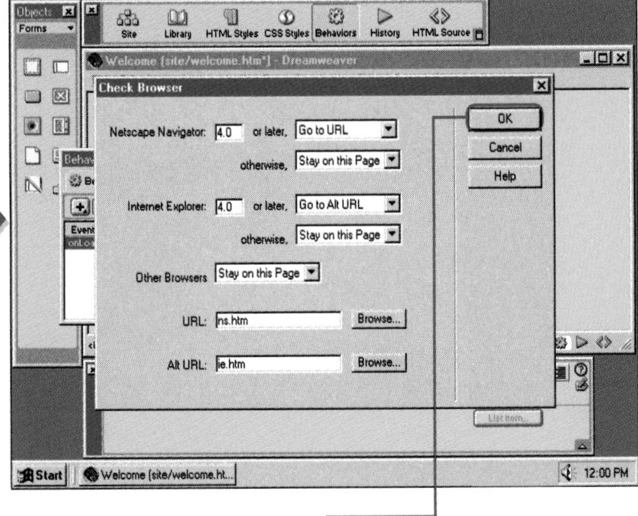

1 Click inside the Web page and click the **<body>** tag selector.

2 Click ⚙ to open the Behaviors inspector.

3 Click ▼ and select a browser.

4 Click ▼ and select **Check Browser**.

5 Select page destinations for the different browser types.

■ Users of newer versions of Navigator are sent to one custom page.

■ Users of newer versions of Internet Explorer go to another custom page.

■ Users of other browsers stay on the current page.

6 Click **OK**.

Why would you want to test the browser brand and version?

Some Web features work in some browser brands but not in others. For instance, Netscape's `<blink>` feature does not function in Internet Explorer, and Microsoft's `<marquee>` feature will not work in Navigator. Other features, such as style sheets and layers, only operate in newer browser versions. Testing the browser enables you to display alternate pages for users who cannot see certain content.

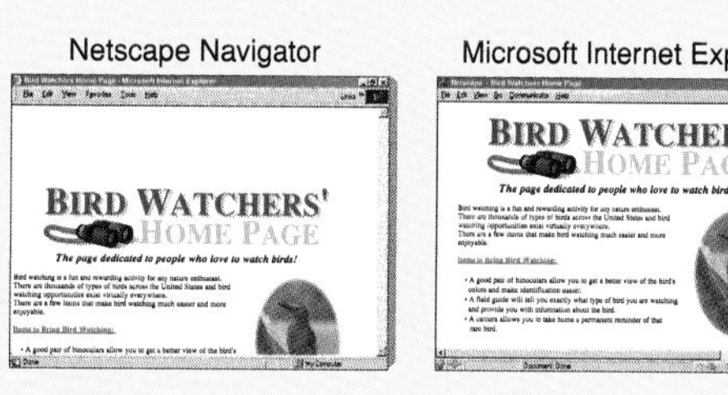

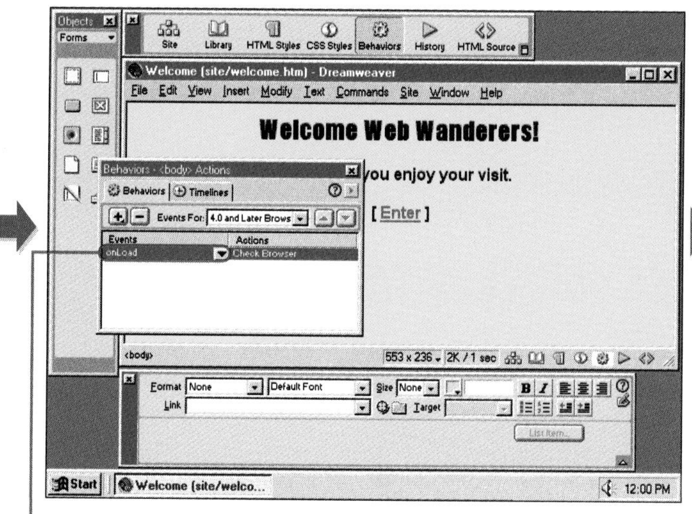

■ The `onLoad` event checks the browser after the Web page has loaded.

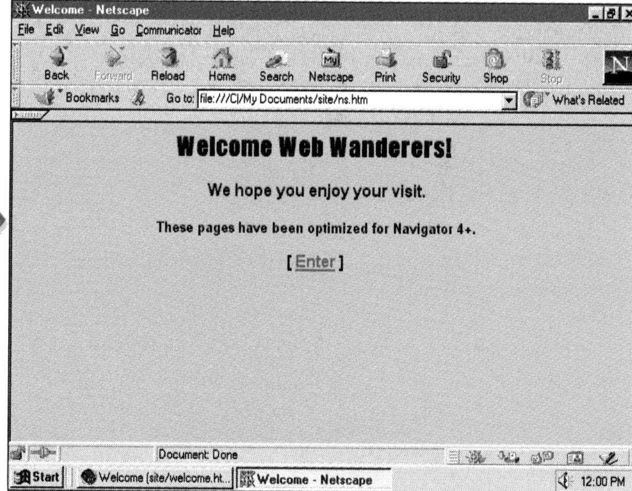

7 Save the Web page. (See Chapter 2.)

■ When the page opens in a Web browser, the browser loads the original page, checks the browser's brand and version, and forwards the user to a new page if required.

■ In this example, the Web page is opened in Netscape Navigator 4.7. The browser forwards the user to a page customized for Navigator 4.0 or later.

CHAPTER 13

Implementing Timelines

Would you like to enhance your Web site with animation? Learn how in this chapter.

ABOUT TIMELINES

You can add animation to your Web page by using Dreamweaver's timelines.

TIMELINES AND LAYERS

Timelines allow you to manipulate the placement, visibility, and other attributes of a Web page's layers over time. (For an introduction to layers, see Chapter 11.) Because timelines rely on layers, timeline animation only works on Version 4.0 or later browsers.

ABOUT JAVASCRIPT

Dreamweaver creates timeline animation with JavaScript, a popular programming language for adding dynamic features to Web sites. You create a timeline by using the Timelines Inspector; Dreamweaver then writes the JavaScript code behind the scenes to create the animation.

The Timelines inspector lets you apply special effects to layers on your page.

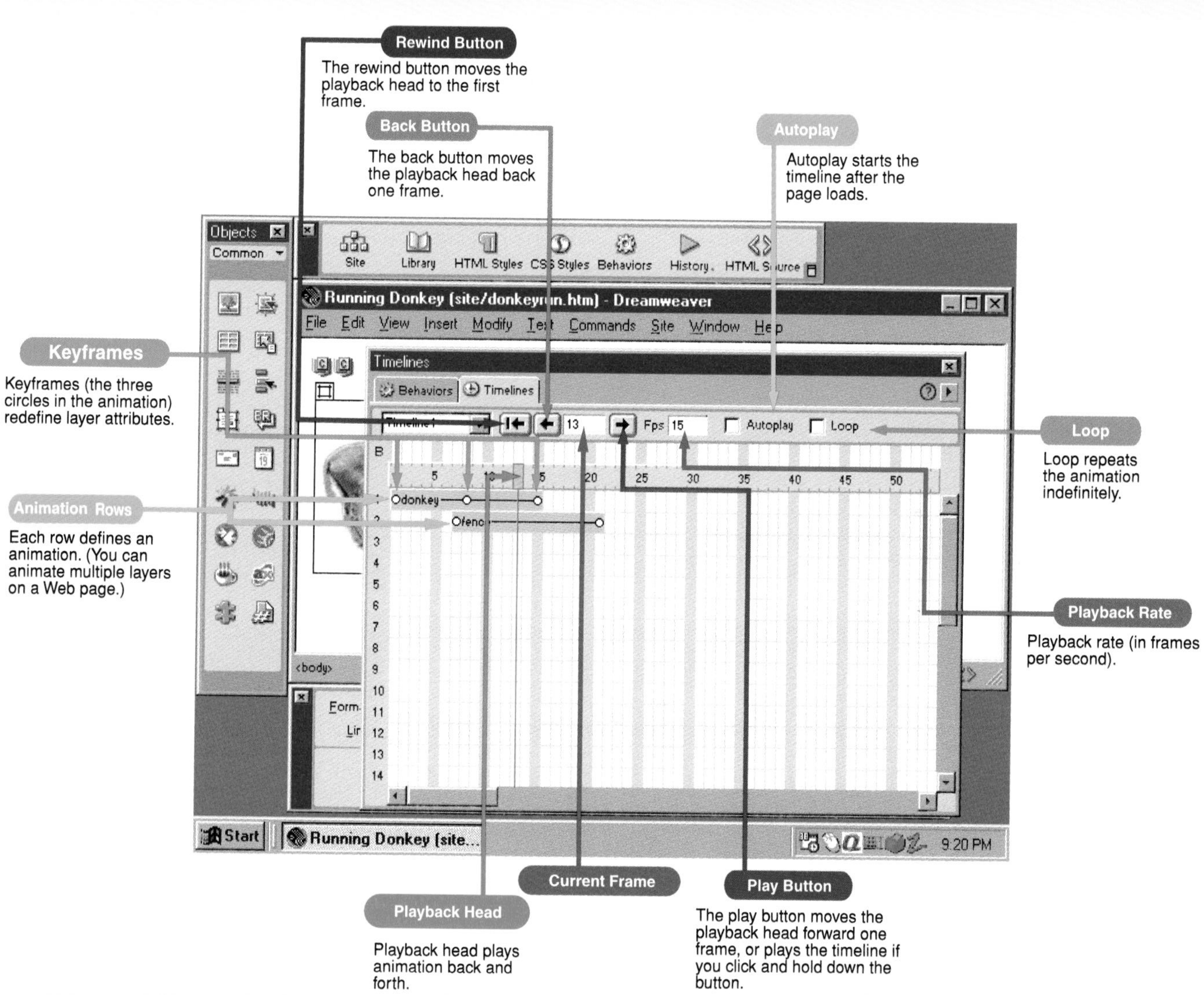
Rewind Button
The rewind button moves the playback head to the first frame.
Back Button
The back button moves the playback head back one frame.
Autoplay
Autoplay starts the timeline after the page loads.
Keyframes
Keyframes (the three circles in the animation) redefine layer attributes.
Loop
Loop repeats the animation indefinitely.
Animation Rows
Each row defines an animation. (You can animate multiple layers on a Web page.)
Playback Rate
Playback rate (in frames per second).
Current Frame
Play Button
The play button moves the playback head forward one frame, or plays the timeline if you click and hold down the button.
Playback Head
Playback head plays animation back and forth.
Running Donkey (site/donkeyrun.htm) - Dreamweaver
Timelines
Behaviors
Timelines
Fps
Autoplay
Loop
Start
9:20 PM

CREATE A STRAIGHT-LINE ANIMATION

You can use timelines to move a layer in a straight line on your Web page.

CREATE A STRAIGHT-LINE ANIMATION

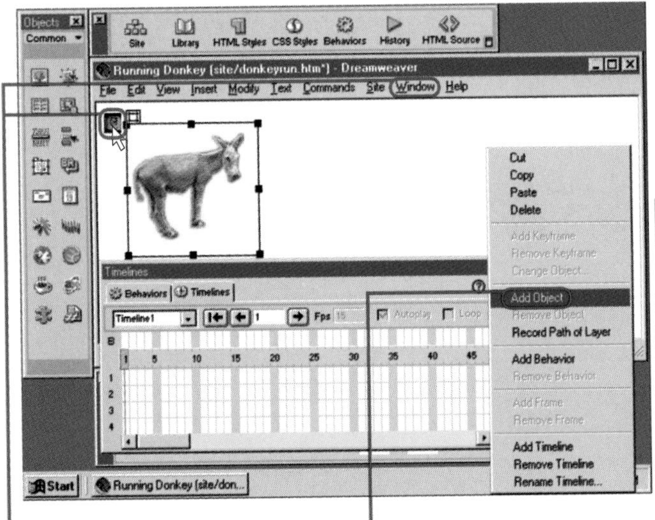

1 Open the Timelines Inspector by selecting **Window⇨Timelines**.

2 Click the layer's icon.

Note: For more about layers, see Chapter 12.

3 Click ▶ in the upper-right corner of the inspector and select **Add Object**.

■ If an alert dialog box appears with information about layer attributes, click **OK**.

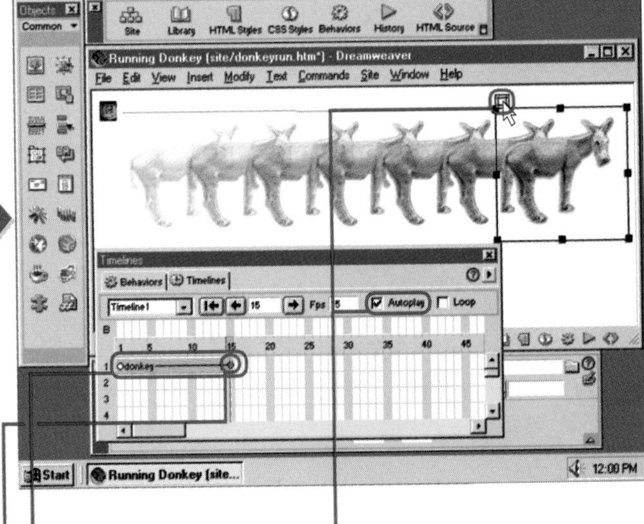

■ Dreamweaver adds an animation bar to the timeline with a default of 15 frames and rate of 15 frames per second.

4 Click the final keyframe of the animation.

5 Click and drag your layer to its final position in the Document window.

6 Click **Autoplay** (☐ changes to ☑).

Can I create straight-line animations in any direction?

Yes. You can make layers move horizontally, vertically, or diagonally. The first keyframe represents the starting position; the last keyframe represents the ending position. The layer moves between the two positions.

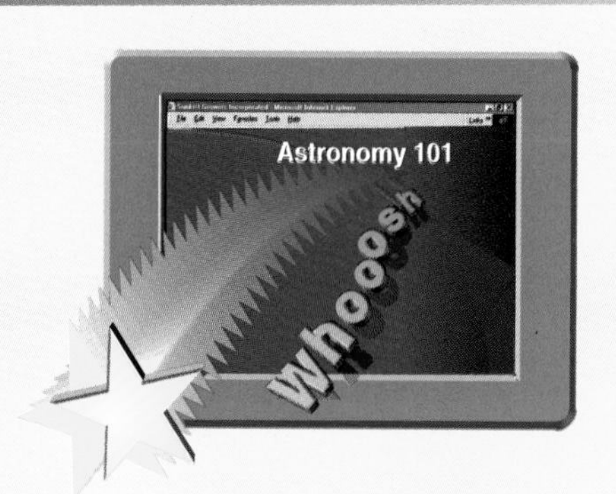

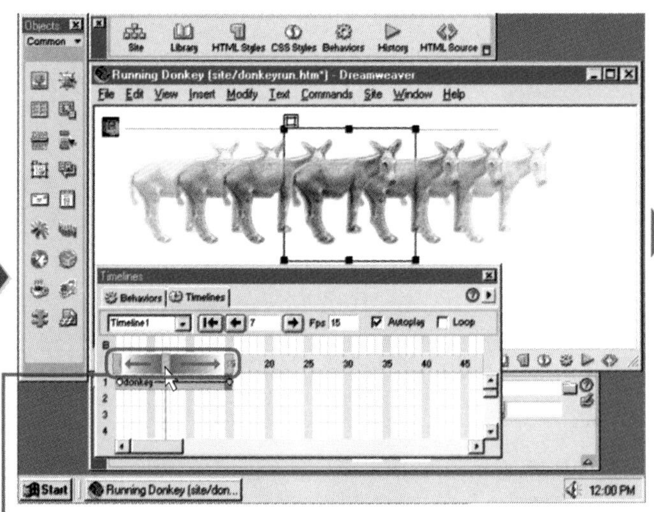

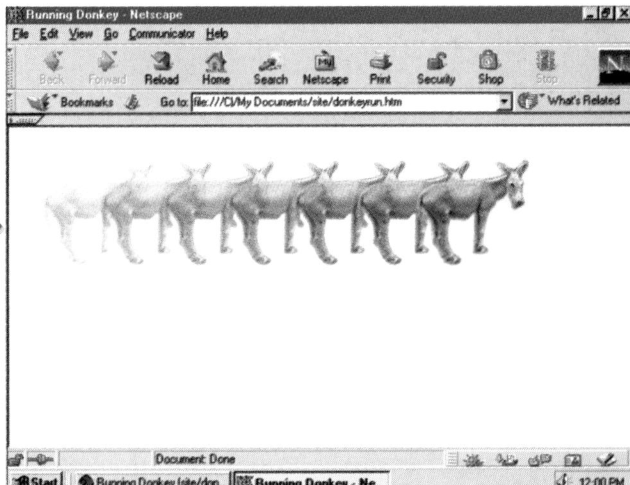

7 To preview the animation, click and drag the Playback Head.

■ The layer moves across the Document window in a straight line.

■ When you save your document and open it in a Web browser, the layer moves across the page once and then stops.

■ The animation starts automatically because Autoplay was checked.

CREATE A CURVED ANIMATION

You can use timelines to move a layer in a curved path across your Web page. Creating a curved animation involves adding an extra keyframe to a straight-line animation.

CREATE A CURVED ANIMATION

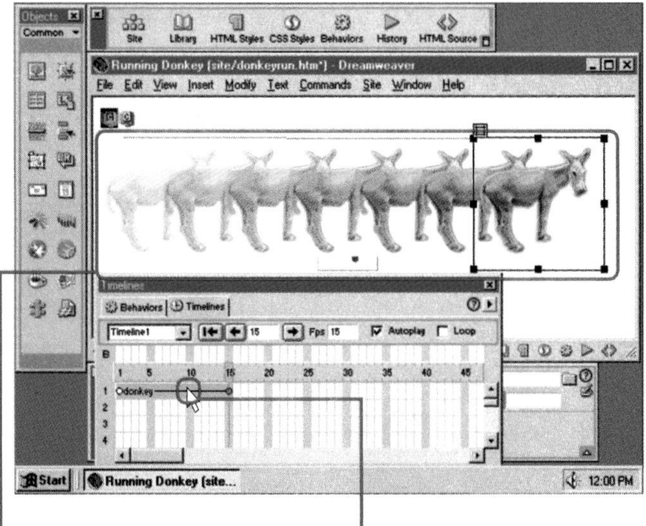

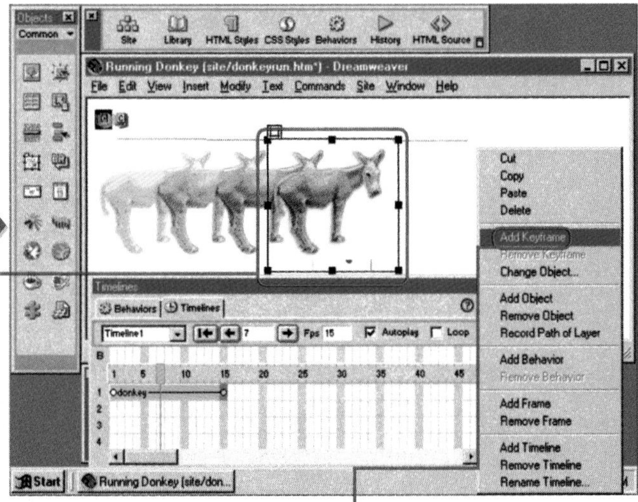

1 Create a straight-line animation using instructions from the Section "Create a Straight-Line Animation."

2 Click in the middle of the animation bar.

■ The layer moves to the middle of its animation sequence in the Document window.

3 Click ▶ in the upper-right corner of the inspector and select **Add Keyframe**.

How do I create animations that zigzag?

Add multiple keyframes between the animation's beginning and end. Stagger the layer's position at each keyframe to cause the layer to zigzag.

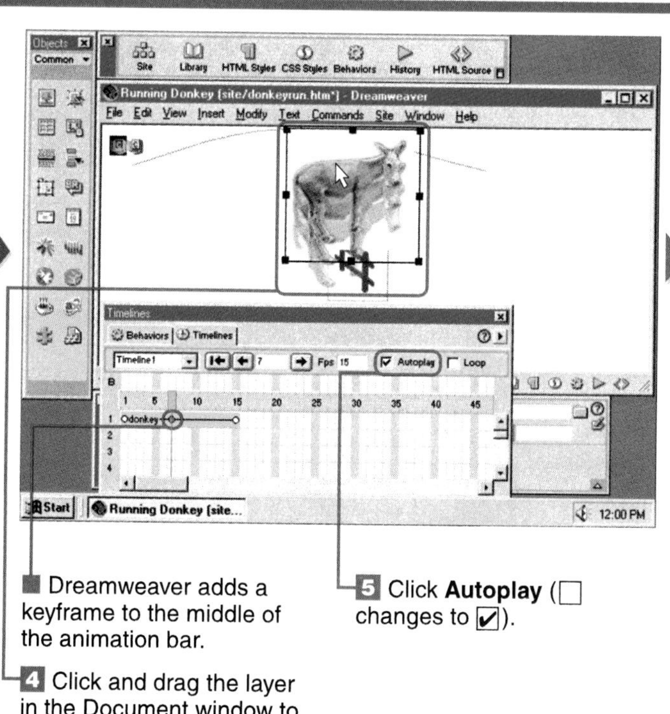

■ Dreamweaver adds a keyframe to the middle of the animation bar.

4 Click and drag the layer in the Document window to define a new position for the middle keyframe.

5 Click **Autoplay** (☐ changes to ☑).

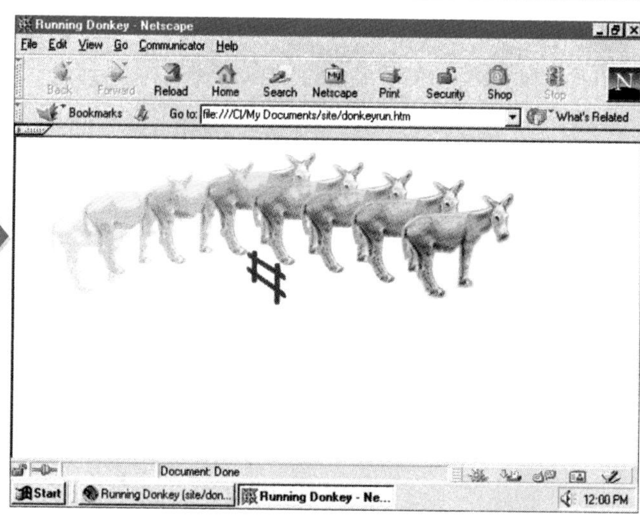

■ When you save your document and open it in a Web browser, the image moves in an arc defined by the first, middle, and last keyframes of the animation.

■ The animation starts automatically because Autoplay was checked.

CREATE A FLASHING ANIMATION

By changing a layer's visibility in a timeline, you can make content on a page flash on and off.

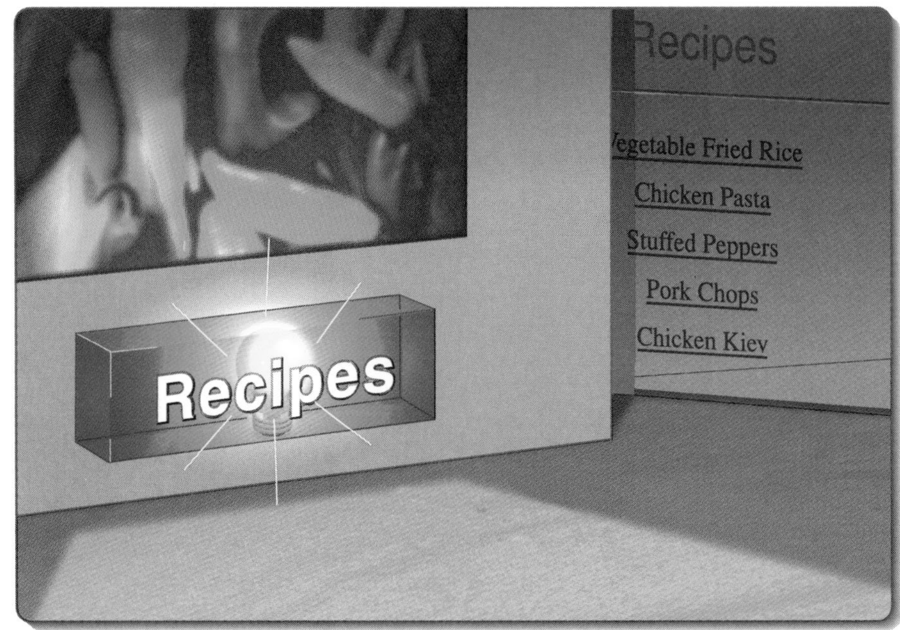

CREATE A FLASHING ANIMATION

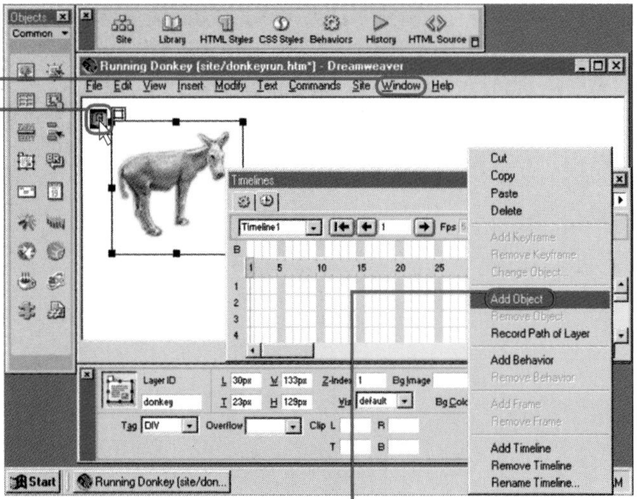

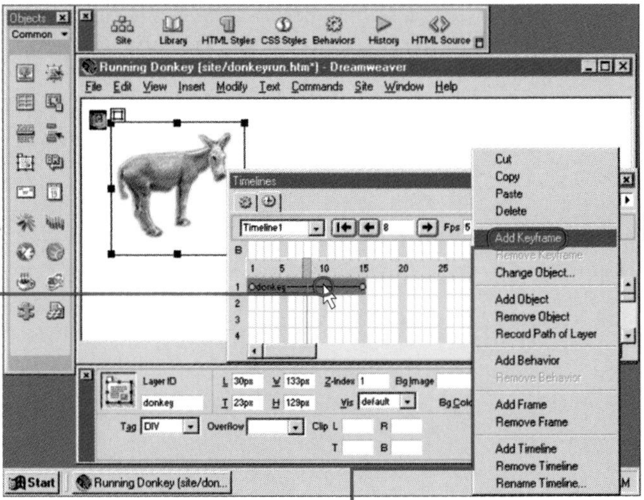

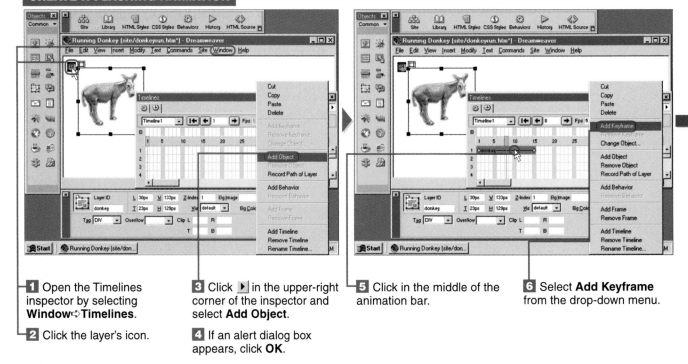

1 Open the Timelines inspector by selecting **Window⇨Timelines**.

2 Click the layer's icon.

3 Click ▶ in the upper-right corner of the inspector and select **Add Object**.

4 If an alert dialog box appears, click **OK**.

5 Click in the middle of the animation bar.

6 Select **Add Keyframe** from the drop-down menu.

How do I make a moving animation flash on and off?

Insert several keyframes in the middle of the moving animation and then alternate the layer's visibility on and off in the keyframes.

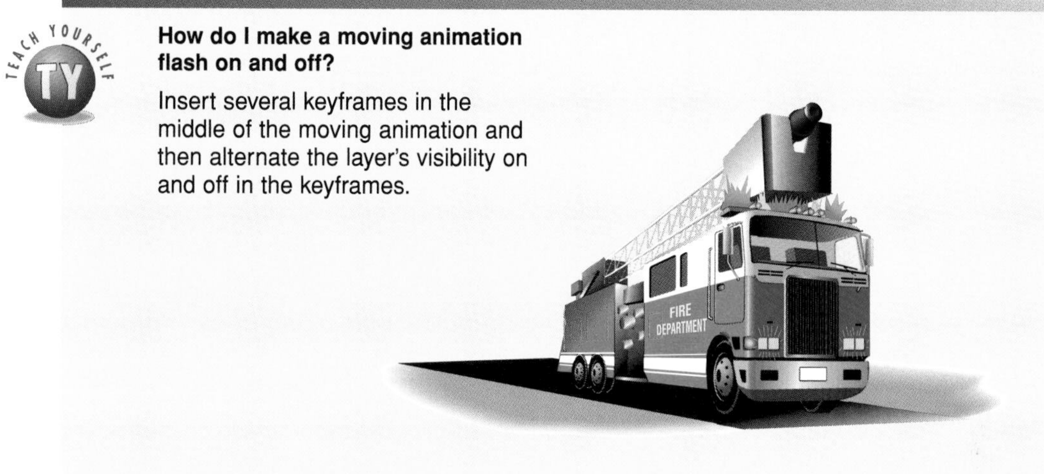

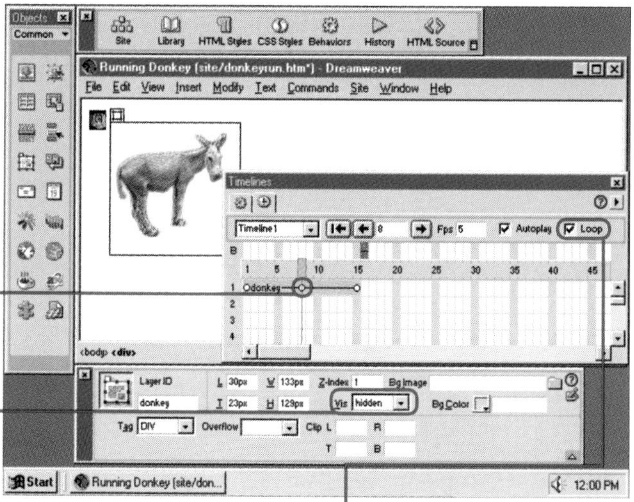

7 Click the middle keyframe.

8 Click ▼ and select **hidden** from the Vis menu.

9 Select **Loop** (☐ changes to ☑). This makes the animation repeat indefinitely.

10 If an alert dialog box appears, click **OK**.

■ The layer is visible at the beginning of the animation, disappears in the middle, and reappears at the end. The animation then repeats.

■ When you save your document and open it in a Web browser, the image flashes on and off.

CHANGE THE ANIMATION SPEED

You can change an animation's speed by changing the frame rate or by changing the number of frames in the animation.

CHANGE THE FRAME RATE

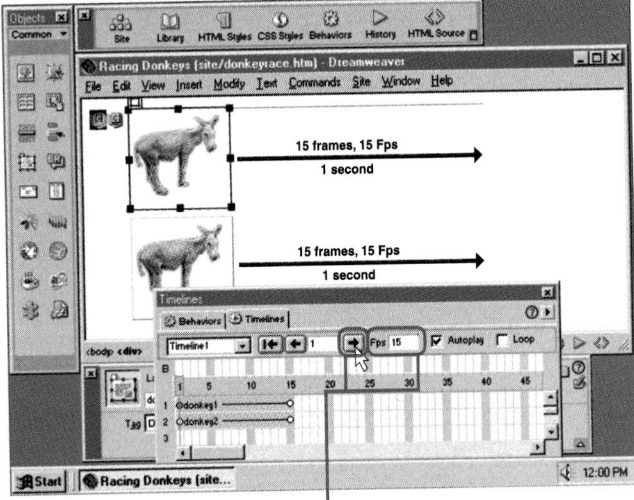

■ In this animation example, two layers cross the page at the same speed.

■ To preview the animation, click and hold ➡.

1 To change the speed of all the animations in the timeline type a new **Fps** (frames-per-second) value.

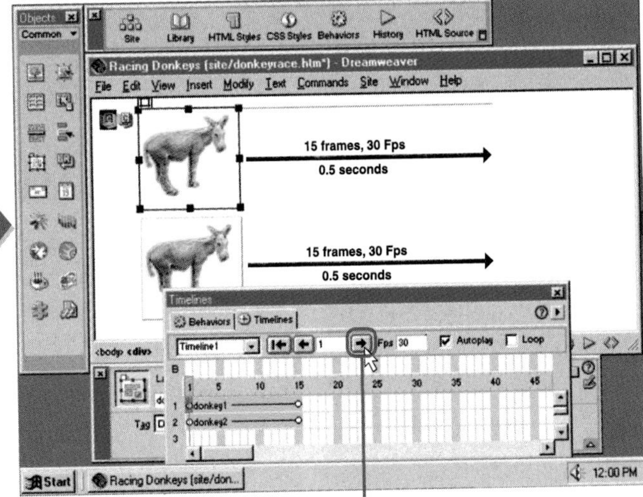

■ In this example, the two animations are defined in the same timeline and both their speeds change.

2 To preview the modified animation, click and hold the Playback button.

How does the frame rate affect the appearance of an animation?

The lower the frame rate, the choppier the animation. Keep the frame rate at 15 fps or greater if you want your animations to appear smooth.

CHANGE THE NUMBER OF FRAMES

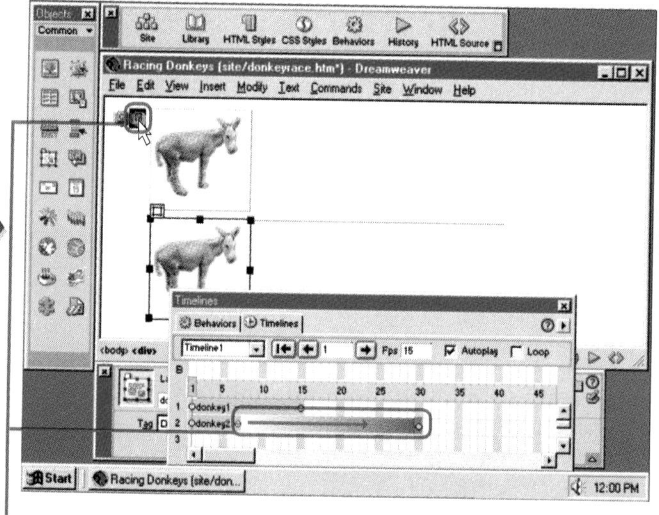

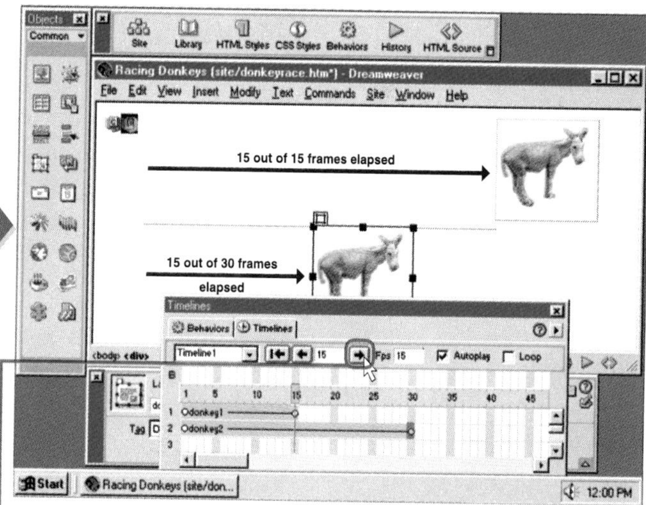

1 Click a layer icon to select an animation.

2 Click and drag the ending keyframe of the selected animation.

■ This adds frames to the animation. The frames-per-second rate stays the same.

3 To preview the animation, click and hold ➡.

■ In the example, the modified animation moves at a decreased speed because it takes longer for the increased number of frames to elapse.

TRIGGER AN ANIMATION WITH A BEHAVIOR

You can make a mouse click trigger an animation using Dreamweaver's behaviors. For more about behaviors, see Chapter 12.

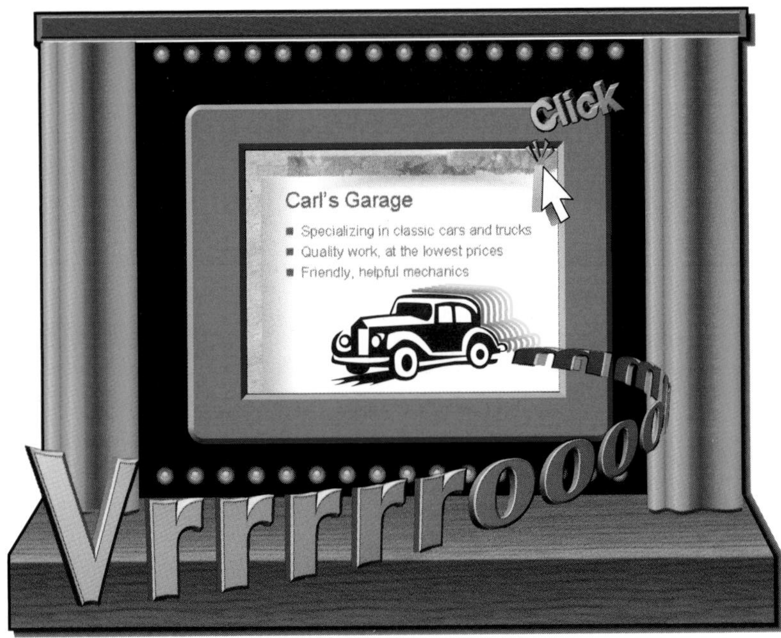

TRIGGER AN ANIMATION WITH A BEHAVIOR

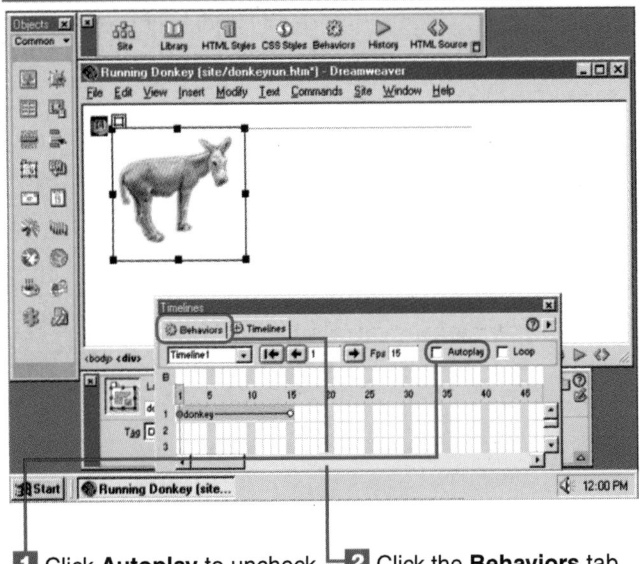

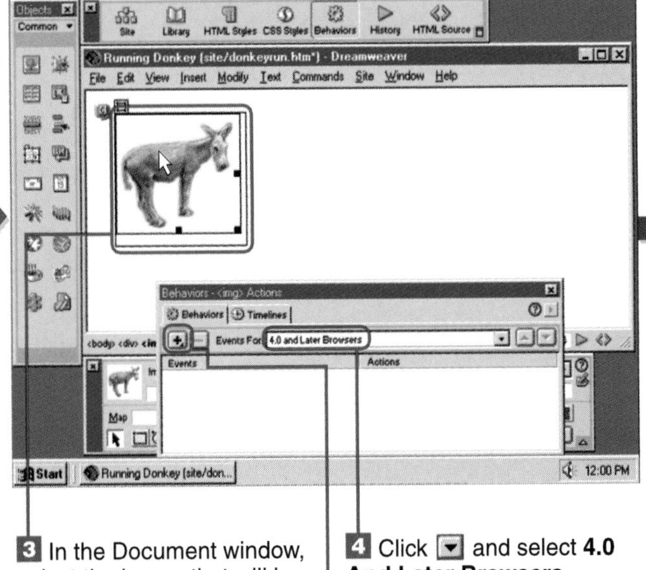

1 Click **Autoplay** to uncheck it (☑ changes to ☐).

2 Click the **Behaviors** tab to switch from the Timelines inspector to the Behaviors inspector.

3 In the Document window, select the image that will be clicked to play the animation. (Do not select the layer that contains the image.)

4 Click ▼ and select **4.0 And Later Browsers**.

5 Click + and select **Timeline⇨Play Timeline**.

How do I create an animation that is stopped with a mouse click?

To create an animation that is stopped with a mouse click, follow Steps 1 through 6 in this section, but select **Timeline⇨Stop Timeline** in Step 5. Make sure the **Autoplay** box is checked in Step 1 so the animation runs when the browser opens the page.

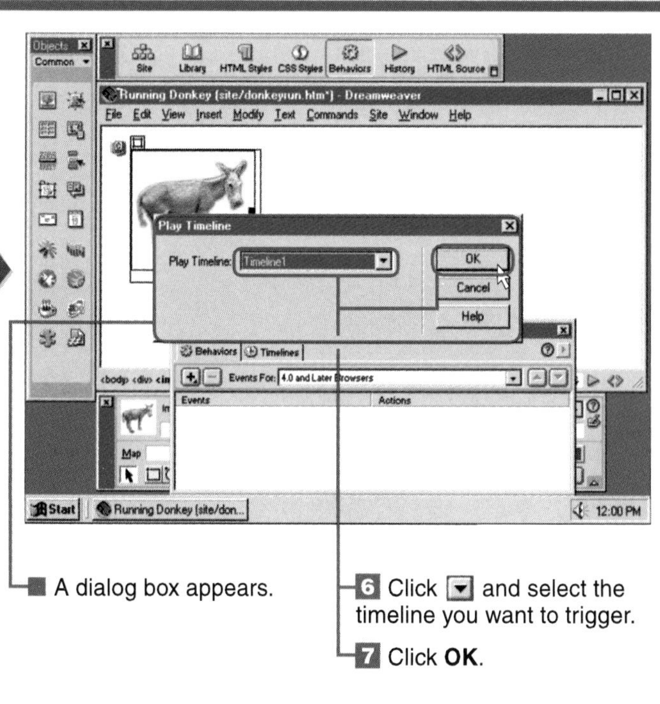

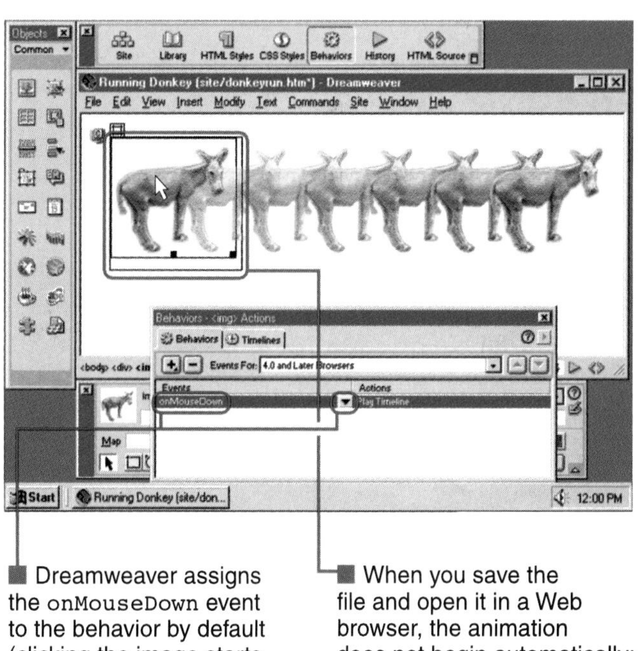

■ A dialog box appears.

6 Click ▼ and select the timeline you want to trigger.

7 Click **OK**.

■ Dreamweaver assigns the `onMouseDown` event to the behavior by default (clicking the image starts the timeline). You can select a different event to trigger the timeline by clicking ▼.

■ When you save the file and open it in a Web browser, the animation does not begin automatically; you must click the image to start it.

Welcome To The
SMITH FAMILY
Web Page
Our Latest Addition
We are pleased to announce there's a new addition to our family. His name is Jack and he was born nine months ago! He is our first child and has brought us nothing but happiness since he arrived.
About Us
We are Jason & Brenda Smith, owners of a 50 acre horse farm. We breed thoroughbred horses and enjoy showing them at national horse shows.
E-mail
ISP

CHAPTER 14

Publishing Your Web Site

Are you ready to publish your finished pages for the rest of the world to see? This chapter shows you how to transfer pages to a live Web server. It also shows you how to keep the pages up to date once they are online.

PUBLISH YOUR SITE

To make your pages accessible to other people on the Web, you can transfer them to a Web server. A Web server is an Internet-connected computer running special software that enables it to serve files to Web browsers.

STEPS FOR PUBLISHING YOUR WEBSITE

Publishing your site content using Dreamweaver involves the following steps:

1. **Specify where on your computer the site files are kept.**
2. **Specify the Web server to which you want to publishyour files.**
3. **Connect to the Web server and transfer the files.**
4. **After uploading your site, you can update to it by editing the copies of the site files on your computer (the local site) and then transferring those copies to the Web server (the remote site).**

In addition to handling file transfer duties, Dreamweaver makes sure that the files are organized on the Web server the same way they were organized on your local computer when you created them. This ensures that images display correctly and that hyperlinks work.

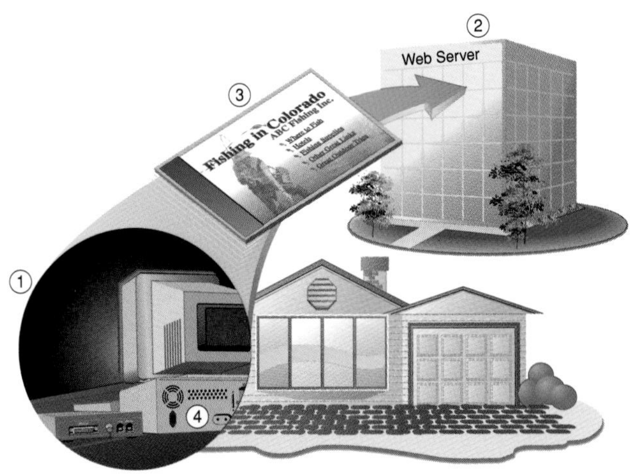

In Dreamweaver, you can see an overview of your site's content and architecture in the Site window.

Remote and Local Site Menus

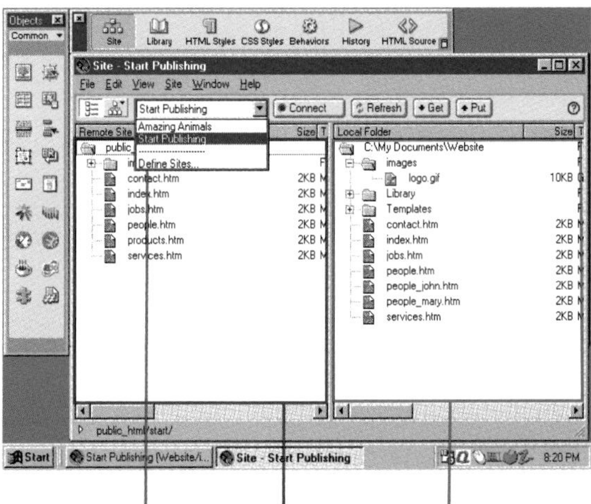

Site Menu

A menu lets you select among different sites stored on your local computer.

Local Site Menu

The right pane displays the content of your site as it exists on your local computer. (To define your local site, see Chapter 2.)

Remote web site menu

The left pane displays the contents of your site as it exists on the remote Web server. (To define your remote site, see the section "Setting Up a Remote Site.")

Site Window

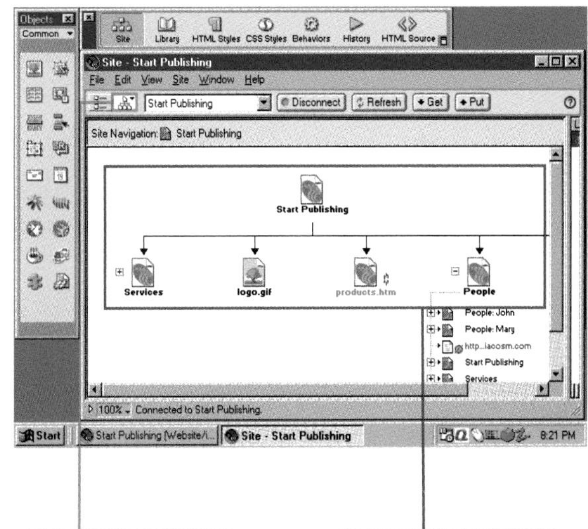

Site Map

Click [icon] to display a site map in the Site window.

View your Web Site Architecture

The site map lets you visualize the architecture of your Web site and easily pinpoint broken links. See "View a Site Map" in this chapter for details.

SET UP A REMOTE SITE

You can associate your site with a directory on a remote Web server where you publish your Web pages.

To set up your remote site, you need certain information about the Web server, such as the name of the FTP host and host directory. The network administrator at your Internet service provider or your company can give you this information.

SET UP A REMOTE SITE

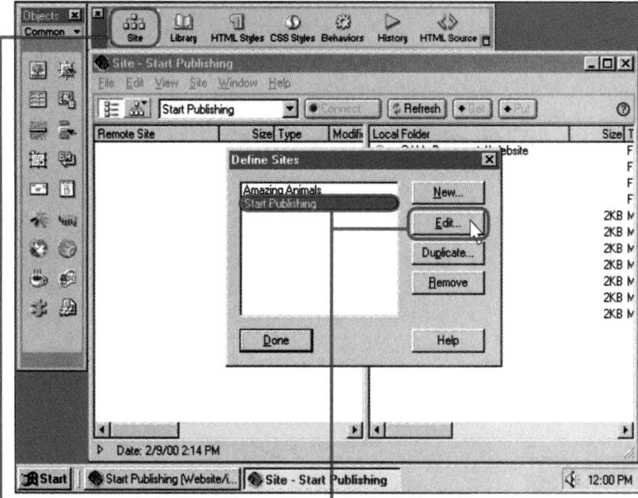

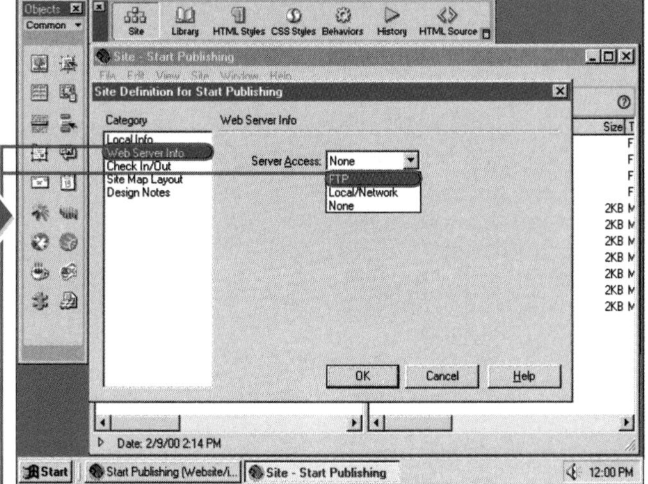

1 Before setting up a remote site, you must define a local site (see Chapter 2).

2 Click the **Site** icon to open the Site window.

3 Select **Define Sites** from the Site menu to open the Define Sites dialog box.

4 Select the site name from the list.

5 Click **Edit**.

■ Dreamweaver opens the Site Definition dialog box.

6 Click **Web Server Info**.

7 Click ▼ and select **FTP** from the Server Access menu.

■ If your Web server is mounted as a network drive (Windows) or as an AppleTalk or NFS server (Macintosh), or if you are running a Web server on your local machine, select **Local/Network**.

What is a Web server?

A Web server is an Internet-connected computer running software that enables it to serve Web pages to browsers that request them. A single Web server can host many different Web sites, each stored in a different directory on the server.

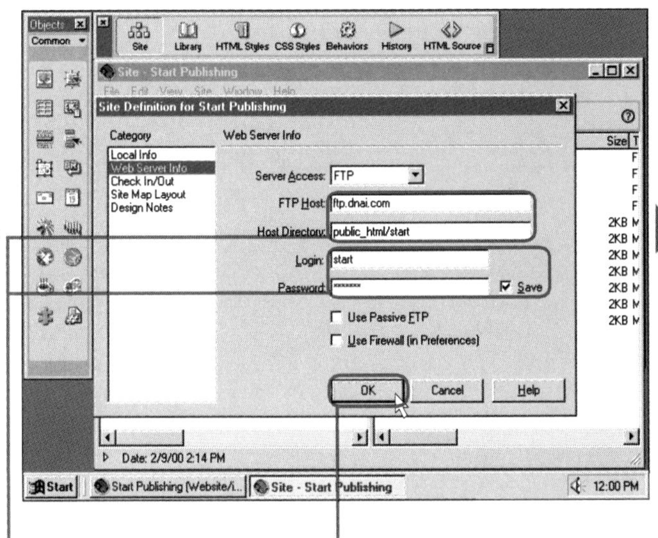

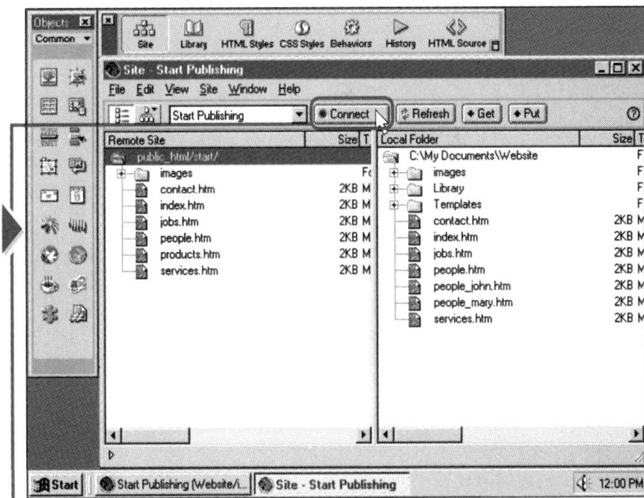

8 Type the name of the FTP host (Web server) and enter your site's directory path on the Web server.

9 Enter your login name and password. Check **Save** to have Dreamweaver save your password (○ changes to ◉).

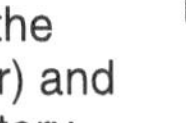

10 Click **OK**.

11 Click **Done** in the Defines Sites window.

12 Click **Connect**.

■ Dreamweaver connects to the remote Web server and displays the contents of your site's directory in the left pane of the window.

You can access a remote site and upload and download files. Dreamweaver connects to the remote site by a process known as File Transfer Protocol, or FTP.

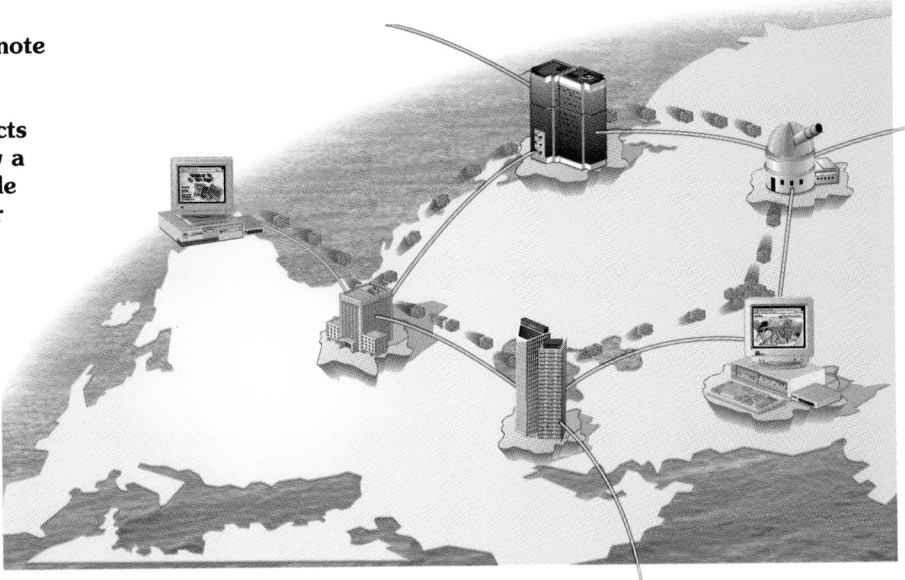

CONNECT TO A REMOTE SITE

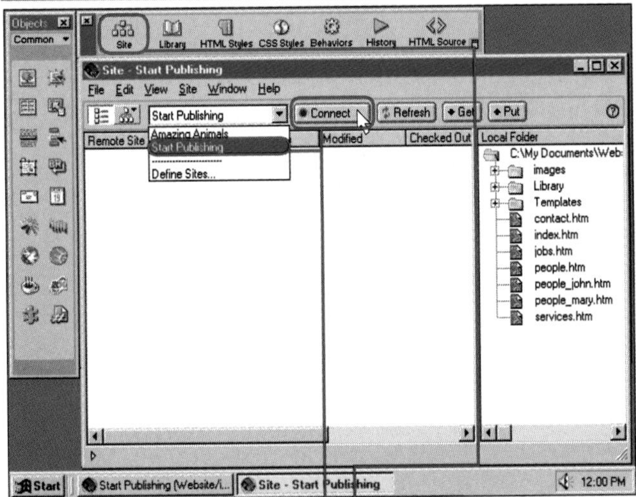

■ Before connecting, you must set up a local site (see Chapter 2) and a remote site (see the Section "Set Up a Remote Site").

1 Click the **Site** icon to open the Site window.

2 Click ▼ and select your Web site.

3 Click **Connect**.

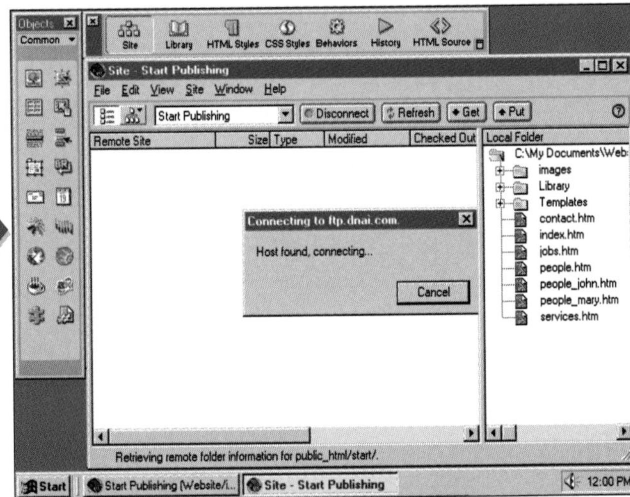

■ Dreamweaver attempts to connect to the remote site.

■ If it cannot connect to the site, Dreamweaver displays an alert box. If you have trouble connecting, double-check the host information you entered for the remote site (see the Section "Set Up a Remote Site").

What is FTP?

Short for File Transfer Protocol, FTP is a method of transferring information between Internet-connected computers. (HTTP, or Hypertext Transfer Protocol, is a different method used by Web browsers and servers.) Some of the commands found in Dreamweaver's Site window (such as Get and Put) are FTP-specific terminology.

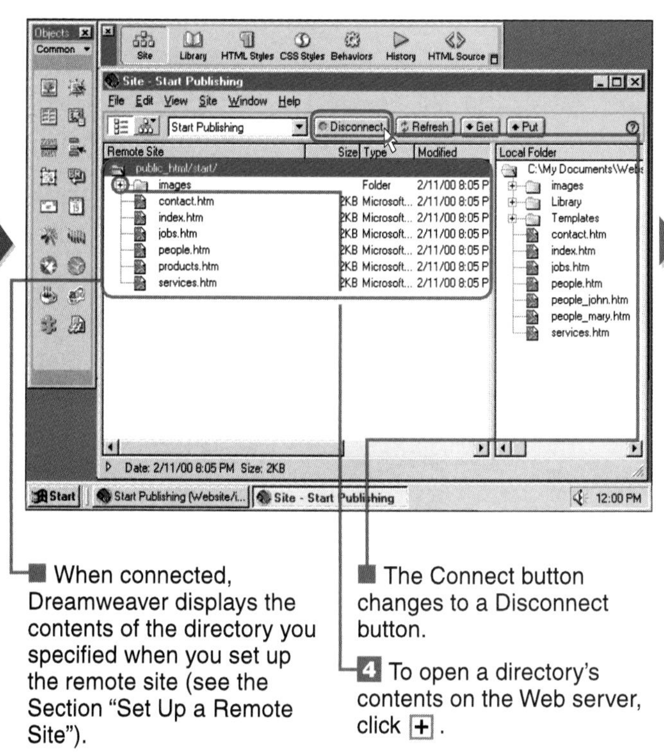

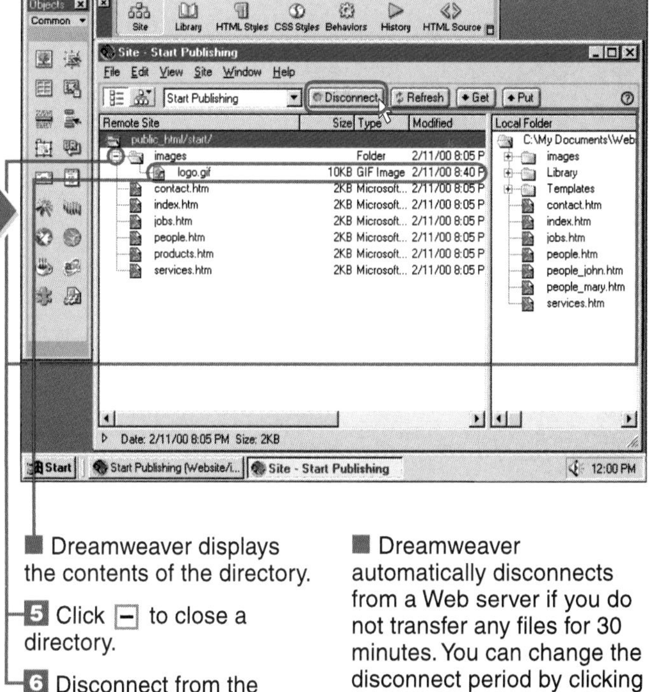

■ When connected, Dreamweaver displays the contents of the directory you specified when you set up the remote site (see the Section "Set Up a Remote Site").

■ The Connect button changes to a Disconnect button.

4 To open a directory's contents on the Web server, click ⊞.

■ Dreamweaver displays the contents of the directory.

5 Click ⊟ to close a directory.

6 Disconnect from the Web server by clicking **Disconnect**.

■ Dreamweaver automatically disconnects from a Web server if you do not transfer any files for 30 minutes. You can change the disconnect period by clicking **Edit⇨Preferences** and selecting **Site FTP**.

UPLOAD FILES

You can upload site files from your computer to the Web server.

UPLOAD FILES

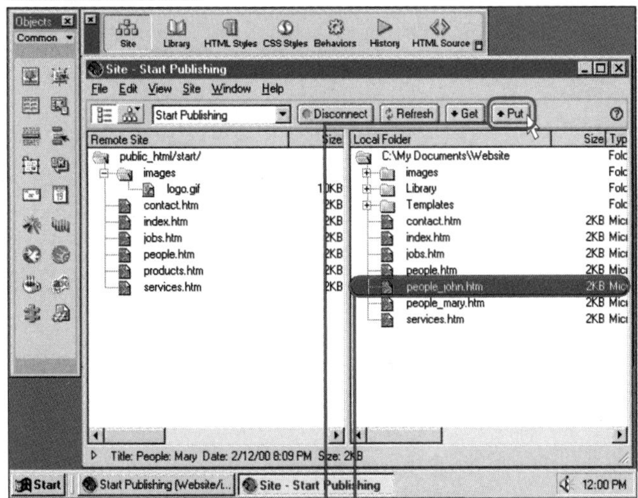

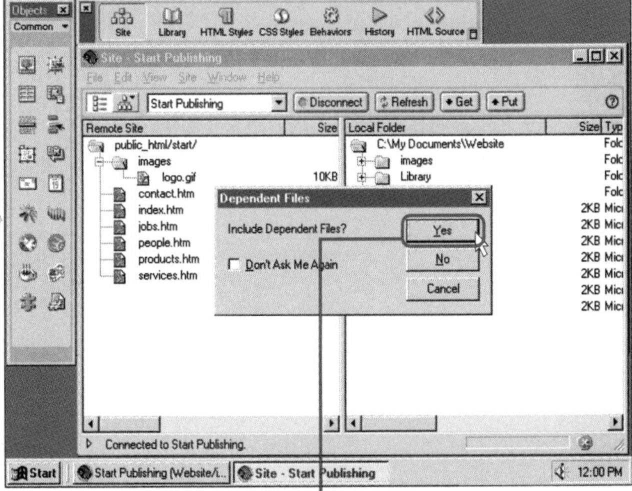

UPLOAD FILES

1 Connect to the Web server by using the Site window (see the Section "Connect to a Remote Site" for details).

2 In the right pane of the Site window, click the file or folder you would like to upload.

3 Click **Put**.

■ Dreamweaver displays an alert box asking if you want to include *dependent files*.

■ Dependent files are images and other files associated with a particular Web page.

■ If you are uploading a frameset, dependent files include files for each frame in the set.

4 Click **Yes** to upload the dependent files. Click **Don't Ask Me Again** to stop seeing the alert box.

When do uploaded files become accessible on the Web?

Files are accessible as soon as you upload them (assuming you upload them to the correct directory on the Web server). After a file is uploaded, Web users can access it by entering a URL in their Web browser (for instance, http://www.startpublishing.com/uploadedfile.htm).

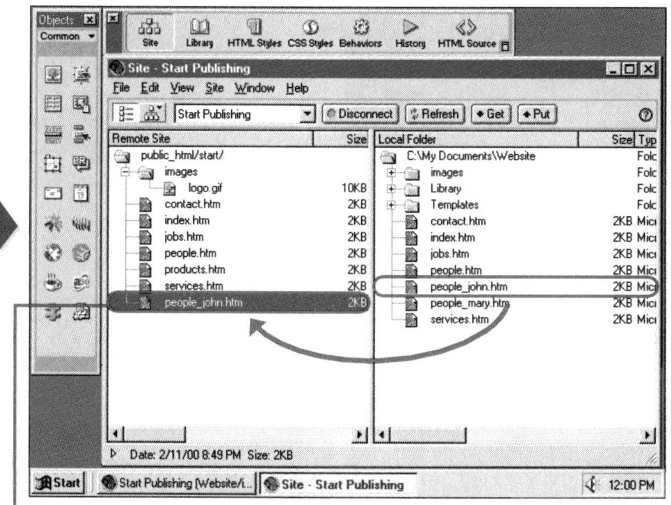

■ Dreamweaver transfers the file or folder from your computer to the Web server.

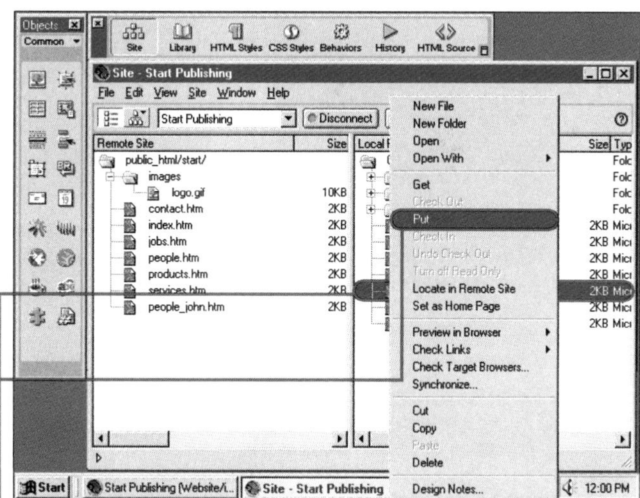

UPLOAD FILES SHORTCUT

1 Right-click the file or folder in the right pane.

2 Select **Put** from the pop-up menu.

■ Dreamweaver transfers the file or folder from your computer to the Web server.

DOWNLOAD FILES

Downloading your site files from the Web server to your computer gives you back-up copies if files on your local site are accidentally changed or lost.

DOWNLOAD FILES

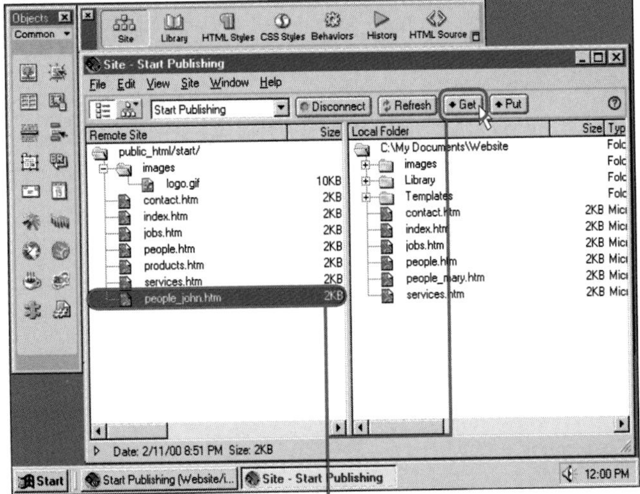

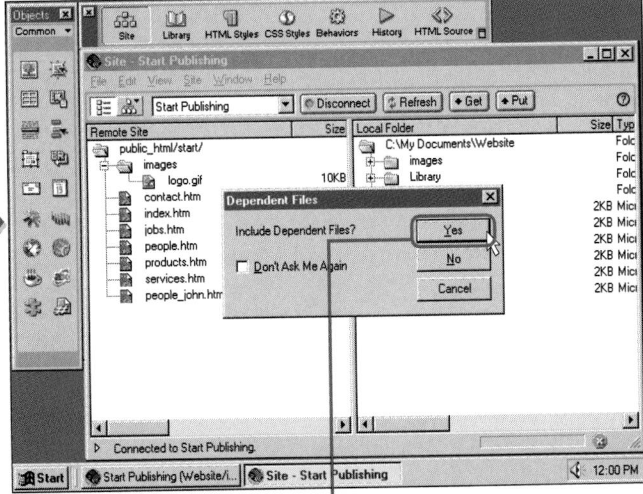

DOWNLOAD FILES

1 Connect to the Web server by using the Site window (see the Section "Connect to a Remote Site" for details).

2 In the left pane of the Site window, click the file or folder you would like to download.

3 Click **Get**.

■ Dreamweaver displays an alert box asking if you want to include *dependent files*.

■ Dependent files are images and other files that are associated with a particular Web page.

■ If you are downloading a frameset, dependent files include files for each frame in the set.

4 Click **Yes** to download dependent files. Click **Don't Ask Me Again** to stop seeing the alert box.

How can I troubleshoot problems resulting from transferred files?

Dreamweaver records all downloads and uploads in an FTP log. The log can help you determine what might be going wrong during transfer. To view the FTP log, select **Window⇨FTP Log** from the Site window (**Site⇨FTP Log** on a Macintosh).

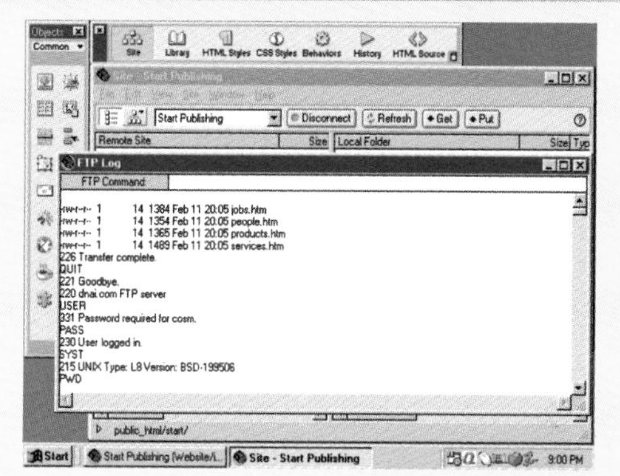

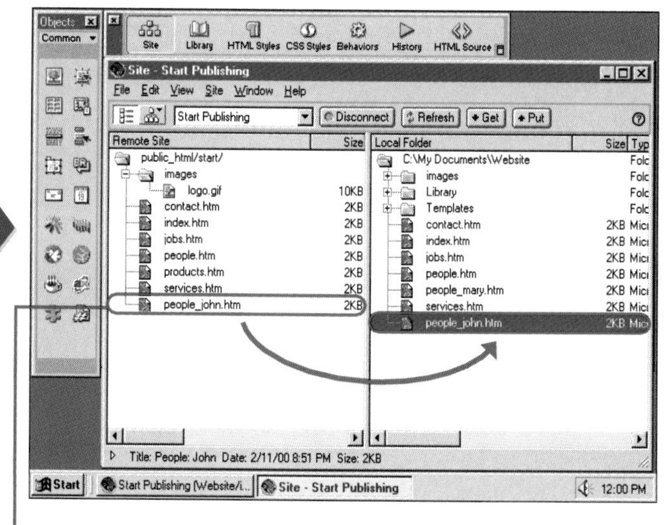

■ Dreamweaver transfers the file or folder from the Web server to your computer.

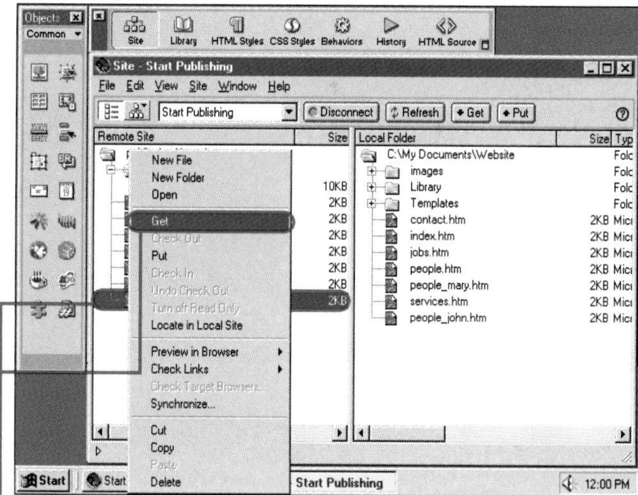

DOWNLOAD FILES SHORTCUT

1 Right-click the file or folder in the left pane.

2 Select **Get** from the pop-up menu.

■ Dreamweaver transfers the file or folder from the Web server to your computer.

VIEW A SITE MAP

You can view the files of your site in flowchart form as a site map.

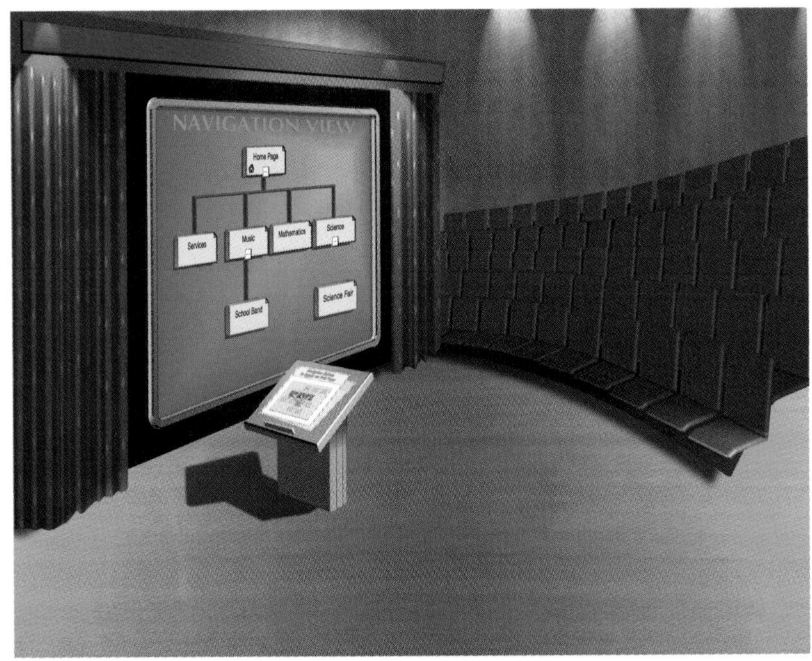

VIEW A SITE MAP

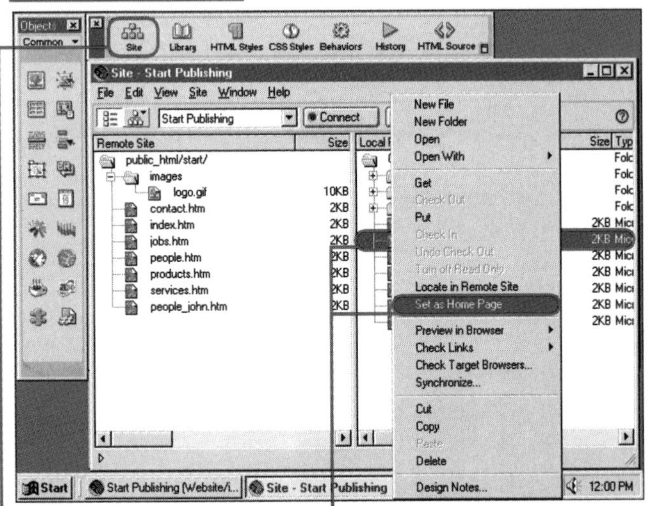

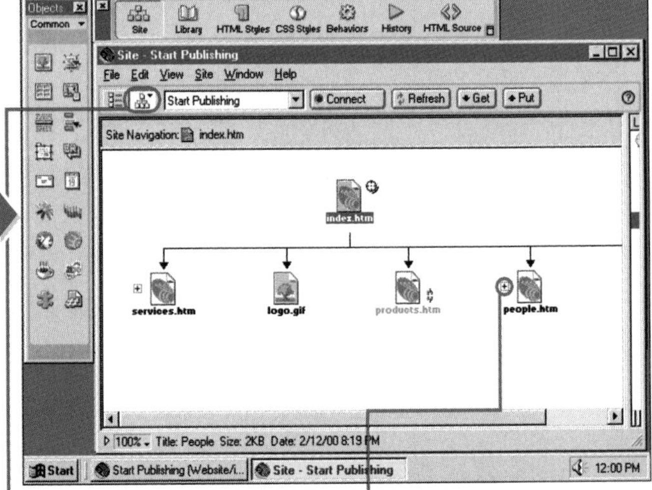

1 Click the **Site** icon to open the Site window.

Note: To create a site map in Dreamweaver, you must first define your site's home page. It serves as the root file of your site map.

2 In the right pane, right-click the file that serves as your home page.

3 Click **Set As Home Page** in the menu.

■ In this example, index.htm is set as the home page.

4 Click .

■ Dreamweaver displays a site map in the left pane. By default, the site map displays the site structure two levels deep beginning from the home page.

5 To view files below the second level, click + .

■ You can save the site map as an image by selecting **File⇨Save Site Map**.

How do I fix a broken link in the site map?

A broken chain in the site map means the link to a page is broken. Links can break because a destination page is renamed or deleted. You can fix a broken link by right-clicking the destination page and selecting **Change Link**.

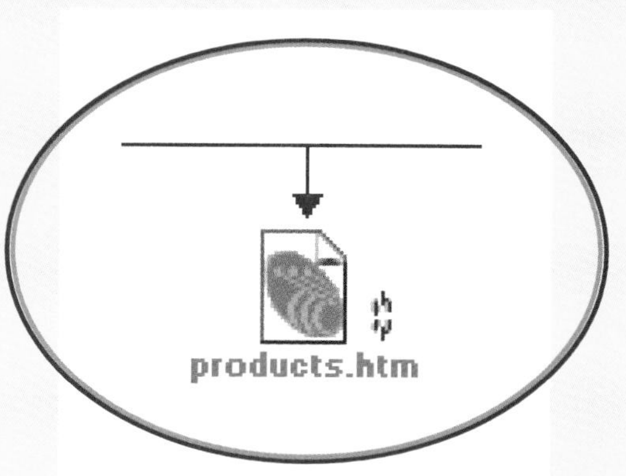

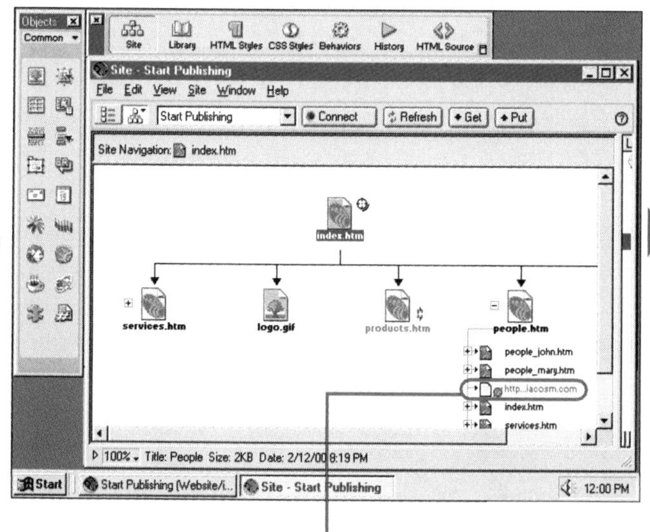

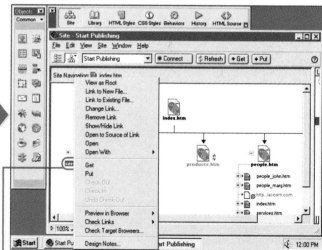

■ Dreamweaver displays the files linked from the second-level page.

■ External links are marked with a special icon ().

6 For more options, right-click a file in the site map.

CREATE LINKS WITH THE SITE MAP

You can create hyperlinks between pages in your site by clicking and dragging between icons in the site window.

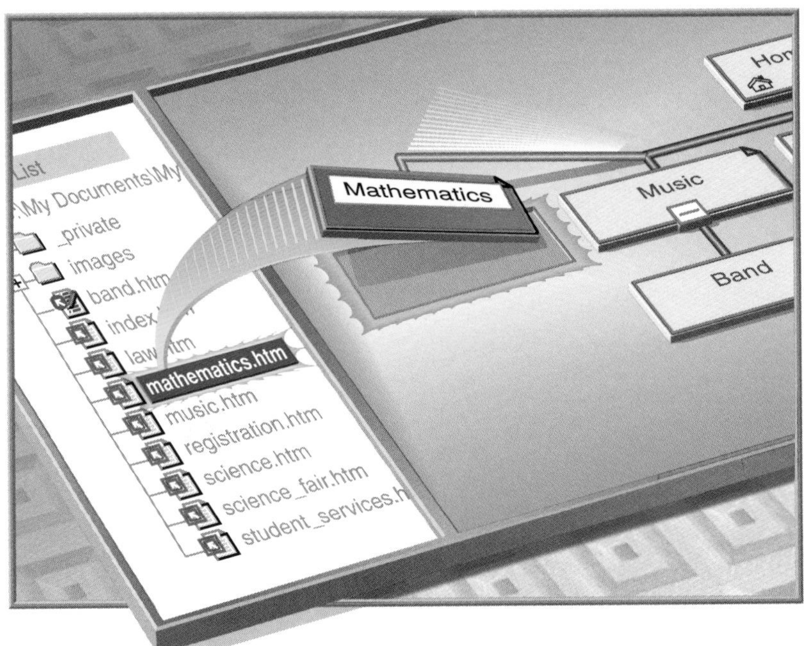

CREATE LINKS WITH THE SITE MAP

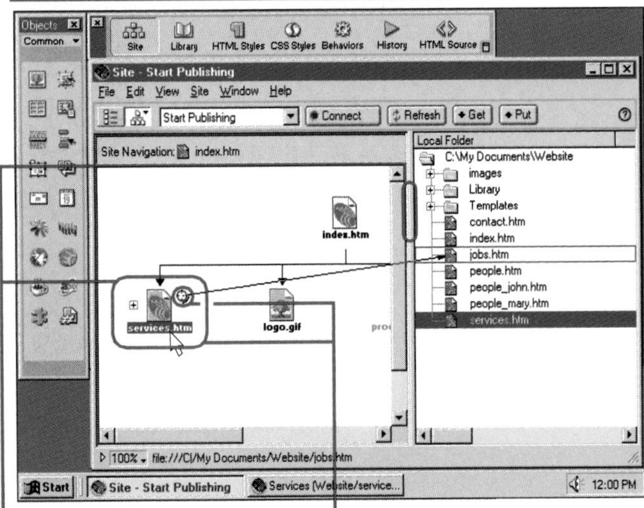

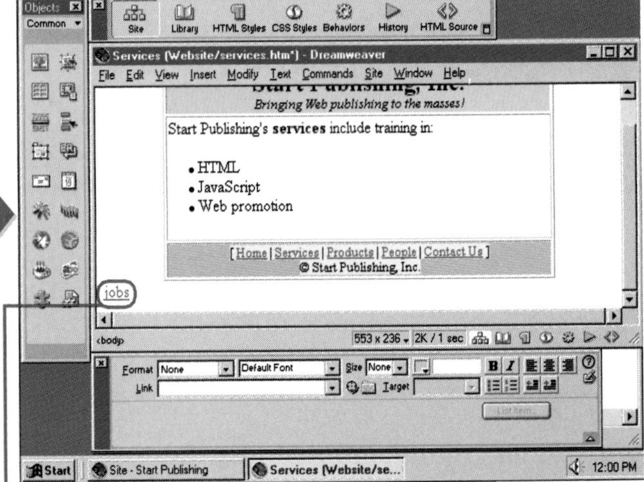

1 Open a site map in the Site window.

2 If necessary, click and drag the window border to adjust the sizes of the panes.

3 Select a file icon in the site map.

4 Click and drag ⊕ to connect the page that will contain the link with the destination file's icon in the right pane.

5 Double-click the linking page's icon to open it in its own Document window.

■ The new link appears on the bottom of the page.

*Note: You can also add a hyperlink to a page by right-clicking its icon in the site map window and choosing **Link To New File** or **Link To Existing File**.*

You can change all the hyperlinks that point to a specific file at once.

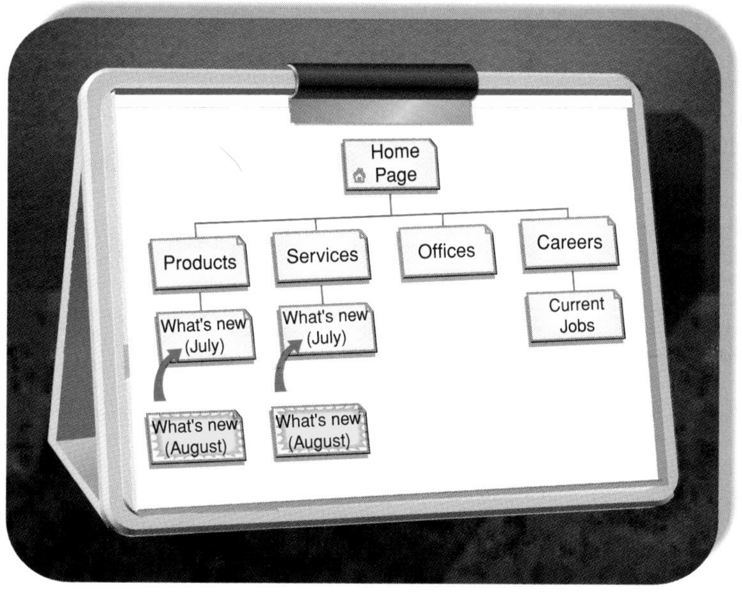

CHANGE LINKS SITEWIDE

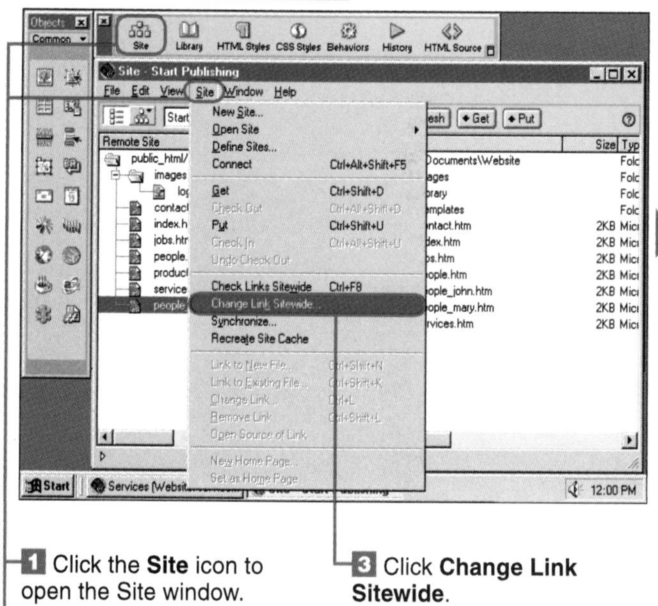

1 Click the **Site** icon to open the Site window.

2 Click **Site**.

3 Click **Change Link Sitewide**.

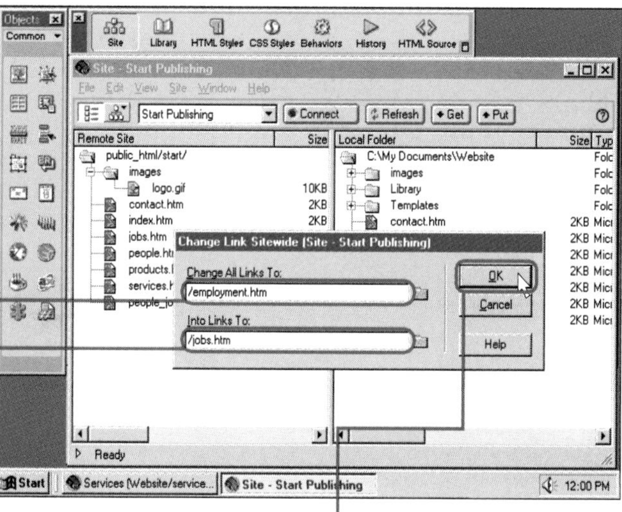

4 Type the hyperlink destination you want to change.

5 Type the new hyperlink destination.

Note: Hyperlinks must start with a /, a mailto: link, or a full URL.

6 Click **OK**.

■ Dreamweaver finds and replaces all instances of the original destination. A dialog box asks you to confirm the changes.

SEARCH FOR TEXT

Dreamweaver has a find option that allows you to search for text in your Web pages. The search text can be regular text, HTML code, or a specific HTML tag.

SEARCH FOR TEXT

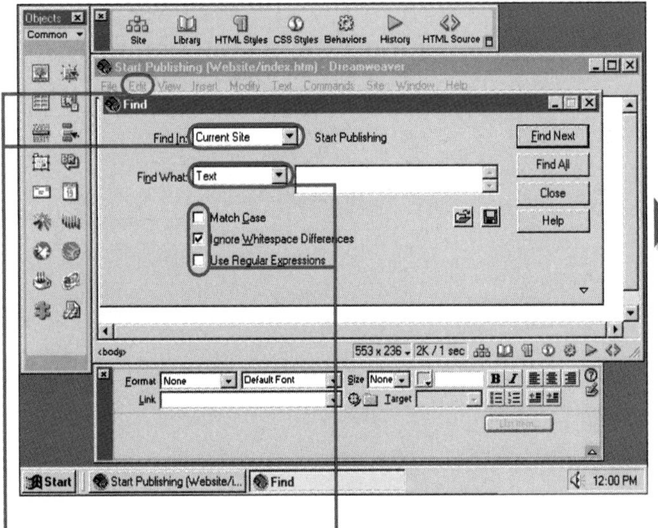

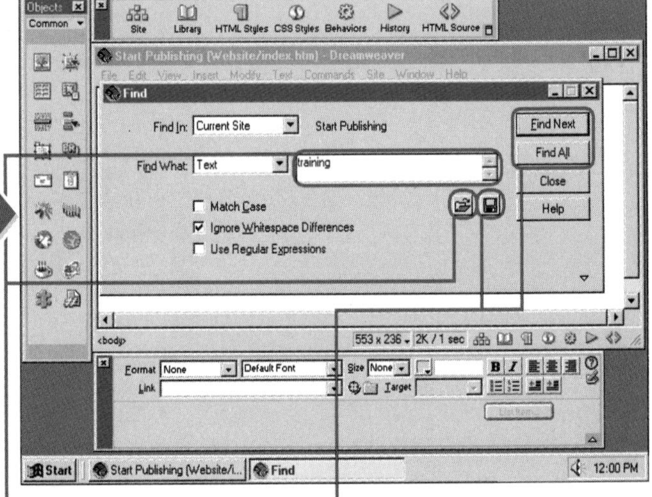

1 Select **Edit⇨Find**.

■ The Find dialog box appears.

2 Click ▼ and select a search for text in the current document, the current site, or a particular folder. The find dialog box appears.

3 Click ▼ and select a search for regular text, HTML source, or a specific HTML tag.

4 Specify whether you want to match case, ignore whitespace differences, or use regular expressions.

5 Type a search term.

■ You can click 📂 to load previously saved search queries.

■ You can click 💾 to save a search query for later use.

6 Click **Find Next** to find the next instance of the search term or **Find All** to find all instances.

What is the difference between searching text and searching HTML source?

Searching text does not consider HTML tags or other code not visible in the Document window. For instance, searching the text for *body* will find instances of "body" in the page content but not instances of the <body> HTML tag.

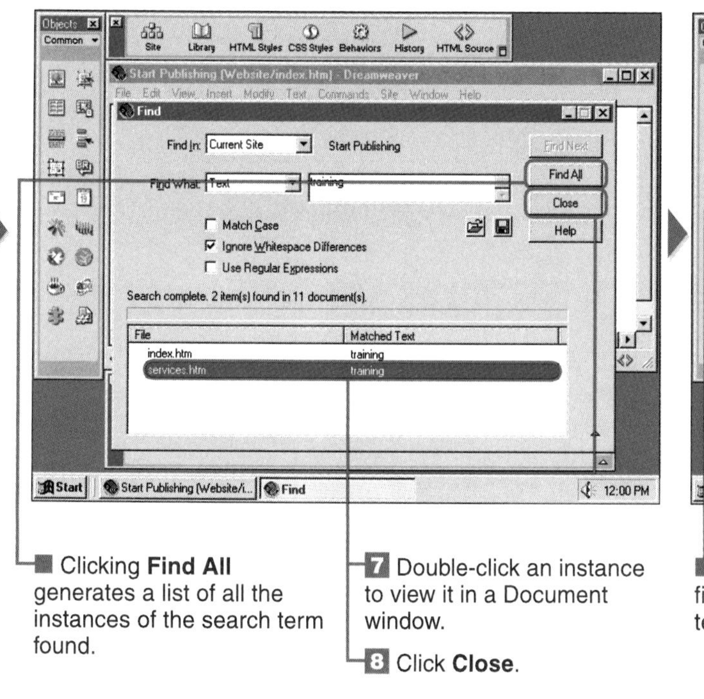

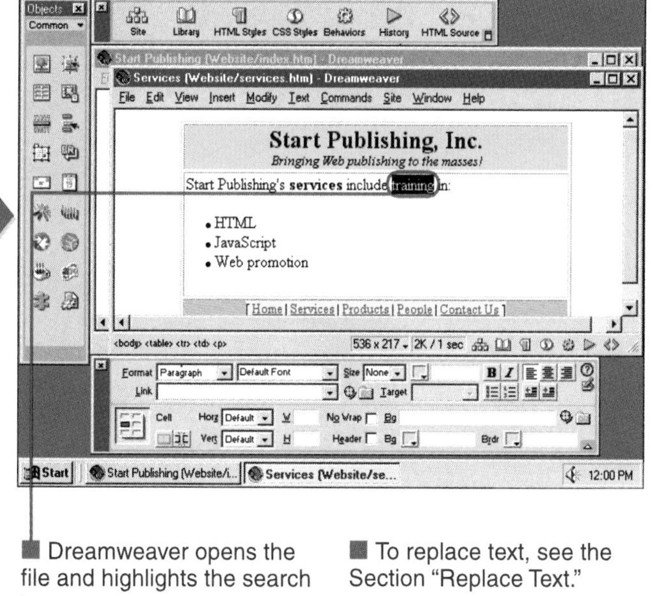

■ Clicking **Find All** generates a list of all the instances of the search term found.

7 Double-click an instance to view it in a Document window.

8 Click **Close**.

■ Dreamweaver opens the file and highlights the search term.

■ To replace text, see the Section "Replace Text."

REPLACE TEXT

You can search for and replace text in your Web pages. The text can be regular text, HTML code, or a specific HTML tag.

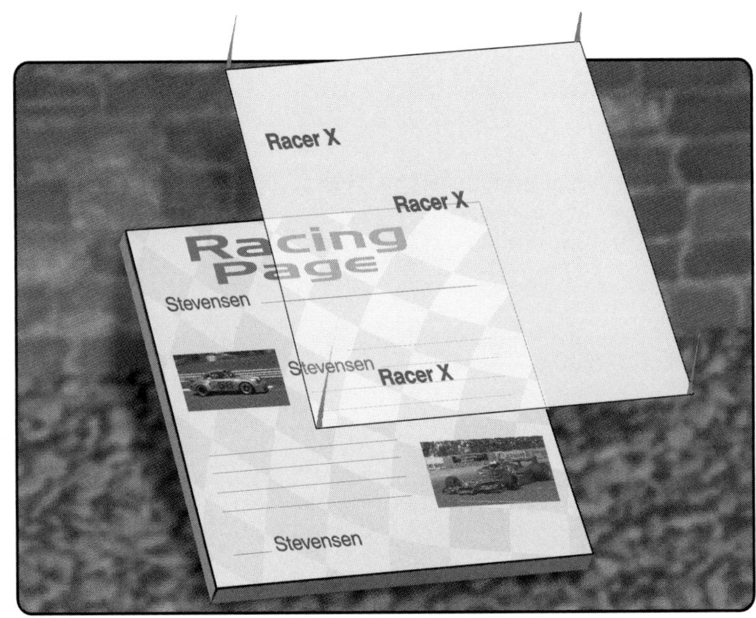

REPLACE TEXT

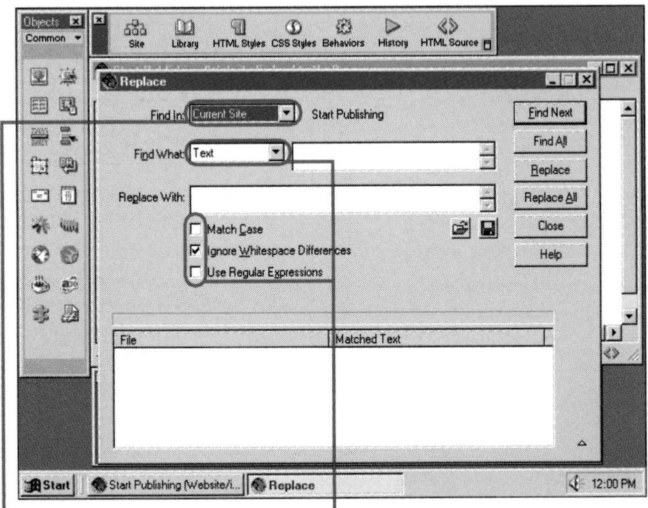

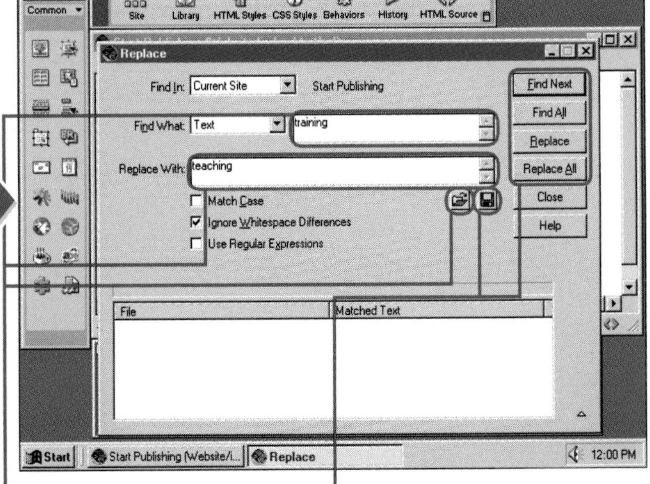

1 Select Edit⇨Replace.

■ The Replace dialog box appears.

2 Click ▾ and select a search for text in the current document, the current site, or a particular folder.

3 Click ▾ and select a search for regular text, HTML source, or a specific HTML tag.

4 Specify whether you want to match case, ignore whitespace differences, or use regular expressions.

5 Type a search term.

6 Type the text that will replace the search term.

■ You can click 📂 to load previously saved search queries.

■ You can click 💾 to save a search query for later use.

7 Click a button to start the search.

How do I resize all of my level-two headings to level-three headings?

In HTML, level-two headings look like `<h2>Some text</h2>` while level-three headings look like `<h3>Some text</h3>`. To resize your level-two headings, you could perform a search in the HTML source for "h2>" (to target both the opening and closing tags) and replace it with "h3>."

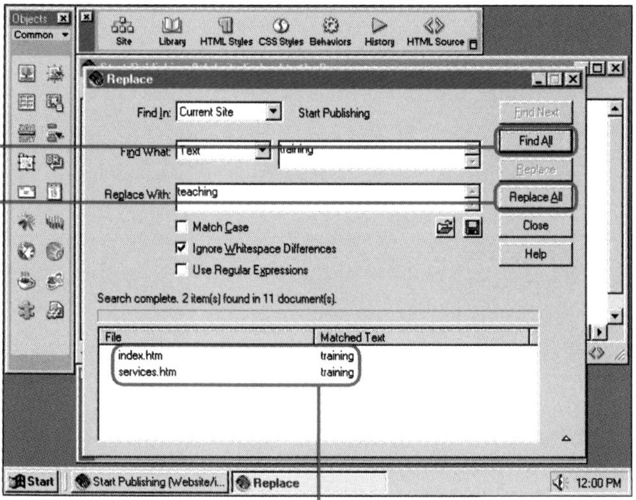

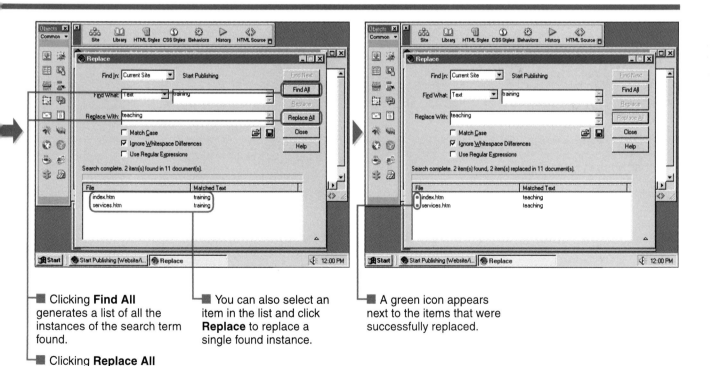

■ Clicking **Find All** generates a list of all the instances of the search term found.

■ Clicking **Replace All** replaces all of the instances of the search term.

■ You can also select an item in the list and click **Replace** to replace a single found instance.

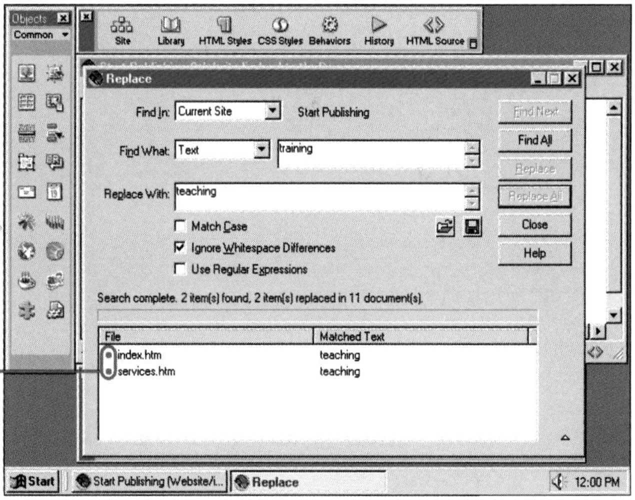

■ A green icon appears next to the items that were successfully replaced.

INDEX

E

F

H

I

J

L

M

N

O

P

Q

R

S

T

U

V

W

(continued)

Z

Read Less, Learn More™

Simplified®

Simply the Easiest Way to Learn

For visual learners who are brand-new to a topic and want to be shown, not told, how to solve a problem in a friendly, approachable way.

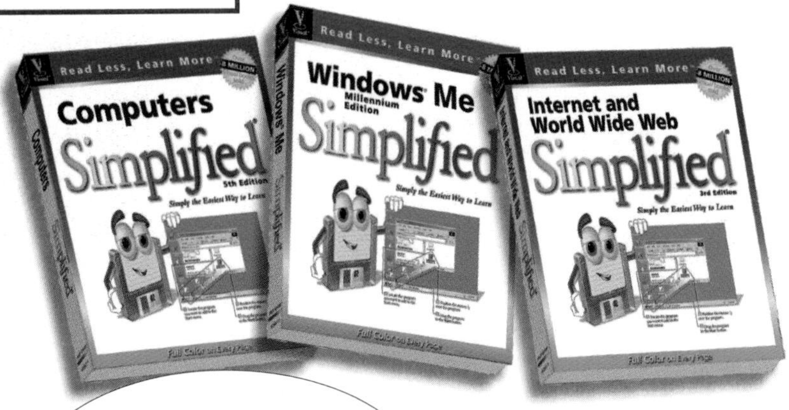

All *Simplified®* books feature friendly Disk characters who demonstrate and explain the purpose of each task.

Title	ISBN	Price
America Online® Simplified®, 2nd Ed.	0-7645-3433-5	$24.99
Computers Simplified®, 4th Ed.	0-7645-6042-5	$24.99
Creating Web Pages with HTML Simplified®, 2nd Ed.	0-7645-6067-0	$24.99
Excel 97 Simplified®	0-7645-6022-0	$24.99
Excel for Windows® 95 Simpified®	1-56884-682-7	$19.99
FrontPage® 2000® Simplified®	0-7645-3450-5	$24.99
Internet and World Wide Web Simplified®, 3rd Ed.	0-7645-3409-2	$24.99
Lotus® 1-2-3® Release 5 for Windows® Simplified®	1-56884-670-3	$19.99
Microsoft® Access 2000 Simplified®	0-7645-6058-1	$24.99
Microsoft® Excel 2000 Simplified®	0-7645-6053-0	$24.99
Microsoft® Office 2000 Simplified®	0-7645-6052-2	$29.99
Microsoft® Word 2000 Simplified®	0-7645-6054-9	$24.99
More Windows® 95 Simplified®	1-56884-689-4	$19.99
More Windows® 98 Simplified®	0-7645-6037-9	$24.99
Office 97 Simplified®	0-7645-6009-3	$29.99
PC Upgrade and Repair Simplified®	0-7645-6049-2	$24.99
Windows® 95 Simplified®	1-56884-662-2	$19.99
Windows® 98 Simplified®	0-7645-6030-1	$24.99
Windows® 2000 Professional Simplified®	0-7645-3422-X	$24.99
Windows® Me Millennium Edition Simplified®	0-7645-3494-7	$24.99
Word 97 Simplified®	0-7645-6011-5	$24.99

Over 9 million *Visual* books in print!

with these full-color Visual™ guides

The Fast and Easy Way to Learn

Discover how to use what you learn with "Teach Yourself" tips

Title	ISBN	Price
Teach Yourself Access 97 VISUALLY™	0-7645-6026-3	$29.99
Teach Yourself Computers and the Internet VISUALLY™, 2nd Ed.	0-7645-6041-7	$29.99
Teach Yourself FrontPage® 2000 VISUALLY™	0-7645-3451-3	$29.99
Teach Yourself HTML VISUALLY™	0-7645-3423-8	$29.99
Teach Yourself the Internet and World Wide Web VISUALLY™, 2nd Ed.	0-7645-3410-6	$29.99
Teach Yourself VISUALLY™ Investing Online	0-7645-3459-9	$29.99
Teach Yourself Microsoft® Access 2000 VISUALLY™	0-7645-6059-X	$29.99
Teach Yourself Microsoft® Excel 97 VISUALLY™	0-7645-6063-8	$29.99
Teach Yourself Microsoft® Excel 2000 VISUALLY™	0-7645-6056-5	$29.99
Teach Yourself Microsoft® Office 2000 VISUALLY™	0-7645-6051-4	$29.99
Teach Yourself Microsoft® PowerPoint® 97 VISUALLY™	0-7645-6062-X	$29.99
Teach Yourself Microsoft® PowerPoint® 2000 VISUALLY™	0-7645-6060-3	$29.99
Teach Yourself More Windows® 98 VISUALLY™	0-7645-6044-1	$29.99
Teach Yourself Netscape Navigator® 4 VISUALLY™	0-7645-6028-X	$29.99
Teach Yourself Networking VISUALLY™	0-7645-6023-9	$29.99
Teach Yourself Office 97 VISUALLY™	0-7645-6018-2	$29.99
Teach Yourself Red Hat® Linux® VISUALLY™	0-7645-3430-0	$29.99
Teach Yourself Windows® 95 VISUALLY™	0-7645-6001-8	$29.99
Teach Yourself Windows® 98 VISUALLY™	0-7645-6025-5	$29.99
Teach Yourself Windows® 2000 Professional VISUALLY™	0-7645-6040-9	$29.99
Teach Yourself VISUALLY™ Dreamweaver® 3	0-7645-3470-X	$29.99
Teach Yourself VISUALLY™ iMac™	0-7645-3453-X	$29.99
Teach Yourself VISUALLY™ Windows® 2000 Server	0-7645-3428-9	$29.99
Teach Yourself Windows® Me Millennium Edition VISUALLY™	0-7645-3495-5	$29.99
Teach Yourself Windows NT® 4 VISUALLY™	0-7645-6061-1	$29.99
Teach Yourself Word 97 VISUALLY™	0-7645-6032-8	$29.99

For visual learners who want to guide themselves through the basics of any technology topic. *Teach Yourself VISUALLY* offers more expanded coverage than our bestselling *Simplified* series.

The Visual™ series is available wherever books are sold, or call 1-800-762-2974. Outside the US, call 317-572-3993

ORDER FORM

IDG BOOKS

TRADE & INDIVIDUAL ORDERS

Phone: **(800) 762-2974**
or **(317) 572-3993**
(8 a.m. – 6 p.m., CST, weekdays)
FAX : **(800) 550-2747**
or **(317) 572-4002**

EDUCATIONAL ORDERS & DISCOUNTS

Phone: **(800) 434-2086**
(8:30 a.m.–5:00 p.m., CST, weekdays)
FAX : **(317) 572-4005**

CORPORATE ORDERS FOR 3-D VISUAL™ SERIES

Phone: **(800) 469-6616**
(8 a.m.–5 p.m., EST, weekdays)
FAX : **(905) 890-9434**

Qty	ISBN	Title	Price	Total

Shipping & Handling Charges

	Description	First book	Each add'l. book	Total
Domestic	Normal	$4.50	$1.50	$
	Two Day Air	$8.50	$2.50	$
	Overnight	$18.00	$3.00	$
International	Surface	$8.00	$8.00	$
	Airmail	$16.00	$16.00	$
	DHL Air	$17.00	$17.00	$

Subtotal ______

CA residents add applicable sales tax ______

IN, MA and MD residents add 5% sales tax ______

IL residents add 6.25% sales tax ______

RI residents add 7% sales tax ______

TX residents add 8.25% sales tax ______

Shipping ______

Total ______

Ship to:

Name ______

Address ______

Company ______

City/State/Zip ______

Daytime Phone ______

Payment: □ Check to IDG Books (US Funds Only)

□ Visa □ Mastercard □ American Express

Card # ______ Exp. ______ Signature ______

maranGraphics™